DO EMOTIONS HELP OR HURT DECISION MAKING?

DO EMOTIONS HELP OR HURT DECISION MAKING?

A Hedgefoxian Perspective

KATHLEEN D. VOHS, ROY F. BAUMEISTER,
AND GEORGE LOEWENSTEIN

Editors

RUSSELL SAGE FOUNDATION   NEW YORK

The Russell Sage Foundation

The Russell Sage Foundation, one of the oldest of America's general purpose foundations, was established in 1907 by Mrs. Margaret Olivia Sage for "the improvement of social and living conditions in the United States." The Foundation seeks to fulfill this mandate by fostering the development and dissemination of knowledge about the country's political, social, and economic problems. While the Foundation endeavors to assure the accuracy and objectivity of each book it publishes, the conclusions and interpretations in Russell Sage Foundation publications are those of the authors and not of the Foundation, its Trustees, or its staff. Publication by Russell Sage, therefore, does not imply Foundation endorsement.

Library of Congress Cataloging-in-Publication Data

Do emotions help or hurt decision making? : a hedgefoxian perspective / Kathleen D.
   Vohs, Roy F. Baumeister, George Loewenstein, editors.
     p. cm.
   ISBN 978-0-87154-877-1
   1. Emotions. 2. Decision making. 3. Cognition. I. Vohs, Kathleen D. II. Baumeister,
Roy F. III. Loewenstein, George.

   BF531.D59 2007
   152.4—dc22

                                                                              2007018762

Text design by Suzanne Nichols.

RUSSELL SAGE FOUNDATION
112 East 64th Street, New York, New York 10021
10 9 8 7 6 5 4 3 2 1

Table of Contents

About the Authors

Kathleen D. Vohs is the McKnight Land-Grant Professor of the University of Minnesota and assistant professor at the Carlson School of Management, University of Minnesota.

Roy F. Baumeister is the Francis Eppes Eminent Scholar and Professor of Psychology at Florida State University.

George Loewenstein is the Herbert A. Simon Professor of Economics and Psychology at Carnegie Mellon University.

Christopher J. Anderson is assistant professor psychology at Temple University.

Eduardo B. Andrade is assistant professor of marketing at the Haas School of Business, University of California, Berkeley.

Jennifer S. Beer is an assistant professor in psychology at the University of Texas at Austin.

Joel B. Cohen is professor of marketing and director of the Center for Consumer Research at the Warrington College of Business Administration, University of Florida.

C. Nathan DeWall is an assistant professor in the Department of Psychology at the University of Kentucky.

Matthew T. Gailliot is assistant professor of psychology at the University of Amsterdam.

Karen Gasper is an associate professor of psychology at the Pennsylvania State University, and has received the Nancy Hirschberg Award for Outstanding Scholarship and Research and her university's Psi Chi's Professor of the Year Award.

Lorenz Goette is a senior economist at the Federal Reserve Bank of Boston and visiting assistant professor of economics at the Massachusetts Institute of Technology.

David Huffman is a senior research associate at the Institute for the Study of Labor in Bonn, Germany.

Linda M. Isbell is an associate professor in the Department of Psychology at the University of Massachusetts at Amherst.

Quinn Kennedy is a research affiliate at the Department of Psychiatry and behavioral sciences, Stanford University School of Medicine.

Peter Kerkhof is associate professor at the Department of Communication science, VU University, Amsterdam.

Jonathan Levav is an associate professor of business at the Columbia Business School.

Debra Lieberman is an assistant professor of psychology at the University of Hawai'i.

Mara Mather is associate professor of psychology at University of California, Santa Cruz and is the associate editor of *Journal of Experimental Psychology: General.*

Nicole L. Mead is a graduate student in the Department of Psychology at Florida State University.

Benoît Monin is an assistant professor in psychology at Stanford University.

Robert Oum is a doctoral candidate at the Department of Psychology, University of Hawai'i.

David A. Pizarro is assistant professor of psychology at Cornell University.

Catherine D. Rawn is a Ph.D. student in the department of psychology at the University of British Columbia.

Dianne M. Tice is professor of psychology at Florida State University.

Jennifer L. Trujillo is a doctoral student in the Department of Psychology at the University of California, San Diego.

Piotr Winkielman is professor of psychology, University of California, San Diego.

John M. Zelenski is associate professor of psychology at Carleton University in Ottawa, Canada.

Liqing Zhang is an assistant professor of psychology at Peking University in Beijing, China.

Overview

Introduction: The Hedgefox

George Loewenstein, Kathleen D. Vohs,
and Roy F. Baumeister

I N A PERHAPS overused metaphor, academics are sometimes classified as "hedgehogs" and "foxes." Playing on a famous, albeit somewhat mysterious, statement by the seventh century BC philosopher Archilochus that "the fox knows many things, but the hedgehog knows one big thing," the prototypical hedgehog is a system addict on a quest for a unified theory of everything. Foxes, in contrast, have an appreciation of the complexities of reality which prevents them from even entertaining the possibility of any grand unifying scheme.

Belying their physical image, hedgehogs are the life of the party. They take outrageous positions and push their arguments to the limit, generating heated debate. Foxes, despite their slyness, are party duds; they stand on the sidelines shaking their heads and rolling their eyes at the naivety of the hedgehogs' wild speculations. One more strike against foxes.

As the party extends into the waning hours, however, the frantic repartee of the hedgehogs can wear thin, even to the hedgehogs themselves. At this time, the host begins to long for the arrival of a third species of party animal: the "hedgefox." Hedgefoxes combine the best properties of their two mammalian relatives. Like the hedgehog, the hedgefox is a synthesizer; but like the fox, the hedgefox cares about, and advances theories that take account of, and make sense of, the complexities of reality.

If research on emotions is a party (and the explosive growth of the topic over the past few decades has lent the topic something of a party

3

atmosphere), the time is ripe for the entry of the hedgefox. Research on emotions has made enormous strides, stimulated by debates between researchers who have taken extreme stands on a variety of central issues. There are hedgehog emotion researchers who argue for the primacy of emotions over cognition, and others who argue, instead, that all emotions are derivative of cognition. (There is also a third group which denies the validity of the distinction; see Oum and Lieberman, chapter 6, this volume.) There are advocates of the idea that moral judgments are the product of emotion, perhaps justified ex post by reasons, as well as those who argue that morality is a matter of logic. And, most central to the basic theme of this book, there are hedgehogs whose research focuses almost exclusively on the destructive effects of emotions, and there are others who focus as selectively as the first group on the vitally beneficial functions that emotions serve.

Of course the foxes are right; each of these polar positions is simplistic in its extremity. But that observation doesn't take us far. In the waning hours of the emotion research party, we have arrived at the point where debates between extreme and obviously untenable positions are not as productive as they once were. In short, we need answers to the When question. *When* do emotions or cognitions predominate? *When* are moral judgments driven by reflexive emotional reactions and *when* by logical thought? And, when are emotions helpful or harmful? This book provides nuanced synthetic answers to these types of questions.

Decision making is the other half of our topic. It too has seen explosive growth in research interest in recent years. As with emotion, its few early hedgehogs (for example, groupthink, rational choice, framing) have had to withstand a stampede of foxes. Some decision making researchers are starting to think that their field's destiny is merely to develop lists of departures from rationality, without much prospect of integrative theory. Yet others are confident that new grand theories will emerge. The time is ripening for hedgefoxes to impose limited order on decision theory also.

If a party is an imperfect metaphor for describing emotion and decision research, its aptness cannot be debated as a metaphor for the events that led to the creation of this book. The genesis of the book was a five-week summer institute on emotion and decision making for twenty young researchers, codirected by two not-so-young researchers, Roy F. Baumeister and George Loewenstein. The institute was hosted by the Center for Advanced Study in the Behavioral Sciences at Stanford University and funded by the Ford and Andrew W. Mellon Foundations. A highlight of the summer institute was a series of visits and presentations, supported by a separate grant from the Russell Sage Foundation, by eminent researchers interested in emotion and/or decision issues.

These visitors included John Gabrielli, Robert Zajonc, Jonathan Cohen, Gerald Clore, Dacher Keltner, Laura Carstensen, Brian Knutson, Antonio Rangel, Jennifer Lerner, and Paul Slovic. Their presentations became the organizational and, to some extent, the intellectual focus of the summer institute.

The group met every morning for two to three hours. On days when there was a guest speaker, the protocol was for everyone to prepare by reading one or two articles by the visiting speaker and then to meet briefly before the speaker arrived, so as to begin discussion of the assigned readings. Speakers were warned that we wanted to conduct their presentation as a seminar rather than as a colloquium, meaning that there should be ample discussion during the talk. Most speakers prepared a forty-five-minute to one-hour talk, and yet the presentations invariably filled the two hours and many of them could have gone on longer.

Over the course of the five weeks, the group became increasingly cohesive and the atmosphere increasingly festive, with discussions of emotion (as well as a range of less highbrow topics) spilling out of the confines of the Center for Advanced Study to dinner tables, restaurant tables, and the bars of local "watering holes." At the same time, the group began to expand as friends of the scholars, many represented among the coauthors of these chapters, began to show up at social events.

Are hedgefoxes born or made? The events of the summer institute suggested the latter. Most participants arrived at the institute with extreme, hedgehogian, positions on affect, decision making, and their interaction, and clashed with one another over basic issues. Interactions then entered a foxy period in which everyone began to feel somewhat overwhelmed by the seemingly contradictory perspectives and research findings that emerged, and hopeless about the prospects of any kind of reconciliation. However the unusual length of the institute paid off. By the end of the period we began to see the emergence of a hedgefox period with a common language, a shared understanding of a number of issues, and, most characteristically of hedgefoxism, a nuanced theoretical perspective that made sense of, and in fact eliminated, what had previously appeared to be disagreements and contradictions. The benefits of the five weeks can be seen in each of the chapters represented in this volume.

Consider the answer, in chapter 1, by Roy F. Baumeister, C. Nathan DeWall, and Liqing Zhang, to the question of whether emotions improve or hinder the decision process. The answer is, of course, "it depends." It depends on several factors, according to these authors. In particular, the distinction between current emotional state and anticipated emotional outcomes is influential. Current emotional states often lead to hasty or incomplete consideration of information, resulting in poor decisions and sometimes even self-destructive actions. In contrast, anticipated emotional outcomes are often vitally helpful in setting priorities and helping people make sensible decisions. This distinction helps inform a broader understanding of emotional phenomena as a feedback system which processes information and informs decision making. Full-blown conscious emotions guide reflection and evaluation, whereas brief twinges of automatic affect can bring these remembered lessons back in rapid manner to influence current behavioral choices.

Eduardo B. Andrade and Joel B. Cohen, in chapter 2, discuss the role of affect in risk taking, helping behavior, and eating. The authors note that research in each of these areas has produced seemingly contradictory findings: some studies find that positive emotions tend to increase risk taking, helping behavior, and eating, and other studies find the opposite. Andrade and Cohen propose a simple explanation for these contradictory findings—based on the distinction between "affective evaluation" and "affect regulation"—which can explain and predict when positive and negative emotions will tend to have each effect. In a nutshell, current emotions tend to cause people to perceive the world in specific ways (that is, affective evaluation), which produce specific patterns of behavior. However people also have intuitions about how behaving in different ways will affect their future emotions (that is, affect regulation), and these expected effects of behavior on affect often propel behavior in different directions than the more direct influences of affect. Whether emotions promote or reduce a particular behavior, then, depends on the relative strength of these two mechanisms.

Piotr Winkielman and Jennifer L. Trujillo, in chapter 3, add further nuance to Baumeister, DeWall, and Zhang's perspective, arguing that these different phenomena can be understood as different stopping points in a sequence of events. According to these authors, "emotional stimuli are initially differentiated on importance, with the reaction being a nonspecific orienting response. Next, the processing focuses on general valence of the cue, with the reaction being a positive or negative response." Baumeister, DeWall, and Zhang would refer to this point of the process as a conscious emotion. Winkielman and Trujillo see it slightly differently, and they suggest that even relatively complex emotions can be unconscious, and yet can still exert their influence on behavior.

Karen Gasper and Linda M. Isbell, in chapter 4, take an instrumental perspective on the question of when people seek out or avoid information. They underscore the importance of emotion and mood (as separate concepts) in directing not only how much information people search for, but also what types they seek and favor. The perspective put forth by

Gasper and Isbell allows for more fine-grained predictions of people's choices when they are faced with new information to potentially peruse. Major decisions can thus be powerfully, albeit indirectly, shaped by emotions. If emotions guide information seeking, then the information one has available for subsequent decision making is biased.

Even within psychology, scholars with diverse theoretical perspectives and specific research interests were represented. For example, John M. Zelenski, a personality researcher, argues in chapter 5 that personality serves as a kind of context that moderates the impact of emotion on judgment and choice, and that whether a particular emotion is helpful or destructive in a particular situation depends crucially on the personality of the individual experiencing the emotion. Robert Oum and Debra Lieberman (chapter 6), coming from the perspective of evolutionary psychology, suggest the intuitive distinctions often made between emotion and cognition disappear when one considers an information processing view of the mind. They argue that emotion programs are a subset of cognitive processes evolved to guide decision making and behavior, along with other psychological and physiological processes, in a manner that would have led on average to an increase in survival and reproduction in ancestral environments. Whether emotions help or hurt decision making depends on the metric one employs: effects of decision making on inclusive fitness, well-being, or happiness.

Some authors dealt with the question of how emotion helps or hinders decision making by analyzing potential mechanisms that may shift the balance from one side to the other. Catherine D. Rawn, Nicole L. Mead, Peter Kerkhof, and Kathleen D. Vohs (chapter 7) take an individual differences approach and posit that self-feelings (that is, self-esteem) may be a key component in predicting when and under what circumstances emotions direct decision making.

In chapter 8, Christopher J. Anderson proposes an even more complex sequential perspective on emotion and the role it serves in decision making, with emotion first shaping decisions, then aiding in their implementation, and finally providing feedback about the desirability of the consequences that result from the decision. Of course, these outcomes cease to be a surprise to the seasoned decision maker, and the person may begin to make decisions based on these emotional consequences. This again points up the theme of anticipated emotion proving an important factor in decision processes.

Thus, a basic distinction that is emphasized in many of these chapters is between currently felt emotion, and future, possible, or anticipated emotion. Anderson's emphasis on how decision makers come to use anticipated emotional consequences to guide their decisions is a conclusion that others have reached by different routes. For example,

Baumeister, DeWall, and Zhang suggest that anticipated emotion generally benefits the decision process, whereas current emotions impair it. Andrade and Cohen likewise feature the distinctive benefits of affect regulation, which is based on wanting a future emotional outcome. Moral evaluation can be swayed by the anticipation of possibly feeling guilty over a particular action (see Monin, Pizarro, and Beer, chapter 10). Yet the line is not sharp, because some of the effects of current emotion are sometimes based on trying to feel better. The intensely upset consumer who overspends or overeats, for example, may be seeking to bring about an improved emotional state.

The sometimes harmful effects of seeking to regulate oneself out of a bad emotional state is one theme of chapter 9. Matthew T. Gailliot and Dianne M. Tice argue that much self-destructive behavior that might be perceived as "out of control" can in fact be interpreted as attempts by people to regulate negative affective states. In other words, "people succumb to their impulses in order to feel better."

The final section of the book deals with specific applications in order to shed light on particular sets of problems. Benoît Monin, David A. Pizzaro, and Jennifer S. Beer (chapter 10) tackle the knotty question of the relative role of reason and emotion in moral judgment. Several researchers have taken strong stands on the issue, with Jonathan Haidt arguing that moral reasoning is almost artifactual; he described it as the "tail that wags the emotional dog." At the opposite extreme, many philosophers, and the psychologist Lawrence Kohlberg have argued instead that morality is purely a matter of reasoning. In a classic hedgefoxian statement, Monin, Pizarro, and Beer propose that "the different models of morality that have appeared in the literature over the years may be a direct consequence of the different moral situations considered by the various researchers who have proposed them. Observe humans as they try to solve complex moral dilemmas, and you are likely to propose a model of morality that relies heavily on high-level reasoning; ask them how they feel about disgusting immoral acts, and you are likely to conclude that morality is all about gut reactions that require little rational deliberation."

Quinn Kennedy and Mara Mather are both cognitive psychologists with an interest in aging. In chapter 11, they review the changes in affect that occur in connection with aging, and they examine the consequences of these changes for decision making. Their model highlights the benefits of aging for emotional regulation in that older adults have a better aptitude for improving their emotions as compared to younger adults. This ability is the result of strategic decision making, which has been seen in the recollection and information-processing styles of older adults in contexts such as recalling past decisions, public events, and personal experiences.

Beyond the intensity and length of the summer institute, the diverse backgrounds of the participants made it productive for all involved. Most of the scholars were drawn from the fields of psychology, but economics, marketing, and other business-school disciplines were also well represented, and we were fortunate to have one sociologically-oriented demographer.

The two economists in the group, Lorenz Goette and David Huffman, provided two chapters to this volume, each examining the implication of insights about affect to basic problems in economics. In chapter 12, they examine the role of affect in labor supply decisions, arguing that affect plays a critical role in income targeting, a phenomenon that is otherwise difficult to account for. In chapter 13, they argue that affect actually improves labor-market outcomes, because it addresses limitations inherent in purely self-interested economic behavior. For example, employers cannot track all of their employees' actions, so purely self-interested employees would shirk whenever it was undetectable. This would ultimately lead to lower productivity and wages. Positive affect between the employer and employee can reduce this problem, rescuing employers from the problem of shirking and rescuing employees from the low wages that would result. Harry S. Truman once said he wanted to get advice from a one-handed economist, because his economic advisors would typically give him economic advice of the form, "On the one hand . . . and on the other . . ." Goette and Huffman are two hedgefox economists whom Truman would not have liked to receive advice from (but should have!).

In chapter 14, Jonathan Levav addresses the question of why life events often have an impact on physical and mental health, but do not affect subjective (self-reported) happiness or well-being in the long run. Levav argues that the problem lies with the scales that measure subjective well-being, which fail to pick up the effects that such life events have on subconscious mental structures or "assumptive world schemas."

So what *is* the answer to the question of whether affect helps or hurts decision making? The hedgehog would argue that it either helps or hurts decision making. The fox would argue that both are true, or that the question doesn't make sense. The hedgefoxes who make up the authors of the chapters in this book will tell you, however, that the correct answer is "it depends." If you want to know what it depends on, read on.

· 1 ·

Do Emotions Improve or Hinder the Decision Making Process?

ROY F. BAUMEISTER, C. NATHAN DEWALL,
AND LIQING ZHANG

To ARRIVE at a decision, people use both cognition and emotion. The cognitive aspects of decision making, including the use of such heuristics as availability, representativeness, and anchoring and adjustment, have received considerable attention (Epley and Gilovich 2001; Kahneman, Slovic, and Tversky 1982; Tversky and Kahneman 1974). More recently, social scientists have sought to consider how emotional processes influence decision making. Researchers have to yet to reach a consensus, however, as to whether emotions improve or hinder the decision making process. On the one hand, sometimes emotions impair decision making. A long tradition of folk wisdom suggests that emotions seriously hinder the ability for people to make good decisions. It is thought that people who are emotionally distraught frequently engage in rash, reckless, and even destructive behaviors. They say and do things that they regret later. They take foolish risks and fail to appreciate the potentially harmful consequences of their choices. From this perspective, emotions are inimical to the decision making process.

On the other hand, emotions may facilitate decision making. People who act against their "gut feelings" are often sorry later. People who disregard the emotional impact of their choices (on themselves or others) neglect a crucial aspect of the situation. Emotions help people differentiate right from wrong, and help them learn from their mistakes. Perhaps the most dramatic example of how emotions facilitate decision making is derived from observations of patients with damage to the ventromedial frontal cortices of the brain (Damasio 1994). These patients have retained their intellectual capacity, including aspects of memory and the ability to engage in logical reasoning, but their brain damage has removed their capability to associate affective feelings and emotions with anticipated consequences of their actions. If emotions impair decision making, these neurological patients should be shining examples of judicious, detached, and rational decision making. Against that line of reasoning, these individuals who lack an ability to experience emotions consistently demonstrate impairments in their ability to make choices in a coherent manner and to learn from their mistakes (Damasio 1994).

Thus there are contradictory lines of thought regarding the role of emotions in the decision making process. Can they both be correct? That is, can emotions both improve and impair decision making? In our view, the answer is yes. There is no simple answer to the question of whether emotions are helpful or harmful for decision making. They can be both helpful and harmful. The purpose of this chapter is to explain how different aspects of emotion and different categories of emotional processes can produce both beneficial and harmful effects on decision making.

A full understanding requires an appreciation of different kinds of emotional phenomena and different processes. Some of these are almost indispensable to optimal, effective decision making. Others can so distort the decision maker's thinking as to bring disaster. We begin therefore with the distinctions among different emotional phenomena.

What Is Emotion?

Dual process theories are highly influential in current psychological theories about cognition (that is, thinking), but have not largely been extended to emotion, except for a few theories that have sought to contrast emotional and nonemotional processes (for example, Metcalfe and Mischel 1999). Our view is that there are two profoundly different kinds of emotional phenomena.

The distinction was driven home to one of us during the 2004 Summer Institute on Emotion and Decision Making at the Center for Advanced Study in the Behavioral Sciences. At the institute, a series of eminent experts gave guest lectures on emotion and decision making. Many got around to the same basic questions, such as whether cognition is always involved in emotion, and different answers emerged. Some thought that emotion always involved thinking. Others argued staunchly emotion does not always involve thinking, and that, in the memorable phrase of Robert Zajonc (1980), "preferences need no inference." Yet these seemingly opposite answers invoked supporting evidence that pointed to different kinds of phenomena. Those who dismissed the need for cognition in emotion generally pointed to rapid affective responses such as automatic liking or disliking, some of which were not even conscious. In contrast, those who emphasized the importance of cognition generally cited full-blown, subjectively conscious, mind-and-body emotional states. Thus the most important distinction was apparently between automatic affect and conscious emotion.

Unlike some other theorists, we use the terms *affect* and *emotion* in specific and noninterchangeable ways. Affect refers to the automatic, mainly nonconscious responses to stimuli; these responses are fundamental to the majority of all varieties of behavioral functioning. Automatic affects are the swiftly occurring evaluative reactions that people experience in response to stimuli and events. Affects may not be experienced consciously, and if they enter conscious awareness at all, may only be experienced as momentary twinges of liking or disliking. Automatic affects are rapidly arising in response to a wide variety of stimuli and events. As such, affects may be beneficial for guiding behavioral decisions.

Emotion, in contrast, refers to processes that are more limited in scope than affect. Emotions are the full-blown experiences that correspond to what most laypersons mean when they speak of emotions. Conscious emotions frequently involve a strong subjective feeling in addition to some physical response such as arousal. Emotions contain many attributes that are commonly looked upon as central causes of behavior. To be sure, much empirical research makes attempts (when appropriate) to rule out alternative explanations that emotions cause changes in behavior. Given the slowness with which conscious emotions arise, however, these emotions are not likely to be very effective or helpful as means for guiding behavior.

Similar distinctions have been suggested previously, most notably by Damasio (1994) and Bechara and Damasio (2005). These authors noted that emotional states leave so-called somatic markers which can be reactivated on future decision making occasions. The marker enables the new decision to be guided by the previously felt emotion.

Emotions and Behavior

The present chapter builds on another project by Roy Baumeister et al. (2007), which addresses the fundamental question of how emotion is related to behavior. According to our theory, emotions may have evolved for the direct causation of behavior, but in humans there are other layers of control, including cognition and self-regulation, so the direct link is not needed. Still, this does not mean that emotion is evolutionarily obsolete and is on the way toward disappearing from the human psyche. Emotion is important primarily as a feedback system. Instead of emotion causing behavior, behavior may pursue emotion. It is therefore possible that emotion regulation is a fundamental guiding principle behind some, if not most, behavior. Emotion may occasionally have a direct influence on behavior, but this is not its normal function. (When emotion does directly influence behavior the results may sometimes be problematic. For example, anger may make a person say or do something that will be regretted later.) In general, the influence of emotion on behavior is indirect; it is a feedback system which works more primarily via cognition (Baumeister et al. 2007).

Full-blown conscious emotion may often be too slow to guide on-line behavior effectively. But emotion may arise after the event and help to solidify the lesson to be learned from the situation, partly by keeping the person engaged in mental processing about what happened and why. Emotion keeps one engaged in thinking about the event, and this increases the likelihood that the person will extract the lesson to be learned from it, thereby improving behavior on future occasions. Organisms that are devoid of the capacity for conscious experience, such as the majority of nonhuman animals, live in a comparatively simple world of unequivocal outcomes and might not need to (or be able to) maintain their attention on recent events in order to learn from them. Humans, in contrast, live in a cultural system in which the majority of events and outcomes can be interpreted as positive or negative (Baumeister 2005). Conscious emotion can therefore be considered as beneficial in terms of promoting learning under multifaceted, uniquely human conditions.

Automatic affect, in contrast, is fast enough to guide behavior on-line. If a person encounters a situation that produces an immediate twinge of liking, the person will tend to make choices that increase the likelihood of experiencing further instances of positive affect. Automatic affect does not, however, necessarily stimulate rumination or learning lessons.

We think automatic affect is often helpful and possibly essential for decision making. Without feelings about what is good or bad, it is hard to choose effectively. In contrast, the influence of a conscious emotional state is more variable. Baumeister et al. (2007) have speculated that one function of conscious emotion is to create emotional residues that give rise to affective memory traces which will guide future behavior (Damasio 1994). For example, if a person performs an action that results in a strong subjective experience of sadness, guilt, or regret, it will not be necessary for the person to experience the full-blown conscious emotional episode again the next time a similar opportunity arises. Instead, the emotional residue from the first emotional experience causes an automatic affective reaction that, being negative, will aid the person in altering their behavior in order to avoid the type of behavior that previously generated the unpleasant emotional experience. Positive emotional experiences likely produce emotional residues which give rise to future automatic affective reactions. But given that negative events and unpleasant reactions are more psychologically powerful than good events and reactions (Baumeister et al. 2001), people likely possess more emotional tags for negative events, and are more strongly guided by them than emotional tags for positive events.

Although an emotional feedback system is beneficial in terms of guiding future behavior, such a feedback system may be imprecise and occasionally misleading. Decisions that produced a bad outcome once will not inevitably produce a bad outcome in the future. If, for example, a young man plans to meet an attractive woman for a date and she stands him up, then he may feel a twinge of negative affect when considering whether to ask another woman for a date. This automatic affective response is largely beneficial in terms of directing behavior on-line and increasing the chances for the man to avoid a subsequent negative emotional experience. But there is no guarantee that he will again be stood up for a date, and he may in fact encounter a person who enjoys being in his company. In this way, automatic affect is fast enough to guide behavior on-line, but learning to develop the most advantageous strategies for making complex decisions may be beyond the reach of the system of automatic affect. Still, people would probably benefit from avoiding decisions that produced negative emotional experiences and approaching those that created positive emotional experiences, even if they were occasionally misled by their pangs of automatic affect.

The proposal that conscious emotions and automatic affects operate within the context of an emotional feedback system raises the possibility that decisions are guided by anticipated emotion, instead of by the emotions felt at the time of the decision.

Current Versus Anticipated Emotion

When considering the role of emotion in decision making, an important distinction is between current emotional states and anticipated emotions. The feedback system theory (Baumeister et al. 2007) suggests that anticipated emotion may play a prominent and beneficial role in the human decision making process. From this perspective, it is not what a person feels right now, but what he or she anticipates feeling as a result of a particular behavior that can be a powerful and effective guide to choosing well.

Anticipated emotion is directly linked to what we have termed conscious emotions. People anticipate whether and to what degree a decision will produce a positive or negative subjective emotional experience. In other words, people make decisions based on the conscious emotional experience that they anticipate. Anticipated emotion may represent one adaptive subcategory of influential conscious experiences. Indeed, one of the current authors suggested that the arrival of human consciousness altered a variety of motivational patterns (Baumeister 2005). Animals that are devoid of conscious attention and awareness respond to inner drives to perform basic actions meant to increase the likelihood of survival and reproductions. Humans, in contrast, engage in behaviors that are motivated by the pursuit of anticipated conscious experiences.

It is our view that current emotional states probably do more harm than good in terms of shaping the decisions that people make. The traditional folk wisdom that emotions produce irrational behavior, as well as much of the evidence for destructive effects of emotion, both emphasize current emotional states (e.g., Leith and Baumeister 1996). When people make decisions while feeling emotionally distraught, or even possibly euphoric, they may do foolish things and make irrational decisions. Anticipated emotions, in contrast, will have a beneficial effect on the decision making process. This proposal strikes at the core of the argument that emphasizes the role of emotion as a feedback system. People who make choices based on past emotional experiences as well as anticipated future emotional outcomes will frequently arrive at a reasonable and wise decision. Without the anticipation of feeling guilty, people might perform immoral or antisocial acts. Without the anticipation of regret, people might do things that will make them feel sorry in the future. In contrast, making a choice based on one's current emotional state may impair the decision making process and lead to suboptimal choices.

A long tradition of folk wisdom suggests that emotions seriously hinder the ability for people to make good decisions. Recent evidence has also demonstrated that people escape from intense emotional states into neutral ones when to do so would produce a more beneficial outcome (Erber and Markunas 2005). People may therefore be aware that their current emotional state could be detrimental to the choices they make, and, as a result, refrain from making choices at all. Insofar as people habitually lessen their emotional reactions before making choices, current emotional states may be considered a general hindrance to the decision making process.

While automatic twinges of affect may facilitate decision making, we also propose that anticipated emotion may likewise be beneficial. Automatic twinges of affect and anticipated emotions may be linked. That is, a small twinge of automatic affect may be an important signal to help the person anticipate future, full-blown emotional states that may result from a particular course of action.

Magnitude Versus Probability of Outcome

To understand the impact of emotion on decision making, one must also understand the distinction between the magnitude of outcomes and the probabilities. Most theories hold that optimal, effective decision making requires a balanced and integrated appreciation of both the magnitude of outcomes and the probabilities. For example, a five hundred dollar reward is more appealing than a four hundred dollar one; however, if the odds of the former are only one in ten, whereas the odds of the latter are eight in ten, one would be ill-advised to pursue the former. In general, emotional phenomena (both conscious emotion and automatic affect) appear to capture people's awareness of the magnitude of possible outcomes, but they leave people essentially uninterested to changes in probabilities. The only exception is that the difference between certainty versus a mere possibility does have emotional power and impact. But apart from this distinction, the emotion system is virtually numb to the vast range of probabilities.

In an early demonstration of emotional indifference to probabilities, Monat, Averill, and Lazarus (1972) showed that research participants became physiologically aroused as they approached the moment at which they anticipated that they might receive an electric shock. Although the probability of receiving a shock was high, medium, or low, participants showed essentially the same level of arousal regardless of the probability of receiving a shock. Participants failed to become aroused only when there was no chance of receiving an electric shock.

Emotional blindness to probabilistic outcomes, as opposed to certain outcomes, was illustrated by Viscusi and Magat (1987; Loewenstein et al. 2001). Participants were presented with a decision concerning a pesticide which allegedly caused some degree of risk and would likely cause poisoning to a small portion of people who were using the pesticide. The researchers then asked participants to decide how much they would be willing to pay to reduce the risk of poisoning to human users of the pesticide from fifteen in ten thousand to five in ten thousand, or, instead, from five in ten thousand to zero in ten thousand. The majority of participants were willing to pay more to reduce the risk of poisoning to zero, even though the former plan was twice as powerful in saving lives. This finding implies that reducing the chance of risk to zero possesses a particular emotional appeal, and draws out a stronger reaction than a larger improvement that still contained an element of probabilistic risk.

In a recent series of studies, Hsee and Rottenstreich (2004) demonstrated that affect and cognition play different roles in judgments which vary in scope. The basic finding was that people are insensitive to the scope (that is, the magnitude) of a judgment when the judgment activates the emotion system. In contrast, when the judgment only calls into play cognition, people are properly sensitive to scope. Participants in these between-subject studies said that they would give four times as much money to save four pandas as they would to save one panda. This rational decision making only occurred, however, when the pandas were represented by abstract dots. When the pandas were represented by pictures of cute, amiable, real pandas, people said that they would give amounts of money that were in between the one and four panda amounts in the purely cognitive dot conditions. Hsee and Rottenstreich replicated this finding in other domains, and suggested that these findings help to explain the concave shape of most value judgments in the world, presumably because some decisions have elements of emotions in them and therefore are not linear. These findings provide additional evidence that emotions lead to irrational and foolish decisions. When attaching value to an object—or to four cuddly pandas—one ought to increase the amount of worth proportionally with the number of objects on which the value will be distributed. These findings suggest that when emotions play a role in decision making, this does not happen; thus, current emotional states impair the decision making process.

One explanation for these findings is that the neurocircuitry responsible for emotional responding evolved before the cognitive system had become capable of appreciating variations in probability. Our ancestors evolved from animals that had sophisticated emotion systems but little or no higher-order cognition. This lag time in evolution leaves modern humans with an emotion system that is well attuned to the magnitude of rewards and costs, but not well attuned to probabilities.

Current Emotions and Decisions

Emotions alter decisions. It remains uncertain, however, which types of emotions present the most harmful influence to effective decision making. We believe that current emotional states are often detrimental to the decision making process. The deleterious effects of emotion on decision making are often so damaging that if the main function of current emotions was to influence decision making, evolution would have phased out the role of emotion in mammalian species long before our primate ancestors evolved into humans. If current emotional states are mainly harmful to the choices people make, then people with fewer and less intense emotions would have been placed at an advantage in terms of their ability to survive and reproduce compared to people who allowed their current emotions to guide their decisions.

Several studies have directly tested whether one's current emotional state has a positive or negative effect on decision making. Leith and Baumeister (1996) manipulated participants' emotions, and then had participants select among different lotteries that varied in the degree of risk and reward. The lotteries also differed in another important aspect: expected gain. Lottery selections were intentionally arranged so that lotteries with high rewards were statistically less promising in terms of expected gain. Choosing these high-reward, low-gain lotteries could have therefore been considered as irrational, self-defeating, and high-risk decision making. If current emotions improve the capacity for people to make wise, reasonable decisions, participants who were exposed to the mood manipulations would have exhibited more rational, optimal, and low-risk decision making than participants in the emotionally-neutral control conditions. The results from these studies showed that participants whose mood was experimentally manipulated did not make better decisions than participants whose mood was essentially neutral. In fact, participants who were made to feel high-arousal negative emotions such as anger and embarrassment were more likely to choose the high-reward, high-risk lotteries compared to the other participants. Thus, some emotions, particularly those linked with personal distress, caused people to take foolish risks.

Leith and Baumeister (1996) conducted an additional study to identify the mechanism that might account for the link between current emotional state and impaired decision making. In their study, participants were exposed to a mood manipulation to elicit either anger or a neutral emotion, and then were asked to choose among a set of lotteries as in the previous studies. Before making their decision, however, some participants were instructed to list the costs and benefits of each lottery option before making their decision. The results replicated the shift toward foolish risk taking among people who were experiencing anger, and showed that this effect was mediated by reduced cognitive processing. Thus, emotional distress impaired the capacity for optimal decision making by reducing cognitive processing. This pattern of responding supports the common thought that emotional states do more harm than good in terms of facilitating rational, optimal decision making.

Additional research on the relationship between negative emotions and their effect on decision making has been investigated by Luce and colleagues (Luce 1998; Luce, Bettman, and Payne 1997). Participants in these studies were exposed to a mood manipulation in which the decision task they faced involved either high or low conflict between important options.

The mood manipulation was therefore the resultant negative affect that accompanied the trade-off of difficulties with which participants were confronted, as opposed to an ambient mood manipulation. Results from these studies revealed that participants chose avoidant decision options more often when they were faced with a decision that might produce negative affect (the high difficulty trade-off condition, as opposed to the low difficulty trade-off condition). Participants who were currently experiencing negative affect selected the relatively "easy" options offered to them. In these cases, they selected (a) a status quo option (that is, participants relied on information that they had liked one of the options immensely, choosing this before viewing the other options), (b) an option that was clearly better than one other option, but would entail making difficult trade-offs with the third option in the set, or (c) an option to prolong the search. Results from these studies also indicated that choosing the relatively "easy" option decreased negative emotion, which supports our theory that behavior pursues future emotional states.

These results show that people are more likely to make easier decisions when they are experiencing negative emotions as the result of having to make a difficult choice—even when this choice is not the optimal one. Many decades ago, Easterbrook (1959) proposed that emotions can impair information processing. Easterbrook sought to explain the curvilinear relationship between arousal and performance, which he asserted was a result of emotional arousal narrowing the range of information that was processed. According to this perspective, a certain amount of arousal could have a beneficial effect on performance by aiding people in screening out information that is irrelevant to the performance domain. Once the irrelevant information has been screened out, however, any additional arousal can cause a person to overlook potentially helpful, task-relevant information. This perspective fits with the results of Leith and Baumeister (1996), namely that high-arousal emotions have a deleterious effect on decision making as a result of reduced cognitive processing.

These previous results demonstrated that emotions impair decision making through reducing cognitive processing, but this is not the only manner in which emotions influence decisions. In addition to diminishing cognitive processing, emotions can shift a person's priorities toward immediate mood improvement. This goal of feeling better can have a detrimental effect on the choices people make.

Emotions can impair decision making even when they are irrelevant to the domain of interest. Lerner, Small, and Loewenstein (2004) argued that certain emotions, such as sadness and disgust, have functional value in terms of aiding people in avoiding circumstances that might reduce their likelihood of surviving and reproducing. Specifically, sadness and disgust indicate negative appraisals that should motivate people to want to make a change. In their studies, participants were induced to feel sadness or disgust and were then instructed to make a decision as to the asking price for an item that they were required to sell. Results from these studies indicated that sad participants set lower selling prices compared to participants who were feeling a neutral emotional state, presumably as a result of sadness naturally motivating people to seek change. That is, sad people set a relatively low selling price because this would increase the likelihood of the item being sold, thereby bringing about a change in one's circumstances. Sad participants were also more likely to agree to buy the same item at a higher price, apparently as a result of sadness creating a positive attitude toward change. This pattern of results amounts to a reversal of the endowment effect, which has been shown to be robust across a wide variety of manipulations. Disgusted participants had lower buying and selling prices compared with participants in a neutral emotional state, presumably in agreement with their goal of expelling owned objects and avoiding ownership of novel objects. Participants who were induced to experience disgust also demonstrated a choice pattern of buying and selling prices that were not statistically different from each other, which also diverges from the standard endowment effect. The results also highlighted the significance of emotion specificity in the decision making process. Sad participants set higher choice prices than disgusted participants, but sad and disgusted participants did not differ with regard to their selling prices. These findings demonstrate how current emotional states can take priority over rationality in decision making even when the emotions are irrelevant to the task-domain. Emotions take precedence over the cognitive scrutiny, which is necessary for considering proper market values and calculations of long-term self-interest.

Additional evidence has shown how current emotional states, particularly negative emotions, can lead people to abandon their long-term priorities for immediate gratification. In their study, Knapp and Clark (1991) had participants complete a resource-management task that took the form of a simulated fishing game. The optimal strategy in the game would be to harvest fish somewhat slowly and on sporadic occasions, which would allow the lake to replenish its fish and sustain one's profits over time. An alternative, less optimal strategy would be to take as much profit as possible from the start, which would deplete the lake of its capacity to replenish its fish and would reduce the long-term gain. Knapp and Clark found that participants who were induced to feel sad chose the less optimal, short-term benefit strategy more often than participants in neutral moods. Thus, a current emotional state caused people to make shortsighted, irrational decisions.

In a subsequent study, Tice, Bratslavsky, and Baumeister (2001) demonstrated that the short-term strategy used by sad people in the resource-management task was due to participants placing a higher priority on immediately improving their moods than taking full advantage of the long-term gains that could be obtained by careful, rational decision making. These authors replicated the effect of sadness on resource management (Knapp and Clark 1991), and further showed that this effect could be eliminated when participants were led to believe that they were temporarily unable to change their current emotional states. Believing that one's current emotional state is "frozen" apparently reduces the appeal of engaging in behaviors meant to improve one's mood. This finding provides additional evidence in support of our second postulate that behavior pursues future emotional states. Sadness does not impair the neurological mechanisms responsible for decision making, but instead shifts people's priorities from maximizing long-term goals to improving one's mood immediately. Human decision making pursues emotional states in a plastic and goal-directed fashion.

Bad moods have negative consequences for decision making when people feel as though they can improve their mood by engaging in short-sighted, frequently irrational behavior. Several studies have extended the effects of mood "freezing" to other domains that have shown to be affected by negative moods. People who are sad often behave in helpful ways, but not when they believe that helpful behavior will not improve their mood (Manucia, Baumann, and Cialdini 1984). That is, sad people help others to make themselves feel better. Helpful behavior is therefore not the direct result of being in a sad mood, but it is instead a means of attaining an improved emotional state. The tendency for people to overeat unhealthy foods is also contingent on their belief that such behavior will improve their mood. When people believe that their mood is immune to change (that is, it is "frozen"), they do not engage in overeating of unhealthy foods (Tice, Bratslavsky, and Baumeister 2001). The same pattern is true for aggressive behavior: angry people behave aggressively only when they believe that such behavior will improve their mood (Bushman, Baumeister, and Phillips 2001).

The results from these studies make one point abundantly clear: behavior frequently pursues future emotional states. Current emotional states produce consistent alterations in decision making and other behaviors. However, the power of emotions over behavior only exists insofar as people believe that their behavior will cause a desired change in their mood. These findings suggest that one function of emotions is to serve as a feedback system. Basing one's decisions on anticipated emotional outcomes is a beneficial decision making strategy. The rewards that are gained from the capacity to anticipate future emotional outcomes are partially (or entirely) lost, however, when people's current emotional states disrupt the capacity for careful consideration of long-term self-interest and other calculations. Current emotional states do not necessarily damage the ability of people to engage in thoughtful decision making; rather, they merely shift people's priorities to engage in immediate mood reparation strategies instead of maximizing long-term gains.

Anticipated Emotion

While research shows that current emotional states can have unfavorable effects on decision making, anticipated emotional outcomes, in contrast, can facilitate effective, optimal decision making. We believe that choices that are aimed at increasing positive and decreasing negative future emotions will likely have beneficial effects. Why might this be the case? Put simply, emotions calculate outcomes. Positive emotions represent positive outcomes, whereas negative emotions signify negative outcomes. It would follow that choices made with the intention of maximizing positive future emotions and minimizing negative future emotions would result in good (as opposed to bad) outcomes.

The view that anticipated emotional outcomes inform the decision making process has been proposed by Mellers, Schwartz, and Ritov (1999). They asserted that in addition to people seeking to maximize gains and minimize losses, anticipated emotions play a role in shaping the choices that people make. Mellers, Schwartz, and Ritov demonstrated some minor and subtle departures from material rationality, in which anticipated emotional payoffs were used as the basis for making choices. With some exceptions, the most sensible decisions are often those that promise the best emotional outcomes.

The tendency for people to base their choices on anticipated emotional outcomes fits with a broader perspective recently proposed by Baumeister (2005). Baumeister regarded the human capacity for living in a complex cultural system as reliant upon being able to make choices in a more meaningful and far-sighted manner than our evolutionary forebears had. These choices can seem fairly straightforward, such as comparing the price of two cars made by the same company. Other choices, however, are between options that on the surface may have little or nothing in common. For example, one might have to decide whether to occupy an afternoon making love with one's spouse, shopping for a colleague's retirement party, or mastering a complicated piece of classical music. Regardless of its processing speed or available bandwidth, even a supercomputer would have immense difficulty deciphering which of these three options would yield the best possible outcome, because there is no common dimension that can be used to compare the options and select the best one. To resolve this impasse, evolution seems to have endowed humans with an emotion system that can supply a "common currency" into which seemingly disparate values can be transformed and interpreted. The human emotion system fulfills this need precisely. That is, anticipated emotions offer a basis for comparing various options that in cognitive or informational terms have little in common. One can then choose whatever option seems likely to yield the best emotional outcomes.

Within the context of judgment and decision making, anticipated regret has been investigated more than the anticipation of any other emotions. The logic is simple: people adjust their decisions so as not to experience regret in the future. Although people are not left regretting the choices they make, this decision making strategy is not foolproof in terms of guaranteeing the optimal decision. In a study by Anderson (2004), participants were given a choice between two lotteries. The first lottery offered participants a 90 percent chance of winning sixty dollars and a 10 percent chance of winning one dollar. The second lottery offered participants a 90 percent chance of winning forty dollars and a 10 percent chance of winning one hundred dollars. Thus, the first lottery had the better expected gain and, from a purely rational perspective, it was therefore the better choice. Participants overwhelmingly chose the second lottery, however, presumably because they anticipated a higher level of regret if they chose the first lottery and earned a paltry one dollar. This finding supports the idea that anticipated emotion informs decision making, and decision making is not solely dependent upon cognitive processing (Mellers, Schwartz, and Ritov 1999).

Although this finding showed that anticipated emotion led to a nonoptimal decision, we regard such effects as exceptions to what is generally an effective and adaptive decision making strategy of avoiding regret. The Anderson (2004) study also illustrates the relative clumsiness of the emotion system in terms of effectively considering probabilistic outcomes. Participants selected the forty dollar lottery (that is, the second lottery option) most likely to avoid the regret that would follow from gaining only one dollar. Emotions keep people attuned as to how they might feel about best- and worst-case outcomes. The emotion system is relatively deficient, however, in terms of fine tuning these judgments.

An apparent detraction from professing one's faith in the beneficial effect of anticipated emotions on decision making is that anticipations may not be entirely accurate. The research reviewed thus far has demonstrated that anticipated emotions facilitate effective decision making to a greater extent than current emotional states. Still, it is necessary to investigate the ways in which anticipated emotions are systematically inaccurate, and to investigate the degree to which the imprecision of anticipated emotions detracts from rational decision making. Two of the most prominently documented inaccuracies are *affective forecasting* and the *hot-cold empathy gap*.

Affective forecasting refers to the ways in which people predict their future feelings (Wilson and Gilbert 2003). Research has shown consistently that people overestimate the duration and intensity of their emotional responses to future events, an effect termed the *impact bias* (Wilson and Gilbert 2003). People overestimate how happy they will be after winning a date on a simulated dating game (Wilson, Wheatley, Kurtz, Dunn, and Gilbert 2004), predict greater distress following a romantic breakup or a denial for academic tenure than actually occurs (Gilbert, Pinel, Wilson, Blumberg, and Wheatley 1998), and inflate the effect of an important medical procedure on their quality of life (Jepson, Loewenstein, and Ubel, 2001). Thus, people often predict a prolonged and intense emotional response to possible future events, but when those events do come to pass, the emotional reactions may be relatively brief and modest.

These consistent biases in affective forecasting appear to cast doubt on the view that people make decisions based on anticipated emotional outcomes. We believe, however, that the evidence does not contradict the perspective that anticipated emotions inform decision making (Baumeister et al. 2007). If anticipated emotions do not play a role in shaping the decisions that people make, inaccuracies in anticipated emotions should appear random and nonsystematic. Against that line of reasoning, inaccuracies in anticipated emotions follow a consistent and orderly pattern. People correctly predict that they will feel sad after failing to receive academic tenure and happy in response to winning a date. They simply overestimate the duration and intensity of their emotional responses to such events.

The tendency for people to overestimate the intensity and duration of emotional responses to possible future events fits with the view that people often choose based on anticipated emotional outcomes. Overestimation of emotional responses is a beneficial decision making strategy compared with underestimating emotional outcomes. For example, imagine that a person was considering whether to invest her college savings in a risky start-up business. If she underestimated the intensity and duration of the regret she would feel if the business venture turned out badly, the anticipated regret would not be an effective deterrent. Overestimating the regret she would feel if she wasted her college savings on a risky business venture, in contrast, would presumably influence whether she was willing to make such a risky decision. The impact of the anticipated emotional outcome, although it would likely be overestimated, is helpful to decision making insofar as it motivates a person to consider carefully the possible consequences of his or her decisions.

The second well-documented inaccuracy in anticipated emotional outcomes concerns what is commonly referred to as the hot-cold empathy gap

(Bouffard 2002; Loewenstein, Nagin, and Paternoster 1997). The hot-cold empathy gap refers to the tendency for people to neglect the impact that their emotional state will have on how they might act in some possible future situation. In a provocative study, Ariely and Loewenstein (2006) instructed male participants to rate the likelihood that they would engage in a variety of socially controversial and even morally reprehensible sexual behaviors. Participants rated, for example, how appealing it would be to have sex with a child or old woman, an extremely fat partner, and a woman they hated, and further questions assessed what their level of arousal would be when engaging in deviant sexual acts such as spanking, bondage, and urination. Participants were asked whether they would ever attempt to obtain sex by getting a woman drunk, declaring love for her, or persisting in seductive efforts after she said no. The main independent variable of interest was participants' level of arousal. All participants responded to each of the questions once while in a relatively neutral emotional state and once while in a state of high sexual arousal (that is, while they were masturbating and had achieved a level of arousal that was at least seventy-five out of a maximum of one hundred). The majority of male participants reported being more willing to engage in all forms of deviant and immoral actions and rated the stimuli as more appealing when they were in an aroused state than when their mood was relatively neutral. Thus, participants failed to consider how their current emotional state might influence their willingness to partake in behaviors that they would otherwise perceive as undesirable.

The hot-cold empathy gap provides additional evidence that current emotional states can negatively influence decisions. Perhaps the most damaging effect of the hot-cold empathy gap can be in preliminary decisions, in which the person has not made a commitment to engage or not engage in a particular behavior. For example, a man may not intend to meet or have sex with a prostitute, and, as a result, he fails to bring a condom along when going to a Las Vegas casino. The decision to not bring a condom to the casino was based on the assumption that he does not perceive sexual intercourse with a prostitute as a likely or even appealing behavior. After flirting with a cocktail server, however, the man's arousal level may be increased and he might end up having unprotected sex with a prostitute. In this instance, the man fails to anticipate the regret that he will have in the case of an unwanted pregnancy or a sexually transmitted disease. He would be better off choosing by anticipated emotion instead of letting his current emotional state shift his priorities so as maximize his short-term hedonic outcomes. This hypothetical scenario demonstrates how decisions based on anticipated emotions offer people the benefit of considering the long-term costs and benefits of one's decisions.

Emotions and Learning

We believe that conscious emotion, as opposed to automatic affect, is instrumental in enabling people to learn. Conscious emotions develop too slowly to guide behavior on-line, but this does not hinder the learning process. In fact, the slowness of conscious emotions can be beneficial in terms of keeping one's attention focused on the recently concluded event so as to rehash its features and lessons carefully. If humans were more like robots or computers and lacked an emotion system, people might simply redirect their cognitive processes to new situations as soon as the most recent event had ended. Instead, the human emotion system directs one's attention and devotes its services to ruminating about recent events. This rumination allows the person to translate the recent events into an appropriate lesson to be learned from the variety of interpretations that might accompany the situation.

One particularly relevant example of how emotions facilitate learning is the stimulation of counterfactual thinking. Counterfactual thinking frequently arises from a negative emotional experience, which in turn causes a person to reconsider events in their lives and how they might have had different outcomes (Roese 1997). From this perspective, emotion causes people to engage in counterfactual thinking in order to learn from a recent event in terms of how they could have adjusted their behavior so as to bring about a more desirable response. Within the context of decision making, counterfactual thinking could prove extremely beneficial. Indeed, research on answer changing among test takers has shown consistently that the majority of answer changes are from incorrect to correct, and most people who change their answers usually make better choices as indicated by higher test scores (Clark 1962; Kruger, Wirtz, and Miller 2005; Reiling and Taylor 1972; Vispoel 1998). Apparently test takers anticipate the regret that may arise from an incorrect response, and as a result learn why their initially incorrect response was wrong by changing it to a correct response.

An additional example of how emotions facilitate learning was shown in a provocative study by Bechara, Damasio, Damasio, and Lee (1999). Participants in their study drew cards from any of four decks, and gained or lost money depending on the card they selected. Two of the decks bestowed consistent but small monetary gains, whereas the other two decks contained some big rewards but occasionally brought large monetary losses. People with normal emotional responding would sample from the four decks and, once having incurred the significant monetary losses from the so-called dangerous decks, would avoid choosing cards from those decks and instead draw cards from the decks that would be more likely of conferring a monetary gain. Such a pattern of behavior illustrates the fundamental and beneficial nature of learning, in that people are reinforced for refraining from decisions that previously caused a severe negative outcome. Other participants in the study, in contrast, did not learn in the same manner. Instead of avoiding the dangerous decks after experiencing a serious loss of money, these participants failed to learn from their previous negative experience and continued to draw cards from the dangerous decks. These participants had suffered damage to the amygdala ventromedial prefrontal cortex, which left them incapable of experiencing emotional reactions. Thus, the capacity for experiencing emotions conferred a dramatic benefit in decision making in terms of aiding people in learning from their previous negative experiences.

Conclusion

Emotions play a significant role in the choices people make, but researchers continue to disagree as to whether emotions improve or impair the decision making process. Part of the disagreement regarding the positive and negative influence of emotion on decision making is centered on the fact that emotional reactions began to develop long before our ancestors had evolved into humans. Humans are therefore equipped with an emotion system that they inherited from animals with simpler lives, and this system must somehow be retrofitted or adapted to cope with the far more complex choices presented by human culture. Conscious attention and awareness, language-based meaning systems, and an extended perception of time are only a few of the aspects that make human decision making more complex than that of animals, and which place new demands on the emotion system.

The current work is founded on the assumption that humans evolved to live in culture (Baumeister 2005). People are continually confronted with a variety of complex decisions embedded within an intricate and multifaceted cultural meaning system. Nonhuman animals, which lack consciousness, a sophisticated language, and the ability to mentally transcend their current situation, depend on their current emotions as a direct guide of their immediate behavior. Humans, in contrast, are equipped with the neurological mechanisms that allow for mental time travel, and they therefore have the ability to transform the relationship between past, present, and anticipated future events into a lesson from which one can learn.

The current chapter has assumed that the genesis of human consciousness dramatically altered the ways in which humans experience emotion and make decisions, as compared to other animals. Whereas nonhuman animals choose on the basis of whether an action will provide immediate gratification, human decision making is often motivated by anticipated conscious experiences. A dog may become hungry and frantically seek to consume the requisite amount of food to sate his appetite. Humans, in contrast, seek to quench their appetite and the concomitant conscious experience that is linked to certain combinations of foods, prepared in a certain manner, and ingested with a particular set of companions. Conscious emotion also becomes the goal of human behavior. People choose on the basis of how they anticipate the decision will make them feel.

Animals are forced to make decisions based on their current emotional and motivational states, and these choices are shaped by patterns that evolution and learning have rewarded, such as by promoting immediate chances of survival and reproduction. However, choosing on the basis of one's current emotional state is not an effective decision making strategy for humans. Humans constantly face decisions that are imbued with intricate culture meaning, whereas animals mainly react to concrete events in their immediate environment. Human decision making that makes use of lessons learned from emotional experiences and consideration of anticipated emotional states may be a beneficial and successful decision making strategy.

References

Anderson, Christopher J. 2004. "Inaction Inertia Is a Rational Choice: Regret, Self-regulation, and the Problem of the Non-referential Reference." Presented to the Society for Judgment and Decision Making, November 2004, Minneapolis, Minn.

Ariely, Dan, and George Loewenstein. 2006. "The Heat of the Moment: The Effect of Sexual Arousal on Sexual Decision Making." *Journal of Behavioral Decision Making* 19(2): 87–98.

Baumeister, Roy F. 2005. *The Cultural Animal: Human Nature, Meaning, and Social Life.* New York: Oxford University Press.

Baumeister, Roy F., Ellen Bratslavsky, Catrin Finkenauer, and Kathleen D. Vohs. 2001. "Bad Is Stronger than Good." *Review of General Psychology* 5(4): 323–70.

Baumeister, Roy F., Kathleen D. Vohs, C. Nathan DeWall, and Liqing Zhang. 2007. "How Emotion Shapes Behavior: Feedback, Anticipation, and Reflection, Rather than Direct Causation." *Personality and Social Psychology Review* 11(2): 167–203.

Bechara, Antoine R., and Antonio R. Damasio. 2005. "The Somatic Marker Hypothesis: A Neural Theory of Economic Decision." *Games and Economic Behavior* 52(2): 336–72.

Bechara, Antoine R., Hanna Damasio, Antonio Damasio, and Gregory P. Lee. 1999. "Different Contributions of the Human Amygdala Ventromedial Prefrontal Cortex to Decision-making." *The Journal of Neuroscience* 19(13): 5473–81.

Bouffard, James A. 2002. "The Influence of Emotion on Rational Decision Making in Sexual Aggression." *Journal of Criminal Justice* 30(2): 121–34.

Bushman, Brad J., Roy F. Baumeister, and Colleen M. Phillips. 2001. "Do People Aggress to Improve their Mood? Catharsis Beliefs, Affect Regulation Opportunity, and Aggressive Responding." *Journal of Personality and Social Psychology* 81(1): 17–32.

Clark, Carl A. 1962. "Should Students Change Answers on Objective Tests?" *Chicago Schools Journal* 43: 382–85.

Damasio, Antonio 1994. *Descartes' Error: Emotion, Reason, and the Human Brain.* New York: Grosset/Putnam.

Easterbrook, John A. 1959. "The Effect of Emotion on Cue Utilization and the Organization of Behavior." *Psychological Review* 66(3): 183–201.

Epley, Nicholas, and Tom Gilovich. 2001. "Putting Adjustment Back in the Anchoring-and-Adjustment Heuristic: Self-generated Versus Experimenter Provided Anchors." *Psychological Science* 12(5): 391–6.

Erber, Ralph, and Susan Markunas. 2005. *Managing Affective States.* Unpublished manuscript. Department of Psychology, DePaul University.

Gilbert, Daniel T., Elizabeth C. Pinel, Timothy D. Wilson, Stephen. J., Blumberg, and Thalia P. Wheatley. 1998. "Immune Neglect: A Source of Durability Bias in Affective Forecasting." *Journal of Personality and Social Psychology* 75(3): 617–38.

Hsee, Christopher K., and Yuval Rottenstreich. 2004. "Music, Pandas, and Muggers: On the Affective Psychology of Value." *Journal of Experimental Psychology: General* 133(1): 23–30.

Jepson, Christopher, George Loewenstein, and Peter Ubel. 2001. "Actual Versus Estimated Differences in Quality of Life Before and After Renal Transplant." Unpublished manuscript. Department of Social and Decision Sciences, Carnegie Mellon University.

Kahneman, Daniel, Paul Slovic, and Amos Tversky. 1982. *Judgment Under Uncertainty: Heuristics and Biases.* Cambridge: Cambridge University Press.

Knapp, Andreas, and Margaret S. Clark. 1991. "Some Detrimental Effects of Negative Mood on Individuals' Ability to Solve Resource Dilemmas." *Personality and Social Psychology Bulletin* 17(6): 678–88.

Kruger, Justin, Derrick Wirtz, and Dale T. Miller. 2005. "Counterfactual Thinking and the First Instinct Fallacy." *Journal of Personality and Social Psychology* 88(5): 725–35.

Leith, Karen P., and Roy F. Baumeister. 1996. "Why Do Bad Moods Increase Self-defeating Behavior? Emotion, Risk Taking, and Self-regulation." *Journal of Personality and Social Psychology* 71(6): 1250–67.

Lerner, Jennifer S., Deborah A. Small, and George Loewenstein. 2004. "Heart Strings and Purse Strings. Carryover Effects of Emotions on Economic Decisions." *Psychological Science* 15(5): 337–41.

Loewenstein, George F., Daniel Nagin, and Raymond Paternoster. 1997. "The Effect of Sexual Arousal on Expectations of Sexual Forcefulness." *Journal of Research in Crime and Delinquency* 34(4): 443–73.

Loewenstein, George F., Elke U. Weber, Christopher K. Hsee, and Ned Welch. 2001. "Risk as Feelings." *Psychological Bulletin* 127(2): 267–86.

Luce, Mary F. 1998. "Choosing to Avoid: Coping with Negatively Emotion-laden Consumer Decisions." *Journal of Consumer Research* 24(4): 409–33.

Luce, Mary F., James R. Bettman, and John W. Payne. 1997. "Choice Processing in Emotionally Difficult Decisions." *Journal of Experimental Psychology: Learning, Memory, and Cognition* 23(2): 384–405.

Manucia, Gloria K., Baumann, Donald J., & Cialdini, Robert B. (1984). Mood influences on helping: Direct effects or side effects? *Journal of Personality and Social Psychology*, 46(2), 357–64.

Mellers, Barbara, Alan Schwartz, and Ilana Ritov. 1999. "Emotion-based Choice." *Journal of Experimental Psychology: General* 128(3): 332–45.

Metcalfe, Janet, and Walter Mischel. 1999. "A Hot/Cool-system Analysis of Delay of Gratification: Dynamics of Willpower." *Psychological Review* 106(1): 3–19.

Monat, Alan, James R. Averill, and Richard S. Lazarus. 1972. "Anticipatory Stress and Coping Reactions Under Various Conditions of Uncertainty." *Journal of Personality and Social Psychology* 24(2): 237–53.

Reiling, Eldon, and Ryland Taylor. 1972. "A New Approach to the Problem of Changing Initial Responses to Multiple Choice Questions." *Journal of Educational Measurement* 9(1): 67–70.

Roese, Neal J. 1997. "Counterfactual Thinking." *Psychological Bulletin* 121(1): 133–48.

Tice, Dianne M., Ellen Bratslavsky, and Roy F. Baumeister. 2001. "Emotional Distress Regulation Takes Precedence over Impulse Control: If You Feel Bad, Do It!" *Journal of Personality and Social Psychology* 80(1): 53–67.

Tversky, Amos, and Daniel Kahneman. 1974. "Judgment Under Uncertainty: Heuristics and Biases." *Science* 185(4157): 1124–31.

Viscusi, W. Kip, and Wesley A. Magat. 1987. *Learning About Risk.* Cambridge, Mass.: Harvard University Press.

Vispoel, Walter P. 1998. "Reviewing and Changing Answers on Computer-adaptive and Self-adaptive Vocabulary Tests." *Journal of Educational Measurement* 35(4): 328–45.

Wilson, Timothy D., and Daniel T. Gilbert. 2003. "Affective Forecasting." In *Advances in Experimental Social Psychology*, Volume 35, edited by Mark P. Zanna. New York: Elsevier.

Wilson, Timothy D., Thalia P. Wheatley, Jaime. L. Kurtz, Elizabeth W. Dunn, and Daniel T. Gilbert. 2004. "When to Fire: Anticipatory Versus Post-event Reconstrual of Uncontrollable Events." *Personality and Social Psychology Bulletin* 30(3): 340–51.

Zajonc, Robert B. 1980. "Feeling and Thinking: Preferences Need No Inferences." *American Psychologist* 35(2): 151–75.

Integrative Frameworks

· 2 ·

Affect-Based Evaluation and Regulation as Mediators of Behavior: The Role of Affect in Risk Taking, Helping, and Eating Patterns

Eduardo B. Andrade and Joel B. Cohen

Consider the following dilemma: To get people's attention and motivate action, a charity organization decides to use vivid pictures of orphaned and starving children in Africa along with somber background music. A primary research stream within the affect literature suggests, first, that such stimuli are likely to put people in a bad mood and that bad moods produce mood congruent information retrieval and explanatory attributional processes (for example, "I guess I didn't like the appeal"), all of which could work to the disadvantage of the charity. However, a second research stream proposes that people in bad moods pursue strategies likely to improve their moods, so people could feel much better if they called the charity and made a donation to help the children. But which of these opposing outcomes is most likely to occur?

In this chapter we apply a unified theoretical conceptualization (Andrade 2005) that relates both informational and goal-directed properties of affect to three important substantive research streams: risk taking, helping others, and eating patterns. These behaviors have not previously been brought together to observe their common affective underpinnings.

We propose that the integration of these two established affective mechanisms—where informational aspects are treated as affective evaluation (AE) and goal-directed aspects are treated as affect regulation (AR)—can help us account for many of the findings linking affect to observed differences in these behavioral domains. In the previous example, the AE mechanism works against calling the charity, as negative aspects of donating money (for example, fraud or failure to have a meaningful impact) become more salient as one experiences a more negative affective state. However, if donating money is perceived as a mood-lifting opportunity, the AR mechanism comes into play and may reverse the effect. As we will explain, positive affect produces mirror-image effects. It encourages behavioral activity via the affective evaluation mechanism. Donating money may seem easier (it would possibly lead to fewer "rainy day" thoughts) and more appealing when one is happy. However, when mood threatening cues are made salient (for example, risks of providing too much information over the phone), the effects reverse due to the impact of the affect regulation mechanism. In this case, AR leads people to protect their current positive feelings.

Thus, this chapter focuses on a broader understanding of the behavioral consequences of positive and negative feeling states, and how two general affect-related mediating mechanisms interact with one another to influence individual decision making. Contrary to other chapters in this volume (for example, Baumeister, DeWall, and Zhang, chapter 1), the proposed framework does not make general normative judgments about a particular affect-driven (or biased) choice. The reason is twofold: First, helping, eating, or taking risks are not necessarily appropriate or inappropriate behavioral activities by default. Second, whether affect will help or hurt decision making will depend on whether the combination of its informational and goal-directed properties leads to better outcomes than would follow from some other decision heuristic.

Affective Evaluation and Affect Regulation

A fundamental aspect of affective states is their ability to stimulate or discourage behavior (Frijda 1999). However, it is clear that no unique pattern of behavior can be expected from a valenced affective state: positive affect has been shown to both stimulate and mitigate risk taking and helping, just as negative affect has been shown to both encourage and discourage helping and food intake. While each of the three substantive domains we examine has important distinguishing characteristics, we believe this integrative conceptual approach may provide a parsimonious account of how affect influences behavior both here and elsewhere.

Studies examining the behavioral consequences of affect have, surprisingly, received very limited attention. There has been much more extensive research on the impact of affect on memory, information processing, and judgments and attitudes (Martin and Clore 2001) than on the impact of affect on choices and behavioral activities. For example, Norbert Schwarz and Gerald L. Clore's (1996) twenty-seven page review of the affect literature in social psychology allocated about half of a page to the impact of feelings on behavior: "As reflected in this review, most of the research has focused on the influence of feelings on cognitive processing. Attention to the impact of feelings on behavior has been more limited" (458). Also, behavioral models have usually focused either on a single behavioral activity (for example, helping; Schaller and Cialdini 1990) or on one pole of the affective spectrum (for example, positive affect; Isen 2000). Finally, and probably as an outgrowth of highly specialized research, the focus of resulting theories diverges, though each can call upon some supportive data. Looking across theories, domains, and studies, for example, there are disagreements as to whether negative affect enhances or inhibits helping as a result of mood regulation (Gendolla 2000; Schaller and Cialdini 1990) and whether mood maintenance leads to behavioral encouragement (Clark and Isen 1982; Manucia, Baumann, and Cialdini 1984).

Although a small number of alternative interpretations can be found in the literature, most theoretical accounts fall into one of the two major categories: static affective evaluation theories and dynamic affect regulation theories, each with its own underlying mechanism to explain the impact of affect on behavior (for an exception, see Forgas 1995). Affective evaluation theories rely most strongly on the role of affect as information (Schwarz and Clore 1983) and mood-congruency processes (Bower 1981; Isen et al. 1978). These models focus on the impact of affective states on cognition during an evaluative judgment (that is, at a single point in time), the results of which either stimulate or discourage a specific behavior. They suggest that affect influences cognition and action tendencies either directly, by providing people with unique information (Schwarz and Clore 1983), or more indirectly, by making mood congruent information more accessible in people's minds (Bower 1981; Isen et al. 1978).[1] The second major category, dynamic affect regulation theories, includes the negative relief model (Cialdini, Darby, and Vincent 1973), mood-maintenance (Clark and Isen 1982), coping (Lazarus and Folkman 1984), mood management (Zillmann 1988), the social constraint model of mood regulation (Erber and Erber 2001), and emotion regulation (Gross 1998). Although they vary in many details, these theories incorporate dynamic aspects such that individuals' hedonic goals (that is, preferences for feeling good and positive self-regard) lead them to consider possible affect discrepancy between two points in time (for example, what they feel now and what they could feel in the future as a result of the behavioral activity), and this anticipated affective change is likely to influence behavior.

Looking across all these theories, the affect-behavior relationship can be summarized by thinking about four combinations: positive affect-action, positive affect-inaction, negative affect-action, and negative affect-inaction (see figure 2.1). None of the theories within either of the two categories (together with their assumed mediating processes), can resolve the apparent "conflicting" findings. For instance, whereas the affect as information or mood congruency hypothesis can help us explain why negative mood discourages action or positive mood encourages action (represented in the lower-right and upper-left quadrants of figure 2.1), it is harder for these theories to explain how negative affect stimulates action or how positive mood mitigates action (represented in the lower-left and upper-right quadrants of figure 2.1). The opposite holds true for theories

Figure 2.1   Behavioral Consequences of Positive and Negative Affect

		BEHAVIORAL CONSEQUENCE	
		Encourages Behavior/ Behavioral Intentions	Discourages Behavior/ Behavioral Intentions
AFFECT	POSITIVE	Helping (Isen and Levin 1972) Eating patterns (Patel and Schlundt 2001)	Mood-threatening helping activity (Isen and Simmonds 1978) Risk-taking with low prob. and/or high stakes (Nygren et al. 1996)
	NEGATIVE	Helping (Manucia et al. 1984) Impulsive behavior (Tice et al. 2001)	Helping among children (Cialdini and Kenrick 1976) Chocolate intake among men (Grunberg and Straub 1992)

☐ Usually influenced by affective evaluation (AE)
☐ Usually influenced by affect regulation (AR)

Source: Authors' compilation.

based exclusively on affect regulation principles. These theories explain why, compared to a control condition, sad people are more willing to act and happy people are less willing to act (represented in the lower-left and upper-right quadrants of figure 2.1). However, they cannot easily account for a decrease in behavioral activity when people experience negative affect, nor can they easily account for the impact of positive affect on behavior encouragement (represented in the lower-right and upper-left quadrants of figure 2.1).

In our integrative framework, on the other hand, affect regulation and affective evaluation represent parallel mediators of behavioral response. Empirical evidence from research on helping (Cialdini and Kenrick 1976), risk taking (Nygren et al. 1996), and eating behavior (Willner et al. 1998) is reviewed in order to assess the framework's ability to explain relevant behavioral reactions (those resulting from current as well as anticipated affective states). In addition to clarifying apparent inconsistencies within each body of research, we hope to integrate seemingly isolated findings across these different substantive research streams. For example, understanding the reasons why people's willingness to help may increase or decrease as a function of a bad mood should allow us to understand the apparent "non-reliable" results relating negative mood and eating behavior. More generally, we provide an explanation of how the two processes interact, and we identify the critical moderating variables attached to each mediating process.

Scope of Analysis

The scope of analysis of our framework is defined by the independent variable (affect), the level of analysis of the mediating processes (affective evaluation and affect regulation), and the dependent variable (behavior and behavioral intentions).

Affect

Affect is defined as "positively or negatively valenced subjective reactions that a person experiences at a given point in time" (Wyer, Clore, and Isbell 1999, 3). Therefore, it represents the conceptual umbrella for both mood and emotions (for a different definition of affect, see Baumeister, DeWall, and Zhang, chapter 1, this volume). Although distinctions between mood and emotions vary somewhat, researchers tend to agree that the source of the affective experience represents a critical distinction. While subjects experiencing emotions are consciously aware that it emanates from some source, subjects experiencing moods are not.

For example, whereas people are *in* a bad or good mood, they are angry *at* someone or something (Schwarz and Clore 1996). Furthermore, emotions have several subcategories which may vary in intensity, duration, or cognitive participation (Ortony, Clore, and Collins 1988). Moods, however, usually represent a unique, indivisible, positive or negative state. This implies that specific types of emotions are likely to trigger different sets of behavior, depending on their arousing or cognitive properties (Raghunathan and Pham 1999; Lerner, Small, and Loewenstein 2004). For instance, as we will see, depressed people, compared to subjects who are simply in a bad mood, may behave differently when a mood-repair opportunity presents itself, since the chronic properties of the former probably mitigate the impact of affect regulation on behavior. Although it is beyond the scope of this chapter to assess the impact of specific types of emotions, the proposed framework does recognize the uniqueness of each type of emotion in producing behavioral consequences.

Mediational Processes

We believe it is useful to make the simplifying assumption that affect can potentially mediate evaluative and behavioral patterns at three different levels of processing (Cohen and Areni 1991; Pham et al. 2001). At the most basic level (Type I-Affect), affective information is conveyed via sensory-motor programs critical to bio-regulation. Bodily information is captured by the peripheral nervous system and sent to the central nervous system, which sends back signals that help regulate organs and biorhythmic activities. People are usually unaware of these automatic mechanisms. A midlevel of analysis (Type II-Affect) refers to basic affective reactions learned through conditioning or mere association, such as fear responses or alertness triggered by danger identification. This type of information may follow a "low road," departing from the thalamus where sensory information is processed to the amygdala, responsible for triggering emotional responses. As minimal cortical processing takes place, individuals have no more than a rough representation of the stimulus, but are capable of reacting fairly quickly to it (LeDoux 1996). Finally, affective information can be processed at a higher level (Type III-Affect), involving subjective appraisal of the stimulus. In this case, affective information requires significant participation of the neocortex, where most of the cognitive functions operate, before any behavioral activity takes place.

Though recognizing the importance of all three levels of psychophysiological processes, we focus on the impact of affect on behavior via a deliberate cognitive process, rather than more automatic affective reactions. Specifically, the propositions and empirical evidence discussed rely on cognitive processes in which individuals deliberately use affect as a signal to evaluate the environment around them (affective evaluation mechanism), or to regulate their affective experiences (affect regulation mechanism), or to do both.

Behavior

The focus here is given to behavior and behavioral intentions as the primary dependent measures. As mentioned earlier, behavior has received much less attention than cognition in research on affect (Forgas 2002; Schwarz and Clore 1996). Since many of the available studies have investigated the impact of affect on behavioral intentions rather than on final action, it made sense to include this empirical evidence. Moreover, there is compelling evidence of a reasonable relationship between intentions and behavior (Eagly and Chaiken 1993). Finally, for the sake of simplicity, we divide people's choice alternatives or intentions into two broad categories: action and inaction. This can mean helping versus not helping, eating more versus eating less, or being risk seeking versus being risk averse. Our analysis assumes that action will be more likely to produce affective changes than inaction (that is, doing something makes someone feel better or worse than if they didn't do anything). Thus, we do not incorporate important special circumstances in which inaction may actually perform a mood-lifting function (for example, procrastination; Tice, Bratslavsky and Baumeister 2001). Although our focus is on behavioral reactions, our hypothesized interaction between affective evaluation and affect regulation may also help to explain some of the observed inconsistencies at an information processing level (for example, mood congruent or incongruent recall; Isen 1984). However, that is beyond the scope of this chapter.

Theoretical Development

Historically, the relationship between affect and its behavioral consequences has been examined from three different perspectives, each highlighting one major property of affect (see also Baumeister, DeWall, and Zhang, chapter 1, this volume). The first, and probably the oldest tradition, stresses the disruptive properties of affect on judgment and behavior. Judson S. Brown and I. E. Farber (1951) suggested, for example, that hunger produced an affective impact if the goal was not reached. Two drives were hypothesized to operate in parallel: hunger (the "relevant drive") and frustration (the "irrelevant drive"). People were seen as striving for the relevant goal, to satisfy their hunger, while avoiding the negative effects of frustration, the irrelevant drive. Following the same rationale, action control theory (Kuhl and Beckmann 1984) considered frustration to be a "competing tendency" that must be controlled. Affect (typically negative affect) was therefore reduced to a disrupting psychological mechanism leading to negative cognitive and behavioral outcomes in such research programs.

The critique of the disruptive perspective challenges the treatment of feelings as maladaptive or irrational (and therefore, "to be avoided") components of human nature. Moreover, it disputes the assumption that individuals' goals can best be met by controlling for internal and environmental "emotional temptations." The conception of disruptive feelings tends to overlook the functional aspects of feelings and constrains our understanding of the importance of feelings to judgment and behavior (Carver, Lawrence, and Scheier 1996; Frijda 1999; Pham et al. 2001). Although it is clear that affect can lead to disruptive and nonadaptive consequences (for example, Shiv et al. 2005), feelings are, under many circumstances, indispensable for optimal decision making, and ". . . the absence of emotions and feeling is no less damaging, no less capable of compromising the rationality that makes us human" (Damasio 1994, xii).

Two more recent perspectives have attempted to understand the "rationality" behind affectively-influenced behavior. The first has focused on the *static evaluative properties* of the affective experience and the second has relied on the *dynamic regulatory properties* of affect. To a certain extent, these two bodies of knowledge have followed somewhat independent paths. As a result, many inconsistencies have emerged in the literature.

The Static Affective Evaluation Approach

Within this paradigm, a common assumption is that current affective states at a single point in time are likely to bias any evaluative judgment, and eventually behavior. Two rather complementary hypotheses have emerged to account for the processes underlying affective evaluations: one direct process—affect as information—and one indirect process—mood congruency. The affect as information hypothesis proposes that affect itself may provide unique information that is directly retrieved during evaluation (Schwarz and Clore 1983). Individuals ask themselves "How do I feel about it?" and use this information to make evaluative judgments. The mood congruency hypothesis proposes that concepts congruent with an individual's current affective state become more accessible in memory (Bower 1981; Isen et al. 1978). As evaluation typically requires a retrieval process, the likelihood of using mood congruent concepts during an evaluative judgment increases, thereby biasing judgment. In short, affect is assumed to influence evaluation directly as newly supplied information, as well as indirectly via changes in the accessibility of mood congruent information. Since the predictions are usually similar across these two information-based mediators of evaluation, we focus on their similar effects on evaluation as a precursor to behavior rather than on information-processing distinctions. First, positive affect can lead to more positive evaluations, thereby stimulating action (represented in the upper-left quadrant of figure 2.1). Different research streams have provided evidence consistent with this rationale. People experiencing positive feelings are, under certain circumstances, more willing to eat (Cools, Schotte, and McNally 1992; Patel and Schlundt 2001), gamble (Isen and Geva 1987), and help (Manucia, Baumann, and Cialdini 1984). Similarly, negative affect can lead to more negative evaluation, thereby discouraging action (represented in the lower-right quadrant of figure 2.1). Convergent with this hypothesis, negative affect has been shown, under certain circumstances, to reduce helping (Cialdini and Kenrick 1976), risk taking (Raghunathan and Pham 1999), and food consumption (Grunberg and Straub 1992).

The Dynamic Affect Regulation Approach

Whereas affective evaluation approaches focus both on direct and on indirect informational effects, the affect regulation mechanism captures the motivational aspect of specific affective states. Moreover, it moves from a static conception of the role of affect to a dynamic approach in which the current affective state and the anticipated affective state, as well as the discrepancy between them, play major roles in guiding behavior (Atkinson 1957, 1964; Bagozzi, Baumgartner, and Pieters 1998). The dynamic affect regulation approach proposes two basic effects, both of which contrast with the effects suggested by the affective evaluation approach. First, negative affect can stimulate action (represented in the lower-left quadrant of figure 2.1). People experiencing negative affect are, under certain circumstances, more willing to take actions such as watch comedies (Weaver and Laird 1995; Zillmann 1988), listen to uplifting music (Knobloch and Zillmann 2002), eat (Grunberg and Straub 1992; Tice, Bratslavsky and Baumeister 2001), exercise (Hsiao and Thayer 1998), aggress (Bushman, Baumeister, and Phillips 2001), self-gift (Mick and DeMoss 1990), help (Cialdini, Darby, and Vincent 1973; Manucia, Baumann, and Cialdini 1984), buy impulsively (Rook and Gardner 1993), and sell (Lerner, Small, and Loewenstein 2004). Second, positive affect can discourage action (represented in the upper-right quadrant of figure 2.1), such that people experiencing positive affect can, under certain circumstances, be less willing to take risks (Isen and Geva 1987) and to help (Forest et al. 1979; Isen and Simmonds 1978). This is probably in an attempt to protect their current affective states.

In order to address the four combinations of the affect-behavior relationship (that is, positive and negative affect, and stimulation and inhibition, represented in the four quadrants of figure 2.1), it seems critical to integrate both the static evaluation and the dynamic regulation research traditions, each with their focus on a separate key property of affect.

An Integrated Affect Evaluation and Regulation Framework

We assume that affective states have both motivational and evaluative influences, and that the interaction between these two mechanisms directs behavior. In an attempt to understand the impact of positive affect on risk taking, Alice M. Isen and colleagues (Isen and Geva 1987; Isen, Nygren, and Ashby 1988; Nygren et al. 1996) provided initial evidence of the interaction between these two mechanisms. However, there is no theoretical reason to believe that the same principles would not also apply to negative affective states, or to virtually any type of behavioral activity (Gendolla 2000; Schaller and Cialdini 1990).

In our model, AE arises from people's congruent use of affective information (whether through associational processes or inferential reasoning) during an evaluative judgment. AR relies on a hedonic goal pursuit assumption, in which positive affect represents a goal or the achievement of a goal. Thus, individuals spontaneously attempt to achieve this desired affective state when feeling bad, and protect it once the state has been attained.

At the core of the distinction between these two mechanisms is their static versus dynamic character. Because the affective evaluation mechanism is essentially driven by people's current affective states, either directly (as information) or indirectly (via mood congruent information), immediate feelings are responsible for the impact of AE on judgment and behavior. This is the case even when people project themselves into some imagined or alternative state of affairs and use an affective heuristic to make future affect salient in order to judge how much they like an outcome, because in this case they still rely on a onetime, static affect-congruent appraisal (Pham 1998). For affect regulation to operate, individuals must assess their current feelings as well as forecast the affective consequences likely to be produced by the subsequent behavioral activity, and they must focus on the direction of the difference.

Intuitive theories about affective consequences of behavior are critical to this dynamic analysis. For instance, when people are led to believe that the upcoming behavior will not change their mood because their mood is "frozen," the impact of AR is mitigated (Manucia, Baumann, and Cialdini 1984; Tice, Bratslavsky, and Baumeister, 2001). This is also the case if some individuals fail to perceive an activity as mood lifting. Robert B. Cialdini and Douglas T. Kenrick (1976) showed that children in a bad mood were less willing to help than young adults, probably because they have not yet learned the hedonic benefits associated with helping (that is, for these children altruistic behaviors did not represent an affect regulation opportunity). Finally, studies examining chronic affective states have shown that depressed people do not perceive themselves as capable of upwardly regulating their current negative affective states (Davidson et al. 2002; Kanfer and Zeiss 1983), which may also mitigate the impact of AR on behavior.

In short, the extent to which AR will strongly mediate the impact of affect on behavior is highly contingent on the perceived affect changing properties of the upcoming behavioral activity (Andrade 2005). Moreover, this moderator interacts with people's current affective states and the respective affective gains or losses that are expected to result from action. Thus, mood-lifting cues associated with the behavioral activity are more likely to lead to action encouragement for those experiencing negative (versus neutral) affect, as people have more to gain (represented in the lower-left quadrant of figure 2.1), whereas mood-threatening cues are more likely to discourage action for those experiencing positive (versus neutral) affect, as these people have more to lose (represented in the upper-right corner of figure 2.1).

It is also clear that moderating variables other than expected affective changes are likely to influence the impact of both mechanisms. For instance, the salience of the current affective experience is predicted to influence both mechanisms in a similar way. Affective evaluation tends to produce stronger evaluative and behavioral effects compared to a control (that is, a neutral affect) condition when a given positive or negative affective state is vividly experienced (Forgas and Fiedler 1996). The same pattern holds true for the affect regulation mechanism, in which polarized (versus neutral) affective states more strongly influence people's willingness to regulate their moods (Cohen and Andrade 2004). However, while the strength of the affective signal makes it more accessible and indicates a potentially stronger impact of affect on behavior (for example, greater potency or activation potential), the intensity and direction of behavior itself (that is, action versus inaction) results from the interaction between the accessible affective signal and specific situational factors associated with both AE and AR.

Both mechanisms are influenced by the perceived informational value of current feelings vis-à-vis the judgment or behavior at stake. AE becomes less influential when the diagnosticity of affect is reduced. This happens, for instance, when people realize they are mistakenly using their feelings (Schwarz and Clore 1983), or when they simply do not trust their feelings (Avnet and Pham 2004). On the other hand, it becomes more influential when the diagnosticity of affect is increased, such as when judgment or behavior is linked to hedonic goals and outcomes (Adaval 2001; Pham 1998; Yeung and Wyer 2004). The essence of diagnosticity for AE is the subjective appropriateness of using an affective signal as the basis for the decision to behave or not (for a similar "functional sufficiency" assessment of the attitude-behavior relationship, see Cohen and Reed 2006). Diagnosticity could have the same type of contingent impact for dynamic assessments linked to AR, although direct evidence for this is scant.

Finally, an analysis of diagnosticity assumes that the evaluative relevance of affective information must be seen in relation to the relevance of competing (non affective) information in the environment. Although researchers have focused more often on changing the relevance (or representativeness) of affective information (Pham 1998; Schwarz and Clore 1983), changes in the amount and quality of competing information should produce mirror image effects. More relevant information about the stimulus should weaken the impact of the affective evaluation mechanism, as less relevant information should strengthen the impact. For instance, affective evaluation tends to have a stronger impact when people judge ambiguous (versus unambiguous) stimuli (Gorn, Pham, and Sin 2001), or when cognitive resources are depleted (Siemer and Reisenzein 1998). Though diagnosticity of competing information is also germane to affect regulation, it is important to note that the impact of AR on behavior should also vary as a function of other competing and complementary goals. As the strength or number of competing goals increases, the impact of AR tends to decrease (for example, one might forgo shopping in favor of saving). Moreover, competing goals may influence not only the strength of the affect regulation mechanism, but also the direction of the effort. For example, happy people might try to feel worse prior to a task requiring careful analytical thinking (Cohen and Andrade 2004).

In summary, the guiding premise of our model is that affect impacts behavior via two mediating mechanisms: affective evaluation (AE) and affect regulation (AR). The impact of these mechanisms is moderated by several factors, including affect accessibility, affect diagnosticity, competing goals, and the perceived affective consequences of the behavioral activity.

Using the Framework to Resolve Inconsistencies Across Three Research Streams

Research has focused mostly on two moderators: accessibility, using orthogonal mood manipulations; and perceived affective consequences, by providing mood-lifting or mood-threatening cues. The interactions between these and our two key mediators of affect-behavior outcomes (AE and AR) help explain and integrate research findings in each of the four quadrants of figure 2.1 across disparate substantive domains. We start with the largest of the literatures, research on helping behavior, which accounts for a substantial amount of the inconsistent findings in this area.

Helping

One of the prevalent findings in the helping literature is that current affective states influence individuals' willingness to help. However, the effects do not follow a single pattern (Batson 1990; Salovey, Mayer, and Rosenhan 1991; Schaller and Cialdini 1990). Researchers tend to agree that the relationship between positive mood and helping is, in general, well established, and that positive mood increases people's propensity to help (Isen, Clark, and Schwartz 1976; Isen and Levin 1972; Levin and Isen 1975). However, there is some evidence that the opposite may also be true, and that there can be a decrease in helping due to individuals' positive feelings (Isen and Simmonds 1978). The impact of negative affect on helping is also bidirectional; it sometimes increases helping (Cialdini, Darby, and Vincent 1973; Cunningham, Steinberg, and Grev 1980; Manucia, Baumann, and Cialdini 1984), and sometimes decreases helping (Berkowitz 1972; Berkowitz and Connor 1966; Isen 1970). Several hypotheses have been proposed to account for these inconsistent patterns. However, the proposed mechanisms seem to vary almost as much as the results themselves; these mechanisms include positive mood maintenance, guilt reduction, negative state relief, aversive arousal reduction, positive affective priming, and negative affective priming (Batson 1990; Salovey, Mayer, and Rosenhan 1991).

Positive Affect and Helping Increase. In a field study, Alice M. Isen and Paula F. Levin (1972) showed that subjects who found a dime in the coin return of a public telephone were subsequently more willing to pick up papers dropped off in front of them by a confederate. Similarly, after manipulating mood through false feedback, Isen (1970) showed that happy students were more willing to give money to the "Junior High

Air-Conditioning Fund" compared to sad students. Indeed, the positive impact of good mood on prosocial behavior is quite robust (Aderman 1972; Berkowitz and Connor 1966; Levin and Isen 1975; Moore, Underwood, and Rosenhan 1973; Rosenhan, Underwood, and Moore 1974). Two underlying mechanisms leading to this effect have been advanced: cognitive mechanisms such as priming effects, and motivational mechanisms such as positive mood maintenance. The cognitive/priming explanation is based essentially on mood congruency effects (Isen, Clark, and Schwartz 1976; Isen 1978), through which positive information becomes more accessible during evaluation and influenced behavior (Clark and Waddel 1983).

The competing motivational explanation for the effects of positive affective states on helping adopts a regulatory process approach. This explanation proposes that people in a good mood try to remain in their current affective states, and therefore are more willing to help (Clark and Isen 1982; Isen 1984; Levin and Isen 1975). This hypothesis has two major drawbacks. From a theoretical point of view, it fails to explain why people experiencing positive (versus neutral) affect would be more willing to take actions, such as helping, that impact mood, since those in a neutral mood have more to gain (for a strength of signal rationale, see Cohen and Andrade 2004). Moreover, from an empirical standpoint, "evidence is scarce that happy subjects help as a means to maintain positive moods" (Schaller and Cialdini 1990, 282). Helping as a mood maintenance alternative (that is, people's willingness to help in order "to fuel" their otherwise decaying positive feelings) requires people to perceive the behavioral activity as mood lifting. Gloria K. Manucia, Donald J. Baumann, and Robert B. Cialdini (1984) used a "mood-freezing pill" technique to test the extent to which people's willingness to help would vary depending on their affect regulation beliefs. After instantiation of positive, neutral, or negative affective states, subjects were asked to take a placebo pill. Half the subjects were informed that this pill would "freeze" their current affective states for a while. The results showed effects of the "mood-freezing pill" manipulation only among those in the negative affect conditions. Positive affect tended to increase helping even when people were led to believe that their affective states would not change as a result of the behavioral activity (see Gailliot and Tice, chapter 9, this volume, for a detailed description of the "mood freezing" procedure). In summary, biases in evaluative judgment rather than anticipated changes in current affective states seem to play the key role in happy people's increased propensity to help (Batson 1990; Salovey, Mayer, and Rosenhan 1991; Schaller and Cialdini 1990). As no study has contrasted affect as information versus mood-congruency mechanisms, and both predict the same effects, it seems premature to claim which process, if not both, is responsible for the impact of positive mood on helping.

Positive Affect and Helping Decrease.   Little evidence is available showing that being in a good mood can decrease helping. However, Alice M. Isen and Stanley F. Simmonds (1978) found that when the helping scenario displays situational cues that threaten subjects' current positive mood, these individuals were indeed less likely to help than were subjects in a neutral mood. The authors suggested that a challenging helping task may have led happy subjects to anticipate negative affect and triggered a self-protective regulatory mechanism (see also Andrade 2005, study 2). This type of effect will be further examined under the risk taking literature review where the impact of positive affect on behavioral discouragement is well established.

Negative Affect and Helping Increase.   Studies showing that negative affect increases helping have generated several related hypotheses to account for the underlying mechanisms; these mechanisms include guilt reduction (Carlsmith and Gross 1969; Regan, Williams, and Sparling 1972), negative mood relief (Baumann, Cialdini, and Kenrick 1981; Cialdini, Darby, and Vincent 1973; Cialdini and Kenrick 1976; Manucia, Baumann, and Cialdini 1984), and aversive arousal reduction (Piliavin et al. 1981, 1982). Although adopting different research approaches, these researchers all share the basic assumption that upward affect regulation is at the core of people's disposition to help. Helping is conceived to be an affect regulation strategy aimed at achievement of hedonic goals (in other words, feeling good in general or about oneself).

Robert B. Cialdini, Betty Lee Darby, and Joyce E. Vincent (1973) were among the first to categorize helping as a mood-repair strategy. They showed that subjects in a bad mood were more likely than those in control conditions to help in response to another person's request. Most importantly, as soon as hedonic benefits, such as an unexpected monetary reward or approval for task performance, were interposed between the mood manipulation and the help request, the effects of negative affect on helping disappeared. The authors asserted that helping, monetary reward, and positive feedback each perform a similar functional goal: mood relief (Baumann, Cialdini, and Kenrick 1981). Manucia, Baumann, and Cialdini (1984) provided further, and perhaps even more compelling, evidence implicating an upward affect regulation strategy as the mediating mechanism linking a bad mood to helping. Subjects in a bad mood who were told about the "freezing" effects of the drug helped much less compared to those in the "nonfrozen" bad-mood condition, and they helped a similar amount as those in the neutral condition.

Finally, these results are also consistent with the findings of Alice M. Isen, Nancy Horn, and David L. Rosenhan (1973). After exposing children to a success, control, or failure feedback, those exposed to a failure condition were more generous only when an "opportunity for image repair" was present.

Negative Affect and Helping Decrease.   There is evidence that negative affect can also decrease helping under certain circumstances (Cialdini and Kenrick, 1976; Isen 1970; Moore, Underwood, and Rosenhan 1973). However, purely cognitive approaches have been used to account for the effect. Similar to positive moods, negative moods are also known to prime congruent thoughts: "Thoughts of deprivation, helplessness, and uselessness may become especially available, rendering such sad and self-focused individuals less likely to help" (Salovey, Mayer, and Rosenhan 1991, 222). In summary, whereas upward affect regulation is typically identified as responsible for instigating helping behavior, affective evaluation is identified as playing a major role when opposite results are found.

There has been a failure to find evidence consistent with affect regulation (that is, a helping increase) in certain studies in which negative mood had been induced. However, in many studies where negative mood decreased helping, children were used as subjects (Cialdini and Kenrick 1976; Moore, Underwood, and Rosenhan 1973; Rosenhan, Underwood, and Moore 1974). It is possible that children do not usually perceive helping as an effective affect regulation strategy. If that is the case, affective evaluation should have a stronger impact. Indeed, Cialdini and Kenrick (1976) showed that age and levels of socialization are critical moderating variables. In one experiment, the authors found an interaction between age and mood on helping. The youngest group (six- to eight-year-olds) was less willing to help when feeling sad (vs. neutral). The effect reversed among the oldest participants. Fifteen- to eighteen-year-old subjects in a bad mood helped more than those in a neutral condition. No difference emerged among participants aged ten to twelve. As the authors predicted, individuals whose socialization process is still incipient do not perceive helping as self-gratifying. In short, the youngest subjects in a bad mood do not help because they do not perceive altruistic behaviors as a viable affect regulation strategy. Consequently, the negative thoughts elicited by a bad mood operate to reduce helping.

Theoretical Integration.   The helping literature shows that both positive and negative affect can stimulate or discourage helping depending on situational cues available in the environment (that is, there is support for each of the four quadrants in figure 2.1). It is possible to reconcile these effects if we begin with the basic assumption that two interdependent mechanisms underlie the impact of affect on behavior. Situational cues and internal affective signals determine which mechanism will prevail.

Our framework suggests that positive affect leads to helping increase (represented in the upper-right quadrant of figure 2.1) via an AE mechanism. That is, a positive mood positively biases subjects' evaluations of the helping task—either via affect as information or mood congruency—both of which should increase subjects' willingness to help (Isen 1970; Isen and Levin 1972; Moore, Underwood, and Rosenhan 1973). However, when situational cues lead subjects to anticipate negative affect, AR becomes the dominant mechanism, and helping behavior is discouraged (represented in the upper-left quadrant of figure 2.1). As originally proposed by Isen and Simmonds (1978), the reason for such protective reaction is that subjects in a positive mood have more to lose than those in control conditions. Although this type of effect is rather sporadic in the helping literature, the study of risk taking offers consistent theoretical and empirical evidence of the impact of anticipated negative affect on behavior.

For people in a negative mood, upward affect regulation is usually a reasonably important motivator and is likely to dominate the impact of the affective evaluation mechanism. As a result, individuals attempt to improve their current negative affective states (represented in the lower-left quadrant of figure 2.1). Several studies provide evidence of a helping increase for sad subjects (Baumann, Cialdini, and Kenrick 1981; Cialdini, Darby, and Vincent 1973; Cialdini and Kenrick 1976; Manucia, Baumann, and Cialdini 1984). However, in our framework, affect regulation is contingent on people's recognition of the behavior as an effective upward affect regulation strategy. When sad subjects are incapable of perceiving the mood-lifting benefits of helping, affect regulation is mitigated, and the affective evaluation mechanism (that is, the negative evaluation of the environment) leads to a decrease in helping (represented in the lower-right quadrant of figure 2.1). This was the case when children were used in the experiments (Cialdini and Kenrick 1976; Moore, Underwood, and Rosenhan 1973), as well as when people's moods were "frozen" (Manucia, Baumann, and Cialdini 1984).

In short, the proposed framework accounts for the bulk of effects in the helping literature, by suggesting that positive affect increases helping via affective evaluation (that is, through priming effects or affect as information, or through both); positive affect decreases helping via affect regulation when accompanied by anticipated negative affect; negative affect increases helping via upward affect regulation when accompanied by anticipated positive affect; and negative affect decreases helping via negative affective evaluation when subjects are unable to perceive the mood-lifting benefits of helping.

Risk Taking

The relationship between affective states and expected outcomes is well established (Loewenstein et al. 2001). Eric J. Johnson and Amos Tversky (1983) found that when asked to evaluate the subjective probability of positive future events, subjects in positive moods reported a higher subjective probability compared to control subjects, and a much higher subjective probability compared to subjects in a negative mood. The opposite was true when they were asked to evaluate the subjective probability of negative future events. In this case, subjects in negative moods reported a higher subjective probability compared to those in neutral moods, and a much higher subjective probability than subjects in a positive mood. After tracking cognitive processes by means of thought listing, William F. Wright and Gordon H. Bower (1992) showed that individuals focused more on mood-congruent information during the assessment of subjective probabilities. In other words, happy (sad) people seem to have a more optimistic (pessimistic) view of the world.

Thus, based on prevailing evidence one would expect that people in bad moods, who tend to perceive situations as riskier, should be less inclined toward risk taking. The opposite should be true for subjects experiencing a positive affective state. Individuals in good moods, who usually perceive a safer environment, should be more prone to risk taking. Yet, findings in the literature do not fully confirm either of these two predictions. Although the results are rather consistent as to the impact of affect on risk *perception* (for example, Constans and Matthews 1993; Johnson and Tversky 1983; Mayer et al. 1992; Pietromonaco and Rook 1987; Wright and Bower 1992), they vary significantly when it comes to the relationship between affect and risk *taking*.

Negative Affect and Risk Taking.   Negative affective states have been shown to increase risk taking (Gehring and Willoughby 2002; Leith and Baumeister 1996; Mittal and Ross 1998; Raghunathan and Pham 1999). Rajagopal Raghunathan and Michel T. Pham (1999) investigated the impact of sadness and anxiety on risk taking. When presented with two gamble options—a low-risk, low-payoff option and a high-risk, high pay off option—in a consumer-decision task, sad subjects preferred the riskier alternative with a higher payoff compared to anxious subjects, who were strongly risk averse. The authors suggested that different goals are primed for sad versus anxious people: sad subjects focused on reward replacement (that is, mood repair), whereas anxious subjects focused on uncertainty reduction. Sad subjects thus perceived the high-risk, high-payoff option as more attractive because of the mood-lifting potential, whereas anxious subjects preferred the low-risk, low-payoff alternative because it could reduce their uncertainty (that is, their anxiety). This rationale is in line with the studies of Michael W. Eysenck, Colin MacLeod, and Andrew Matthews (1987), in which anxiety led to attentional and interpretational biases. Highly anxious people tend not only to have an attentional bias toward threat-related words but also to interpret ambiguous information as more threatening. Nazanin Derakshan and Michael W. Eysenck (1997) also found that highly anxious people display an interpretative bias for their own behavior in social situations; they perceive their behavior as more anxious.

These findings highlight a critical assumption of the proposed framework: the affective evaluation and affect regulation mechanisms are interdependent. Anxious people appear to evaluate risky action even more negatively, lowering the likelihood of taking action to regulate affect in the absence of an almost certain mood lifting opportunity. Thus, any potential mood-lifting properties which might be associated with a high-risk bet are dissipated, and the impact of the affect regulation mechanism is mitigated. Simultaneously, anxious subjects arrive at a rather threatening assessment of the environment, which further strengthens the impact of the affective evaluation mechanism. The impact of strong negative affective evaluation, combined with the perceived absence of an upward affect regulation opportunity, leads to risk-averse behavioral patterns (represented in the lower-right quadrant of figure 2.1). However, when people experience sadness, the mood-lifting properties of similar risk taking may remain stable or even intensify, offsetting the negative impact of affective evaluation on risk perceptions, and leading people to choose more risk-prone behaviors (represented in the lower-left quadrant of figure 2.1).[2] Thus, the type of affective state experienced may well produce different interpretations of, or attention to, available mood-lifting opportunities, making the affect regulation mechanism either more or less influential.

Risk taking has also been shown to increase as a result of losses. In a gambling scenario, William J. Gehring and Adrian R. Willoughby (2002) showed that choices made after experiencing losses were riskier. Since losses may trigger negative feelings of disappointment, sadness, frustration, etc., people might be using risk taking opportunities as a strategy to improve their current affective states. In line with this rationale, Eduardo B. Andrade and Ganesh Iyer (2007) have recently shown that people plan to bet less in anticipation of a loss but end up betting more than planned once the loss is eventually *felt*. The authors adopt an empathy gap rationale to argue that actual negative feelings (experienced

after a loss) are stronger than anticipated, leading to greater than anticipated efforts to upwardly regulate their affective states. In fact, when
participants in the experiment were asked to control for the potential
impact of feelings on betting decision, the difference between planning
and actual betting (after losses) disappeared. Thus, risk taking might
under certain circumstances represent a mood-lifting opportunity which
may stimulate the affect regulation mechanism and overcome potentially countervailing forces based on the affective evaluation mechanism. This rationale is also supported by recent evidence from
neuroscience, in which the pleasure and reward areas of the brain (that
is, the nucleus accumbens) are activated in the anticipation of a financial
benefit (Knutson et al. 2001a, 2001b).

Positive Affect and Risk Taking.   Barbara Kahn and Alice M. Isen (1993)
showed that individuals in a positive mood (compared to a neutral
mood) were stimulated to seek more variety among safe and enjoyable
food products. Hal R. Arkes, Lisa Tandy Herren, and Alice M. Isen
(1988) also demonstrated that, compared to subjects in a neutral mood,
happy subjects were more willing to pay for lottery tickets. These and
similar results show that people in a good mood are apparently more
prone to risk taking. Since we know that people in a good mood are
more optimistic (Johnson and Tversky 1983; Wright and Bower 1992),
this pattern might be labeled as rather intuitive. However, not all studies
have shown this risk-prone behavior among happy people. For example, Kahn and Isen (1993) showed that the increase of variety-seeking
behavior among happy subjects disappeared as soon as a product's
negative features were included or made salient in the choice context.
Similarly, Thomas E. Nygren and his colleagues (1996) showed that subjects in a positive mood are more risk seeking than subjects in a neutral
mood, provided that the potential losses are not salient or too high.
When larger amounts are at stake, positive affect makes subjects more
cautious (Isen, Nygren, and Ashby 1988). Research on this topic has
used a motivational rationale to account for the findings: people in a
good mood facing threatening stimuli become more self-protective of
their current feelings, thereby discouraging risky behaviors which may
lead them to feel bad.

The pattern of results is consistent with the proposed framework,
which predicts that affect regulation is activated not only when subjects
experience negative feelings, but also when subjects anticipate negative
feelings. As the positive side of the spectrum represents the desired
affective state, subjects in a positive mood have more to lose than those
in a neutral affective state. Thus, when losses are likely, such as in a
high-risk condition, people in a good mood face a greater relative loss

than people in a neutral mood (Isen and Geva 1987). Such anticipatory negative emotional reactions reduce the likelihood of engaging in risky behavior to achieve affect regulation goals, and hence counteract the impact of positive affect-based evaluations. Nygren et al. (1996) used the seemingly contradictory expression "cautious optimism" to underscore the dual and, here, opposing mechanisms at work. They summarize their first study by saying that, on the one hand, "positive affect participants significantly overestimated the probabilities," but on the other hand, "[they] were less likely to gamble than were controls when a real loss was possible" (Nygren et al. 1996, 59). Whereas "optimism" is a result of affective evaluation (that is, affective priming effects), "caution" represents a consequence of affect regulation, and it is triggered by anticipated negative affect.

In summary, being in a good mood may promote both risk-averse behavior (represented in the upper-right quadrant of figure 2.1) as well as risk-seeking behavior (represented in the upper-left quadrant of figure 2.1). The outcome depends on mediating effects linked primarily to affect regulation, which have been shown to be contingent on the perceived mood-threatening consequences associated with the behavioral activity. When no threats are made salient, affective evaluation leads to risk-prone behaviors; in contrast, when environmental cues signal threats, affect regulation goals are activated, promoting negative mood avoidance through risk-averse behaviors.

Eating Patterns

Although many goals and situational variables can influence eating patterns, the impact of affect, particularly that of negative affect, on food intake has been widely investigated (Canetti, Bachar, and Berry 2002; Christensen 1993; Greeno and Wing 1994). Researchers' interests vary significantly: They range from the effects of stress on psychopathological behaviors (for example, obesity and bulimia), to normal influences of mild mood swings on food preferences (for example, cravings for sweets or carbohydrates). They include studies ranging from tail-pinch stressors and animal eating responses, to unpleasant movies and human propensity to eat snack food.

As our analysis and proposed model focuses on the impact of mild affective states on everyday behavior, we concentrate on how negative and positive affective states influence normal food intake. Consistent with the evidence reviewed above, the first conclusion to be drawn from this body of research is that affect does not lead to a unique behavioral outcome. Positive and negative affective states each may stimulate or discourage food intake.

Negative Affect and Eating Patterns. There are a far greater number of studies dealing with the impact of negative affect on eating behavior than those dealing with positive affect. The underlying assumption in most of the literature is that food acts as mood regulator, lifting subjects' current affective state after intake (Bruch 1973; Greeno and Wing 1994; Kaplan and Kaplan 1957; Morris and Reilly 1987; Polivy and Herman 1976; Thayer 1989; Tice, Bratslavsky and Baumeister 2001; Gailliot and Tice, chapter 9, this volume). Thus, compared to a control condition, negative affect is expected to encourage eating behavior. Traditionally, it has been suggested that negative affect stimulates unhealthy eating behaviors (Vohs et al. 1999, 2001). Recently, however, studies have emerged to suggest that the consequences of negative affect on people's eating behavior could also be extended to typical everyday activities.

Neil E. Grunberg and Richard O. Straub (1992) exposed subjects to a film about industrial accidents (to induce a negative affect), or to a pleasant travelogue (as a control), while snack foods were available in the room. They found that eating consumption increased as a result of negative affect only among women. The results actually reversed for male subjects, who reduced the amount of food intake as a consequence of negative affect. Although the authors did not advance a systematic theoretical explanation for the effects, the results have proven quite robust. Whereas negative affect tends to increase food intake among women (Macht 1999; Patel and Schlundt 2001; Weinstein, Shide, and Rolls 1997; Willner et al. 1998), this effect is either canceled (Pine 1985) or reversed among men (Abramson and Wunderlich 1972; Macht, Roth, and Ellgring 2002; Reznick and Balch 1977).

A potential explanation for such variation is that strategic affect regulation through food intake is stronger in women than men, at least for certain types of food (Macht 1999; Steptoe, Pollard, and Wardle 1995). As we have shown in the other streams of research, pursuing a single explanatory mechanism may be at the root of the apparent inconsistency. In this case, however, the main explanatory mechanism has been affect regulation rather than affective evaluation. Once again, our framework proposes that understanding the interaction between affective evaluation and affect regulation is critical to explain the bidirectional pattern.[3] Whereas upward affect regulation accounts for the increase in food intake as a result of negative affect (represented in the lower-left quadrant of figure 2.1), negative affective evaluation is likely to explain food intake inhibition (represented in the lower-right quadrant of figure 2.1). Affect regulation, as a goal, is contingent on the availability of efficacious affect regulation strategies. If men are less likely to perceive certain types of food (for example, chocolate) as mood lifters, the impact of affect regulation will be mitigated and affective evaluation will most likely drive the effects (for example, they would eat less if they felt sad). Oliver and Wardle (1999) showed that whereas stress increased the consumption of snack-type foods—which are perceived both as "quick energy products" and "treats"—it decreased the consumption of typical meal-type foods (such as fruits, vegetables, meat, and fish). Relatedly, Paul Willner and Sarah Healy (1994) showed that after negative affect induction, subjects lowered their own evaluation of cheese in terms of pleasantness and desirability. This also suggests that affective behavior toward food that has no subjective mood-lifting attributes will be mostly directed by the affective evaluation mechanism. So, as bad feelings produce a worsening evaluation of focal objects such as food, eating should decline. Eduardo B. Andrade (2005) addressed this issue by exposing participants to a "virtual sampling promotion" procedure after a negative, neutral, or positive affect manipulation. Participants were asked to imagine themselves in a sampling-promotion setting; a picture of chocolate bar was presented to them, and they indicated the extent to which they would be willing to try it. At the end of the experiment respondents reported the extent to which they typically ate chocolate to try to feel better. In the negative affect condition, those who were less prone to perceive chocolate as mood lifting (this group was mostly made up of men) were less willing to try the chocolate compared to those in the control condition (that is, neutral affect). However, the effects reversed for participants who acknowledged using chocolate as a mood-lifting strategy (this group was mostly made up of women); the participants in this group were more willing to taste the chocolate if they were in the negative affect condition than if they were in the control condition.

Positive Affect and Eating Patterns. Eating disorders that are normally associated with negative affect (such as obesity, binge eating, bulimia, and anorexia) have been at the forefront of the research in this field from the 1970s through the 1990s. Only recently have researchers devoted attention to the consequences of positive affect. The general pattern of results suggests that positive mood stimulates eating (represented in the upper-left quadrant of figure 2.1; Cools, Schotte, and McNally 1992; Macht 1999; Macht, Roth, and Ellgring 2002; Patel and Schlundt 2001), though null effects have also been reported (Frost et al. 1982). Based on two-week food diaries, K. A. Patel and D. G. Schlundt (2001) found that obese women more often increased food intake when experiencing both positive and negative affect than when in a control condition. Contrary to the authors' expectations of an interaction between mood and social context (that is, eating alone versus eating in a social context), the impact of valenced moods occurred under both social context scenarios. No explanation was provided to account for the results. Michael Macht, S. Roth, and Heinrich Ellgring (2002) provided a compelling mood congruent explanation for such effects. They showed that male subjects experiencing positive affect (versus those experiencing negative affect) provided higher ratings on two general dimensions for chocolates they were eating: affective responses to chocolate (for example, taste pleasantness) and motivation to eat (for example, appetite). The authors suggested that the positive impact of affect on food intake was probably a result of mood-congruent evaluation effects. This effect could also be driven by mood maintenance if people are eating more in an attempt to maintain their good mood. However, evidence for this is lacking, and Andrade's (2005) results, described above, contradict this hypothesis. Whereas people's acknowledged use of chocolate as a mood-lifting alternative interacted with participants' negative affective states to increase chocolate consumption intentions (as per AR predictions), it had no impact in the positive affect conditions. Both female (who in general acknowledged using chocolate as a mood-lifting alternative) and male participants (who in general acknowledged not doing so) reported being more willing to try a piece of chocolate when feeling happy as compared to the control conditions, which is a standard AE prediction.

Our analysis of prior research suggests that positive affect probably stimulates eating behavior via the affective evaluation mechanism, though little has been done to isolate mood-congruent effects from affect as information. Finally, good mood might reduce food intake (represented in the upper-right quadrant of figure 2.1). Our framework would predict that this pattern of results is likely when negative consequences of eating become salient (Andrade 2005, study 2). For instance, compared to a neutral mood condition, happy people might be less likely to eat chocolates if negative nutrition or weight gain outcomes are highlighted.

Conclusion

The proposed framework builds on previous theoretical propositions from different research streams to account for the observed consequences of affect on behavior and behavioral intentions across three different bodies of literature: helping, risk taking, and eating patterns. The available evidence indicates that behavioral stimulation for people experiencing positive affect (represented in the upper-left quadrant of figure 2.1) occurs primarily as a result of the affective evaluation mechanism, via affect as information or mood congruent effect. As long as no aversive or threatening cues become salient (that is, when AR is not strongly active, and, hence, people do not consider changes in their affective states), happy people tend to perceive a safer environment and bring positive thoughts to mind. They, therefore, become more likely to help, to take risks, and to exercise food preferences. There is a paucity of evidence to support mood-maintenance models in these domains (in other words, whether people are helping, gambling, or eating in order "to fuel" their otherwise decaying positive feelings). The same affective evaluation mechanism seems to drive the impact of negative affect on behavioral mitigation (represented in the lower-right quadrant of figure 2.1). People with negative affect perceive a more threatening environment and bring more negative thoughts to mind. These people, then, become less likely to help, to take risks, and to exercise food preferences. This is most likely to be the case only when the affect regulation mechanism is inactive or blocked. Blocking or mitigating effects can be a result of participants' inability to perceive specific behavior as an effective mood-lifting opportunity. This probably explains differences in the behavior of sad children versus sad adults when facing a helping opportunity, anxious people versus sad people facing a high-risk, high-payoff opportunity, and sad men versus sad women facing a chocolate consumption opportunity.

When the behavior is perceived to be an effective upward affect regulation strategy, and there are no stronger competing goals in the environment, enactment becomes more likely for those experiencing negative affect. This occurs via the affect regulation mechanism (represented in the lower-left quadrant of figure 2.1), and it often counteracts the impact of the affective evaluation mechanism. In such situations people attempt to improve their current negative affective states, and this accounts for observed increases in helping among sad adults as well as increases in chocolate consumption among those who are in general more likely to perceive chocolate as a mood-lifting alternative (i.e., women). The affect regulation mechanism also drives behavioral discouragement for people experiencing positive affect (represented in the upper-right quadrant of figure 2.1). Happy people should be more sensitive to potential negative affective consequences, because they have more to lose. However, since people in happy moods are less likely to expect negative consequences, this type of signal may need to be stronger. Behavioral discouragement takes place when negative aspects or consequences become salient. This explains a decrease in helping when the task is mood-threatening, as well as risk avoidance when the odds are too high.

In short, by combining the hitherto separately considered affective evaluation and affect regulation mechanisms in our integrative model of affective behavior, we are able to provide a more parsimonious account of this substantial literature. Figure 2.1 shows the evidence in the literature that, to this point, has been more consistent with AE as a main mediator of a relationship between "positive affect, behavioral encouragement" and "negative affect, behavioral discouragement," and with AR as a main mediator of a relationship between "negative affect, behavioral encouragement" and "positive affect, behavioral discouragement." However, we do not assume a dichotomous process in which one or the other "kicks in." Instead, the framework assumes parallel processes with both mechanisms operating within each quadrant. With that in mind, it would be interesting to investigate circumstances under which AE and AR jointly promote or inhibit behavior. For instance, though the literature to this point suggests that the increase in behavioral intentions of a mood-lifting action among happy people (compared to the neutral affect condition) was most likely driven by people's positive assessment of the environment (that is, affective evaluation), rather than a systematic attempt to act in order to maintain a current positive affective state (that is, affect regulation), there may be circumstances in which both mechanisms concurrently encourage or discourage behavior when people experience both positive and negative feelings. Although the proposed model allows for such concomitant effects, direct evidence is lacking. Future research could address this issue.

Notes

1. Affective states have also been shown to alter the way individuals process the information available to them (for a review, see Wyer, Clore, and Isbell 1999). However, these effects are usually attributed to either of the most basic mechanisms proposed above, particularly, affect as information (Schwarz 1990, 2001), and sometimes to affect regulation (Wegener and Petty 1994). Since our interest focuses on behavioral changes rather than information processing changes, this literature will not be reviewed in this chapter.
2. Notice that some authors have used the *affect as disruption* perspective to account for this pattern of results (for example, Mano 1992; Leith and Baumeister 1996). This perspective suggests that negative feelings, especially highly arousing feelings, may disrupt people's ability to properly or rationally make accurate evaluations, thereby leading subjects to choose the poorer or riskier option. While it is possible that, under certain circumstances, disruption may lead to the riskier option, there is also increasing evidence that even highly arousing negative affective states—such as anxi-

ety and fear—can actually reduce risk taking (for evidence on anxiety, see Raghunathan and Pham 1999; for evidence on fear, see Lerner and Keltner 2001). Importantly, such effects are hypothesized to result from the uniqueness of the appraisal process rather than from a cognitive disruption.

3. It is worth noting that these two mechanisms have been recently underscored in the eating behavior literature (Macht, Roth, and Ellgring 2002).

References

Abramson, Edward E., and Richard A. Wunderlich. 1972. "Anxiety, Fear and Eating: A Test of the Psychosomatic Concept of Obesity." *Journal of Abnormal Psychology* 79(3): 317–21.

Adaval, Rashmi. 2001. "Sometimes It Just Feels Right: The Differential Weighting of Affect-Consistent Product Information." *Journal of Consumer Research* 28(1): 1–17.

Aderman, David. 1972. "Elation, Depression, and Helping Behavior." *Journal of Personality and Social Psychology* 24(1): 91–101.

Andrade, Eduardo B. 2005. "Behavioral Consequences of Affect: Combining Evaluative and Regulatory Mechanisms." *Journal of Consumer Research* 32(3): 355–62.

Andrade, Eduardo B., and Ganesh Iyer 2007. "Dynamic Inconsistencies in Gambling and the Role of Feelings." Unpublished Manuscript. University of California, Berkeley.

Arkes, Hal R., Lisa Tandy Herren, and Alice M. Isen. 1988. "The Role of Potential Loss in the Influence of Affect on Risk-Taking Behavior." *Organizational Behavior and Human Decision Processes* 42(2); 181–93.

Atkinson, John W. 1957. "Motivational Determinants of Risk-Taking Behavior." *Psychological Review* 64, Part 1(6): 359–72.

———. 1964. *An Introduction to Motivation*. Princeton, N.J.: Van Nostrand.

Avnet, Tamar, and Michel T. Pham. 2004. "Should I Trust My Feelings or Not? The Metacognition of Affect-as-Information." Working paper. Columbia University.

Bagozzi, Richard P., Hans Baumgartner, and Rik Pieters. 1998. "Goal-Directed Emotions." *Cognition and Emotion* 12(1): 1–26.

Batson, C. Daniel. 1990. "Affect and Altruism." In *Affect and Social Behavior Studies in Emotion and Social Interaction*, edited by Bert S. Moore and Alice M. Isen. New York: Cambridge University Press.

Baumann, Donald J., Robert B. Cialdini, and Douglas T. Kenrick. 1981. "Altruism as Hedonism: Helping and Self-Gratification." *Journal of Personality and Social Psychology* 40(6): 1039–46.

Berkowitz, Leonard. 1972. "Social Norms, Feelings, and Other Factors Affecting Helping and Altruism." In *Advances in Experimental Social Psychology*, Volume 6, edited by Leonard Berkowitz. San Diego, Calif.: Academic Press.

Berkowitz, Leonard, and William H. Connor. 1966. "Success, Failure, and Social Responsibility." *Journal of Personality and Social Psychology* 4(6): 664–9.

Bower, Gordon H. 1981. "Mood and Memory." *American Psychologist* 36(2): 129–48.

Brown, Judson S., and I. E. Farber. 1951. "Emotions Conceptualized as Intervening Variables—With Suggestions Toward a Theory of Frustration." *Psychological Bulletin* 48(6): 465–95.

Bruch, Hilde. 1973. *Eating Disorders: Obesity, Anorexia Nervosa and the Person Within*. New York: Basic Books.

Bushman, Brad J., Roy F. Baumeister, and Collen M. Phillips. 2001. "Do People Aggress to Improve Their Mood? Catharsis Beliefs, Affect Regulation Opportunity, and Aggressive Responding." *Journal of Personality and Social Psychology* 81(1): 17–32.

Canetti, Laura, Eytan Bachar, and Elliot M. Berry. 2002. "Food and Emotion." *Behavioural Processes* 60(2): 157–64.

Carlsmith, J. Merrill, and Alan E. Gross. 1969. "Some Effects of Guilt on Compliance." *Journal of Personality and Social Psychology* 11(3): 232–9.

Carver, Charles S., John W. Lawrence, and Michael F. Scheier. 1996. "A Control-Process Perspective on the Origins of Affect." In *Striving and Feeling: Interactions Among Goals, Affect, and Self-Regulation,* edited by Leonard L. Martin and Abraham Tesser. Mahwah, N.J.: Lawrence Erlbaum Associates, Inc.

Christensen, Larry. 1993. "Effects of Eating Behavior on Mood: A Review of the Literature." *International Journal of Eating Disorders* 14(2): 171–83.

Cialdini, Robert B., and Douglas T. Kenrick. 1976. "Altruism and Hedonism: A Social Development Perspective on the Relationship of Negative Mood State and Helping." *Journal of Personality and Social Psychology* 34(5): 907–14.

Cialdini, Robert B., Betty Lee Darby, and Joyce E. Vincent. 1973. "Transgression and Altruism: A Case for Hedonism." *Journal of Experimental Social Psychology* 9 (6): 502–16.

Clark, Margaret S., and Alice M. Isen. 1982. "Toward Understanding the Relationship Between Feeling States and Social Behavior." In *Cognitive Social Psychology,* edited by Albert H. Hastorf and Alice M. Isen. New York: Elsevier.

Clark, Margaret S., and Barbara A. Waddell. 1983. "Effects of Moods on Thoughts About Helping, Attraction and Information Acquisition." *Social Psychology Quarterly* 46(1): 31–35.

Cohen, Joel B., and Eduardo B. Andrade. 2004. "Affective Intuition and Task-Contingent Affect Regulation." *Journal of Consumer Research* 31(2): 358–67.

Cohen, Joel B., and Charles S. Areni. 1991. "Affect and Consumer Behavior." In *Handbook of Consumer Behavior,* edited by Thomas S. Robertson and Harold H. Kassarjian. Englewood Cliffs, N.J.: Prentice Hall.

Cohen, Joel B. and Americus Reed II. 2006. "A Multiple Pathway Anchoring and Adjustment (MPAA) Model of Attitude Generation and Recruitment" *Journal of Consumer Research.* 33(1): 1–15.

Constans, Joseph I., and Andrew M. Matthews. 1993. "Mood and Subjective Risk of Future Events." *Cognition and Emotion* 7(6): 545–60.

Cools, Joseph, David E. Schotte, and Richard J. McNally. 1992. "Emotional Arousal and Overeating in Restrained Eaters." *Journal of Abnormal Psychology* 101(2): 348–51.

Cunningham, Michael R., Jeff Steinberg, and Rita Grev. 1980. "Wanting to and Having to Help: Separate Motivations for Positive Mood and Guilt-Induced Helping." *Journal of Personality Social Psychology* 38(2): 181–92.

Damasio, Antonio. 1994. *Descartes's Errors: Emotion, Reason, and the Human Brain.* New York: G. P. Putnam's Sons.

Davidson, Richard J., Diego Pizzagalli, Jack B. Nitschke, and Katherine Putnam. 2002. "Depression: Perspectives from Affective Neuroscience." *Annual Review of Psychology* 53(February): 545–74.

Derakshan, Nazanin, and Michael W. Eysenck. 1997. "Interpretative Biases for One's Own Behavior and Physiology in High-Trait-Anxious Individuals and Repressors." *Journal of Personality and Social Psychology* 73(4): 816–25.

Eagly, Alice H., and Shelly Chaiken. 1993. *The Psychology of Attitudes.* Orlando, Fla.: HBJ.

Erber, Ralph, and Maureen W. Erber. 2001. "The Role of Motivated Social Cognition in the Regulation of Affective States." In *Affect and Social Cognition,* edited by Joseph P. Forgas. Mahwah, N.J.: Lawrence Erlbaum Associates, Inc.

Eysenck, Michael W., Colin MacLeod, and Andrew Matthews. 1987. "Cognitive Functioning and Anxiety." *Psychological Research* 49(2/3): 189–95.

Forest, Duncan, Margaret S. Clark, Judson Mills, and Alice M. Isen. 1979. "Helping as a Function of Feeling State and Nature of the Helping Behavior." *Motivation and Emotion* 3(2): 161–9.

Forgas, Joseph P. 1995. "Mood and Judgment: The Affect Infusion Model (AIM)." *Psychological Bulletin* 117(1): 39–66.

———. 2002. "Feeling and Doing: Affective Influences on Interpersonal Behavior." *Psychological Inquiry* 13(1): 1–28.

Forgas, Joseph P., and Klaus Fiedler. 1996. "Us and Them: Mood Effects on Intergroup Discrimination." *Journal of Personality and Social Psychology* 70(1): 28–40.

Frijda, Nico. 1999. "Emotion and Hedonic Experience." In *Well Being: The Foundations of Hedonic Psychology,* edited by Daniel Kehneman, Ed Diener, and Norbert Schwarz. New York: Russell Sage Foundation.

Frost, Randy O., Gail A. Goolkasian, Robin J. Ely, and Fletcher A. Blanchard. 1982. "Depression, Restraint and Eating Behavior." *Behavior Research and Therapy* 20(2): 113–21.

Gehring, William J., and Adrian R. Willoughby. 2002. "The Medial Frontal Cortex and the Rapid Processing of Monetary Gains and Losses." *Science* 295(5563): 2279–82.

Gendolla, Guido H. E. 2000. "On the Impact of Mood on Behavior: An Integrative Theory and a Review." *Review of General Psychology* 4(4): 378–408.

Gorn, Gerald, Michel T. Pham, and Leo Y. Sin. 2001. "When Arousal Influences Ad Evaluation and Valence Does Not (and Vice Versa)." *Journal of Consumer Psychology* 11(1): 43–55.

Greeno, Catherine G., and Rena R. Wing. 1994. "Stress-Induced Eating." *Psychological Bulletin* 115(3): 444–64.

Gross, James J. 1998. "The Emerging Field of Emotion Regulation: An Integrative Review." *Review of General Psychology* 2(3): 271–99.

Grunberg, Neil E., and Richard O. Straub. 1992. "The Role of Gender and Taste Class in the Effects of Stress on Eating." *Health Psychology* 11(2): 97–100.

Hsiao, Evana T., and Robert E. Thayer. 1998. "Exercising for Mood Regulation: The Importance of Experience." *Personality and Individual Differences* 24(6): 829–36.

Isen, Alice M. 1970. "Success, Failure, Attention, and Reaction to Others: The Warm Glow of Success." *Journal of Personality and Social Psychology* 15(4): 294–301.

———. 1984. "Toward Understanding the Role of Affect on Cognition." In *Handbook of Social Cognition*, edited by Robert S. Wyer, Thomas Srull, and Alice M. Isen. Hillsdale, N.J.: Lawrence Erlbaum Associates, Inc.

———. 2000. "Positive Affect and Decision Making." In *Handbook of Emotions*, 2nd edition, edited by Michael Lewis and Jeannette M. Haviland-Jones. New York: Guilford Press.

Isen, Alice M., and Nehemia Geva. 1987. "The Influence of Positive Affect on Acceptable Level of Risk: The Person with a Large Canoe Has a Large Worry." *Organizational Behavior and Human Decision Processes* 39(2): 145–54.

Isen, Alice M., and Paula F. Levin. 1972. "Effect of Feeling Good on Helping: Cookies and Kindness." *Journal of Personality and Social Psychology* 21(3): 384–88.

Isen, Alice M., and Stanley F. Simmonds. 1978. "The Effect of Feeling Good on a Helping Task that is Incompatible with Good Mood." *Social Psychology* 41(4): 346–9.

Isen, Alice M., Margaret Clark, and Mark F. Schwartz. 1976. "Duration of the Effect of Good Mood on Helping: Footprints on the Sands of Time." *Journal of Personality and Social Psychology* 34(3): 385–93.

Isen, Alice M., Nancy Horn, and David L. Rosenhan. 1973. "Effects of Success and Failure on Children's Generosity." *Journal of Personality and Social Psychology* 27(2): 239–47.

Isen, Alice M., Thomas E. Nygren, and F. Gregory Ashby. 1988. "Influence of Positive Affect on the Subjective Utility of Gains and Losses: It Is Just Not Worth the Risk." *Journal of Personality and Social Psychology* 55(5): 710–7.

Isen, Alice M., Thomas E. Shalker, Margaret Clark, and Lynn Karp. 1978. "Affect, Accessibility of Material in Memory and Behavior: A Cognitive Loop?" *Journal of Personality and Social Psychology* 36(1): 1–12.

Johnson, Eric J., and Amos Tversky. 1983. "Affect, Generalization, and the Perception of Risk." *Journal of Personality and Social Psychology* 45(1): 20–31.

Kahn, Barbara, and Alice M. Isen. 1993. "The Influence of Positive Affect on Variety Seeking Among Safe, Enjoyable Products." *Journal of Consumer Research* 20(2): 257–70.

Kanfer, Ruth, and Antonette M. Zeiss. 1983. "Depression, Interpersonal Standard Setting, and Judgment of Self-Efficacy." *Journal of Abnormal Psychology*, 92(3): 319–29.

Kaplan, Harold I., and Helen S. Kaplan. 1957. "The Psychosomatic Concept of Obesity." *Journal of Nervous and Mental Disease* 125(2):181–201.

Knobloch, Silvia, and Dolf Zillmann. 2002. "Mood Management via the Digital Jukebox." *Journal of Communication* 52(2): 351–66.

Knutson, Brian, Charles S. Adams, Grace W. Fong, and Daniel Hommer. 2001a. "Anticipation of Monetary Reward Selectively Recruits Nucleus Accumbens." *Journal of Neuroscience* 21(159): 1–5.

————. 2001b. "Disassociation of Reward Anticipation Versus Outcome with Event-Related FMRI." *NeuroReport* 12(17): 3683–7.

Kuhl, Julius, and Jurgen Beckmann. 1984. *Action Control: From Cognition to Behavior*. Berlin, Germany: Springer-Verlag.

Lazarus, Richard S., and Susan Folkman. 1984. *Stress, Appraisal, and Coping*. New York: Springer.

LeDoux, Joseph. 1996. *The Emotional Brain: The Mysterious Underpinnings of Emotional Life*. New York: Touchstone.

Leith, Karen P., and Roy F. Baumeister. 1996. "Why Do Bad Moods Increase Self-Defeating Behavior? Emotion, Risk-Taking, and Self-Regulation." *Journal of Personality and Social Psychology* 71(6): 1250–67.

Lerner, Jennifer S., and Dacher Keltner. 2001. "Fear, Anger, and Risk." *Journal of Personality and Social Psychology* 81(1): 146–59.

Lerner, Jennifer S., Deborah A. Small, and George Loewenstein. 2004. "Heart Strings and Purse Strings: Carryover Effects of Emotions on Economic Decisions." *Psychological Science* 15(5): 337–41.

Levin, Paula R., and Alice M. Isen. 1975. "Further Studies on the Effect of Feeling Good on Helping." *Sociometry* 38(1): 141–7.

Loewenstein, George F., Elke U. Weber, Chris K. Hsee, and Ned Welch. 2001. "Risk as Feelings." *Psychological Bulletin* 127(2): 267–86.

Macht, Michael. 1999. "Characteristics of Eating in Anger, Fear, Sadness and Joy." *Appetite* 33(1): 129–39.

Macht, Michael, S. Roth, and Heinrich Ellgring. 2002. "Chocolate Eating in Healthy Men During Experimentally Induced Sadness and Joy." *Appetite* 39(2): 147–58.

Mano, Haim. 1992. "Judgment Under Distress: Assessing the Role of Unpleasantness and Arousal in Judgment Formation." *Organizational Behavior and Human Decision Processes* 52(2): 216–45.

Manucia, Gloria K., Donald J. Baumann, and Robert B. Cialdini. 1984. "Mood Influences on Helping: Direct Effects or Side Effects?" *Journal of Personality and Social Psychology* 46(2): 357–64.

Martin, Leonard L., and Gerald L. Clore. 2001. *Theories of Mood and Cognition*. Mahwah, N.J.: Lawrence Erlbaum Associates, Inc.

Mayer, John D., Yvonne N. Gaschke, Debra L. Braverman, and Temperance W. Evans. 1992. "Mood-Congruent Judgment Is a General Effect." *Journal of Personality and Social Psychology* 63(1): 119–32.

Mick, David G., and Michelle DeMoss. 1990. "Self-Gifts: Phenomenological Insights from Four Contexts." *Journal of Consumer Research* 17 (3): 322–32.

Mittal, Vikas, and William T. Ross. 1998. "The Impact of Positive and Negative Affect and Issue Framing of Issue Interpretation and Risk-Taking." *Organizational Behavior and Human Decision Processes* 76(3): 298–324.

Moore, Bert S., Bill Underwood, and David L. Rosenhan. 1973. "Affect and Altruism." *Developmental Psychology* 8(1): 99–104.

Morris, Williams N., and Nora P. Reilly. 1987. "Toward the Self-Regulation of Mood: Theory and Research." *Motivation and Emotion* 11(3): 215–49.

Nygren, Thomas E., Alice M. Isen, Pamela J. Taylor, and Jessica Dulin. 1996. "The Influence of Positive Affect on the Decision Rule in Risky Situations:

Focus on Outcome (and Especially Avoidance of Loss) Rather Than Probability." *Organizational Behavior and Human Decision Processes* 66(1): 59–72.

Oliver, Georgina, and Jane Wardle. 1999. "Perceived Effects of Stress on Food Choice." *Physiology and Behavior* 66(3): 511–5.

Ortony, Andrew, Gerald L. Clore, and Allan Collins. 1988. *The Cognitive Structure of Emotions.* New York: Cambridge University Press.

Patel, K. A., and D. G. Schlundt. 2001. "Impact of Moods and Social Context on Eating Behavior." *Appetite* 36(2): 111–8.

Pham, Michel T. 1998. "Representativeness, Relevance, and the Use of Feelings in Decision Making." *Journal of Consumer Research* 25(2): 144–59.

Pham, Michel T., Joel B. Cohen, John W. Pracejus, and G. David Hughes. 2001. "Affect Monitoring and the Primacy of Feelings in Judgment." *Journal of Consumer Behavior* 28(2): 167–88.

Pietromonaco, Paula R., and Karen S. Rook. 1987. "Decision Style in Depression: The Contribution of Perceived Risks Versus Benefits." *Journal of Personality and Social Psychology* 52(2): 399–408.

Piliavin, Jane A., John F. Dovidio, Samuel L. Gaertner, and Russell D. Clark III. 1981. *Emergency Intervention.* New York: Academic Press.

———. 1982. "Responsive Bystanders: The Process of Intervention." In *Cooperation and Helping Behavior,* edited by Valerian J. Derlega and Janusz Grzelak. New York: Academic Press.

Pine, Charles J. 1985. "Anxiety and Eating Behavior in Obese and Nonobese American Indians and White Americans." *Journal of Personality and Social Psychology* 49(3): 774–80.

Polivy, Janet, and C. Peter Herman. 1976. "Clinical Depression and Weight Change: A Complex Relation." *Journal of Abnormal Psychology* 85(3): 338–40.

Raghunathan, Rajagopal, and Michel T. Pham. 1999. "All Negative Moods Are Not Equal: Motivational Influences of Anxiety and Sadness on Decision Making." *Organizational Behavior and Human Decision Processes* 79(1): 56–77.

Regan, Dennis T., Margo Williams, and Sondra Sparling. 1972. "Voluntary Expiation of Guilt: A Field Experiment." *Journal of Personality and Social Psychology* 24(1): 42–45.

Reznick, Harrell, and Philip Balch. 1977. "The Effects of Anxiety and Response Cost Manipulations on the Eating Behavior of Obese and Normal Weight Subjects." *Addictive Behaviors* 2(4): 219–25.

Rook, Dennis W., and Meryl P. Gardner. 1993. "In the Mood: Impulse Buying's Affective Antecedents." In Vol. 6 of *Research in Consumer Behavior,* edited by Janeen Arnold Costa and Russell W. Belk. Greenwich, Conn.: JAI Press.

Rosenhan, David L., Bill Underwood, and Bert Moore. 1974. "Affect Moderates Self-Gratification and Altruism." *Journal of Personality and Social Psychology* 30(4): 546–52.

Salovey, Peter, John D. Mayer, and David L. Rosenhan. 1991. "Mood and Helping: Mood as a Motivator of Helping and Helping as a Regulator of Mood." In *Review of Personality and Social Psychology: Prosocial Behavior,* Volume 12, edited by Margaret S. Clark. Newbury Park, Calif.: Sage.

Schaller, Mark, and Robert B. Cialdini. 1990. "Happiness, Sadness, and Helping: A Motivational Integration." In *Handbook of Motivation and Cognition: Foundations of Social Behavior,* edited by Richard M. Sorrentino and E. Tory Higgins. New York: Guilford Press.

Schwarz, Norbert. 1990. "Feelings as Information: Informational and Motivational Functions of Affective States." In *Handbook of Motivation and Cognition: Foundations of Social Behavior,* edited by Richard M. Sorrentino and E. Tory Higgins. New York: Guilford Press.

———. 2001. "Feelings as Information: Implications for Affective Influences on Information Processing." In *Theories of Mood and Cognition,* edited by Leonard L. Martin and Gerald L. Clore. Mahwah, N.J.: Lawrence Erlbaum Associates, Inc.

Schwarz, Norbert, and Gerald L. Clore. 1983. "Mood, Misattribution, and Judgment of Well-Being: Informative and Directive Functions of Affective States." *Journal of Personality and Social Psychology* 45(3): 513–23.

———. 1996. "Feelings and Phenomenal Experiences." In *Social Psychology: Handbook of Basic Principles,* edited by E. Tory Higgins and Arie W. Kruglanski. New York: Guilford Press.

Shiv, Baba, George Loewenstein, Antoine Bechara, Hanna Damasio, and Antonio R. Damasio. 2005. "Investment Behavior and the Dark Side of Emotion." *Psychological Science,* 16(6): 435–9.

Siemer, Matthias, and Rainer Reisenzein. 1998. "Effects of Mood on Evaluative Judgments: Influence of Reduced Processing Capacity and Mood Salience." *Cognition and Emotion* 12(6): 783–805.

Steptoe, Andrew, Tessa M. Pollard, and Jane Wardle. 1995. "Development of a Measure of the Motives Underlying the Selection of Food: The Food Choice Questionnaire." *Appetite* 25(3): 267–84.

Thayer, Robert E. 1989. *The Biopsychology of Mood and Arousal.* New York: Oxford.

Tice, Diane M., Ellen Bratslavsky, and Roy F. Baumeister. 2001. "Emotional Distress Regulation Takes Precedence over Impulse Control: If You Feel Bad, Do It!" *Journal of Personality and Social Psychology* 80(1): 53–67.

Vohs, Kathleen D., Anna M. Bardone, Thomas E. Joiner, Jr., Lyn Y. Abramson, and Todd F. Heatherton. 1999. "Perfectionism, Perceived Weight Status, and Self-Esteem Interact to Predict Bulimic Symptoms: A Model of Bulimic Symptom Development." *Journal of Abnormal Psychology* 108(4): 695–700.

Vohs, Kathleen D., Zachary R. Voelz, Jeremy W. Pettit, Anna M. Bardone, Jennifer Katz, Lyn Y. Abramson, Todd F. Heatherton, and Thomas E. Joiner, Jr. 2001. "Perfectionism, Body Dissatisfaction, and Self-Esteem: An Interactive Model of Bulimic Symptom Development." *Journal of Social and Clinical Psychology* 20(4): 476–97.

Weaver, James B., and Elizabeth A. Laird. 1995. "Mood Management During the Menstrual-Cycle Through Selective Exposure to Television." *Journalism and Mass Communication Quarterly* 72(1): 139–46.

Wegener, Duane T., and Richard E. Petty. 1994. "Mood Management Across Affective States: The Hedonic Contingency Hypothesis." *Journal of Personality and Social Psychology* 66(6): 1034–48.

Weinstein, Suzanne E., David J. Shide, and Barbara J. Rolls. 1997. "Changes in Food Intake in Response to Stress in Men and Women: Psychological Factors." *Appetite* 28(1): 7–18.

Willner, Paul, and Sarah Healy. 1994. "Decreased Hedonic Responsiveness During a Brief Depressive Mood Swing." *Journal of Affective Disorders* 32(1): 13–20.

Willner, Paul, David Benton, Emma Brown, Survjit Cheeta, Gareth Davies, Janine Morgan, and Michael Morgan. 1998. " 'Depression' Increases 'Craving' for Sweet Rewards in Animal and Human Models of Depression and Craving." *Psychopharmacology* 136(3): 272–83.

Wright, William F., and Gordon H. Bower. 1992. "Mood Effects on Subjective Probability Assessment." *Organizational Behavior and Human Decision Processes* 52(2): 276–91.

Wyer, Robert S., Gerald L. Clore, and Linda M. Isbell. 1999. "Affect and Information Processing." In *Advances in Experimental Psychology*, Volume 31, edited by Mark P. Zanna. San Diego, Calif.: Academic Press.

Yeung, Catherine W. M., and Robert S. Wyer, Jr. 2004. "Affect, Appraisal, and Consumer Judgment." *Journal of Consumer Research* 31(2): 412–24.

Zillmann, Dolf 1988. "Mood Management: Using Entertainment to Full Advantage." In *Communication, Social Cognition, and Affect*, edited by Lewis Donohew and Howard E. Sypher. Hillsdale, N.J.: Lawrence Erlbaum Associates, Inc.

Emotional Influence on Decision and Behavior: Stimuli, States, and Subjectivity

PIOTR WINKIELMAN AND JENNIFER L. TRUJILLO

HUMANS ARE passionate beings whose thoughts, decisions, and actions are shaped by emotion, sometimes with wonderful and sometimes with disastrous consequences. In this chapter we illustrate some of the major ways in which experimental psychologists, including ourselves, conceptualize and investigate basic mechanisms of emotional influence. Our focus is on basic mechanisms as we believe that figuring out the fundamental relation between emotion and cognition is critical for developing systematic accounts of when and how emotion helps or hurts decision making.

The chapter is organized as follows. We start with some historical observations and then highlight a few conceptual distinctions that help organize thinking about the complex question of emotional influence. Next, we briefly review the most influential theoretical accounts of emotional influence and illustrate them with a few studies. Then, we come to the central topic of our chapter—how judgments, decisions, and behaviors are influenced by salient emotional stimuli in the environment, with special emphasis on the role of facial expressions. We will make several points. First, emotional stimuli can influence a variety of outcomes, ranging from simple preference judgments and behaviors to complex risky decisions. Second, emotional stimuli can have a range of effects, from influences that are differentiated only on a positive-negative dimension to influences that are highly differentiated in emotion quality and highly dependent on a situational context. Third, emotional stimuli can exert their influence via rudimentary affective and motivational mechanisms. They can be processed automatically, without attention and intention, and influence behavior without mediation of conscious subjective experience. Throughout our chapter, we address the rationality of emotional influence, psychological and neural underpinnings of emotion-cognition interactions, and highlight open questions and future research directions.

History: The Good and the Ugly of Emotion

Humanity has long been fascinated by the beneficial and harmful effect of emotions on behavior. Consider sacred texts, such as the Bible, Koran, and Vedas, as well as great literature, such as the Greek tragedies and Shakespeare's plays. The central themes of these works is often the destructive power of anger, pride, envy, or jealousy, but the themes also include the constructive power of love, compassion, or humility. The bright and the dark side of emotion have also been debated in philosophical texts, starting with the classics. For example, in Plato's *Phaedrus* (1973), Socrates compares the human soul to a charioteer steering a pair of horses: one soars towards heaven, powered by godlike feelings, while the other is earthbound, driven by animal passions.

One of the central themes in philosophical discussions of emotion is its relation to rationality and morality (Solomon 2003). On the one hand, there are many troubles with emotion in considering rationality. Instead of following coherent and externally verifiable rational principles, emotion can be governed by some obscure "emotion logic," as expressed in Blaise Pascal's famous quote that "the heart has reasons that the reason does not know." In fact, beliefs based on emotion are often used as paradigmatic illustrations of irrationality.[1] Emotions also seem to live in their own encapsulated world. After involuntarily jumping away from a viper in a zoo kept safely behind glass, Charles Darwin (1872/1998) wrote that his "will and reason were powerless against the imagination of a danger which had never been experienced" (44). Baruch Spinoza (1677/1883) noted that "affect cannot be restrained nor removed unless by an opposed and stronger affect." Even the legal system recognizes the negative effects of emotions on self-control by considering the "heat of passion" as a mitigating circumstance.[2] In short, it is not surprising that given all of these troubling aspects of emotion, Adam Smith (1759) stated that human existence amounts to a struggle between the "passions" and the "impartial spectator."

On the other hand, many have noted that emotions might also promote morality and rationality. Aristotle (1985) thought that a mark of a fully human soul is to respond to injustice with righteous anger, or to respond to suffering with compassion. David Hume (1739/1961) famously argued that "reason is, and ought only to be, the slave of the passions, and can never pretend to any other office than to serve and obey them" (415). Further, just as the law recognizes impairments due to "heat of passion," it also considers "cold-blooded" deeds particularly inhumane. Similarly, society has a name for individuals who fail to show emotions concerning the fate of others: "sociopaths." In a recent paper, Timothy Ketelaar (2006) points out that in many Western traditions, moral philosophers have long considered action based on "emotion" (that is, not only on love and compassion, but also on fearfulness and humility) as a normative standard, not a violation of normative behavior. In fact, the modern conception of normative behavior as based on rational calculations of an action's costs and benefits only goes back as far as the development of formal economic models of human behavior. Finally, many modern philosophical accounts highlight the close connection between emotion and rationality. For example, de Sousa (1987) emphasizes that emotions reflect the results of sophisticated computations that may at times exceed the powers of the conscious mind. Similarly, evolutionary approaches highlight that general affective states (such as moods), as well as specific emotions (for example, fear or guilt) may reflect adaptations which ensure long-term benefits not easily apprehended with logical considerations (Cosmides and Tooby 2000).

In sum, from historical and philosophical perspectives, emotion's influence on normative behavior and rational thinking has been treated with mixed feelings. This ambivalence highlights the need for empirical approaches aimed at understanding exactly how emotions operate on psychological and neural levels, and accordingly, when emotions are beneficial or harmful to decisions.

Some Useful Distinctions

Before we review empirical research which provides background for our studies, it is useful to highlight several distinctions. These will help to keep conceptual clarity as we review research on emotional influences on decisions.

Arousal, Valence, Mood, Emotion, Affect

Researchers use a variety of emotion-related terms. *Arousal* typically refers to a hedonically undifferentiated somatic state that varies on excitation. This term is also used to refer to the activation dimension of emotion, ranging from low to high. *Valence* refers to the hedonic dimension of emotion, ranging from positive to negative. *Mood* refers to a low-intensity, diffuse, and relatively long-lasting state which is primarily differentiated on valence (for example, feeling good or feeling bad). *Emotion* typically refers to an intense state with qualitatively differentiated phenomenology (for example, within negative valence, one can differentiate between fear, anger, sadness, and disgust). However, emotion is also used as a generic umbrella term, encompassing arousal, valence, and qualitatively differentiated states. Similarly, the term *affect* often functions as an umbrella term, but is also used to refer to states and reactions that are primarily differentiated on valence. Finally, it is useful to keep in mind that researchers vary greatly in how they apply these terms. For example, many studies that explore emotional underpinnings of decisions only manipulate or measure nonspecific arousal.

Emotional States Versus Reactions to Emotional Stimuli

The question of "emotional influence" is very broad, and accordingly researchers focus on different parts of the answer. For conceptual clarity, we will distinguish between research that focuses on emotional states and research that focuses on reactions to emotional stimuli. This point will be particularly relevant as we contrast the focus of our own research with some of the other traditions.

The central goal of much research is to characterize the influence of a particular emotional state (for example, high arousal, positive mood, fear, anger, or happiness) on judgment and behavior. In these types of studies, it is relatively unimportant which mediating processes lead to the state. Consequently, researchers use whichever manipulations are handy to induce a particular state that is relatively enduring and strong enough to influence the behavior or judgment in question.

In other research, including ours, the interest is to characterize the process that leads from emotional stimulus to an emotional reaction. That is, we aim to discover how the organism responds to an emotional stimulus (for example, an angry word, a happy face, a rotten carcass, a snake), and consequently how this exposure to an emotional stimulus impacts subsequent behavior and judgments. Note that this tradition of research allows for a more complicated conceptualization of the relationship between stimulus and outcome. Indeed, an emotional stimulus may not always elicit an emotional reaction (for instance, seeing an angry word might or might not elicit anger). Further, if an emotional reaction is induced, it may not have the same quality as the stimulus (for example, a disgusting picture may induce only a generalized negative state). Most importantly, the influence of a stimulus on behavior may, or may not, be mediated by an emotional reaction. This is because an emotional stimulus can function as a "signal." For example, a cat's whiny meow can move the owner to give her food; however, this could happen without the cat or the owner experiencing any underlying emotion (Owren, Rendall, and Bachorowski 2005).

Components of Emotion

When an emotional state is induced, it is important to ask which components of the emotion are present as well as which specific component is causally responsible for the emotion's impact on behavior. Researchers generally agree that emotion has several components. The *cognitive component* refers to changes in perceptual, attentional, and semantic aspects of emotion (for example, attentional biases, primed appraisals). The *behavioral component* refers to activated motor programs and action tendencies (for example, facial or postural expressions). The *physiological component* refers to underlying changes in emotion-relevant bodily and brain responses (for example, cardiovascular or limbic activation). Finally, the *experiential component* refers to the subjective emotional experience, or the "felt," phenomenological aspect of emotion. Emotion can include all or only some of these components, and it can exert its influence via any of them.

Integral Versus Incidental

Finally, it helps to distinguish emotions (in the broad sense that includes mood and other affective states) that are integral and incidental to the decision (Bodenhausen 1993). Integral emotions are generated by causes that are intrinsic to the task. For example, if thinking about how many people get cancer elicits a fear reaction in a task that includes estimating the prevalence rate of cancer, the fear reaction is integral to the task at hand. In that sense, integral emotions are normatively relevant to decision, though they still might be helpful or hurtful (for example, they might lead to overestimation or underestimation of cancer risks). On the other hand, incidental emotions are generated by causes extrinsic to the task (that is, experiences from a prior situation). For example, a lingering fear elicited by the question about cancer might influence how a person subsequently estimates the prevalence of deaths from lightning. Again, although incidental emotions are normatively irrelevant to the current situation, they may be helpful or hurtful in terms of some external criterion for the decision.

Emotional States

With these distinctions in mind, let us now review some studies on how emotion influences judgments, decisions, and behavior. This brief review does not aim to be comprehensive. We simply want to illustrate the major theoretical approaches, highlight the underlying mechanisms identified in the previous studies, and places our work in this general context.

Arousal Effects

Many studies on emotional influence explore the most basic state: arousal.

Excitation Transfer.   Some of the earliest studies on emotional influence explored the effects of nonspecific arousal using the excitation transfer paradigm. Inspiration for these studies came from the two-factor theory of emotion (Schachter and Singer 1962). This theory posits that the physiological component of emotion consists primarily of undifferentiated general arousal, which, depending on contextual cues, is cognitively shaped into a specific emotion such as happiness or anger. Although the original two-factor theory was concerned with explaining contextual effects on the experience of emotion, the studies done in this tradition also show that misattribution of incidental arousal can be a powerful influence on judgments. Thus, arousal induced in some previous context (for example, riding an exercise bike, crossing a bridge, exercising, injesting caffeine, or being in a dangerous environment) can influence a variety of judgments, ranging from attractiveness to aggressiveness (Zillman 1978). Importantly, these excitation-transfer effects occur primarily when participants are not aware of the proper source of arousal (Martin, Harlow, and Strack 1992). Thus, they can be understood in the framework of the feeling-as-information account (Schwarz and Clore 2003). This account proposes that a person may form a judgment of a target by asking herself, "How do I feel about it?" and then can use his current feeling as a shortcut to judgment. However, in doing so, the individual may mistake, or misattribute, feelings from a preexisting state as a genuine reaction to the target. This can occur unless the diagnostic value of the feeling has been put into question.

Somatic Feedback.   The studies on excitation transfer focus on incidental arousal that was sufficiently "free-floating" to transfer from one set of stimuli to another. In addition, those studies relied on subjective ratings (that is, preferences), which disallow claims about the rationality of the effect. In contrast, more recent studies on somatic feedback have explored effects of an arousal that is integral to the task at hand and that arises in the process of considering an option. Further, the arousal in this task is bound to a particular stimulus. These studies attempted to assess the rationality of the effects using some normative criteria (for example, the amount of money made in a task).

One influential line of such research was conducted in patients with brain lesions to the prefrontal cortex, an area associated with processing of arousal and other somatic feedback (Damasio 1994). For instance, Bechara et al. (1997) compared the performance of controls to that of patients with damage to the ventromedial prefrontal cortex (vmPFC) on a repeated gambling task in which an initially attractive option was later associated with occasional but substantial losses. Despite similar cognitive abilities and task comprehension compared to control patients, vmPFC lesioned patients chose the risky option more frequently, presumably due to an inability to process somatic feedback associated with losses.

Interestingly, even integral (that is, task-related) arousal can be hurtful. Recently, Baba Shiv et al. (2005) showed that given the right task, vmPFC patients can also make more profit-maximizing decisions. Specifically, in a myopic loss-aversion task, typical control participants show excessive caution about choosing risky but profitable options (Gneezy and Potters 1997). In this task, participants start with an endowment (for example, twenty dollars), and they are asked to decide during each subsequent round to either invest one dollar or to advance to the next round without investing. If the participant decides to invest, they have a 50 percent chance of losing the one-dollar investment, and a 50 percent chance of winning an additional one dollar and fifty cents. Thus, from a profit-maximizing perspective, it is better to invest than to pass (the expected value is one dollar and twenty-five cents, versus one dollar). However, consistent with the notion of loss aversion, typical participants sometimes fail to invest. Using the myopic loss-aversion paradigm, Shiv et al. (2005) showed that compared to healthy controls, vmPFC patients invested more frequently, presumably because the absence of somatic feedback reduced their risk aversion.

Mood Effects

Other studies have explored the effects of generalized valenced states, such as positive-negative mood (for reviews, see Forgas 1995; Slovic et al.

2002). The vast majority of these studies investigate the impact of incidental mood that is induced by stimuli such as weather, recall of emotional memories, or exposure to emotionally evocative mood or music.

Mood-Congruency Effects.   The most frequently reported finding in the mood literature is that judgments and behaviors are mood congruent. For example, participants in positive rather than negative moods give higher ratings of general life satisfaction (Schwarz and Clore 1983), make more optimistic estimates of risk (Johnson and Tversky 1983), and act in a more cooperative and confident manner (Forgas 2006).

There are two major explanations of the mood-congruency effects. One account, called *affect-priming,* suggests that affective states are linked to related cognitive categories within an associative network of memory. Thus, being in an affective state can bias access to categories which then guide the encoding, retrieval, and use of information in construction of a judgment and generation of a behavior. The evidence for the priming account comes primarily from studies that found mood effects on measures of attention, perception, and memory (Forgas 1995). Another explanation for the mood-congruency effect is the feeling-as-information model, which assumes that people use current feelings as a shortcut to judgment (Schwarz and Clore 2003). The model's explanation of affective influence is supported by findings that affect-congruency effects are eliminated when subjects are given an alternative attribution for their feelings, thus undermining their diagnostic value for judgment (for example, Schwarz and Clore 1983).

Mood-Regulation Effects.   Several mood effects do not fit the congruency pattern and are better conceptualized as emotion-regulation or mood-management effects (Andrade and Cohen, chapter 2, this volume; Erber and Markunas 2006). For example, Erber, Wegner, and Therriault (1996) first made participants happy or sad, and then told them to expect they would be working on an unrelated task either alone or with another participant. Next, participants were asked to indicate their preference for a set of newspaper stories, identified by their headlines as uplifting, depressing, or neutral. Participants who expected to work alone showed the standard mood-congruency pattern: happy participants chose cheerful stories, and sad participants chose depressing ones. However, participants who expected to work with a stranger showed the opposite preference: happy participants chose depressing stories, and sad participants chose cheerful ones, presumably reflecting an attempt to neutralize their mood before a novel social interaction. In another example, Andrade (2005) put participants in a negative, neutral, or positive mood, and then asked them to judge their willingness to try a new brand of chocolate. Participants who did not perceive the chocolate as mood lifting showed the standard mood-congruency pattern, and they were less likely to try the novel product when in a negative mood. However, the reverse finding was obtained for participants who perceived chocolate as a mood lifter (this group was mostly made up of women). Those participants were more willing to try the chocolate when in a negative, rather than neutral, mood.

Emotion Effects

While many studies focus on affective states differentiated on valence, such as mood, some work also considers how judgments and decisions are influenced by qualitatively different emotions, such as sadness, anger, fear, and happiness. Again, several underlying mechanisms have been identified.

Priming Effects. As mentioned earlier, associative memory accounts assume that affective states influence judgments by priming related categories (Forgas 1995). Interestingly, most studies that test this account relied on very general positive-negative mood manipulations. However, how specific is such priming? Niedenthal and Setterlund (1994) found that participants' performance on lexical decision making is facilitated in an emotion-specific way, but not in a general valence way. For example, participants primed with happy music responded faster to words that are directly related to happiness, but not faster to all positive words (for example, love).

Appraisal Effects. The priming accounts are mostly concerned with how emotions facilitate retrieval of associated cognitive content, without much interest in the specific nature of that content. More specific predictions are made by appraisal theories of emotion, which assume that different emotions result from a combination of unique patterns of cognitive assessments or appraisals (Arnold 1960; Lazarus 1991). For example, Craig A. Smith and Phoebe C. Ellsworth (1985) suggest that different emotions are cognitively represented by assessments of six dimensions including pleasantness, anticipated effort, certainty, attentional activity, responsibility and control over self and others, and situational control. On this scheme, fear and anger both have negative valence, but fear is characterized by a lower certainty and control than anger; in that respect, anger has similar qualities to happiness.

The appraisal framework was applied by Jennifer S. Lerner and Dacher Keltner (2001) in their investigations of how incidental fear, anger, and happiness influence risk judgments. They found, across dispositional and experimentally induced emotion, that fearful participants made more pessimistic risk assessments of future negative events, and they made more risk-averse choices than angry and happy participants. Interestingly, angry and happy participants made similarly optimistic assessments and risk-seeking choices, presumably reflecting the high certainty appraisal associated with these two emotions.

Regulation Effects.   Just like mood, specific emotions can also influence choice by promoting different action aimed at emotion management (that is, maintenance or removal). This idea was explored by Rajagopal Raghunathan and Michael Tuan Pham (1999), who contrasted sadness (which presumably promotes seeking of reward) and fear (which increases the need to reduce the uncertainty of the situation). Consistent with these ideas, inducing sadness resulted in high-risk, high-reward choices, while inducing fear led to low-risk, low-reward choices.

Affective Reactions

The previously described studies focused on how the emotional state influences judgments and decisions. Accordingly, these studies typically attempted to induce an enduring emotional change, using manipulations such as exposure to evocative movies or music, recall of autobiographical memories, or changes in weather. In contrast, other research focuses on characterizing the nature of more immediate reactions to emotional stimuli, and the consequences of such reactions for judgments and decisions. Next, we briefly review a general theoretical model governing such reactions, and then discuss related research.

Processing of Emotional Stimuli

Emotional stimuli are processed in a highly complex and interactive fashion. However, it is easiest to characterize this processing as a sequence of events (Scherer 2005). It is assumed that emotional stimuli are initially differentiated on importance, with the reaction being a nonspecific orienting response. This reaction may lead to changes in allocation of attention and in other cognitive resources, as well as a general physiological mobilization; this leads to enhancement of nonspecific arousal (Oehman, Hamm, and Hugdahl 2000). Next, the processing focuses on general valence of the cue, with the reaction being a positive-negative response. This reaction can trigger general biphasic tendencies, with negative stimuli facilitating avoidance and positive stimuli facilitating approach (Cacioppo and Berntson 1999; Hamm, Schupp, and Weike 2003; Lang 1995).[3] Finally, as more features are extracted from the stimulus, the stimulus can be considered in its situational context, and the resulting response becomes differentiated into specific emotions (Ellsworth and Scherer 2003).

This model has found support in a variety of experiments. These experiments show that affective cues can influence a variety of affective responses, ranging from simple preference judgments and immediate approach-avoidance behaviors, to complex decisions and deliberated actions.

Effects on Simple Preference Judgments and Immediate Behavior

Investigations of immediate effects of affective cues use several common paradigms.

Affective Priming.   Several studies have explored the nature of early affective reactions and their impact on simple judgments using the paradigm of affective priming. In this paradigm, participants are briefly presented with an emotional stimulus (for example, a happy or scowling face), which is immediately followed by a neutral judgmental target (for example, a Chinese ideograph or a drawing). The general finding is that even a brief, subliminal presentation of a valenced prime can influence judgments of a subsequent target. Hence, participants primed with a subliminal happy face, as opposed to a subliminal angry face, give more favorable ratings to a variety of novel stimuli (Murphy and Zajonc 1993; Niedenthal 1990; Winkielman, Zajonc, and Schwarz 1997). Interestingly, this research suggests that basic affective reactions elicited by such emotional stimuli are organized mainly on a positive-negative dimension (Zajonc 2000). Accordingly, judgment effects of happy versus angry subliminal facial expressions combine additively with effects of other basic affect inductions, such as mere exposure (Murphy, Monahan, and Zajonc 1995). Furthermore, changes in global positive-negative judgments of stimuli can be obtained with qualitatively different negative facial expressions, such as anger or disgust (Murphy and Zajonc 1993; Niedenthal 1990). Finally, under subliminal-presentation conditions, participants have trouble extracting more than general negativity from different expressions, such as anger, fear, disgust, or sadness (Murphy 2001).

Stimulus-Response Compatibility.   Other studies explored the impact of affective stimuli on simple approach-avoidance behaviors using the stimulus-response compatibility paradigm. In one of the first studies exploring this issue, Andrew K. Solarz (1960) asked participants to move cards with words either toward themselves or away from themselves. Participants responded faster with the pulling (approach) movement to positive words, and faster with the pushing (avoidant) movement to negative words. Mark Chen and John A. Bargh (1999) replicated these effects by asking participants to respond to positive and negative words by either pushing or pulling a joystick towards the body. Participants were faster to pull the lever in response to positive stimuli than to negative stimuli, even when evaluation was not the explicit goal in the task.

Although findings like these may suggest a relatively direct link between valence and movement, the story is more complicated (Niedenthal et al. 2005). For example, in a similar paradigm, Dirk Wentura, Klaus Rothermund, and Peter Bak (2000) asked participants to respond to positive and negative words by either reaching out their hand to press a button, or by withdrawing their hand from the button. Note that in this case, pressing the button required an extension movement, away from the body, and withdrawing required a flexion movement, toward the body. Yet, participants pressed the button faster for positive stimuli than for negative stimuli, but withdrew their hand faster for negative stimuli than positive stimuli. This finding suggests that there is no simple connection between positive-and-negative valence and flexion-and-extension (pull-and-push) movement. Instead, the connection seems to be dependent on participants' understanding of what the movement means in terms of relation between the stimulus and the participant. This point was recently demonstrated by Arthur B. Markman and C. Miguel Brendl (2005), who found that both the push and pull movements can be facilitated by positive valence if the respective action brings the stimulus closer to the self, regardless of whether the self (as represented by participant's name) is in the same or in a different relation to the movement as the participant's physical body.

Effects on Complex Actions and Decisions

Many studies in this area have focused on relatively simple behaviors and judgments. However, recent research from our lab has attempted to examine how exposure to emotional stimuli, such as facial expressions, can modify even more complex actions and decisions.

Subliminal Affective Priming of Consumption Behavior.   In a recent study, we explored the impact of affective reactions on complex actions using consumption behavior (Winkielman, Berridge, and Wilbarger 2005). We selected consumption because it allowed us to construct a task involving multiple steps (for example, pouring and drinking), and also because consumption has potentially important consequences (after all, it involves putting a novel substance into the body). Specifically, under the cover story of a "gender detection task," we first exposed participants to multiple trials of subliminal happy, neutral, or angry facial expressions, immediately followed by a supraliminal "masking" female or male face with a neutral expression. After the exposure phase, participants in experiment 1 were asked to pour a fruit-flavored beverage from a pitcher into a cup, and then to drink as much as they wanted. In experiment 2, participants were given a single sip of the beverage, and were then asked to rate various aspects of the drink. In both experiments, the results depended on the participants' levels of thirst, as determined by a preexperimental measure. Thirsty participants poured and consumed more of the drink after subliminal happy expressions than after subliminal angry facial expressions. Parallel effects of the subliminal stimuli were found on ratings of the single sip of the beverage. Thirsty participants wanted to consume more drink after happy than after angry expressions. Further, those participants reported willingness to pay more than twice as much after happy than after angry expressions. None of these results were obtained for nonthirsty participants, suggesting that the impact of subliminal affective primes depends on the presence of a relevant motivational state. In sum, this study presents clear evidence that complex and consequential actions, as well as ratings of monetary value, can be influenced by subliminal affective primes.

Unobtrusive Affective Priming of Risky Decisions.   Recently we have also explored the impact of basic affective stimuli on complex decisions under risk, involving choices from multiple options (Trujillo et al. under review). In those studies, participants were shown faces varying on gender, with gender detection as the ostensible goal of the task. In addition, however, the faces also varied on expressions (happiness, anger, fear, and neutral), though the emotional dimension of faces was not mentioned to participants as it presumably was "irrelevant to the task." Following each face trial, participants were given a gambling trial on which they decided between options varying in risk. Specifically, we employed three different decision making tasks from the risky choice literature. In one task, participants chose among three simultaneously presented options; the options were equal in probability, but they varied in the variance of outcomes, with the largest variance option being, by definition, the riskiest. In another task, participants chose among three sequentially presented options: the first option was relatively safe, and the subsequent options became progressively more valuable, but also more risky. Finally, in the third task, participants performed the earlier described myopic loss-aversion task, and were asked to choose between a low-risk, low-payoff option, or a high-risk, high-payoff option (Gneezy and Potters 1997). Our results showed that in all three tasks, the likelihood of a risky choice was greater after exposure to positive versus negative expressions. Together, these results suggest that the impact of basic emotional stimuli goes beyond simple preferences; rather, they can influence even complex risk decisions in a valence specific way, with positive expressions enhancing risk seeking and negative expressions reducing it.

From Undifferentiated Reactions to Specific Emotions

One interesting effect in these risky choice studies was that different negative expressions (fear and anger) reduced risk seeking to a similar extent. This suggests that basic affective reactions to facial expressions are differentiated on a general positive-negative dimension, consistent with earlier reported research on affective priming (Murphy 2001).

However, the effects of different expressions may change as participants are given more opportunity to process the stimulus and its implications. For example, Abigail A. Marsh, Nalini Ambady, and Robert E. Kleck (2005) examined reactions to angry and fearful facial expressions using the earlier discussed stimulus-response compatibility paradigm. In their study, angry faces were associated with a shorter latency to push away the lever (that is, avoidance). Interestingly, fearful faces were associated with faster pulling (that is, approach). The authors interpret these results in light of theories suggesting that the anger expression is generally perceived as a threatening stimulus, whereas the fear expression may function not only as a signal of environmental danger, but also as a signal of submission and elicit approach.[4]

Importantly, the Marsh, Ambady, and Kleck (2005) study explicitly required participants to categorize faces as angry or fearful, thus drawing participants' attention to their qualitative difference. Thus, the observed behavioral effects probably reflect a more complex processing of the stimulus, rather than more basic reactions explored in the affective priming studies discussed earlier. In fact, such interpretation is consistent with results of Mark Rotteveel and R. Hans Phaf (2004) who obtained response compatibility effects only when emotional expression (happy versus angry) was an explicit target of evaluation. When the expression was implicit, and participants focused on the gender of the face, no compatibility effects were observed, even though affective processing of the faces was still evident from affective priming effects. Similarly, in our studies participants did not have the motivation or capacity to process the specifics of the expression, as our tasks presented the emotional dimension of the face as irrelevant and put time pressure on participants. Under conditions of greater motivation or capacity, we would predict that different expressions of the same valence might have more specific effects on risk decisions (this possibility awaits empirical testing).

Finally, our findings that both angry and fearful faces reduce risky decisions might seem inconsistent with findings from the appraisal studies reviewed earlier. In those studies, inducing feelings of anger versus fear has opposite effects on risk, with anger leading to more optimistic estimates (Lerner and Keltner 2001). However, note that our studies manipulated the qualitative nature of the emotional stimulus (that is, an angry or fearful face). As discussed earlier, presentation of such faces does not necessarily induce a differentiated state of fear or anger, but only a general valenced reaction. In sum, these issues once again highlight the importance of distinguishing between the emotional stimulus, the reaction, and the state.

Unconscious Affect

Another question raised by the preceding findings is, how conscious are the reactions triggered by rudimentary affective stimuli? That is, do such stimuli change how participants feel? This question raises the possibility of unconscious affect: a reaction caused by valenced stimuli that has valenced behavioral consequences, but which nonetheless is not subjectively felt, even upon introspection (Winkielman and Berridge 2004). Unconscious affect, in this sense, has been proposed by several researchers based on studies of animals and psychiatric and neurological patients (Berridge 1999; Damasio 1994; Kihlstrom 1999). However, few studies have explicitly tested whether truly unconscious affective reactions can occur in typical participants.

Our initial attempt to examine this question relied on the affective priming paradigm, in which participants rate neutral stimuli preceded by subliminally flashed happy or angry faces (Winkielman, Zajonc, and Schwarz 1997). In those studies, we asked some participants to monitor changes in their conscious feelings, and told them not to use their feelings as a source of their preference ratings. Typically, such instructions eliminate the influence of conscious feelings on judgments (Schwarz and Clore 2003). However, even for participants who were told to disregard their feelings, the subliminally presented happy faces increased preference ratings of the neutral stimuli, while subliminally presented angry faces decreased them. This failure to correct for invalid feelings indicates that participants might not have experienced any conscious reactions in the first place. Indeed, after the experiment, participants did not remember experiencing any mood changes when asked about what they had felt during the rating task. Still, memory is not infallible. A skeptic could argue that participants had conscious feelings immediately after subliminal exposure to emotional faces, but they simply failed to remember the feelings later.

We agreed and sought to obtain more substantial evidence for unconscious affect in our subliminal affective priming of consumption behavior (Winkielman, Berridge, and Wilbarger 2005). Specifically, after the exposure to subliminal primes, we asked participants to report on their hedonic state using standard mood questionnaires which ask about conscious feelings such as pleasantness, arousal, hostility, fear, irritability, enthusiasm, and pride. The results showed that changes in behavior and ratings were not accompanied by changes in conscious mood. Thus, happy subliminal faces did not make participants feel better in general, nor did subliminal angry faces make them feel worse. Yet, after seeing a happy versus an angry face, participants poured and drank more of the beverage, and they also wanted and valued it more. This remarkable dissociation between the influence of affective stimuli on behavior and subjective feelings suggests that rudimentary affective processes can indeed be "unconscious" in the strong sense of the term.

Finally, it is worth emphasizing that affective stimuli are not unique in their ability to drive behavior independent of conscious experience. As documented in research on vision for action (Goodale and Milner 2004) and blindsight (Weiskrantz 1996), under certain conditions visual information can control behavior without the vision ever becoming conscious. For example, a patient with a visual form of agnosia, caused by damage to the ventral stream regions of the temporal lobe, is unable to provide a correct perceptual report of the orientation of a letter slot. However, the patient shows no difficulty when asked to insert an actual letter into the slot (Goodale and Milner 2004).

Psychological Mechanisms by Which Affective Reactions Influence Decisions

The studies discussed in this section suggest that unobtrusive exposure to basic affective stimuli, such as emotional facial expressions, influences how a person judges and behaves towards a subsequent target. These findings are particularly important given that emotional facial expressions are ubiquitous, potent, and highly familiar social stimuli (Ekman 1984). Further, it appears that such influences are not mediated by changes in conscious experience. Thus, our findings fall outside the domain of models that postulate a critical role for conscious feelings in affective influences (for example, the feeling-as-information model, Schwarz and Clore 2003).

So, what are the underlying mechanisms? We are currently addressing this question in our lab, so all we can offer are speculations. One possibility involves processes that are not specific to the target, such as changes in a general activation of the "approach-system, avoidance-system." For example, exposure to a smile could enhance a general propensity for exploratory behavior, which could lead participants to favor any novel object. Another possibility involves change in perception of the value, or probability, of a specific primed target. That is, after a smile, an option could either seem more valuable or less risky. Both of these explanations are consistent with our findings that smiles enhance ratings of neutral stimuli, willingness to try a novel drink, and propensity to choose a risky option. Importantly, the underlying psychological process could be direct in the sense that the affective reaction could modify participants' responsiveness to a value or probability of the stimulus via "front end" perceptual, attentional, or motivational mechanisms.

There are several other questions to be addressed by future research. For instance, would giving participants more time to process facial expressions result in qualitatively different effects? This is possible given the earlier results suggesting that explicitly processed expressions are discriminated in terms of their specific valence. It is also interesting how the impact of facial expressions would change depending on whether or not they induce a conscious state in participants. It is also interesting whether similar effects on behavior and decisions would be obtained with other, nonfacial emotional cues, either of basic nature (for example, snakes, spiders, or food), or of socially constructed nature (for example, patriotic flags or disliked groups). Yet another question is whether distinct affective mechanisms push people towards (that is, approach) and away (that is, avoid) from risky options (Cacioppo, Priester, and Berntson 1993).

Neural Mechanisms by Which Affective Reactions Influence Decisions

We can also briefly speculate about the neural underpinnings of the psychological processes responsible for these results (Winkielman et al. 2007). Figure 3.1 shows the approximate location in the brain of the relevant structures, and might be helpful to readers less familiar with affective neuroscience.

It is known that affective stimuli, such as facial expressions, can activate the amygdala, even when they are presented subliminally (Whalen et al. 1998), or when they are presented supraliminally but participants' attention is focused on some irrelevant dimension, such as gender (Critchley et al. 2000). It is also known that the amygdala projects to adjacent structures, such as the nucleus accumbens, which is involved in processing incentives (Berridge 2003), and to the prefrontal cortex, which is involved in representation of value and probability (Knutson and Wimmer 2007). Thus, for example, an emotional face could activate the amygdala and alter responsiveness of the nucleus accumbens when participants are exposed to an incentive stimulus (for example, the sensations of the novel beverage, Rolls 1999; or a risky gamble, Knutson and Wimmer 2007). Importantly, all these neural events could either bypass, or operate independently from, mechanisms that underlie conscious affective experience. Conscious experience presumably involves a complex interaction between cortical and subcortical structures. Specifically, it may require first creating a map of current conditions of one's body,

Figure 3.1   Approximate Locations of Neural Regions Involved in Affective Influence

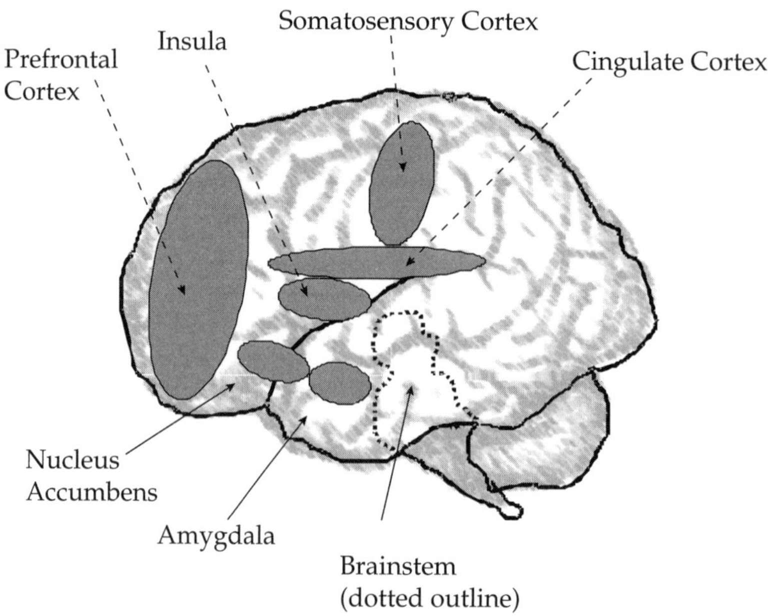

Source: Authors' compilation.
Note: Regions indicated with dashed lines are believed to be critical for the conscious affective experience. The figure shows only the left side of the brain and does not indicate the depth or connections of any structure (for a detailed presentation, see Berridge 2003).

involving the insula and somatosensory cortices (Critchley 2005), and then integrating this map with the representation of the self, presumably involving the prefrontal and cingulate cortex (Damasio 1994).

Conclusion

In this chapter, we reviewed some major theoretical approaches to emotional influence and placed our work in this context. We started by discussing research on how judgments and decisions are influenced by subjectively conscious, enduring emotional states, including arousal, mood, or specific emotions. Next, we covered research including our own, characterizing the nature of basic affective reactions. This research body suggests that basic affective reactions are best understood as resulting from a process that gradually increases in complexity, with basic reaction reflecting analysis of only rudimentary stimulus characteristics. Accordingly, basic affective reactions can be triggered by unconscious stimuli, are qualitatively undifferentiated, and do not necessarily involve subjective experience. Yet, such reactions can influence both simple and more complex behavior, including decision making when risk is involved. There are several important questions yet to be answered regarding the nature of basic affective reactions. However, our understanding is progressing in terms of both psychological mechanisms and neural underpinnings. With this growing knowledge about the basic mechanisms, the field is not only much more capable to formulate exact predictions of when emotion will influence judgment and decision, but also whether the influence will be beneficial or harmful—thus making headway on the questions posed for centuries by writers and philosophers.

Notes

1. A popular online encyclopedia states that "believing that something is true based on emotion may be regarded as epistemological mysticism. An instance of this may be when one bases one's belief in the existence of something merely on one's desire that it should exist. Another example might be the use of a daisy's petals and the phrase 'he loves me/he loves me not' while they are plucked to determine whether Romeo returns Juliet's affections." (Wikipedia Contributors 2006).
2. "Heat of passion" is typically defined as a mental state provoked by fear or anger that, combined with adequate provocation, causes a reasonable person to lose self-control, and to act on impulse and without reflection (Samaha 1999).
3. John T. Cacioppo and Gary G. Berntson (1999) suggest some biases in the functioning of the basic affective system. In a resting state, the system is biased towards exploratory behavior, and thus may evaluate neutral stimuli more favorably (positivity offset). This tendency is counteracted by a negative bias, or the relatively greater sensitivity to negative stimuli.
4. Because this study did not include neutral or happy expressions, it is unclear whether angry and fearful faces influenced immediate behavioral reactions in opposite directions, or had a directionally similar effect relative to neutral or happy faces, with a larger effect for the angry than fearful faces.

References

Andrade, Eduardo B. 2005. "Behavioral Consequences of Affect: Combining Evaluative and Regulatory Mechanisms." *Journal of Consumer Research* 32(3): 355–62.

Aristotle. 1985. *Nicomachean Ethics*. Indianapolis, Ind.: Hackett.

Arnold, Magda B. 1960. *Emotion and Personality*. Volumes 1 and 2. New York: Columbia University Press.

Bechara, Antoine, Hanna Damasio, Daniel Tranel, and Antonio R. Damasio. 1997. "Deciding Advantageously Before Knowing the Advantageous Strategy." *Science* 275(5304): 1293–5.

Berridge, Kent C. 1999. "Pleasure, Pain, Desire, and Dread: Hidden Core Processes of Emotion." In *Well-Being: The Foundations of Hedonic Psychology,* edited by Daniel Kahneman, Ed Diener, and Norbert Schwarz. New York: Russell Sage Foundation.

———. 2003. "Comparing the Emotional Brain of Humans and Other Animals." In *Handbook of Affective Sciences,* edited by Richard J. Davidson, Klaus Scherer, and H. Hill Goldsmith. New York: Oxford University Press.

Bodenhausen, Galen V. 1993. "Emotions, Arousal, and Stereotypic Judgments: A Heuristic Model of Affect and Stereotyping." In *Affect, Cognition, and Stereotyping,* edited by Diane M. Mackie and David L. Hamilton. San Diego, Calif.: Academic Press.

Cacioppo, John T., and Gary G. Berntson. 1999. "The Affect System: Architecture and Operating Characteristics." *Current Direction in Psychological Science* 18(5): 133–7.

Cacioppo, John T., Joseph R. Priester, and Gary G. Berntson. 1993. "Rudimentary Determinants of Attitudes: II. Arm Flexion and Extension Have Differential Effects on Attitudes." *Journal of Personality and Social Psychology* 65(1): 5–17.

Chen, Mark, and John A. Bargh. 1999. "Consequences of Automatic Evaluation: Immediate Behavior Predispositions to Approach or Avoid the Stimulus." *Personality and Social Psychology Bulletin* 25(2): 215–24.

Cosmides, Leda, and John Tooby. 2000. "Evolutionary Psychology and the Emotions." In *The Handbook of Emotions,* edited by Michael Lewis and Jeannette M. Haviland-Jones. New York: Oxford University Press.

Critchley, Hugo D. 2005. "Neural Mechanisms of Autonomic, Affective, and Cognitive Integration." *Journal of Comparative Neurology* 493(1): 154–66.

Critchley, Hugo, Eileen Daly, Mary Phillips, Michael Brammer, Edward Bullmore, Steven Williams, Therese Van Amelsvoort, Dene Robertson, Anthony David, and Declan Murphy. 2000. "Explicit and Implicit Neural Mechanisms for Processing of Social Information from Facial Expressions: A Functional Magnetic Resonance Imaging Study." *Human Brain Mapping* 9(2): 93–105.

Damasio, Antonio R. 1994. *Descartes' Error: Emotion, Reason, and the Human Brain.* New York: Grosset/Putnam.

Darwin, Charles. 1872/1998. *The Expressions of Emotion in Man and Animals.* New York: Oxford University Press.

de Sousa, Ronald. 1987. *The Rationality of Emotions.* Cambridge, Mass.: MIT Press.

Ekman, Paul. 1984. "Expression and the Nature of Emotion." In *Approaches to Emotion,* edited by Klaus Scherer and Paul Ekman. Hillsdale, N.J.: Lawrence Erlbaum Associates, Inc.

Ellsworth, Phoebe C., and Klaus R. Scherer. 2003. "Appraisal Processes in Emotion." In *Handbook of Affective Sciences,* edited Richard J. Davidson, Klaus Scherer, and H. Hill Goldsmith. New York: Oxford University Press.

Erber, Ralph, and Susan Markunas. 2006. "Managing Affective States." In *Affect in Social Thinking and Behavior,* edited by Joseph P. Forgas. Philadelphia, Pa.: Psychology Press.

Erber, Ralph, Daniel M. Wegner, and Nicole Therriault. 1996. "On Being Cool and Collected: Mood Regulation in Anticipation of Social Interaction." *Journal of Personality and Social Psychology* 70(4): 757–66.

Forgas, Joseph P. 1995. "Mood and Judgment: The Affect Infusion Model (AIM)." *Psychological Bulletin* 117(1): 39–66.

———. 2006. "Affective Influences on Interpersonal Behavior: Towards Understanding the Role of Affect in Everyday Interactions." In *Affect in Social Thinking and Behavior*, edited by Joseph P. Forgas. Philadelphia, Penn.: Psychology Press.

Gneezy, Uri, and Jan Potters. 1997. "An Experiment on Risk Taking and Evaluation Periods." *Quarterly Journal of Economics* 112(2): 631–45.

Goodale, Melvyn A., and A. David Milner. 2004. *Sight Unseen: An Exploration of Conscious and Unconscious Vision.* Oxford: Oxford University Press.

Hamm, Alfons O., Harold T. Schupp, and Almut I. Weike. 2003. "Motivational Organization of Emotions: Autonomic Changes, Cortical Responses, and Reflex Modulation." In *Handbook of Affective Sciences*, edited by Richard J. Davidson, Klaus Scherer, and H. Hill Goldsmith. New York: Oxford University Press.

Hume, David. 1739/1961. *A Treatise on Human Nature.* New York: Doubleday and Co.

Johnson, Eric J., and Amos Tversky. 1983. "Affect, Generalization, and the Perception of Risk." *Journal of Personality and Social Psychology* 45(1): 20–31.

Ketelaar, Timothy. 2006. "The Role of Moral Sentiments in Economic Decision Making." In *Social Psychology and Economics*, edited by David DeCremer, Marcel Zeelenberg, and J. Keith Murnighan. Mahwah, N.J.: Lawrence Erlbaum Associates, Inc.

Kihlstrom, John F. 1999. "The Psychological Unconscious." In *Handbook of Personality: Theory and Research*, edited by Lawrence A. Pervin and Oliver P. John. 2nd edition. New York: The Guilford Press.

Knutson, Brian, and G. Elliott Wimmer. 2007. "Reward: Neural Circuitry for Social Valuation." In *Social Neuroscience: Bridging Psychological and Biological Explanations of Social Behavior*, edited by John T. Cacioppo, Penny S. Visser, and Cynthia L. Pickett. New York: Guilford Press.

Lang, Peter J. 1995. "The Emotion Probe: Studies of Motivation and Attention." *American Psychologist* 50(5): 372–85.

Lazarus, Richard S. 1991. *Emotion and Adaptation.* New York: Oxford University Press.

Lerner, Jennifer S., and Dacher Keltner. 2001. "Fear, Anger, and Risk." *Journal of Personality and Social Psychology* 81(1): 146–59.

Markman, Arthur B., and C. Miguel Brendl. 2005. "Constraining Theories of Embodied Cognition." *Psychological Science* 16(1): 6–10.

Marsh, Abigail A., Nalini Ambady, and Robert E. Kleck. 2005. "The Effects of Fear and Anger Facial Expressions on Approach- and Avoidance-Related Behaviors." *Emotion* 5(1): 119–24.

Martin, Leonard L., Thomas F. Harlow, and Fritz Strack. 1992. "The Role of Bodily Sensations in the Evaluation of Social Events." *Personality and Social Psychology Bulletin* 18(8): 412–9.

Murphy, Sheila T. 2001. "The Nonconscious Discrimination of Emotion: Evidence for a Theoretical Distinction Between Affect and Emotion." *Polish Psychological Bulletin* 32(1): 9–15.

Murphy, Sheila T., and R. B. Zajonc. 1993. "Affect, Cognition, and Awareness: Affective Priming with Optimal and Suboptimal Stimulus Exposures." *Journal of Personality and Social Psychology* 64(5): 723–39.

Murphy, Sheila T., Jennifer L. Monahan, and R. B. Zajonc. 1995. "Additivity of Nonconscious Affect: Combined Effects of Priming and Exposure." *Journal of Personality and Social Psychology* 69(4): 589–602.

Niedenthal, Paula M. 1990. "Implicit Perception of Affective Information." *Journal of Experimental Social Psychology* 26(6): 505–27.

Niedenthal, Paula M., and Marc B. Setterlund. 1994. "Emotion Congruence in Perception." *Personality and Social Psychology Bulletin* 20(4): 401–11.

Niedenthal, Paula M., Lawrence W. Barsalou, Piotr Winkielman, Sylvia Krauth-Gruber, and François Ric. 2005. "Embodiment in Attitudes, Social Perception, and Emotion." *Personality and Social Psychology Review* 9(3): 184–211.

Oehman, Arne, Alfons Hamm, and Kenneth Hugdahl. 2000. "Cognition and the Autonomic Nervous System." In *Handbook of Psychophysiology*, edited by John T. Cacioppo, Louis G. Tassinary, and Gary G. Berntson. 2nd edition. New York: Cambridge University Press.

Owren, Michael J., Drew Rendall, and Jo-Anne Bachorowski. 2005. "Conscious and Unconscious Emotion in Nonlinguistic Vocal Communication." In *Emotion and Consciousness*, edited by Lisa Feldman Barrett, Paula M. Niedenthal, and Piotr Winkielman. New York: Guilford Publications.

Plato. 1973. *Phaedrus and Letters VII and VIII*. Translated by Walter Hamilton. Harmondsworth, England: Penguin.

Raghunathan, Rajagopal, and Michael Tuan Pham. 1999. "All Negative Moods Are Not Equal: Motivational Influences of Anxiety and Sadness on Decision Making." *Organizational Behavior and Human Decision Processes* 79(1): 56–77.

Rolls, Edmund T. 1999. *The Brain and Emotion*. Oxford: Oxford University Press.

Rotteveel, Mark, and R. Hans Phaf. 2004. "Automatic Affective Evaluation Does Not Automatically Predispose for Arm Flexion and Extension." *Emotion* 4(2): 156–72.

Samaha, Joel. 1999. *Criminal Law*. 6th edition. Belmont, Calif.: West/Wadsworth.

Schachter, Stanley, and Jerome Singer. 1962. "Cognitive, Social, and Physiological Determinants of Emotional State." *Psychological Review* 69(5): 379–99.

Scherer, Klaus R. 2005. "Unconscious Processes in Emotion: The Bulk of the Iceberg." In *Emotion and Consciousness*, edited by Lisa Feldman Barrett, Paula M. Niedenthal, and Piotr Winkielman. New York: Guilford.

Schwarz, Norbert, and Gerald L. Clore. 1983. "Mood, Misattribution, and Judgments of Well-Being: Informative and Directive Functions of Affective States." *Journal of Personality and Social Psychology* 45(3): 513–23.

———. 2003. "Mood as Information: 20 Years Later." *Psychological Inquiry* 14(3/4): 294–301.

Shiv, Baba, George Loewenstein, Antoine Bechara, Hanna Damasio, and Antonio R. Damasio. 2005. "Investment Behavior and the Dark Side of Emotion." *Psychological Science* 16(6): 435–9.

Slovic, Paul, Melissa Finucane, Ellen Peters, and Donald G. MacGregor. 2002. "Rational Actors or Rational Fools: Implications of the Affect Heuristic for Behavioral Economics." *Journal of Socio-Economics* 31(4): 329–42.

Smith, Adam. 1759. *The Theory of Moral Sentiments.* Indianapolis, Ind.: Liberty Classics.

Smith, Craig A., and Phoebe C. Ellsworth. 1985. "Patterns of Cognitive Appraisal in Emotion." *Journal of Personality and Social Psychology* 48(4): 813–38.

Solarz, Andrew K. 1960. "Latency of Instrumental Responses as a Function of Compatibility with the Meaning of Eliciting Verbal Signs." *Journal of Experimental Psychology* 59(4): 239–45.

Solomon, Robert C. 2003. *Not Passion's Slave: Emotions and Choice.* New York: Oxford University Press.

Spinoza, Baruch. 1677/1883. *The Ethics.* Trans. R. H. M. Elwes. London: George Bell and Sons.

Trujillo, Jennifer L., B. Knutson, M. P. Paulus, and Piotr Winkielman. "Taking Gambles at Face Value: Effects of Emotional Expressions on Risky Decisions." Journal article under review.

Weiskrantz, Lawrence. 1996. "Blindsight Revisited." *Current Opinion in Neurobiology* 6(2): 215–20.

Wentura, Dirk, Klaus Rothermund, and Peter Bak. 2000. "Automatic Vigilance: The Attention-Grabbing Power of Behavior-Related Social Information." *Journal of Personality and Social Psychology* 78(6): 1024–37.

Whalen, Paul, Scott L. Rauch, Nancy L. Etcoff, Sean C. McInerney, Michael B. Lee, and Michael A. Jenike. 1998. "Masked Presentations of Emotional Facial Expressions Modulate Amygdala Activity Without Explicit Knowledge." *The Journal of Neuroscience* 18(1): 411–8.

Wikipedia Contributors. 2006. "Epistemology." Wikipedia: The Free Encyclopedia. Accessed at http://en.wikipedia.org/w/index.php?title=Epistemology&oldid=36365103.

Winkielman, Piotr, and Kent C. Berridge. 2004. "Unconscious Emotion." *Current Directions in Psychological Science* 13(3): 120–3.

Winkielman, Piotr, Kent C. Berridge, and Julia Wilbarger. 2005. "Unconscious Affective Reactions to Masked Happy Versus Angry Faces Influence Consumption Behavior and Judgments of Value." *Personality and Social Psychology Bulletin* 31(1): 121–35.

Winkielman, Piotr, Robert B. Zajonc, and Norbert Schwarz. 1997. "Subliminal Affective Priming Resists Attributional Interventions." *Cognition and Emotion* 11(4): 433–65.

Winkielman, Piotr, Brian Knutson, Martin Paulus, and Jennifer L. Trujillo. 2007. "Affective Influence on Judgments and Decisions: Moving Towards Core Mechanisms." *Review of General Psychology* 11(2): 179–92.

Zajonc, R. B. 2000. "Feeling and Thinking: Closing the Debate over the Independence of Affect." In *Feeling and Thinking: The Role of Affect in Social Cognition,* edited by Joseph P. Forgas. Cambridge: Cambridge University Press.

Zillman, Dolf. 1978. "Attribution and Misattribution of Excitatory Reactions." In *New Directions in Attribution Research,* Volume 2, edited by John H. Harvey, William J. Ickes, and Robert F. Kidd. Hillsdale, N.J.: Lawrence Erlbaum Associates, Inc.

· 4 ·

Feeling, Searching, and Preparing: How Affective States Alter Information Seeking

KAREN GASPER AND LINDA M. ISBELL

I NDIVIDUALS MAKE an astonishing number of decisions each day. They decide on mundane matters (what to wear, drink, and read), important matters (whether one has prepared enough for a test, whether to hire a person, and whether one is persuaded by an argument), and occasionally on life-altering matters (whom to marry, where to move, and if one should have children). To help them make these decisions, people can access a seemingly endless amount of information. The simple decision of what to eat for breakfast, for example, might require a person to search the refrigerator, cabinets, and pantry, and to identify appropriate foods. The person may read the nutritional labels to learn the salt, carbohydrate, fat, and calorie content of the food. Once the person decides to have eggs for breakfast, the individual might consult a cookbook to determine whether the eggs should be scrambled, sunny side up, or made into a tasty frittata. Because people's lives are so demanding, they often do not have the time or the cognitive resources to devote much conscious attention toward all the decisions that have to be made on a daily basis. Luckily, unconscious processes often operate in conjunction with conscious thought to help people navigate through this complex informational world, shaping what information they seek out, how much information they seek out, and how they use this information to form a decision.

One factor that might act as a navigational guide, gently shaping the type of information that people seek out and how they process the information, is people's feelings. In fact, the key purpose of affective states is to sustain, guide, and direct action (Arnold 1960). Nevertheless, many people wonder whether affective states are appropriate guides. This wonderment inspired the central question of this book: Do feelings help or hurt the decision making process?

Like many questions, the answer to this one is complicated because affect can both help and hurt decision making depending on the situation. The goal of the chapter is to use research on moods and information seeking as an illustration of some of the broader conceptual issues that should be taken into account when addressing the question of whether emotions help or hurt decision making. In describing how affect, in particular moods, might influence decision making, we propose some basic principles that determine how moods function to alter decisions. We focus on how mood might alter a relatively unexplored facet of decision making: the process of information seeking (Schwarz 1990). Specifically, we delineate how mood should alter the degree to which people seek out detailed information, diagnostic information, confirmatory information, preparatory task information, and competency information.

Mood States and How They Inform Decisions

First, we want to define mood and distinguish it from emotions. Moods and emotions are two different types of affective experiences. Moods, unlike emotions, are transitory, mild, and diffuse affective states that do not have a readily accessible or salient cause (Frijda 1994). Because moods are not clearly linked to any eliciting conditions in the way that emotions are, moods tend to operate in the background of one's daily activities, whereas emotions operate in the foreground, where they attract one's attention. For instance, individuals experience a sad mood as a global sense of unpleasantness due to reasons that are not clearly identifiable (for example, "I got up on the wrong side of the bed this morning"), whereas they experience a sad emotion as a more highly differentiated affective response to something that is specific and identifiable (for example, "I feel sad because I did not win the award"). Because mood states lack a specific salient cause, people are likely to experience them as a reaction to whatever is in one's focus at the time (Clore, Gasper, and Garvin 2001).

Given that mood states are common experiences that easily can be perceived as part of one's reaction to a task at hand, they have the potential to alter many decisions in subtle ways. If affect operates as an informational tour guide, then mood states are the guides that are most likely to be on duty. For this reason, we limit our discussion to mood states rather than emotional states. We focus on the two most commonly experienced mood states: happy moods (feeling mildly happy, pleasant, and positive) and sad moods (feeling mildly sad, unpleasant, and negative). In addition, we focus on several general principles that shape the way that affect alters decisions. It is these principles that lead us to conclude that the answer to the question "Do feelings help or hurt decisions?" is that it depends.

How Does Affect Alter Decisions?

Affective states occur as a result of an unconscious appraisal process in which individuals assess the goodness or badness of their environment (for a discussion of the unconscious aspects, see Winkielman and Trujillo, chapter 3, this volume). The feelings that result from this assessment direct action, typically toward what is appraised as good and away from what is appraised as bad (Arnold 1960; Frijda 1994). Thus unlike cognitions, affective states provide people with a felt and highly personalized assessment of their environment (Clore and Gasper 2000; Gasper and Bramesfeld 2006a).

According to the affect-as-information perspective (Schwarz and Clore, 1983, 1988, 1996), affective states alter individuals' thoughts and actions when people experience their states as providing relevant information about the task at hand (Clore, Gasper, and Garvin 2001; Wyer, Clore, and Isbell 1999). For example, imagine a scenario in which individuals are asked to rate how likely it is that some negative events will happen to them. When thinking about the events, people may experience their sad moods as providing information indicating that the negative events are likely. This affective information then informs individuals' judgments, leading those in sad moods to rate negative events as more likely to occur compared to those in happy moods (Gasper and Clore 1998; Johnson and Tversky 1983; for a discussion on the differential role that specific emotions, such as fear versus anger, may play in this process, see Lerner and Keltner 2000).

The Basic Principles

When considering whether affect might help or hurt one's decisions, it is important to consider several basic principles that can influence the ways in which affect functions. These factors include whether the task typically elicits judgment or processing effects, which strategies are conducive to task success, the relevance of the affect to the task, and the contextualized meaning of affective information within the given task.

Judgment Versus Processing Effects.   The role that affect plays in the decision making process depends, in part, on the type of decision to be made. Affective states do not serve only one role. Like all tour guides, they can shape people's opinions through a variety of different routes. For example, an important distinction within the literature concerns whether affect alters how people judge a person, place, or object (referred to as a *judgment effect*), or whether affect alters how people process information about a person, place, or object (referred to as a *processing effect*).

Judgment effects occur when mood provides information that alters an opinion at the time of evaluation. Typically, when moods provide information at the time of judgment, they lead individuals to render a mood-congruent judgment (Mayer et al. 1992). For example, research indicates that people are happier with their lives (Schwarz and Clore 1983), report better health (Croyle and Uretsky 1987), perceive the world as less dangerous (Johnson and Tversky 1983), and hold more favorable opinions of various couples (Forgas 1995b) when they are in happy, rather than in sad, moods.

In addition to altering people's judgments, mood also alters how people process information en route to judgment. Processing effects occur when mood states provide information indicating the type of processing strategy that should be employed to encode, interpret, and organize incoming information. When processing information, positive moods provide information to people indicating that the environment is benign, that they should proceed freely without constraints, and that they should go forward with their gut reactions. In contrast, sad moods signal to people that the environment is problematic, that they should proceed with caution, and that they should be conservative in their approach (Bless 2000, 2001; Bless et al. 1996; Fiedler 2001; Gasper and Clore 2002; Schwarz and Clore 1996; Schwarz 2001; Schwarz and Bless 1991; Wyer, Clore, and Isbell 1999). The sense that the environment is safe leads individuals in happy moods to feel free to explore their environment (Fredrickson 1998, 2001), and to rely on global, abstract information that has served them well in the past, such a stereotypes, scripts, and schemas (Bless et al. 1996; Bodenhausen, Kramer, and Susser 1994; Gasper and Clore 2002; Melton 1995). In contrast, the sense that the environment is problematic leads individuals in sad moods to be cautious in their exploration of the environment (Gasper 2003, 2004b), and to rely on local, detailed information as a means to solve the problem (Bless 2000, 2001; Gasper and Clore 2002; Gasper 2004a).

A good example of the effects of mood on information processing is found in persuasion research (Bless et al. 1990; Bless, Mackie, and Schwarz 1992; Bohner et al. 1992; Mackie and Worth 1989; Sinclair, Mark, and Clore 1994). When individuals are in a sad mood, their mood conveys information that the message is potentially more problematic than would be the case if they were in a happy mood. To address these potential problems, individuals in sad moods may pay relatively more attention to argument strength than those in happy moods. Consistent with this hypothesis, the psychologists Robert Sinclair, Melvin Mark, and Gerald Clore (1994) found that individuals in sad moods based their evaluations of a persuasive argument on the strength of the message, agreeing with the strong message more than the weak one; in contrast, those in happy moods were not influenced by message strength and they endorsed both messages equally. Thus, moods influence the manner in which people process information.

Depending on whether affect alters judgment or how information is processed, different conclusions may be drawn from the same information. For example, suppose respondents are asked to form an impression of an African American named Stan. If mood serves to influence judgment directly, than happy moods should confer more favorable information about Stan than do sad moods, leading to more positive evaluations. In contrast, if mood activates a specific processing style, then happy moods should lead individuals to rely on their negative stereotype of African Americans to a greater extent than those in sad moods.[1] In this situation, individuals in happy moods should judge Stan more negatively than individuals in sad moods. Thus, when happy moods directly influence judgment, they may increase liking of Stan relative to sad moods, but when happy moods alter processing, they may decrease liking of Stan. Therefore, to determine how mood will alter decision making, one not only needs to consider the mood state, but also whether the influence of mood is on judgment or information-processing style.

Which Strategies Are Conducive to Task Success.   When considering the question of whether affect is good or bad for decision making, one must also consider that the same affective state could be beneficial or detrimental depending on which types of processes and outcomes lead to task success. For example, because happy moods signal that the environment is safe and that one should proceed, happy moods facilitate performance on tasks for which it is beneficial to view the situation as being safe and free of constraints, such as creativity tasks (Gasper 2004b; Isen 1984; Murray et al. 1990). Meanwhile, they would hinder performance on tasks for which it is important to exercise caution and be conservative, such as solving syllogisms (Melton 1995). Conversely, because sad moods indicate that the environment is problematic, they facilitate performance on tasks in which it is beneficial to view the situation cautiously and conservatively, such as solving syllogisms (Melton 1995). In contrast, sad moods hinder performance on tasks in which it is important to operate without constraints, such as creativity tasks (Gasper 2004b). Therefore, mood states cannot be easily classified as being beneficial or detrimental to the decision making process. Their influence depends on whether the mood state activates strategies that benefit the task at hand.

Relevance.   Moods alter action only when they are experienced as relevant to or informative about the judgment or task at hand (Clore et al. 2001; Schwarz and Clore 1988; Gasper and Clore 2000). Moods do not alter judgments on tasks in which affective information is not needed, such as when an outcome is already known (for example, mood is clearly irrelevant in determining the sum of two and two), or when a judgment is already available and easily retrievable from memory (Forgas 1995a). Mood is also unlikely to influence judgment and processing under conditions in which people want to arrive at a certain decision (for example, a juror who is motivated to find a defendant guilty). Finally, they tend not to have an influence when a particular processing motivation is highly activated (Forgas 1995a). For example, individuals in happy moods tend to process information systematically when they are held accountable for their judgments (Bodenhausen, Kramer, and Susser 1994), are explicitly told to process information carefully (Bless et al. 1990), or are led to believe that careful processing will enhance or maintain their moods (Wegener, Petty, and Smith 1995).

Because mood states have to be experienced as relevant to or informative about a judgment or task, mood effects should not appear when they are experienced as irrelevant to the situation at hand. For example, in the Norbert Schwarz and Gerald Clore (1983) study cited earlier, the effect of mood on life-satisfaction ratings was eliminated when participants were led to attribute their mood to a judgment-irrelevant source. Importantly, this attribution did not alter individuals' mood states; it only altered the relevance of their mood to their judgment. In a similar vein, research by Sinclair, Mark, and Clore (1994) demonstrated that the effects of mood on information-processing style are also eliminated under conditions in which mood is attributed to something other than the task at hand. These findings suggest that mood states do not randomly hijack people's thoughts and actions. Rather, mood states only influence thoughts and actions when people experience mood states as providing relevant information.

The powerful influence of mood attributions on eliminating the impact of mood on judgment and processing also may explain why it might be particularly difficult for some researchers to create mood effects in the laboratory. In order to examine mood in the laboratory, the first challenge is to create the desired mood state. However, creating the state is not enough. The second challenge is to create an environment in which participants misattribute their feelings to the experimental task. Any part of the experiment that draws undo attention to one's feelings could result in the participant seeing those feelings as irrelevant to the task; this could easily eliminate the effect under investigation (Berkowitz and Troccoli 1990; Gasper and Clore 2000). Thus, some researchers may successfully alter participants' affective states, but they would not find mood effects because they failed to create an environment in which the mood state was experienced as relevant to the experimental task. In sum, moods do not always exert an influence; they only do so when people experience them as being relevant to the task.

Affective Meaning.   Finally, the meaning of affective information is context dependent (Martin and Stoner 1996). Just as the word "bank" can refer to the side of a river or a financial institution, the meaning of mood states, and hence the effect that they might exert, depends on context. A multitude of factors can influence the meaning of affective cues, including one's goals (Martin et al. 1993), personality (Gasper and Bramesfeld 2006b; Gasper and Clore 1998; Tamir and Robinson 2004; Rawn et al. chapter 7, this volume; Zelenski, chapter 5, this volume), and the nature of the task (Martin et al. 1997). A good example of how the meaning of the mood state may depend on the nature of the task is to consider how people might determine whether they liked a sad movie, such as *Schindler's List*. Given that happy mood states confer more favorable information than do sad, it is reasonable to predict that people should like the movie more when they feel happy than sad. This prediction, however, fails to consider the context. The hallmark of an excellent sad movie is that it evokes sadness. If a person feels happy after watching a sad movie, then the movie failed to meet this important evaluative marker. With this principle in mind, Leonard Martin and his colleagues (1997) hypothesized and found that sad movies are rated more favorably by individuals in sad moods than those in happy moods. Another example of the importance of context comes from research by Jennifer Lerner, Deborah Small, and George Loewenstein (2004). They reasoned that sad moods encourage individuals to change their circumstances. Thus, they predicted and found that people in sad moods accept lower selling prices, in an effort to change one's circumstances by getting rid of an item; meanwhile, they would increase buying prices, in an effort to change one's circumstance by obtaining a new good. Thus, both experiments illustrate that sad moods do not have a singular effect; instead, their role depends on how moods inform the particular context.

Taken together, this review indicates that affective states do not have a simple, single effect on decision making. Moods may either help or hurt decision making depending on whether the mood influences judgment or processing, whether the information provided by one's mood is conducive to task success, what the relevance of the mood is to the task, and what the contextual meaning of the affective information is within a given task or situation. These basic principles not only influence how people process and judge information, but also how they seek it out.

Information Seeking

When individuals acquire information, they have to decide whether they need information, what information to look for, and how much information to acquire. Given the potential complexities that might exist in this process, it makes sense that mood states might provide individuals with information which helps them navigate through it. Mood can alter the degree to which people seek detailed information, diagnostic information, confirmatory information, preparatory task information, and competence information. Because people can seek out information in a wide array of domains, we focus solely on how mood may operate within two key domains: *impression formation* and *task preparations.*

Impression Formation

Everyday, individuals form impressions of others. In fact, when people see a person for even a few seconds, they form an impression that can have long-lasting effects (Ambady and Gray 2002). This impression can be based on an immediate reaction to the person (Ambady and Gray 2002), or on countless pieces of information, such as specific behaviors that the person performed, groups that the person is a member of, or the person's physical appearance (Fiske, Lin, and Neuberg 1999). Often when people form impressions of others, they have the opportunity to seek out a wide range of information. Building on extant research, we review evidence that indicates that mood alters the types of information that people seek out about others by influencing their quest for detailed, diagnostic, and confirmatory information.

Detailed Information.   Research demonstrates that individuals' feelings influence the extent to which they rely on different types of information as a basis for their judgments. Given that happy moods indicate that the environment is safe, people use information that typically serves them well, such as general, global, and abstract information. In contrast, because sad moods indicate that the environment is problematic, people use information that will help them to achieve a greater understanding of the problem at hand, such as specific and detailed information. Consistent with this view, research on impression formation indicates that individuals in happy moods tend to rely on global abstract information, such as stereotypes or traits, as a basis for their target judgments, whereas sad participants tend to rely on more detailed behavioral information (Bodenhausen, Kramer, and Susser 1994; Isbell 2004). In fact, this preference occurs regardless of the order in which individuals receive this information (Isbell 2004). Given that such findings are well established under conditions in which target information is explicitly provided to participants by an experimenter, it makes sense to hypothesize that these results may extend to situations in which individuals are given the opportunity to actively seek out information about a target. That is, individuals in happy moods should seek out global information, whereas those in sad moods should seek out detailed information.

To investigate this hypothesis, the psychologists Linda Isbell, Kathleen Burns, and Thomas Haar (2005) conducted an impression formation study (study 1) in which relatively happy and unhappy participants were asked to form an impression of a target on the basis of two types of information. Some of the information about the target was general (that is, traits that described her), whereas other information was specific (that is, details of the behaviors that she performed). Participants were told that they would receive both types of information, but could choose the type of information that they wanted to receive first. Consistent with predictions, the results revealed that relatively happy participants selected the global information before the specific behavioral information significantly more often than did relatively unhappy participants. This finding suggests that the results obtained in earlier impression-formation studies may generalize to information-seeking contexts. However, it is important to keep in mind that individuals in relatively unhappy or sad moods are likely to seek out detailed information because they believe that it will help them solve a problem. If this hypothesis holds true, then individuals in sad moods may seek global information if it provides diagnostic and helpful information about the problem at hand.

Diagnostic Information. Isbell, Burns, and Haar (2005) tested the hypothesis that happy moods may promote a desire to seek out global information regardless of its diagnosticity, whereas sad moods may lead individuals to seek out diagnostic information regardless of whether it is global or detailed. To explore this possibility, they manipulated the diagnosticity of

the global information. Extant research in the impression-formation literature (Skowronski and Carlston 1989) indicates that negative information
is more diagnostic than positive information. Based on this work, Isbell,
Burns, and Haar (2005) manipulated the diagnosticity of the information
by allowing participants to select global target information that was either
negative (relatively diagnostic) or positive (relatively non-diagnostic).
They reasoned that happy participants would show a greater preference
for global information than sad participants when the global information
was positive (non-diagnostic), but happy and sad participants would
not differ in their preference for global information when it was negative (diagnostic).

To test this hypothesis, participants were given the opportunity to
choose up to thirty-two pieces of information about a target from two
boxes on a computer. One box contained sixteen traits that described
the target, and the other box contained sixteen behaviors that the target
recently performed. All of the traits were either consistently positive (for
example, kind, warm, and intelligent) or consistently negative (for example, hostile, cold, and unintelligent), whereas the behaviors were eval-
uatively mixed (and thus relatively more diagnostic than the positive
set of traits, and relatively less diagnostic than the negative set of traits).
Consistent with past results, happy participants were more likely to
select a trait initially, whereas sad participants were more likely to select
a behavior; however, these results did not generalize to all of the information that participants selected. As expected, when the traits were positive (non-diagnostic), happy participants selected a greater proportion
of traits than did sad participants. However, when the traits were negative
(diagnostic), both happy and sad participants selected a similar proportion
of traits. Participants' later reports of which information they found to be
most useful in forming their impressions of the target were consistent with
the diagnosticity interpretation. Furthermore, even though the composition of the selected information differed as a function of affect and trait
valence, the total amount of information selected was uninfluenced by
these factors. On the basis of these findings, Isbell, Burns, and Haar (2005)
suggest that individuals in sad mood may be more attuned to the diagnosticity of information as a consequence of their affect informing them
that careful processing is necessary.

These state effects may even generalize to trait affect. Research on
depression (Edwards et al. 2000; Hildebrand-Saints and Weary 1989) is
consistent with the assertion that negative moods promote attention to
and selection of detailed and diagnostic information relative to positive
moods. For example, John Edwards and his colleagues (2000) found
that depressed participants were more sensitive to the diagnosticity of
experimenter-provided trait information when forming an impression.

In a social-information-gathering study, Lorraine Hildebrand-Saints and Gifford Weary (1989) examined the types of questions that depressed participants choose to ask a target during an interview. The results revealed that depressed individuals selected more highly diagnostic questions than did nondepressed participants. Thus, not only do sad moods promote the quest for diagnostic social information, but trait differences in depression do so as well.

Confirmatory Information.   Oftentimes when people seek out information, they have some preexisting knowledge about the target, such as a hypothesis, a stereotype, or some other general expectation (trait-based knowledge). When this knowledge exists, people have a tendency to confirm it (Johnston 1996; Johnston and Macrae 1994; Snyder and Swann 1978; Klayman and Ha 1987; Trope and Liberman 1996). Research by Lucy Johnston and her colleagues (Johnston 1996; Johnston and Macrae 1994) nicely illustrates how this confirmation bias alters information seeking. In this research, respondents select questions to ask to a stereotyped target. The results revealed that respondents selected questions that confirmed their stereotype rather than questions that disconfirmed or were irrelevant to it. As a result of asking questions that confirm their beliefs, people are likely to maintain their stereotype-based evaluations of targets. This work suggests that seeking out confirmatory evidence is a general strategy that people employ.

Given that sad moods signal that one should be cautious, Linda Isbell, Kathleen Burns, and Lanell James (2007) hypothesized that individuals in sad moods may forgo such a confirmatory strategy, and may seek to test their default assumptions more actively than those in happy moods. To test this hypothesis, they investigated whether happy moods would lead individuals to seek more stereotype-confirming information than would sad moods. In this experiment, they manipulated participants' moods and then, in an ostensibly unrelated study, told participants that they would review a job applicant's resume and then interview the applicant. To activate a stereotype about the applicant, participants were told that the applicant was either Tameka, an African American woman, or Laura, a Caucasian woman. Other than the name and race information, the applicants' resumes were identical. After reviewing the resume, participants received a list of sixteen "standard interview questions" and were asked to select eight questions to ask the applicant. Eight of the sixteen questions were designed to elicit positive information from the applicant (for example, "What is your greatest strength?"), and eight were designed to elicit negative information (for example, "What is your greatest weakness?"). Based on prior research which suggests that the evaluative implications of the African American stereotype are negative (Bargh, Chen, and Burrows 1996; Devine, 1989), Isbell, Burns, and James (2007) hypothesized that individuals in happy moods would select a greater number of negative questions to ask the African American target than the Caucasian target, whereas individuals in sad moods would select a similar number of negative questions to ask the two targets. The results were consistent with these predictions, suggesting that an interviewer who is in a bad mood might actually be fairer than one who is in a good mood, because negative moods seem to reduce the preference for confirmatory information.

Task Preparations

In addition to continuously forming impressions of others, people often are engaged in preparatory activities. Employees prepare for the next big presentation, students prepare for their classes, and athletes prepare for the upcoming competition. These individuals prepare to acquire information and feedback. They can acquire information about how to do the task or information about how well they are doing the task (Ashford and Cummings 1983). When people begin working on a novel task, they initially engage in task assessment. Here, they want to acquire information as a means to learn about the task. Once people understand what they are supposed to do, they switch from the process of task assessment to the process of competency assessment. Here, they want to learn if they have the skills and abilities needed to do the task (Ashford and Cummings 1983; Greller and Herold 1975; Ruble and Frey 1991). Research on mood and information processing suggests that mood may alter both of these processes. Specifically, sad moods may promote task assessment by encouraging individuals to acquire preparatory task information; meanwhile, happy moods may promote competency assessment by encouraging individuals to prepare in order to acquire information about their competencies and skills.

Preparatory Task Information.   When people encounter a new task, they engage in the process of task assessment. They want to learn what the task entails, especially if they foresee that the task might be problematic. If sad moods signal that the task might be more problematic than happy moods, then individuals in sad moods might be more likely to seek out additional task information. Given the belief that sad moods undermine motivation, it may seem surprising that sad moods could potentially foster learning about a task. However, this hypothesis can be explained in the context of research indicating that sad moods may promote the quest for detailed, diagnostic, and disconfirmatory information in an effort to understand the task. Additionally, Mary Luce, James Bettman, and John

Payne (1997) found that negative emotions encouraged individuals to acquire information using a systematic, attribute-based processing strategy. Given this focus on understanding the details of the task, it seems reasonable that the desire to understand the task would even apply to a situation in which a person is required to prepare for a task.

Building upon this work, Karen Gasper and Kosha Bramesfeld (2007) hypothesized that, because sad moods signal that an upcoming task is problematic, individuals in sad moods should be more likely than those in happy moods to seek out task-relevant information as a means to learn about the problem. To test this hypothesis, individuals in happy and sad moods were given an opportunity to practice an anagram task prior to engaging in the "real" anagram task. As predicted, individuals in sad moods practiced more than those in happy moods. In addition, individuals in happy and sad moods got the same overall percentage of practice problems correct and averaged the same amount of time per problem. This experiment reveals that individuals in sad moods practiced more than those in happy moods, and this effect was not the result of mood altering people's ability to perform the task.

Even though individuals in sad moods prepared more than those in happy moods in Gasper and Bramesfeld's (2007) first experiment, this study did not explicitly test the hypothesis that these differences were due to the desire of individuals in sad moods to acquire information that would help them learn about the task. To examine this hypothesis, Gasper and Bramesfeld (2007) ran a second study in which they varied the diagnosticity of the information gleaned from practicing by telling participants that practicing either did or did not promote learning. If individuals in sad moods practiced to acquire information that would help them learn about the task, then they should practice more when they are led to believe that doing so will promote learning than when they are led to believe that it does not promote learning. The results were consistent with these predictions. Participants prepared more in sad than in happy moods when practicing promoted learning, but not when practicing failed to promote learning. These findings also coincide with Isbell, Burns, and Haar's (2005) finding that sad moods promote the acquisition of diagnostic information.

It is important to note that sad moods may not always enhance information seeking relative to happy moods. Individuals in sad moods are hypothesized to want to acquire diagnostic and task-relevant information. Therefore, they may not want to acquire information that is interesting but irrelevant to the task at hand. In contrast, because happy moods promote a global focus and encourage people to broaden and build their extant knowledge (Fredrickson 1998, 2001), individuals in happy moods might be more interested in obtaining information that is irrelevant to their primary goals but is potentially interesting in light of alternative goals. Consistent with this prediction, research indicates that individuals in happy moods are more likely to seek out interesting but not highly pertinent information. For example, happy moods resulted in pedestrians picking up a free pamphlet containing interesting facts about Kansas (Batson et al. 1979), students desiring additional information about psychology experiments (Rodrigue, Olson, and Markley 1987), and doctors providing diagnoses for more patients than required (Isen, Rosenzweig, and Young 1991). Thus, the relevance of the task information may be just one factor that moderates the effect of mood on acquiring preparatory task information. Overall, these findings support the hypothesis that individuals in sad moods will acquire relevant and diagnostic information in an effort to learn about the task.

Competency Information.   Recall that people may practice not only to assess the task, but also to assess their competency. In this situation, happy moods may promote preparations more than sad moods because they are less likely to confer negative information about oneself and one's abilities. For example, research indicates that people in sad moods hold less positive views of their life (Schwarz and Clore 1983), their health (Salovey and Brinbaum 1989), and their future (Gasper and Clore 1998) relative to those in happy moods. This negative information about the self might exert two effects that could hinder the quest for competency-relevant information.

First, feeling poorly about oneself might impede learning because the feelings are experienced as an indication that one lacks the ability to do a task. When people doubt that they can achieve their goals, they often stop trying to obtain them. A hallmark of depression is that individuals feel like they cannot control their environment and hence are more likely to give up on various tasks (Miller and Seligman 1975). Negative affect might similarly convey information indicating that one lacks the ability or competency to take effective actions, thereby decreasing the degree to which people are motivated to acquire more information about their competence.

Second, feeling poorly about oneself might activate the desire to repair one's mood state and protect one's self-esteem (for discussions of affect regulation, see Andrade and Cohen, chapter 2, this volume; Gailliot and Tice, chapter 9, this volume). People may protect their feelings by avoiding information about their competency, because they fear that it might be negative and may further threaten their self-esteem (Rawn et al., chapter 7, this volume). For instance, social-comparison research reveals that individuals high in negative affectivity (that is, they have low self-esteem, depression, or sad moods) fail to seek out helpful upward comparisons, in part because these upward comparisons highlight one's inferiority and hence are mood threatening (Smith LeBeau and Gasper 2005; Wills 1981; Wood and Lockwood 1999). Similar to the findings in social comparison research, individuals in sad moods may avoid assessing their competency because such information might be threatening and could hurt their feelings.

In contrast, positive moods may promote a sense of self-competency. They signal that all is well, and they foster efforts that help individuals grow by encouraging them to broaden and build their skills (Aspinwall 1998; Fredrickson 1998, 2001). They also act as a resource (Trope, Ferguson, and Raghunathan 2001). According to the *mood-as-a-resource hypothesis* (Trope, Ferguson, and Raghunathan 2001), when people feel happy, they may be more likely to seek out helpful negative information; this is because their happy moods help buffer them against any short-term pain so that they can obtain long-term benefits. Consistent with this notion, Yaacov Trope and Efat Neter (1994) found that after individuals in happy moods failed at a task, they were more likely than those in negative moods to express interest in seeing negative information that could help them improve their performance. Taken together, this research suggests that when individuals are focused on assessing their competency, individuals in happy moods may feel that they can benefit from information more than those in sad moods, and they may be more likely to seek it out.

At first glance, this prediction may seem incongruent with the prediction that sad moods help learning. That is, if sad moods promote learning about a task, why not promote learning about one's competency? To answer this question, it is important to keep in mind that the meaning of affective cues depends on context (Martin and Stoner 1996). When people focus on task assessment, sad moods should signal that there is a problem with their understanding of the task requirements. To solve this problem, it makes sense to acquire more information through preparations. When people focus on assessing their competencies, sad moods should signal that their competencies are problematic. In this instance, more information would not be helpful because negative affect signals that it is doubtful that one would be able to learn from the task. Thus, sad moods may foster a desire to assess the task, but not a desire to assess one's competencies.

To test this hypothesis, Gasper and Bramesfeld (2007) asked people to prepare for an upcoming anagram task, and they manipulated the degree to which participants focused on learning about the task (task assessment) or their competency to do the task (competency assessment). As predicted, when people focused on assessing the task, individuals in sad moods practiced more than those in happy moods. In contrast, when people focused on assessing their competencies, individuals in happy moods increased their preparatory efforts more than those in sad moods. Consistent with predictions, additional analyses revealed that for individuals in sad moods, the desire to learn about the task but not about their competency, predicted preparations; meanwhile, for individuals in happy moods, the desire to learn about their competency but not about the task, predicted preparations. Therefore, both mood states encouraged the quest for information, but the quest depended on which type of information individuals sought.

One potentially interesting, but untested, ramification of these findings is that even though individuals in sad moods may engage in extensive preparations to understand the task, these preparations may not help them feel competent enough to do the task. That is, knowledge about the task need not mitigate one's fear of failing to be able to do the task. If this is the case, then advising people to handle stress by preparing extensively may help them learn about the task but may not ultimately help them feel more competent at doing the task.

This review focuses primarily on the process of gathering information and not on how that information might alter people's final decisions. Researchers who examine people's final decisions should pay close attention to the processes that underlie them, because it is entirely possible for people to arrive at the same conclusions using very different decision making processes. For example, a couple may be booking reservations for their honeymoon. The bride, who is in a negative mood, might spend hours researching various travel websites, comparing prices of different tour companies and learning about a wide range of destinations. The groom, who is in a happy mood, may merely go to his favorite travel website and select a vacation in a matter of minutes. They both could pick the exact same vacation but would do so through entirely different processes. This distinction between process and outcome is important, for although in this instance the bride and groom agreed on the vacation, they did so using very different methods. Hence, it is important to understand how people arrived at a decision and the role of affect in the process of seeking out information.

Linking the Basic Principles to Research on Information Seeking

To examine how affect might alter decision making, we focused on just one small aspect of the decision making process: information seeking. We defined information seeking broadly, touching upon how information seeking might be relevant to impression formation and task preparations. We argued that sad moods can increase the degree to which individuals seek out detailed, diagnostic, and preparatory task information, but it can decrease the degree to which these individuals seek out confirmatory and competency information. These findings follow the basic principles guiding affect research and highlight how affect may both help and hurt decision making.

Information Seeking and Judgment Versus Processing Effects

Research on how moods alter both judgment and processing informs research on how moods alter information seeking. For instance, research on mood and judgments sheds light on how mood might alter the acquisition of competency-assessment information. When individuals judge whether they have the competency to do a task, sad moods confer more negative information about one's competency than do happy moods. Research on the role of mood in processing elucidates Isbell, Burns, and Haar's (2005) work on affect and the search for detailed information. Recall that individuals in sad moods tend to process information in a more detailed manner than those in positive moods. This logic inspired their prediction that individuals in sad moods would acquire more detailed information than those in positive moods. Thus, research on how mood alters judgment and processing informs hypotheses concerning the role that mood states may play in entirely different arena: information acquisition. It also helps to elucidate why sad moods may hinder the acquisition of one type of information (that is, competency information) but facilitate the acquisition of another type of information (that is, detailed information).

Information Seeking and Strategies Conducive to Task Success

In this chapter we described mood differences in seeking out detailed, diagnostic, confirmatory, preparatory, and competency information. One might be tempted to deem one of these sources of information to be better than the others. However, the utility of these different types of information depends on the task. For example, recall that Isbell, Burns, and Haar (2005) found that individuals in happy moods tended to seek out confirmatory information. In the context of interviewing an African American job applicant, this confirmatory bias could lead people in happy moods to make a more discriminatory decision than those in sad moods. In other instances, this confirmatory bias could prove to be beneficial, such as when the goal is to support an argument. Thus, whether moods help or hurt decisions may depend, in large part, on whether mood states promote the quest for information that is conducive to task success.

Information Seeking and Relevance

Mood states alter information seeking because people experience them as providing relevant information about the task. Therefore, we propose that when mood states seem to be irrelevant to the task at hand, they should no longer exert an influence on information seeking. One way to test this hypothesis would be to lead participants to experience their feelings as due to a task-irrelevant source (Schwarz and Clore 1983). We predict that when feelings no longer seem to be part of the task, the effect of mood on information seeking will be attenuated. Currently, researchers have yet to examine whether such manipulations would eliminate the effect of mood on information seeking. However, this possibility seems likely because such manipulations can eliminate the effect of mood on both judgment and processing (Gasper 2004a; Schwarz and Clore 1983; Sinclair, Mark, and Clore 1994). If the effect of mood on information seeking depends on relevance, then mood states do not guide information seeking in a haphazard fashion. Rather, mood states only guide information seeking when the information that they provide seems to be helpful and relevant to the process.

Information Seeking and Affective Meaning

Finally, the effect that moods exert on information seeking depends on the context. For example, the effect of mood on preparations depended on whether individuals were engaged in the process of task assessment or competency assessment. Sad moods encouraged preparations when individuals wanted to learn about the task, whereas happy moods encouraged them when individuals wanted to learn about their competency (Gasper and Bramesfeld 2007).

Another illustration of the importance of affective meaning is to consider how the motive to self-verify versus the motive to self-enhance might alter how sad moods influence information seeking. If people are motivated to self-verify (Swann 1990), individuals in sad moods might seek out negative information to verify their mood state. Conversely, if people are motivated to self-enhance, individuals in sad moods may avoid negative, threatening information and seek out positive information in an effort to feel better about themselves (Isen 1984). Consistent with both of these views, research on how depressed individuals seek out information indicates that they may "flip-flop" between these two goals. Depressed individuals seek out negative feedback to verify their negative self-views (Casbon et al. 2005) and positive feedback as a means to console themselves (Joiner, Alfano, and Metalsky 1993). Therefore, the type of information that people seek may depend not only on the information itself, but also on their goals and other contextual factors.

Conclusion

Does affect help or hurt decision making? Our answer to this question is a resounding and firm "it depends." We argue that feelings operate as tour guides by directing, sustaining, and even motivating action (Arnold 1960). Whether these affective tour guides take us down the right path or lead us on a "wild goose chase" depends on a wide range of factors. In particular, one needs to consider whether mood influences information processing or information evaluation, whether the information provided by one's mood is conducive to task success, the relevance of the mood to the task, and the contextual meaning of the affective information within the given task. Research in this field illustrates how these factors can conspire to both help and hurt one small aspect of decision making: the process of information seeking. This work reveals that sad moods can increase the degree to which individuals seek out detailed information, diagnostic information, and preparatory information, but can decrease the degree to which individuals seek out confirmatory information and competency information. Thus, affect sometimes helps decisions and sometimes hurts decisions, depending on the nature of the situation and the role the affective tour guide plays within it.

Preparation of this article was supported in part by NSF Grant 0349048 to Karen Gasper entitled "Mood and Learning: How Feelings Influence Task Preparations."

Notes

1.   Research indicates that the African American stereotype tends to be largely negative (Bargh, Chen, and Burrows 1996; Devine 1989).

References

Ambady, Nalini, and Heather M. Gray. 2002. "On Being Sad and Mistaken: Mood Effects on the Accuracy of Thin-Slice Judgments." *Journal of Personality and Social Psychology* 83(4): 947–61.

Arnold, Magda B. 1960. *Psychological Aspects.* Volume 1 of *Emotion and Personality.* Oxford: Columbia University Press.

Ashford, Susan J., and Larry L. Cummings. 1983. "Feedback as an Individual Resource: Personal Strategies of Creating Information." *Organizational Behavior and Human Performance* 32(3): 370–98.

Aspinwall, Lisa G. 1998. "Rethinking the Role of Positive Affect in Self-Regulation." *Motivation and Emotion* 22(1): 1–32.

Bargh, John A., Mark Chen, and Lara Burrows. 1996. "Automaticity of Social Behavior: Direct Effects of Trait Construct and Stereotype Activation on Action." *Journal of Personality and Social Psychology* 71(2): 230–44.

Batson, C. Daniel, J. S. Coke, Fred Chard, Debra Smith, and Antonia Taliaferro. 1979. "Generality of the 'Glow of Goodwill': Effects of Mood on Helping and Information Acquisition." *Social Psychology Quarterly* 42(2): 176–79.

Berkowitz, Leonard, and Bartholomeu T. Troccoli. 1990. "Feelings, Direction of Attention, and Expressed Evaluations of Others." *Cognition and Emotion* 4(4): 305–25.

Bless, Herbert. 2000. "The Interplay of Affect and Cognition: The Mediating Role of General Knowledge Structures." In *Feeling and Thinking: The Role of Affect in Social Cognition*, edited by Joseph P. Forgas. New York: Cambridge University Press.

———. 2001. "Mood and the Use of General Knowledge Structures." In *Theories of Mood and Cognition*, edited by Leonard L. Martin and Gerald L. Clore. Mahwah, N.J.: Lawrence Erlbaum Associates, Inc.

Bless, Herbert, Diane M. Mackie, and Norbert Schwarz. 1992. "Mood Effects on Encoding and Judgmental Processes in Persuasion." *Journal of Personality and Social Psychology* 63(4): 585–95.

Bless, Herbert, Gerd Bohner, Norbert Schwarz, and Fritz Strack. 1990. "Mood and Persuasion: A Cognitive Response Analysis." *Personality and Social Psychology Bulletin* 16(2): 331–45.

Bless, Herbert, Gerald L. Clore, Norbert Schwarz, Verena Golisano, Christina Rabe, and Marcus Wölk. 1996. "Mood and the Use of Scripts: Does a Happy Mood Really Lead to Mindlessness?" *Journal of Personality and Social Psychology* 71(4): 665–79.

Bodenhausen, Galen V., Geoffrey P. Kramer, and Karin Susser. 1994. "Happiness and Stereotypic Thinking in Social Judgment." *Journal of Personality and Social Psychology* 66(4): 621–32.

Bohner, Gerd, Kimberly Crow, Hans P. Erb, and Norbert Schwarz. 1992. "Affect and Persuasion: Mood Effects on the Processing of Message Content and Context Cues on Subsequent Behavior." *European Journal of Social Psychology* 22(6): 511–30.

Casbon, Todd S., Andrea B. Burns, Thomas N. Bradbury, and Thomas E. Joiner, Jr. 2005. "Receipt of Negative Feedback Is Related to Increased Negative Feedback Seeking Among Individuals with Depressive Symptoms." *Behaviour Research and Therapy* 43(4): 485–504.

Clore, Gerald L., and Karen Gasper. 2000. "Feeling is Believing: Some Affective Influences on Belief." In *Emotions and Beliefs: How Feelings Influence Thoughts*, edited by Nico Frijda, Antony S. R. Manstead, and Sacha Bem. New York: Cambridge University Press.

Clore, Gerald L., Karen Gasper, and Erika Garvin. 2001. "Affect as Information." In *Handbook of Affect and Social Cognition*, edited by Joseph P. Forgas. Mahwah. N.J.: Lawrence Erlbaum Associates, Inc.

Clore, Gerald L., Robert S. Wyer, Bruce Dienes, Karen Gasper, Carol Gohm, and Linda Isbell. 2001. "Affective Feelings as Feedback: Some Cognitive Consequences." In *Theories of Mood and Cognition: A User's Guide*, edited by

Leonard L. Martinand and Gerald L. Clore. Mahwah, N.J.: Lawrence Erlbaum Associates, Inc.

Croyle, Robert T., and Michael B. Uretsky. 1987. "Effects of Mood on Self-Appraisal of Health Status." *Health Psychology* 6(3): 239–53.

Devine, Patricia G. 1989. "Stereotype and Prejudice: Their Automatic and Controlled Components." *Journal of Personality and Social Psychology* 56(1): 5–18.

Edwards, John A., Gifford Weary, William von Hippel, and Jill A. Jacobson. 2000. "The Effects of Depression on Impression Formation: The Role of Trait and Category Diagnosticity." *Personality and Social Psychology Bulletin* 26(4): 462–73.

Fiedler, Klaus. 2001. "Affective States Trigger Processes of Assimilation and Accommodation." In *Theories of Mood and Cognition: A User's Guidebook*, edited by Leonard L. Martin and Gerald L. Clore. Mahwah, N.J.: Lawrence Erlbaum Associates, Inc.

Fiske, Susan T., Monica Lin, and Steven L. Neuberg. 1999. "The Continuum Model: Ten Years Later." In *Dual-Process Theories in Social Psychology,* edited by Shelley Chaiken and Yaacov Trope. New York: Guilford Press.

Forgas, Joseph P. 1995a. "Mood and Judgment: The Affect Infusion Model (AIM)." *Psychological Bulletin* 117(1): 39–66.

———. 1995b. "Strange Couples: Mood Effects on Judgments and Memory About Prototypical and Atypical Relationships." *Personality and Social Psychology Bulletin* 21(7): 747–65.

Fredrickson, Barbara L. 1998. "What Good Are Positive Emotions?" *Review of General Psychology* 2(3): 300–19.

———. 2001. "The Role of Positive Emotions in Positive Psychology: The Broaden-and-Build Theory of Positive Emotions." *American Psychologist* 56(3): 218–26.

Frijda, Nico H. 1994. "Varieties of Affect: Emotions and Episodes, Moods, and Sentiments." In *The Nature of Emotion: Fundamental Questions,* edited by Paul Ekman and Richard J. Davidson. New York: Oxford.

Gasper, Karen. 2003. "When Necessity Is the Mother of Invention: Mood and Problem Solving." *Journal of Experimental Social Psychology* 39(3): 248–62.

———. 2004a. "Do You See What I See? Affect and Visual Information Processing." *Cognition and Emotion* 18(3): 405–21.

———. 2004b. "Permission to Seek Freely? The Effect of Happy and Sad Moods on Generating Old and New Ideas." *The Creativity Research Journal* 16(2–3): 215–29.

Gasper, Karen, and Kosha D. Bramesfeld. 2006a. "Imparting Arnold's Wisdom: Integrating Research on Affect and Motivation." *Cognition and Emotion* 20(7): 1001–26.

———. 2006b. "Should I Follow My Feelings? How Individual Differences in Following Feelings Predict Affective Experience, Affective Well-Being, and Affective Responsiveness." *Journal of Research in Personality* 40(6): 986–1014.

———. 2007. "The Effect of Mood on Practicing." Unpublished paper. Pennsylvania State University.

Gasper, Karen, and Gerald L. Clore. 1998. "The Persistent Use of Negative Affect by Anxious Individuals to Estimate Risk." *Journal of Personality and Social Psychology* 74(5): 1350–63.

————. 2000. "Do You Have To Pay Attention To Your Feelings In Order To Be Influenced By Them?" *Personality and Social Psychology Bulletin* 26(6): 698–711.

————. 2002. "Attending to the Big Picture: Mood and Global Versus Local Processing of Visual Information." *Psychological Science* 13(1): 33–39.

Greller, Martin, and David M. Herold. 1975. "Sources of Feedback: A Preliminary Investigation." *Organizational Behavior and Human Performance* 13(2): 244–56.

Hildebrand-Saints, Lorraine, and Gifford Weary. 1989. "Depression and Social Information Gathering." *Personality and Social Psychology Bulletin* 15(2): 150–60.

Isbell, Linda M. 2004. "Not All Happy People Are Lazy or Stupid: Evidence of Systematic Processing in Happy Moods." *Journal of Experimental Social Psychology* 40(3): 341–9.

Isbell, Linda M., Kathleen C. Burns, and Thomas Haar. 2005. "The Role of Affect on the Selection of Global Versus Specific Target Information." *Social Cognition* 23(6): 529–52.

Isbell, Linda M., Kathleen C. Burns, and Lanell James. 2007. "The Influence of Affect on Interview Question Selection." Raw data. University of Massachusetts, Amherst.

Isen, Alice M. 1984. "Towards Understanding the Role of Affect in Cognition." In *Handbook of Social Cognition,* Volume 3, edited by Robert S. Wyer and Thomas K. Srul. Hillsdale, N.J.: Lawrence Erlbaum Associates, Inc.

Isen, Alice M., Andrew S. Rosenzweig, and Mark J. Young. 1991. "The Influence of Positive Affect on Clinical Problem Solving." *Medical Decision Making* 11(3): 221–7.

Johnson, Eric J., and Amos Tversky. 1983. "Affect, Generalization and the Perception of Risk." *Journal of Personality and Social Psychology* 45(1): 21–31.

Johnston, Lucy C. 1996. "Resisting Change: Information-Seeking and Stereotype Change." *European Journal of Social Psychology* 26(5): 799–825.

Johnston, Lucy C., and C. Neil Macrae. 1994. "Changing Social Stereotypes: The Case of the Information Seeker." *European Journal of Social Psychology* 24(5): 581–92.

Joiner, Thomas E., Jr., Mark S. Alfano, and Gerald I. Metalsky. 1993. "Caught in the Crossfire: Depression, Self-Consistency, Self-Enhancement, and the Response of Others." *Journal of Social and Clinical Psychology* 12(2): 113–34.

Klayman, Joshua, and Young-won Ha. 1987. "Confirmation, Disconfirmation and Information in Hypothesis-Testing." *Psychological Review* 94(2): 211–28.

Lerner, Jennifer S., and Dacher Keltner. 2000. "Beyond Valence: Toward a Model of Emotion-Specific Influences on Judgment and Choice." *Cognition and Emotion* 14(4): 473–93.

Lerner, Jennifer S., Deborah A. Small, and George Loewenstein. 2004. "Heart Strings and Purse Strings: Carry-Over Effects of Emotions on Economic Transactions." *Psychological Science* 15(5): 337–41.

Luce, Mary F., James R. Bettman, and John W. Payne. 1997. "Choice Processing in Emotionally Difficult Decisions." *Journal of Experimental Psychology: Learning, Memory, and Cognition* 23(2): 384–405.

Mackie, Diane M., and Leila T. Worth. 1989. "Processing Deficits and the Mediation of Positive Affect in Persuasion." *Journal of Personality and Social Psychology* 57(1): 27–40.

Martin, Leonard L., and Peggy Stoner. 1996. "Mood as Input: What I Think About How I Feel Determines How I Think." In *Striving and Feeling: Interactions Among Goals, Affect, and Self-Regulation,* edited by Leonard L. Martin and Abraham Tesser. Mahwah, N.J.: Lawrence Erlbaum Associates, Inc.

Martin, Leonard L., Teresa Abend, Constantine Sedikides, and Jeffrey D. Green. 1997. "How Would It Feel If . . . ? Mood as Input to a Role Fulfillment Evaluation Process." *Journal of Personality and Social Psychology* 73(2): 242–53.

Martin, Leonard L., David W. Ward, John W. Achee, and Robert S. Wyer. 1993. "Mood as Input: People Have to Interpret the Motivational Implications of Their Moods." *Journal of Personality and Social Psychology* 64(3): 317–26.

Mayer, John D., Yvonne N. Gaschke, Debra L. Braverman, and Temperance W. Evans. 1992. "Mood-Congruent Judgment Is a General Effect." *Journal of Personality and Social Psychology* 63(1): 119–32.

Melton, R. Jeffrey. 1995. "The Role of Positive Affect in Syllogism Performance." *Personality and Social Psychology Bulletin* 21(8): 788–94.

Miller, William R., and Martin E. Seligman. 1975. "Depression and Learned Helplessness in Man." *Journal of Abnormal Psychology* 84(3): 228–38.

Murray, Noel, Harish Sujan, Edward R. Hirt, and Mita Sujan. 1990. "The Influence of Mood on Categorization: A Cognitive Flexibility Interpretation." *Journal of Personality and Social Psychology* 59(3): 411–25.

Rodrigue, James R., Kenneth R. Olson, and Robert P. Markley. 1987. "Induced Mood and Curiosity." *Cognitive Therapy and Research* 11(1): 101–6.

Ruble, Diane N., and Karin S. Frey. 1991. "Changing Patterns of Comparative Behavior as Skills Are Acquired: A Functional Model of Self-Evaluation." In *Social Comparison: Contemporary Theory and Research,* edited by Jerry Suls and Thomas Ashby Wills. Hillsdale, N.J.: Lawrence Erlbaum Associates, Inc.

Salovey, Peter, and Deborah Brinbaum. 1989. "Influence of Mood on Health-Relevant Cognitions." *Journal of Personality and Social Psychology* 57(3): 539–51.

Schwarz, Norbert. 1990. "Feelings as Information: Informational and Motivational Functions of Affective States." In *Handbook of Motivation and Cognition: Foundations of Social Behavior,* Volume 2, edited by E. Tory Higgins and Richard M. Sorrentino. New York: Guilford Press.

———. 2001. "Feelings as Information: Implications for Affective Influences on Information Processing." In *Theories of Mood and Cognition: A User's Handbook,* edited by Leonard L. Martin and Gerald L. Clore. Mahwah, N.J.: Lawrence Erlbaum Associates, Inc.

Schwarz, Norbert, and Herbert Bless. 1991. "Happy and Mindless, but Sad and Smart? The Impact of Affect States on Analytic Reasoning." In *Emotion and Social Judgments,* edited by Joseph Forgas. Oxford: Pergamon Press.

Schwarz, Norbert, and Gerald L. Clore. 1983. "Mood, Misattribution, and Judgments of Well-Being: Informative and Directive Functions of Affective States." *Journal of Personality and Social Psychology* 45(3): 513–23.

————. 1988. "How Do I Feel About It? Informative Functions of Affective States." In *Affect, Cognition, and Social Behavior,* edited by Klaus Fiedler and Joseph Forgas. Toronto, Canada: Hofgrefe International.

————. 1996. "Feelings and Phenomenal Experiences." In *Social Psychology. A Handbook of Basic Principles,* edited by E. Tory Higgins and Arie Kruglanski. New York: Guilford Press.

Sinclair, Robert C., Melvin M. Mark, and Gerald L. Clore. 1994. "Mood-Related Persuasion Depends on (Mis)attributions." *Social Cognition* 12(2): 309–26.

Skowronski, John J., and Donald E. Carlston. 1989. "Negativity and Extremity Biases in Impression Formation: A Review of Explanations." *Psychological Bulletin* 105(1): 131–42.

Smith LeBeau, Lavonia, and Karen Gasper. 2005. "When Quality Influences Quantity: The Effects of Mood and Information Quality on Upward Social Comparison Seeking." Paper presented to the Society for Personality and Social Psychology, January 2005.

Snyder, Mark, and William B. Swann. 1978. "Hypothesis-Testing Processes in a Social Interaction." *Journal of Personality and Social Psychology* 36(11): 1202–12.

Swann, William B., Jr. 1990. "To Be Adored or To Be Known? The Interplay of Self-Enhancement and Self-Verification." In *Handbook of Motivation and Cognition,* edited by Richard M. Sorrentino and E. Tory Higgins. New York: Guilford Press.

Tamir, Maya, and Michael D. Robinson. 2004. "Knowing Good from Bad: The Paradox of Neuroticism, Negative Affect, and Evaluative Processing." *Journal of Personality and Social Psychology* 87(6): 913–25.

Trope, Yaacov, and Akiva Liberman. 1996. "Social Hypothesis Testing: Cognitive and Motivational Mechanisms."In *Social Psychology: Handbook of Basic Principles,* edited by E. Tory Higgins and Arie W. Kruglanski. New York: Guilford Press.

Trope, Yaacov, and Efrat Neter. 1994. "Reconciling Competing Motives in Self-Evaluation: The Role of Self-Control in Feedback Seeking." *Journal of Personality and Social Psychology* 66(4): 646–57.

Trope, Yaacov, M. Ferguson, and Raj Raghunathan. 2001. "Mood as a Resource in Processing Self-Relevant Information." In *Handbook of Affect and Social Cognition,* edited by Joseph P. Forgas. Mahwah, N.J.: Lawrence Erlbaum Associates, Inc.

Wegener, Diane T., Richard E. Petty, and Stephen M. Smith. 1995. "Positive Mood Can Increase or Decrease Message Scrutiny: The Hedonic Contingency View of Mood and Message Processing." *Journal of Personality and Social Psychology* 68(1): 1092–1107.

Wills, Thomas A. 1981. "Downward Comparison Principles in Social Psychology." *Psychological Bulletin* 90(2): 245–71.

Wood, Joanne V., and Penelope Lockwood. 1999. "Social Comparisons in Dysphoric and Low Self-Esteem People." In *The Social Psychology of Emotional and Behavioral Problems: Interfaces of Social and Clinical Psychology,* edited by Robin M. Kowalski and Mark R. Leary. Washington: American Psychological Association.

Wyer, Robert S., Gerald L. Clore, and Linda M. Isbell. 1999. "Affect and Information Processing." In *Advances in Experimental Social Psychology,* edited by Mark P. Zanna. San Diego, Calif.: Academic Press.

· 5 ·

The Role of Personality in Emotion, Judgment, and Decision Making

JOHN M. ZELENSKI

STATEMENTS about how emotions influence judgment and decision making rarely apply to all persons equally. Individual differences and personality are ubiquitous in these processes, and, as a result, they provide an important context for determining whether emotions help or hurt decision making. Recent judgment and decision making research has incorporated personality, and offers support for the contention that the costs and benefits of emotion often depend on personality. Said another way, in addition to asking when emotions help or hurt decisions, we must also consider for whom they have these effects.

Personality can influence judgments and decisions in multiple ways. First, propensities to experience different emotions are at the core of many well-studied personality characteristics. For example, the traits of extraversion and neuroticism predispose people to experience more frequent and intense positive and negative affect respectively. As a result, these traits may help predict judgments and decisions, even if only indirectly (that is, through emotion states). To the extent that emotions help or hurt decision making, they likely do so to a greater or lesser degree depending on personality, because personality contributes to the experience of these emotion states. In essence, the influence of personality is sometimes mediated by emotion states. It is also clear that personality includes stable differences in cognition (such as biases in appraisal, attention, and memory, which are often intimately connected with emotions), that color or direct judgment and decision processes. Therefore, even in the absence of intense emotional states, these emotion-based traits can predict judgments and decisions in a similar way to their corresponding emotion states. For example, in relatively mild affective states, people scoring high on extraversion or neuroticism tend to judge things more positively or negatively, respectively, compared to people scoring low on these traits. To the extent that these biases lead to good or bad decisions, personality again provides an important context by directly influencing judgments and decisions. Finally, emotion states interact with personality in a way that makes the influence of emotions helpful for some people and deleterious for others. For example, people differ in the extent to which they use or weight their emotions in making judgments and decisions. Therefore, personality helps explain why different people come to different decisions, even when experiencing the same emotions.

Personality and Mood Congruent Judgement

Current work on personality and judgment owes much to earlier theory and research on mood-congruent memory and judgment (that is, the idea that people's judgments are often biased in the same direction as current mood states). In a well-known study, psychologists Eric Johnson and Amos Tversky (1983) asked participants to read a newspaper story about tragic events in order to induce negative mood states. Compared to controls, the participants in bad moods rated other unrelated negative events (for example, getting cancer or going bankrupt) as more frequent in general and more likely to happen to them personally. In other words, negative moods seemed to bias people's judgments in a negative or pessimistic direction (in other words, they increase perceptions of risk). Such mood-congruent judgment effects have been replicated many times; however, the effect is not ubiquitous (Forgas 1995; Rusting 1998).

Mood-congruent effects are often explained in terms of psychologist Gordon Bower's (1981) network theory of affect. Bower suggested that emotions help organize memory. That is, emotions form nodes in an associative network of information (that is, memory). When a node is activated by emotional information in the environment or by emotional experience, similarly valenced memories and information come to mind more easily because they are closely linked through the emotion node. For example, in Johnson and Tversky's (1983) study, reading a newspaper article about a tragic event might activate a negative emotion node, which in turn makes other negative information more accessible (for example, an uncle or neighbor with cancer). These thoughts then cause judgments that are biased in a mood-congruent manner (for example, "Cancer is pretty common, and I am likely to get it"). Although Bower (1981) identifies memory structures as the source of bias, the theory implies that mood congruency will occur across many cognitive processes. Because certain types of information are more accessible (that is, mood-congruent information), they are more likely to be perceived, attended to, and recalled, and, thus, to influence judgment and decision making. This model of mood-state-congruent cognition has been adapted to also predict personality-trait-congruent cognition (Clark and Teasdale 1985; Rusting 1998).

Most trait approaches to personality include two dimensions similar to extraversion (characterized by sociability, positive emotionality, and assertiveness) and neuroticism (characterized by worry, frequent complaints, and negative emotionality). Although propensities to experience positive and negative emotions have always been parts of these traits (particularly in the case of neuroticism), personality psychologists increasingly see them as rooted in motivational or emotional systems (Carver, Sutton, and Scheier 2000).

Neuroscientist Jeffrey Gray and colleagues' (Gray 1981, 1994; Pickering, Corr, and Gray 1999) seminal approach to (or explanation of) extraversion and neuroticism illustrates the central role of motivation and emotion. Drawing on neurophysiology, he suggested that these traits emerged from individual differences in the strengths of two independent motivational systems: The behavioral activation system (BAS) responds to conditioned cues of reward in the environment and creates approach motivation. Furthermore, people who score high on extraversion have a highly sensitive BAS and are thus highly sensitive to reward cues. In other words, the approach-oriented behavior of extraverts stems from their propensity to notice and pursue potential rewards. A second system, the behavioral inhibition system (BIS), monitors the environment for punishment cues, and, upon detection, inhibits ongoing behavior and creates avoidance motivation. People who score high on neuroticism have a highly sensitive BIS, and are thus highly sensitive to punishment cues. Thus, the anxiety and erratic behavior typical of neurotics is due to their tendency to notice and react to potential punishments. (Revisions to Gray's theory suggest that some BIS functions noted here are performed by a fight/flight system; Smillie, Pickering, and Jackson 2006. However, this distinction goes beyond the scope of this chapter.) A number of similar theories highlight individual differences in approach and avoidance motivation as central personality characteristics, likely underlying the more descriptive dimensions of extraversion and neuroticism (Carver 2001; Cloninger 1986; Higgins 1997; Tellegen 1985).

The emotional consequences of strong approach or avoidance tendencies are readily apparent; an approach orientation should create a more positive emotional experience, and an avoidance orientation should create a more negative emotional experience. Consistent with this suggestion, extraversion and neuroticism consistently predict positive and negative emotional experience respectively. This has been found with day-to-day emotions, using experience sampling methods, and with reactions to positive and negative laboratory mood inductions (Larsen and Ketelaar 1989, 1991; Lucas and Fujita 2000; Zelenski and Larsen 1999). In other words, even when the situation is held constant, extraversion and neuroticism predict more intense emotional experiences. These propensities are also evident in naturalistic settings (that is, in the typical ebb and flow of emotional experience).

Combining personality's strong emotion links with Bower's network theory of affect provides a rationale for predicting personality-congruent cognition. That is, extraversion may predict positive judgment biases, and neuroticism may predict negative judgment biases. However, even within the associative-network framework, these predictions could take different forms (Rusting 1998). For example, personality's influence on judgment could be entirely indirect. Accordingly, extraversion and neuroticism would predict the frequency and intensity of moods, and these moods, in turn, produce congruent biases in judgment (because they activate positive or negative emotion nodes). Alternatively, extraversion and neuroticism may include stable individual differences in associative networks. A person who frequently experiences positive or negative affect (stemming from an approach or avoidance orientation) would be expected to have a more elaborated positive or negative node, respectively. As a result, that node is more likely to be activated by stimuli that another person might find neutral, or to have more judgment-relevant associations after the node is activated. In other words, part of extraversion and neuroticism may be the cognitive structures that develop over a lifetime of positive and negative emotional experiences. Such differences in cognitive structures could produce judgment biases over and above momentary mood states.

A few studies have used this reasoning to explore personality-congruent judgment and memory under conditions of naturally occurring differences in mood as well as experimentally manipulated moods (Rusting 1999; Rusting and Larsen 1998, Zelenski and Larsen 2002). In one study, we assessed personality (extraversion/BAS and neuroticism/BIS) and current mood states (positive and negative affect), and asked participants to judge the likelihood of clearly positive and negative events (Zelenski and Larsen 2002). For example, we asked, "What are the chances that you will become very wealthy?" and "What are the chances that you will die before age 50?" Consistent with the mood-congruency hypothesis, state positive and negative affect predicted more optimistic and pessimistic judgments respectively. In addition, extraversion/BAS and neuroticism/BIS measures predicted more optimistic and pessimistic judgments respectively. To test whether personality's influence was indirect (that is, through mood states) or direct (perhaps due to stable differences in associative networks), we performed mediation analyses. (Personality was also significantly related to mood states, as expected.) When personality and mood states were entered into regressions simultaneously, personality remained a significant predictor, while mood states did not. In other words, mediation did not occur, and the results suggested a direct effect of personality. A second study found very similar results when participants underwent positive, sad, fear, and neutral mood inductions. That is, both personality and mood states predicted affect-congruent judgment biases, and personality's influence was direct.

Psychologist Cheryl Rusting (1999) found a similar pattern of results with a series of memory and interpretation tasks, which further suggest that personality differences in associative networks could produce personality-congruent judgment biases. With naturally occurring mood states, participants were more likely to recall positive words from a list, include positive content in a story completion task, and to interpret homophones in a positive way (for example, "sweet" as opposed to "suite") if they reported more state positive affect and if they were extraverted. Negative mood states and neuroticism also predicted affect-congruent biases on these tasks. Moreover, when personality and mood states were entered simultaneously in regression analyses, personality had a direct effect and mood state became statistically insignificant. These results (and other direct effects; Peters and Slovic 2000; Rusting and Larsen 1998; Uziel 2006) suggest the importance of personality variables in mood-congruent cognition, especially under conditions of natural mood states.

Because mood effects became insignificant when personality was controlled (across these studies), earlier findings of naturally occurring mood-congruent cognition (Mayer and Bremer 1985; Mayer, Mamberg, and Volanth 1988; Mayer and Volanth 1985) may have been due to personality differences. However, stronger manipulated emotions, do seem to predict bias even after controlling for personality (Rusting 1999; Zelenski and Larsen 2002). Nonetheless, personality likely remains important under these conditions, as state-congruent biases were stronger among people with dispositional tendencies to experience them (that is, trait-by-state interactions emerged; Rusting 1999). These findings are consistent with the idea that extraversion and neuroticism include more elaborated positive and negative emotion nodes. That is, even after an emotion node is activated (because of the mood induction), some will have more connections in the network, further biasing judgment. In sum, extraversion and neuroticism predict increased likelihood and intensity of positive and negative emotions. Once an affective state is produced, personality predicts the extent to which the state influences cognition. It follows that personality will contribute to good or bad decisions when positive or negative emotions, interpretations, and judgments form the basis of these decisions (for example, Ristvedt and Trinkaus 2005).

Although the extension of Bower's model to personality has generated interesting findings and explanations, other mechanisms could explain personality- and mood-congruent judgment. Another framework popular in the mood-congruent literature is the affect-as-information perspective (Schwarz and Clore 1983), which also has been extended to personality differences in judgment. According to the affect-as-information perspective, moods can provide information that can be useful in making judgments. That is, to the extent that affect is relevant to evaluation, it cues bias in an affect-congruent direction. For example, psychologists Norbert Schwarz and Gerald Clore (1983, 2003) asked participants to judge their life satisfaction on either sunny days or cloudy days. Although evaluation of one's entire life should not change with fluctuations in weather, mood-congruent judgment biases were observed. That is, life satisfaction was rated lower among participants asked on cloudy days—presumably associated with negative moods—compared to those asked on sunny days. This finding is relatively consistent with Bower's (1981) network explanation for mood-congruency, but the affect-as-information perspective makes an additional prediction: Moods should only influence judgment when they are viewed as relevant to the object being evaluated. That is, making affect seem less relevant should reduce mood-congruency effects. Accordingly, when researchers asked participants about the weather prior to life satisfaction judgments (that is, providing a more relevant source of their negative moods), the negative mood-congruent bias disappeared on cloudy days. However, asking participants about the weather did not reduce the positive mood-congruent bias on sunny days. Thus, alternative attributions (such as the weather) do not always remove bias.

Psychologists Karen Gasper and Gerald Clore (1998) demonstrated additional limits to attributional manipulations by investigating individual differences (that is, trait anxiety, which is similar to neuroticism; see also Gasper and Isbell, chapter 4, this volume). They reasoned that, because people who experience frequent anxiety tend to attribute it to stable general sources, these people would place more value on anxious states. In other words, state anxiety is more broadly informative for highly anxious people. Therefore, attempts to provide alternative attributions (that is, attributions other than the object of judgment) might only reduce mood-congruent biases among people with low trait anxiety. A clever series of experiments confirmed this hypothesis. University students were recruited to make risk judgments (for example, the likelihood of getting into a conflict with parents or the likelihood of police violence) shortly before final exams, a time of significant state anxiety. Some participants were asked to rate the extent to which present feelings of anxiety might be due to impending final exams, providing a potentially relevant attribution for their high-anxiety state. This attributional manipulation reduced risk estimates for participants with low trait anxiety, but slightly increased risk ratings for high trait anxiety participants. Moreover, this pattern of results was replicated with more controlled laboratory mood inductions, and depended on participants' beliefs about the relevance of affect to judgments. In sum, trait anxiety seems to predict what people will do with negative moods and how much they use affective information in making judgments.

While not as explicitly based in the affect-as-information perspective, a few other recent findings suggest that broad personality dispositions predict the value that people place on their feelings when making judgments and decisions. For example, given the strong links between extraversion (BAS) and neuroticism (BIS) and emotional experience, it is not surprising that they are very good predictors of life satisfaction (Diener et al. 1999). However, psychologists John Updegraff, Shelly Gable, and Shelley Taylor (2004) suggest that beyond the direct influence of emotional experience on satisfaction, approach-oriented (that is, high-BAS) people may weight this emotion information more heavily when making satisfaction judgments. Using experience sampling data, they found that the intensity of momentary positive emotions (assessed at six times throughout the day) interacted with BAS scores to predict end-of-day satisfaction ratings. That is, the positive relationship between positive emotional experience and satisfaction judgments was stronger for approach-oriented participants. Somewhat surprisingly, the mirror prediction—that avoidance orientation would interact with negative emotional experience to predict satisfaction—was not supported. In any case, this study provides a nice example of how people use their emotional experience differently when making judgments in a more naturalistic context.

Psychologists Ellen Peters and Paul Slovic (2000) similarly suggested that personality influences the weight given to affective information; this study was in a choice (as opposed to judgment) context. They adapted a task in which participants repeatedly chose from four decks of face-down cards that represent large and small gains and losses (compare, Damasio 1994). Decks were "fixed" to yield either a positive or negative expected value (that is, a net gain or loss) and, independently, to include either big or small average gains or losses. In other words, some decks were better choices than others because they yielded more money, but this varied independently of the magnitude of average gains or losses. Participants can win money by learning which decks pay more as they turn cards during the task. Given that extraversion (BAS) and neuroticism (BIS) predict emotional reactivity, Peters and Slovic (2000) reasoned that these dispositions would, respectively, predict choosing "big win" decks and avoiding "big loss" decks. That is, extraverts would value the big gains more (because they experience them more intensely) and thus would be more likely to choose cards from the "big win" decks. Conversely, high-BIS participants would find big losses particularly aversive and would avoid decks that included them. Results supported these predictions. To clarify, extraversion and neuroticism did not predict the number of cards chosen from decks with positive expected value; rather, they only predict whether a participant will choose "big win" and avoiding "big loss" decks, respectively. Unfortunately, the design of this study (that is, the application of many repeated events without emotion-state measures) does not allow us to parse personality, emotion, and cognition very clearly. Nonetheless, it extends personality's predictive power from judgments to decisions (that is, choices between potential gains and losses as opposed to broad judgments of risk and experience). Although personality did not predict winnings (that is, optimal decisions) in this study, changing the expected value of "big win" and "big loss" decks likely would have produced such results. That is, the experimental situation did not favor a high- or low-risk strategy, but many real-life situations do. In these situations, personality would likely provide an important context for optimal decision making.

Beyond Valence

While many studies consider broad personality constructs that are clearly linked with positive or negative emotional experience, narrower traits without clear valences may also influence how people use their emotions in judgment. For example, Gasper and Clore (2000) showed that people who pay more attention to their emotional experience (that is, both positive and negative) are more likely to use the informational value of their moods (unless attributional manipulations make them highly salient). In addition, psychologist Kent Harber (2005) showed that people with high self-esteem seem to place more confidence in their emotions when making judgments. That is, after hearing a series of baby cries, self-esteem interacted with self-reported distress (in participants, not in babies) when making judgments of how distressed the babies were. In essence, correlations between personal distress and estimates of babies' distress were higher among those with high self-esteem. Although these studies are similar to others in that personality predicts more or less use of emotion in judgment, Harber's (2005) studies are particularly interesting in that they link a generally positive trait with ratings of distress. Because the judgment is personality incongruent, the explanation that high self-esteem people value the informational value of their emotions more is particularly convincing. (For further discussion of how self-esteem can moderate decision processes in emotional contexts, see Rawn et al., chapter 7, this volume.)

Going further beyond valence may yield additional insight into personality, emotion, and judgment (Lerner and Keltner 2000). That is, emotions with similar valence (for example, sadness and anger) sometimes produce divergent effects on judgment. DeSteno et al. (2000) found that sad moods increased likelihood judgments of sad events more than angry events, and angry moods increased likelihood judgments of angering events more than sad events. In an even more striking dissociation of similarly valenced emotions, fear, following the events of September 11, 2001, seemed to increase risk estimates of future terrorism, while anger decreased them (Lerner et al. 2003).

Psychologists Jennifer Lerner and Dacher Keltner (2000) draw on appraisal theories of emotion (for example, Ortony, Clore, and Collins 1988; Smith and Ellsworth 1985) to predict when similarly valenced emotions will have divergent influences on judgments. Appraisal theories suggest that each emotion (for example, fear and anger) is associated with a distinct pattern of evaluation along a set of emotion-appraisal dimensions. For example, fear and anger are both low in pleasantness, but they diverge on appraisals of control and certainty, with anger high in these areas and fear low (Smith and Ellsworth 1985). Lerner and Keltner (2000) suggest that when an emotion-appraisal dimension is activated by affective information, the dimension is more likely to be used in evaluating subsequent information. That is, rather than broad affect congruency, emotions influence judgments through greater availability of certain appraisals (specifically, those consistent with recent emotion experience).

The appraisal approach to emotion has typically been applied to emotion states. However, many initial tests of Lerner and Keltner's (2000) framework have used dispositional emotions (that is, stable propensities to experience specific emotion states). Across a series of studies, dispositional fear predicted higher estimates of risk (e.g., that negative events are likely to occur, choosing risk averse options in Amos Tversky and Daniel Kahneman's (1981) Asian disease problem). Conversely, dispositional anger predicted lower perceptions of risk; these people actually responded more similarly to dispositionally happy people than to fearful people (Lerner and Keltner 2000, 2001). These divergent effects for similarly valenced emotions at the dispositional level of analysis are particularly striking. Although distinct negative emotion states are often experienced separately, they typically co-occur in people over time (Scollon et al. 2005; Vansteelandt, Van Mechelen, and Nezlek 2005; Zelenski and Larsen 2000). In other words, people who are dispositionally fearful also tend to be dispositionally sad and angry, and these emotions correlate strongly with neuroticism.

Because neuroticism predicts estimates of high risk (Zelenski and Larsen 2002), there seems to be more similarity to neuroticism with Lerner and Keltner's (2000, 2001) dispositional fear than with anger. This is roughly consistent with the emerging consensus that something like a BIS (that is, punishment sensitivity) underlies the dimension of neuroticism. That is, fear, rather than anger, would be a more likely output of the BIS. Moreover, the fact that anger (as opposed to another negatively valenced dispositional emotion) diverged from fear may also fit within a broader trait framework. Even though anger is often experientially negative, it likely facilitates approach behaviors (for example, attack). Carver (2004) has explicitly linked anger with the BAS, showing that following the attacks of September 11, 2001, BAS (and not BIS) predicted angry reactions. Anger has also been associated with brain activity more similar to an approach, rather than to an avoidance, system (that is, greater left hemisphere activation; Harmon-Jones and Sigelman 2001). That is, anger may dissociate from other negatively valenced emotions (especially fear) because it is generated by a different system, even at a broad disposition level of analysis. In sum, both Lerner and Keltner's (2000) approach and work within the tradition of broad motivational dispositions suggests that personality's influence on emotions and judgment may need to go beyond simple positive and negative congruency. Such work might benefit by combining broad personality dimensions with appraisal theory and more specific emotions (for example, Hemenover 2001; Hemenover and Zhang 2004).

Do Emotions Help or Hurt Decision Making?

Turning more directly to the central question of this volume—"Do emotions help or hurt decision making?"—an important role for personality is revealed. Answers to the general question will almost certainly require qualifications. That is, the extent to which emotions help or hurt depends on context. This chapter has used the word "bias" to describe many of the personality and emotion influences on judgment and decision making. While bias often connotes error or lack of rationality, such effects should not be viewed as universally maladaptive. Such processes likely serve important purposes. For example, a fearful person has likely had much experience with threat, and anxious states presumably have some basis in reality. Adapting estimates of risk based on experience or current states may serve protective functions, even if not completely rational. For example, people's conservative or risky choices may make more sense when considering differences in their ability to cope with potential outcomes. Moreover, laboratory, or even "real-life," situations can be manipulated to make these biases appear more or less adaptive or rational (Funder 1987).

Personality may provide an important context for determining when judgment biases lead to desirable or undesirable outcomes. For example, estimates of risk and potential benefits can be important to health behaviors. Traci Mann, David Sherman, and John Updegraff (2004) showed that approach-oriented people were more persuaded by appeals to floss their teeth daily when these appeals highlighted potential gains of flossing as opposed to potential losses of not flossing. We have found similar results with gain- and loss-framed appeals to engage in safe sex behaviors (Barta, Kiene, and Zelenski 2005) and to behave in more environmentally friendly ways (Zelenski, Nisbet, and Legault 2005). These findings suggest that tailoring appeals to people's motivational dispositions may make their biases more adaptive.

In addition, people low in BIS significantly delay seeking medical assistance after symptoms of rectal cancer appear (Ristvedt and Trinkaus 2005). Although the processes underlying this behavior need to be clarified, emotions, interpretations of symptoms, and judgments of risk (predicted by the same personality characteristics) almost certainly play important roles. People high in BIS typically suffer unpleasant emotional experience, but these emotions and accompanying inflated risk judgments may save their lives through early detection of cancer. In other words, unpleasant emotions or judgment biases may help get a person to the doctor (that is, emotions can sometimes help); however, in the absence of illness, they detract from a person's well-being and waste medical resources (that is, emotions can other times hurt).

To the extent that fast (yet accurate) decisions can be considered "better decisions," personality again seems to provide an important context for determining when emotion states help or hurt decision making. Psychologist Maya Tamir and colleagues (Tamir and Robinson 2004; Tamir, Robinson, and Clore 2002) have examined how quickly people can categorize words along evaluative dimensions (for example, positive versus negative, or desirable versus undesirable). Rather than simple mood- or personality-congruent effects, results indicate an interactive pattern. More specifically, extraverts classify objects as both desirable and undesirable more quickly when in positive moods (Tamir, Robinson and Clore 2002), and people high in neuroticism classify both positive and negative words more quickly when in negative moods (Tamir and Robinson 2004). In other words, moods facilitate these judgments when they are consistent with a person's traits, regardless of the object's valence. To the extent that faster decisions are better decisions (a speed-accuracy tradeoff was not evident in these studies), emotions either improved or hindered decision making, depending on personality. Although it is presently unclear how or if such differences in processing speed impact other decision outcomes, future research may indicate how dispositions and emotion states combine in more consequential decision processes.

To summarize, individual differences in personality are clearly important when considering emotion and judgment generally, as well as in considering more specifically whether or not emotions help decision making. Dispositions (either at the level of specific emotions or broader motivational orientations) describe propensities to experience more frequent and intense emotion states. To the extent that these emotion states influence judgment and decision making biases, dispositions will predict these biases. Surprisingly, very little research has found this pattern (that is, state affect mediating personality's influence). Instead, personality often has direct effects independent of emotion states (typically with naturalistic moods) or interacts with emotion states (typically with manipulated emotions). Said another way, emotion-related individual differences seem to include processing biases (for example, in appraisal patterns and memory), which influence judgments, and these processes often involve the way people use affective information or mood states in making judgments.

Although the goal of this review was to be more illustrative than comprehensive, it reflects the fact that relatively few studies have simultaneously considered stable dispositions and emotion states. That is, the majority of work on emotion and judgment has considered these types of variables independently (Rusting 1998). This has begun to change (compare more recent work reviewed in the chapter with Rusting's 1998 review), but current conclusions must remain tentative. For example, it seems too early to rule out the intuitively likely mediational role of mood states in linking personality and judgment. In addition, the processes responsible for personality's role in judgment remain elusive. Extensions of the affect-as-information perspective (Schwarz and Clore 1983) and network theory of affect (Bower 1981) have provided initial explanations, but the results of many studies are consistent with both (as well as with alternative explanations). The effect of attributional manipulations has helped highlight affect-as-information processes (for example, Gasper and Clore 1998). Exploring memory or accessibility differences as mediators between personality and judgment may provide support for the idea of individual differences in associative networks (compare, Rusting 1999). In any case, there is much more work to be done.

In general, traits like extraversion and neuroticism and their accompanying pleasant and unpleasant emotion states bias people towards "positive" and "negative" judgments and decisions, respectively. However, there are important exceptions. For example, anger as a trait and state often has effects more similar to happiness than to fear or sadness. It is also critically important to recognize that "positive" and "negative" biases do not ubiquitously result in good or bad decisions. The context of individual situations will determine whether or not dispositional propensities help or hurt the decision maker. For example, despite many other undesirable correlates, neuroticism helps people by facilitating decisions to seek treatment for cancer. It is important to recognize that a similar caveat must be made when taking a situational perspective: personality is a context in determining whether emotions help or hurt decision making. For example, negative moods can speed decisions, but only among people scoring high on neuroticism. Further research will benefit by considering both emotion states *and* personality traits.

References

Barta, William D., Susan M. Kiene, and John M. Zelenski. 2005. "Individual Differences Bias Framed Condom Use Messages." Journal manuscript in preparation.

Bower, Gordon H. 1981. "Mood and Memory." *American Psychologist* 36(2): 129–48.

Carver, Charles S. 2001. "Affect and the Functional Bases of Behavior: On the Dimensional Structure of Affective Experience." *Personality and Social Psychology Review* 5(4): 345–56.

———. 2004. "Negative Affects Deriving from the Behavioral Approach System." *Emotion* 4(1): 3–22.

Carver, Charles S., Steven K. Sutton, and Michael F. Scheier. 2000. "Action, Emotion, and Personality: Emerging Conceptual Integration." *Personality and Social Psychology Bulletin* 26(6): 741–51.

Clark, David M., and John D. Teasdale. 1985. "Constraints on the Effects of Mood on Memory." *Journal of Personality and Social Psychology* 48(6): 1595–1608.

Cloninger, C. Robert. 1986. "A Unified Biosocial Theory of Personality and Its Role in the Development of Anxiety States." *Psychiatric Developments* 3: 167–226.

Damasio, Antonio R. 1994. *Descartes' Error: Emotion, Reason, and the Human Brain.* New York: Putnam.

DeSteno, David, Richard E. Petty, Duane T. Wegener, and Derek D. Rucker. 2000. "Beyond Valence in the Perception of Likelihood: The Role of Emotion Specificity." *Journal of Personality and Social Psychology* 78(3): 397–416.

Diener, Ed, Eunkook Suh, Richard E. Lucas, and Heidi L. Smith. 1999. "Subjective Well-Being: Three Decades of Progress." *Psychological Bulletin* 125(2): 276–302.

Forgas, Joseph P. 1995. "Mood and Judgment: The Affect Infusion Model (AIM)." *Psychological Bulletin* 117(1): 39–66.

Funder, David C. 1987. "Errors and Mistakes: Evaluating the Accuracy of Social Judgment." *Psychological Bulletin* 101(1): 75–90.

Gasper, Karen, and Gerald L. Clore. 1998. "The Persistent Use of Negative Affect by Anxious Individuals to Estimate Risk." *Journal of Personality and Social Psychology* 74(5): 1350–63.

———. 2000. "Do You Have to Pay Attention to Your Feelings to Be Influenced by Them?" *Personality and Social Psychology Bulletin* 26(6): 698–711.

Gray, Jeffrey A. 1981. "A Critique of Eysenck's Theory of Personality." In *A Model For Personality*, edited by H. J. Eysenck. New York: Springer-Verlag.

———. 1994. "Personality Dimensions and Emotion Systems." In *The Nature of Emotion: Fundamental Questions*, edited by P. Ekman and R. Davidson. New York: Oxford University Press.

Harber, Kent D. 2005. "Self-Esteem and Affect as Information." *Personality and Social Psychology Bulletin* 31(2): 276–88.

Harmon-Jones, Eddie, and Jonathan D. Sigelman. 2001. "State Anger and Prefrontal Brain Activity: Evidence That Insult Related Relative Left-Prefrontal Activation Is Associated with Experienced Anger and Aggression." *Journal of Personality and Social Psychology* 80(5): 797–803.

Hemenover, Scott H. 2001. "Self-Reported Processing Bias and Naturally Occurring Mood: Mediators Between Personality and Stress Appraisals." *Personality and Social Psychology Bulletin* 27(4): 387–94.

Hemenover, Scott H., and Shen Zhang. 2004. "Anger, Personality, and Optimistic Stress Appraisals." *Cognition and Emotion* 18(3): 363–82.

Higgins, E. Tory. 1997. "Beyond Pleasure and Pain." *American Psychologist* 52(12): 1280–1300.

Johnson, Eric J., and Amos Tversky. 1983. "Affect, Generalization, and the Perception of Risk." *Journal of Personality and Social Psychology* 45(1): 20–31.

Larsen, Randy J., and Tim Ketelaar. 1989. "Extraversion, Neuroticism and Susceptibility to Positive and Negative Mood Induction Procedures." *Personality and Individual Differences* 10(12): 1221–28.

———. 1991. "Personality and Susceptibility to Positive and Negative Emotional States." *Journal of Personality and Social Psychology* 61(1): 132–40.

Lerner, Jennifer S., and Dacher Keltner. 2000. "Beyond Valence: Toward a Model of Emotion-Specific Influences on Judgment and Choice." *Cognition and Emotion* 14(4): 473–93.

———. 2001. "Fear, Anger and Risk." *Journal of Personality and Social Psychology* 81(1): 146–59.

Lerner, Jennifer S., Roxana M. Gonzalez, Deborah A. Small, and Baruch Fischhoff. 2003. "Effects of Fear and Anger on Perceived Risks of Terrorism: A National Field Study." *Psychological Science* 14(2): 144–50.

Lucas, Richard E., and Frank Fujita. 2000. "Factors Influencing the Relation Between Extraversion and Pleasant Affect." *Journal of Personality and Social Psychology* 79(6): 1039–56.

Mann, Traci, David Sherman, and John Updegraff. 2004. "Dispositional Motivations and Message Framing: A Test of the Congruency Hypothesis in College Students." *Health Psychology* 23(3): 330–4.

Mayer, John D., and Deborah Bremer. 1985. "Assessing Mood with Affect-Sensitive Tasks." *Journal of Personality Assessment* 49(1): 95–99.

Mayer, John D., and Alton J. Volanth. 1985. "Cognitive Involvement in the Mood Response System." *Motivation and Emotion* 9(3): 261–75.

Mayer, John D., Michelle H. Mamberg, and Alton J. Volanth. 1988. "Cognitive Domains of the Mood System." *Journal of Personality* 56(3): 453–86.

Ortony, Andrew, Gerald L. Clore, and Allan Collins. 1988. *The Cognitive Structure of Emotions*. New York: Cambridge University Press.

Peters, Ellen, and Paul Slovic. 2000. "The Springs of Action: Affective and Analytical Information Processing in Choice." *Personality and Social Psychology Bulletin* 26(12): 1465–75.

Pickering, Alan D., Philip J. Corr, and Jeffrey A. Gray. 1999. "Interactions and Reinforcement Sensitivity Theory: A Theoretical Analysis of Rusting and Larsen (1997)." *Personality and Individual Differences* 26(2): 356–65.

Ristvedt, Stephen L., and Kathryn M. Trinkaus. 2005. "Psychological Factors Related to Delay in Consultation for Cancer Symptoms." *Psycho-Oncology* 14(5): 339–50.

Rusting, Cheryl L. 1998. "Personality, Mood, and Cognitive Processing of Emotional Information: Three Conceptual Frameworks." *Psychological Bulletin* 124(2): 165–96.

———. 1999. "Interactive Effects of Personality and Mood on Emotion-Congruent Memory and Judgment." *Journal of Personality and Social Psychology* 77(5): 1073–86.

Rusting, Cheryl L., and Randy J. Larsen. 1998. "Personality and Cognitive Processing of Affective Information." *Personality and Social Psychology Bulletin* 24(2): 200–13.

Schwarz, Norbert, and Gerald L. Clore. 1983. "Mood, Misattribution, and Judgments of Well-Being: Information and Directive Functions of Affective States." *Journal of Personality and Social Psychology* 45(3): 513–23.

———. 2003. "Mood as Information: 20 Years Later." *Psychological Inquiry* 14(3/4): 296–303.

Scollon, Christie N., Ed Diener, Shigehiro Oishi, Robert Biswas-Diener. 2005. "An Experience Sampling and Cross-Cultural Investigation of the Relation Between Pleasant and Unpleasant Affect." *Cognition and Emotion* 19(1): 27–52.

Smillie, Luke D., Alan D. Pickering, and Chris J. Jackson. 2006. "The New Reinforcement Sensitivity Theory: Implications for Personality Measurement." *Personality and Social Psychology Review* 10(4): 320–35.

Smith, Craig A., and Phoebe C. Ellsworth. 1985. "Patterns of Cognitive Appraisal in Emotion." *Journal of Personality and Social Psychology* 48(4): 813–38.

Tamir, Maya, and Michael D. Robinson. 2004. "Knowing Good from Bad: The Paradox of Neuroticism, Negative Affect and Evaluative Processing." *Journal of Personality and Social Psychology* 87(6): 913–25.

Tamir, Maya, Michael D. Robinson, and Gerald L. Clore. 2002. "The Epistemic Benefits of Trait-Consistent Mood States: An Analysis of Extraversion and Mood." *Journal of Personality and Social Psychology* 83(3): 663–77.

Tellegen, Auke. 1985. "Structures of Mood and Personality and Their Relevance to Assessing Anxiety, with an Emphasis on Self-Report." In *Anxiety and the Anxiety Disorders,* edited by A. H. Tuma and J. Mason. Hillsdale, N.J.: Lawrence Erlbaum Associates, Inc.

Tversky, Amos, and Daniel Kahneman. 1981. "The Framing of Decisions and the Psychology of Choice." *Science* 211(4481): 453–8.

Updegraff, John A., Shelly L. Gable, and Shelley E. Taylor. 2004. "What Makes Experiences Satisfying? The Interaction of Approach-Avoidance Motivations and Emotions in Well-Being." *Journal of Personality and Social Psychology* 86(3): 496–504.

Uziel, Liad. 2006. "The Extraverted and the Neurotic Glasses Are of Different Colors." *Personality and Individual Differences* 41(4): 745–54.

Vansteelandt, Kristof, Iven Van Mechelen, and John B. Nezlek. 2005. "The Co-occurrence of Emotions in Daily Life: A Multilevel Approach." *Journal of Research in Personality* 39(3): 325–35.

Zelenski, John M., and Randy J. Larsen. 1999. "Susceptibility to Affect: A Comparison of Three Personality Taxonomies." *Journal of Personality* 67: 761–91.

———. 2000. "The Distribution of Basic Emotions in Everyday Life: A State and Trait Perspective from Experience Sampling Data." *Journal of Research in Personality* 34: 178–97.

———. 2002. "Predicting the Future: How Affect-Related Personality Traits Predict Likelihood Estimates of Future Events." *Personality and Social Psychology Bulletin* 28(7): 1000–1010.

Zelenski, John M., Elizabeth K. L. Nisbet, and Mira Legault. 2005. Personality, Framing, and the Persuasiveness of Pro-environmental Messages. Unpublished data.

· 6 ·

Emotion Is Cognition: An Information-Processing View of the Mind

ROBERT OUM AND DEBRA LIEBERMAN

S INCE THE time of Heraclitus in 500 BC, scholars have speculated on and investigated the role that emotions play in shaping human behavior and reasoning abilities. The number of theories of emotion generated since this time is as vast as it is varied: for example, they include David Hume's view of emotion as "master over reason" (Hume 1739), the theory that emotional feelings depend on feedback from the body (James 1884; Lange 1885), cognitive-appraisal theories (for example, Frijda 1986; Lazarus 1991; Schachter 1964; Schachter and Singer 1962), theories of basic universal emotions with associated facial expressions (Tomkins 1963; Izard 1977; Ekman and Friesen 1971), and social-constructionist theories (Averill 1980; Harré 1986; Shweder and LeVine 1984). As diverse as these perspectives are, however, nearly all draw a sharp distinction between emotion and cognition. We address this dualistic account and suggest that the common distinction between emotion and cognition is largely misleading and limits the potential for understanding emotions in general and, in particular, their role in decision making. A more comprehensive conception of emotions needs to incorporate an information-processing model of the mind. In this light, emotions can be viewed not as a separate domain from cognition, but rather as a subset of cognitive processes, guiding decision making and behavior in a manner that would have led to an increase in survival and reproduction in ancestral environments (Tooby and Cosmides 1990; Pinker 1997; Ketelaar 2004; Ketelaar and Clore 1997).

To start out, we briefly review the history and implications of dualistic accounts of emotion versus cognition. This is followed by a discussion of an information processing view of the mind and the levels of analysis it entails. These levels of analysis allow for the dissection of emotions (and other psychological capabilities) according to the function they evolved to perform; the structure and development of their proximate mechanisms (for example, information processing circuitry); and their neurophysiological implementation (for example, neural correlates and hormonal feedback processes). Within this framework, emotions are characterized as superordinate cognitive programs that regulate specific aspects of the psychology and physiology in response to the adaptive problems encountered by our species throughout evolutionary history (Cosmides and Tooby 2000). Rather than privileging facial expressions, subjective feelings and qualia, or temporal duration as defining features of emotions, this approach includes a consideration of the kinds of recurring adaptive problems our ancestors faced (for example, depleted nutritional resources or avoidance of predators); the cues signaling the presence of the specific problem or situation (for example, low blood sugar or a large fanged animal); and the kinds of physiological systems and psychological programs required to solve the particular problem at hand (for example, shifts in perception or changes in oxygen consumption; Tooby and Cosmides, 1990). To illustrate how emotions can be investigated using an information processing view of the mind, the emotion of disgust is used as an example. Finally, in light of the perspective advanced, we address the specific question raised in this volume: do emotions help or hurt decision making?

The Division Between Emotion and Cognition

Philosophers and psychologists have traditionally drawn a sharp distinction between emotion and cognition. Though the precise language varies depending on the model in question, emotions generally have been viewed as a set of primal processes controlling, for example, urges to eat, mate, fight, or flee. Rather than aiding or guiding thought processes, emotions have been charged with the interference of deliberative, controlled, rational thinking, which is considered the domain of cognition (Pinker 1997; Solomon 2000; Frijda 2000; Isen 2000; Johnson-Laird and Oatley 2000; Salovey et al. 2000). This distinction has long shaped the scientific inquiry of how the mind works and is described in the following quote by the anthropologist Geoffrey White (2000): "A great deal of emotion theory is built upon assumptions about irreducible oppositions between thought and feeling, mind and body, rationality and irrationality, conscious and unconscious, nurture and nature, and so forth" (31).

The academic literature is replete with discussions of emotions and how they are viewed as distinct from more general cognitive processes:

- "Emotion is about motivation, cognition about knowledge" (Izard 1994, 204).
- "A proper distinction between affective and cognitive process is essential for neuroscientific progress" (Panksepp 1994, 224).
- "The traditional contrast of emotion and reason is still very much with us in some form or another. 'Reason' is being used to denote several quite different things—for instance, the use of complex thought processes such as logical inference, as well as efforts to achieve optimal solutions. Both have been regarded as being opposed to emotion. It has frequently been argued that emotions do not employ reasoning and may even confuse it" (Frijda 2000, 70).
- "Some authors have treated [emotions] as purposeless; others have treated them as worse than useless, as impediments to the rational governance of life—a notion that runs from Plato to Freud, along with the doctrine that unbridled emotions lead to self-destruction" (Johnson-Laird and Oatley 2000, 461).
- "Furthermore, most people assume that when affect plays a role in their decision processes, such influences are disruptive and tend to make their decisions 'irrational' and less appropriate than otherwise" (Isen 2000, 417).

Though the dualist notion of cognition versus emotion has taken on different nomenclature through time, the essence of the distinction has remained unchanged. For example, the ancient Greek philosophers discussed these two discrete processes as "reason" and "passion," respectively. More recently, the concept of *hot cognition* has been introduced (Abelson 1963). This concept recognizes that emotion is inexorably linked to cognition. Accordingly, social information is stored and retrieved using cognitive *and* affective representations (for example, remembering an individual who cheated you—the cognitive representation—will also cause recall of the anger you experienced—the affective representation). However, hot cognition still calls attention to the distinction between cognition and emotion. This terminology blurs the line by gluing the two concepts together, and, furthermore, it emphasizes that there exist remarkable differences between hot cognition and all other forms of cognition, whatever they may be. In this way, the division between hot cognition and all else is an updated version of the division between passion and reason. Whether it is called passion versus reason, hot versus cold cognition, affect versus cognition, or feeling versus thinking, the line distinguishing emotion from cognition has more or less remained unmoved for centuries (for recent discussions, see chapters in Lewis and Haviland-Jones 2000).

Though there may be sound reasons why humans or people intuitively mark the difference between emotion and cognition (for example, conscious versus unconscious processes, felt versus not-felt processes, controllable versus uncontrollable processes), the distinction between the two is nonetheless problematic. First, the distinction between emotion and cognition is descriptive, not explanatory; it fails to specify the exact processes underlying cognition and emotion and how they differ. It also presumes the distinction made between thinking and feeling translates into separate mental processes. This is a biased position from which to start a scientific investigation. Second, it ignores a computational theory of mind (that is, an information-processing view of the mind; Barrett 2005)—a view that can shed light on, for example, why certain processes are felt and others are not, and why certain processes are cognitively penetrable (that is, influenced by "deliberative" thought processes) and others are not. Brains evolved to process information and guide behavior in adaptively meaningful ways (Clore 1994). As such, to fully understand the nature of emotion and cognition, one must consider an information-processing view of the mind.

An Information-Processing View of the Mind: Levels of Analysis

According to the vision scientist David Marr (1982), to fully understand any information-processing system, naturally evolved or artificial, one must address three distinct yet causally-related levels of analysis: a computational level of analysis which specifies the function or goals of the system; an algorithmic level of analysis which details how the function of the system is carried out in real time (that is, the nature of the information taken as input to the system, how this information is represented, the operations transforming the representations, the order in which information is processed, and the nature of the outputs or end state); and an analysis of the system's physical instantiation (that is, the organization and nature of the hardware required to implement the information processing task, such as neurons or silicon chips).

Though Marr used these levels of analysis to study perceptual systems in particular, these levels can be used as tools to investigate the architecture of the psychological mechanisms naturally selected to perform a particular function with respect to human behavior in general (Cosmides and Tooby 1987). Respectively, these levels translate into an analysis of the adaptive problem, the cognitive programs, and the neurophysiological instantiation (Tooby and Cosmides 1992).

The Adaptive Problem

For a particular aspect of human behavior, the computational level of analysis entails a description of the corresponding adaptive problem our ancestors faced over our species' evolutionary history. An adaptive problem is a problem posed by long-enduring selection pressures (that is, statistically recurring features of the social, biological, or physical world) whose successful solution affected the probability of survival and reproduction, however distally (Tooby and Cosmides 1992). Examples of adaptive problems include finding a mate, avoiding incest, detecting cheaters, forming friendships, avoiding toxins and pathogens, finding food, avoiding predators, and detecting kin. This level of analysis provides an ultimate level of explanation (that is, *why* certain cognitive abilities and behaviors are thought to exist, and how they contributed to reproductive success in the ancestral past). A thorough assessment of each adaptive problem, including the associated selection pressures and the manner in which survival and reproduction were affected, generates testable hypotheses regarding the kinds of behaviors that might exist as well as the nature of the underlying cognitive programs.

Cognitive Programs

The goal of this level of analysis is to develop a rigorous model of the cognitive programs governing a particular ability. This level of analysis specifies the structure of the *proximate* information-processing systems natural selection shaped to perform a particular ability. A useful question to consider when developing a model of the cognitive architecture is, What would a well-engineered system designed to perform a particular function look like? For example, What information is required, what operations are performed on this information, and what kinds of systems do the outputs regulate?

In addition to a description of the kinds of information-processing systems required to perform a particular function, a complete description of the cognitive programs requires a consideration of how the proposed cognitive abilities develop. Just as many perceptual systems require calibration during development (for example, the visual system; Shatz 2002), so too must other cognitive programs, such as those guiding predator avoidance, mate choice, kin detection, food choice, and cheater detection. Understanding the nature of the information required in the development and calibration of these systems can greatly aid investigations into the mature structures as well as causes of individual differences.

Neurophysiology

The last level of analysis is that of neurophysiological instantiation. Somehow, the cognitive programs must be instantiated in the neural architecture. There has been a wide array of work conducted on the neural correlates of behavior in general (Gazzaniga 2000) and emotion in particular (Adolphs 2004; Phillips, Young, and Senior 1997; Vaitl, Schienle, and Stark 2005). Investigations into the function of particular neural tissue can be greatly aided by considering the other two levels of analysis. For example, theoretical considerations of the adaptive problems our ancestors faced and the types of information-processing circuits that are likely to exist can greatly inform investigations exploring the functional architecture of our neural tissue. Similarly, discovery of neural functionality (for example, through studies on diverse populations such as individuals with selective impairments) can provide important information as to the nature of the information processing pathways that perform particular functions.

An Example: Cheater Detection

An information-processing view of the mind that takes into account the different levels of analysis can be used to investigate many aspects of human psychology. For example, the adaptive niche created by the benefits of reciprocal altruism (Trivers 1971) generated the selection pressure of detecting cheaters, individuals who take a benefit without paying the cost or meeting the requirement. As such, detecting cheaters constituted a specific adaptive problem facing our hunter-gatherer ancestors (Cosmides 1989). Consequently, evolution is hypothesized to have shaped our cognitive abilities to detect and prevent the possibility of being cheated in a social exchange.

What would a well-engineered system for detecting cheaters look like? Possible information-processing components include systems for recognizing individuals, systems for storing person-specific memory (for example, whether the individual has cooperated or cheated in the past), and systems for reasoning about cheating (Tooby and Cosmides 1992). Given the specificity of the kinds of operations required to perform this task, it suggests the possibility that circuits underpinning this ability might be dissociable from other kinds of reasoning abilities. Indeed, using this framework, selective impairments in reasoning about cheaters (but not other reasoning abilities such as reasoning about precautions) have been found in patients with damage to specific brain regions (Stone et al. 2002). Cheater detection constitutes one example of how these levels of analysis can provide a guide rail for investigating how the mind works. Just as these levels of analysis can be used to dissect particular reasoning abilities, so too can they be used to dissect the emotions.

Emotions from an Information-Processing View of the Mind

According to anthropologist John Tooby and psychologist Leda Cosmides (Tooby and Cosmides 1990; Cosmides and Tooby 2000), an emotion is a superordinate information-processing program that coordinates the activation of multiple systems (for example, cognitive, physiological, and behavioral systems) in a manner that led to the increased probability of survival and reproduction over our species' evolutionary history. Each emotion program is hypothesized to have evolved in response to a specific adaptive problem that required the concerted activation of multiple independent systems. That is, certain recurring situations (for example, being chased by a predator, falling ill, having few friends, losing face, coordinating a coalition action, and avoiding the sexual advance by a family member) would have led to the evolution of cognitive programs (that is, information-processing systems) that coordinated elements of the psychology and physiology in ways that led to an increase in fitness in ancestral environments. The successful navigation of each situation would have required different patterns of activation across the diverse systems potentially entrained by emotion programs: perceptual and attentional systems, goal and motivational systems, inference systems, information-gathering programs, memory bases, communication processes, physiology, and behavioral decision rules (Tooby and Cosmides 1990).

For example, the adaptive problem of predator avoidance would have required the activation of a specific set of systems (for example, perceptual systems for heightened visual and auditory acuity, memory stores of successful escape routes, increased heart rate and muscle tone for rapid escape, and secretion of analgesics to treat injury and increase the probability of reaching safe harbor). This pattern of activation differs from the constellation of systems deployed to search for food (that is, hunger), assess the sexual fidelity of a mate (that is, sexual jealousy), or reevaluate sources of investment and social support (that is, depression or grieving). Which physiological components and aspects of the psychology (that is, cognitive programs) are activated depend on the nature of the particular adaptive problem. According to this perspective, then, emotion programs *are* cognitive programs. They are like a chord, setting in motion, once activated, a cascade of events specific to an evolutionarily recurring situation associated with fitness consequences.

According to Tooby and Cosmides (1990), emotions can be characterized by the following:

1. The evolutionarily recurring situation and adaptive problem it posed (for example, the presence of predators and their avoidance)
2. The cues that signaled the presence of the situation (for example, nighttime or a large fanged animal)
3. Situation-detecting algorithms that monitor for the cues correlating with the occurrence of a recurring situation (for example, algorithms monitoring for visibility and for large fanged animate creatures)
4. Situation-detecting algorithms that perform a signal-detection analysis to assess whether a situation is occurring given the detection of particular cues (for example, given the condition of nighttime and the large overhangs covering a path, what is the probability that an undetected predator lies in wait?)
5. Algorithms that assign priority (for example, if nutritionally depleted and in the presence of a predator, first flee and then eat)
6. Internal communication systems (for example, hormonally mediated feedback systems regulating different components of the physiology—such as heart rate, oxygen consumption, and vaso-constriction—to solve the adaptive problem at hand)
7. A set of algorithms specific to each adaptive problem that specify how different components of the physiology and psychology are regulated (for example, up-regulate heart rate but not peristalsis of gastro-intestinal tract, increase sensitivity threshold for auditory information but not olfactory information; Cosmides and Tooby 2000)

There are many different types of psychological systems (for example, goals, perceptions, inference procedures, and social communication) that can be entrained by an emotion program; which ones are entrained depends on the recurring situation and the kinds of functions that would have led to an increased probability of survival and reproduction under ancestral conditions. This perspective, then, allows for a rigorous task analysis of how our cognitive architecture is organized to respond to a particular feature of the environment.

This perspective differs from many current models of emotion that suggest an emotion, by definition, possesses a specific facial expression, a particular state or qualia, and occurs for only a brief period of time (longer-enduring states are instead labeled "affect" or "mood"). According to the perspective discussed above, the communication, felt arousal and temporal duration are potential *properties* of an emotion program, not defining features. For example, whether a particular facial expression exists depends on the benefits of communicating that a particular situation is occurring. For those situations in which no value came from communicating one's knowledge of the world, no facial expressions are expected to exist. That is, a unique facial expression may not be associated with each and every emotion program; some may have a characteristic facial expression or vocalization, and some may not. The absence of a facial expression does not necessarily mean that an emotion program is not in play (unless, of course, this is used as the arbitrary defining feature). This may call into question facial feedback hypotheses for the functional explanation of emotions. The fact that facial feedback may occur certainly sheds light onto the organization of our cognitive system, but it does not necessarily constitute a functional explanation. For example, that a car can be jump-started by rolling it forward does not mean it was designed to function that way.

Similarly, it is irrelevant to the status of a particular state as an emotion whether one is able to "feel" the activation of different physiological systems (for example, adrenaline release, increased heart rate, or increased rate of respiration). Some theories of emotion rely on this felt state to appraise the situation and dictate a response; however, an evolutionary perspective suggests that a response is generated through the detection of cues signaling the presence of an evolutionarily recurring situation producing—as a by-product of the activation of different physiological components—a characteristic felt state. Thus, the felt state is a consequence, not a cause, of the deployment of emotion programs.

Finally, the temporal duration of a state depends on the adaptive problem at hand. Whereas some adaptive problems occurred over short durations of time, others persisted over longer durations. For example, accidentally ingesting a source of pathogens (for example, eating meat with maggots) produces a rapid response (that is, disgust) that quickly dissipates once the source of pathogens is removed. However, assessing the status of a cooperative relationship and attempting to renegotiate more equal investments can take weeks, months, or years (this can be the case of post-partum depression, an emotion program hypothesized to have evolved in response to the adaptive problem posed by cooperative child rearing; Hagen 2002). Privileging time as a defining feature of emotion occludes the larger picture gained by viewing emotions as superordinate cognitive programs which regulate components of the physiology and psychology. Though states that endure have been classified as "affect" or "mood," an evolutionary-informed information-processing view of the mind sees emotion, mood, and affect as places along a continuum of one parameter—time duration—which needs to be considered when describing the functional architecture of a program designed to deal with an ancestrally recurring situation.

An Example: Adaptive Problems, Cognitive Programs, and Neurophysiology of Disgust

To demonstrate how emotions can be investigated using an information-processing view of the mind, consider the example of disgust. Disgust is an emotion program that evolved to regulate behavior in a number of domains. Disgust solves a range of different kinds of adaptive problems: pathogen avoidance, the avoidance of costly sexual behavior, and the avoidance of people imposing large fitness costs (that is, people engaging in sociomoral transgressions). We focus on the pathogen avoidance function of disgust to illustrate how emotions can be investigated using an information processing view of the mind.

Adaptive Problem: Pathogen Avoidance

One evolved function of disgust is to motivate the withdrawal from and avoidance of substances associated with disease-causing organisms (for example, bacteria and viruses) and toxins. These agents were a recurrent feature of hominid environments and posed severe threats to the health and reproduction of our ancestors. Certain foods (for example, plants and rotting meat), body products, body fluids, other animals (for example, insects), and dead organisms would have all harbored potential disease-causing organisms. Because pathogens posed an increased threat to the health of a host, a system that prevented an individual from coming into contact with these substances would have conferred a significant fitness advantage. Indeed, many researchers have suggested that the function of disgust is to protect against bacteria and other disease-causing agents (Izard 1977; Plutchik 1980; Frijda 1986; Tooby and Cosmides 1990; Davey 1992; Nesse and Williams 1994; Pinker 1997; Curtis and Biran 2001). Valerie Curtis and Adam Biran (2001) provide empirical support for this claim by detailing the harmful disease agents commonly associated with various cross-cultural elicitors of disgust.

Andra Angyal (1941), one of the early researchers who focused on this emotion, acknowledged that disgust results in the distancing of oneself from sources of microorganisms and toxins. However, he maintained that this could not be the underlying function because disgust reactions occur in individuals who do not understand the biology of microorganisms. Rather, he proposed that "[the disgust] reaction is due to the particular sensory quality: the disgusting object may be disagreeable to touch, it may smell bad, etc." (394). But evidence that individuals lack knowledge of microorganisms does not mean evolution did not shape the disgust response for this purpose. Angyal's discussion of disgust exposes a common confusion between ultimate and proximate levels of analysis. The ultimate adaptive problem that disgust evolved to solve was the avoidance of disease-causing agents. This selection pressure would have led to the evolution of proximate cognitive programs designed to detect substances that were associated with these harmful agents. The cognitive architecture of such detection systems did not require explicit knowledge of microorganisms, but rather knowledge of the kinds of sensory properties (for example, odor and texture) and likely locations (for example, animal waste products) that were highly correlated with disease-causing agents in ancestral environments.

Unfortunately, the failure to distinguish between these different levels of analysis continues to shape many theoretical treatments of disgust. For example, Paul Rozin and April Fallon (1987), echoing Angyal (1941) and current emotion researchers, agree that disease avoidance is a plausible function of disgust. However, they maintain that this could not be its sole purpose; their evidence for this point is the finding that subjects decline drinking from a glass of juice after a sterilized dead cockroach had been dipped in it (Rozin, Millman, and Nemeroff 1986). However, the pathogen-avoidance function of disgust is consistent with this finding. After all, our neural circuits did not evolve in an environment that contained sterilized insects, nor did they evolve to deal with modern artifacts or contrivances designed to mimic the perceptual properties of ancestral threats. In our ancestral past, something with the physical properties resembling a cockroach was, most likely, a cockroach, with all of its potentially harmful resident pathogens. One might as well argue that photographs of attractive people should not activate erotic feelings, because photographs are pieces of paper. Stimulus arrays, which preserve some of the properties of the evolved trigger of a system, are expected to activate, to some degree, the system in question. If anything, these findings provide insight into the cognitive architecture of emotion programs: they suggest that some emotion programs may be cognitively impenetrable to consciously held beliefs. That is, explicitly held beliefs may not update the internal regulatory variables governing the deployment of some emotion programs. This impenetrability and encapsulation may contribute to the intuitive distinction often made between emotions and other cognitive processes.

Adaptive Problem: Avoidance of Costly Sexual Acts

A second evolved function of disgust is the avoidance of sexual behavior that would have negatively impacted one's reproductive success over our species' evolutionary history. Sexual behavior with close genetic relatives (that is, incest) is one category of these costly matings. Disgust, an emotion already motivating withdrawal from substances exhibiting a given set of properties, is well-suited for this function. In addition, disgust is already related to sexual behavior: if other individuals and their bodily fluids represent planets of potentially harmful pathogens, then for sex to even take place, disgust needs to be down regulated. If, instead of down regulating, disgust was up regulated in response to particular individuals, evolution would have been well on its way to fashioning an inbreeding-avoidance mechanism.

Past researchers have suggested that disgust is the emotion involved in the dampening of sexual attraction and the motivation of sexual avoidance. For example, Silvan Tomkins (1963) suggested that disgust is a reaction to unwanted sexual or intimate contact. Similarly, Susan Miller (1993) suggested that disgust serves to reduce the level of intimacy and increase interpersonal distance with another individual. A handful of researchers have found that disgust is antithetical to sexual arousal (Koukounas and McCabe 1997; Vonderheide and Mosher 1988). In a recent study, John Rempel and Barbara Baumgartner (2003) found that sensitivity to disgust is negatively related to the desire to engage in various sexual behaviors. These results suggest that disgust is an emotion that governs the avoidance of costly sexual behaviors.

Adaptive Problem: Avoidance of Individuals Imposing Large Fitness Costs

A final example of an evolved domain of disgust pertains to social transgressions. Jonathan Haidt and colleagues (1997) report that subjects listed sociomoral violations such as lawyers who chase ambulances, Nazis, and drunk drivers as a subset of elicitors of disgust. There is also evidence from different cultures that the term *disgust* (or a synonym) is used to describe various social transgressions (Haidt et al. 1997). This domain of disgust governs reactions to third-party behaviors and, as a result, resides within the arena of morality and moral sentiments. One hypothesis, then, is that the subset of behaviors eliciting negative moral sentiments such as disgust and contempt fall into the category of "costly third-party behaviors." Indeed, in their definition of sociomoral disgust, Haidt et al. (1997) allude to this function as "a kind of character judgment of others, especially of people who violate the basic dignity of other human beings" (118).

Over our evolutionary history, disgust may have been the emotion that was co-opted to distance oneself from other individuals in the social environment whose behaviors imposed large fitness costs; this was useful to prevent incurring any costs personally or perhaps to prevent being associated with individuals engaging in such social transgressions. The social communication of disgust sentiments regarding a particular individual and their behavior may have relayed important information to kin, mates, and social-exchange partners (that is, individuals for whom one has a stake in their well-being). This particular aspect of disgust requires further investigation to determine the types of social behaviors that fall within the bounds of moral judgments and disgust reactions.

Cognitive Programs for Avoiding Pathogens

What would a well-engineered system that functioned to prevent contact with substances associated with disease-causing agents look like? A number of different components would be required: information-processing programs that detected the properties (for example, olfactory, tactile, and visual properties) correlated with the presence of pathogens over our species' evolutionary history; programs that take information regarding pathogen presence as input and activate the appropriate psychological and physiological systems. For example, programs governing motivations and goals can be activated to selectively avoid and withdraw from substances identified as contaminated. Empirical evidence of the redirection of goals when disgust is activated comes from Ira Roseman, Cynthia Wiest, and Tamara Swartz (1994), who found that subjects report a desire to rid the body of something noxious, to remove something from the perceptual field, or to get something away from oneself when thinking of disgusting stimuli. Additionally, unpublished data from a study by Debra Lieberman (2004) found that subjects increased the distance between themselves and a computer monitor when shown statements eliciting disgust. The idea that disgust functions as a distancing emotion is also supported by Jennifer Lerner, Deborah Small, and George Loewenstein (2004), who found that individuals primed with disgust sold items at lower prices than those in the control condition.

Another cognitive system that is expected to be entrained by the emotion program of disgust is memory. Once an object possessing properties that are associated with disease-causing agents has been detected, memory systems can selectively retain information regarding the item and its surroundings in order to facilitate identification in the future. Also, in the event that a toxic substance has been ingested and has caused a physiological response such as nausea, vomiting, or diarrhea, memory systems should be engaged to recall the likely source of the contaminant (for example, the "sauce béarnaise" effect; Seligman and Hager 1972).

There are also many physiological systems that are designed to defend the body against invading pathogens. If disease agents have been ingested, nausea and vomiting are two responses that are designed to expel the contaminated food substances. The immune system and its dedicated army of complement factors and immunoglobulins independently combat bacteria and viruses that have entered the body. Although an emotion program is not necessary for the activation of an immune response, specific aspects of this system may be entrained in the event that contact is made with external substances harboring disease-causing agents. For example, body temperature may be regulated in response to contact with pathogens. Increased body temperature creates a less hospitable environment for pathogens and reduces their ability to replicate while allowing elements of the immune system to mobilize for attack (Kluger 1979). Evidence that thermoregulation occurs during disgust comes from Robert Zajonc and Daniel McIntosh (1992), who found that temperature in the extremities increases when disgust is activated in college-aged subjects.[1]

Another component of the immune response that may become activated when contact is made with specific categories of pathogens is the system designed to decrease the supply of available nutrients required by bacteria to replicate (for example, free iron). Though it has been hypothesized that prolonged anemia may reflect a sustained infection (Nesse and Williams 1994), it is unknown whether brief contact, and hence the potential transmission of pathogens, activates these defense systems.

In summary, an information-processing view of the mind allows for the development of a detailed model of the kinds of systems required to solve a recurring adaptive problem—in this case, the avoidance of pathogens. Specification of the kinds of perceptual mechanisms for detecting the presence of pathogens, the kinds of psychological and physiological components that are entrained once pathogens have been detected, and how each component is affected (for example, up-regulated or down-regulated) generates testable hypotheses regarding how the mind performs this function. In general, this approach provides a standard for determining, among other things, whether characteristic facial expressions are likely to exist, how long the emotion program is likely to be engaged, and whether physiological components, once activated, generate a characteristic felt state. It also provides a potential map of how systems can be impaired, which can be updated with findings from neuroscientific inquiries of the neural correlates of emotion.

Neurophysiology

Recently, researchers have started to discover specialized brain regions involved in the processing of different emotions (Calder 2003; Lawrence, Murphy, and Calder 2004). One of the emotions found to have a distinct neural basis is disgust (Adolphs, Tranel, and Damasio 2003). Andrew Calder, Jill Keane, and Facundo Manes (2000) investigated a patient with brain injuries localized in the insula and putamen and found specific impairments in disgust reactions. Studies on healthy subjects have also implicated the insula. Specifically, the insula has been found to mediate the recognition of facial expressions of disgust (Adolphs, Tranel, and Damasio 2003), to govern responses to pictures showing sources of pathogens (Wright, He, and Shapira 2004), and to govern olfactory responses to items eliciting disgust (Phillips and Heining 2002). Additional evidence that disgust responses are neurally localized comes from studies on populations with specific disorders; for example, studies on those with obsessive-compulsive disorder (Phillips, Marks, and Senior 2000) and those with Huntington's Disease (Sprengelmeyer et al. 1997).

In general, investigations into the neural correlates of emotion can help flesh out models of the cognitive programs underpinning emotional responses. For example, the finding that visual, olfactory, and auditory stimuli relating to disgust all activate the same brain region in healthy subjects suggests that perceptual systems assessing the probability of pathogen concentration take in information from multiple modalities. Significant progress can be made in uncovering the neural architecture of the human brain if findings from neuropsychology and cognitive neuroscience are interpreted alongside rigorous models of the cognitive programs hypothesized to govern specific brain functions.

Summary of Emotions from an Information-Processing View of the Mind

Different from previous models of disgust (Haidt, McCauley, and Rozin 1994), an evolutionary analysis of disgust suggests three distinct functional domains: the avoidance of pathogens, the avoidance of costly sexual partners, and the avoidance of contact or association with people who commit moral offenses. Each disgust system is expected to entrain specific cognitive, behavioral, and physiological systems to solve the particular adaptive problem at hand (for example, avoiding pathogens or avoiding close genetic relatives as sexual partners). There are many questions that remain unanswered. For example, How are elements of the psychology and physiology activated in response to the adaptive problem of pathogen and toxin avoidance? Are these same systems activated to solve the adaptive problem of incest avoidance and sociomoral disgust (if this is indeed found to be a separate functional domain)? Furthermore, Are similar brain regions involved in processing information regarding pathogen avoidance, the avoidance of costly sexual behaviors, and sociomoral transgressions? These questions and others can be answered using the guide rails provided by an information-processing view of the mind.

Do Emotions Help or Hurt Decision Making?

According to the perspective advanced in this chapter, emotions evolved to direct decision making (and a host of other capabilities) in situations that recurred over our species' evolutionary history. For example, when confronted by a predator, the emotion program *fear* sets in motion the courses of action likely to result in survival; when confronted with a piece of rotting meat, the emotion *disgust* regulates decision making systems involved in food choice. In this light, emotions act as heuristics, bounding the infinite set of possible actions and decisions to those that were adaptively meaningful in ancestral environments (for more on bounded rationality, see Gerd Gigerenzer and Rheinhard Selten 2002). Thus, emotions can be said to govern and direct decision making.

Whether emotions help or hurt decision making depends on what one means by helping or hurting. If hurting decision making means that the outcome of a situation in which a person was "emotional" led to a decrease in well-being or greater sadness and frustration, then emotions may hurt decision making. For example, post-partum depression, despite its potential function (Hagen 2002), may have undesirable effects on well-being and esteem. Similarly, if helping decision making means that the outcome of a situation was enhanced (that is, benefits or greater happiness resulted) due to the presence of an emotion, then emotions can also be seen to help decision making. For example, being sexually attracted to someone and deciding to pursue them as a mate may result in the development of a strong and stable relationship.

However, the evolutionary approach uses a very different metric to assess emotions. Rather than measuring the level of well-being or happiness, this perspective of emotions assesses how the particular emotion program led to an increase in survival and reproduction in ancestral environments. Though many emotions that we experience may be "negative" (for example, fear, jealousy, depression, and anger), they nonetheless evolved in response to a recurring adaptive problem facing our hunter-gatherer ancestors. Increasing reproductive success does not necessarily promote happiness or shared moral values. According to Steven Pinker (1997), "we often call an act 'emotional' when it is harmful to the social group, damaging to the actor's happiness in the long run, uncontrollable and impervious to persuasion, or a product of self-delusion. Sad to say, these outcomes are not malfunctions but precisely what we would expect from well-engineered emotions" (370).

However, suggesting that emotions *always* guide decision making in adaptive ways would be a gross oversimplification. For instance, modern environments may differ from the ancestral environments to which we are adapted, rendering decision making processes nonfunctional and potentially harmful. For example, our food-choice systems evolved in environments in which the presence of high-energy sources (such as fruits) varied temporally and spatially. Consequently, mechanisms that motivated the search for such foods would have conferred a selective advantage. In modern environments, however, where there is an endless supply of sugar-rich foods, and a sweet tooth can lead to all kinds of negative consequences. Similarly, sexual disgust may occur between two individuals who, due to cultural practices or the idiosyncrasies of the modern world, are not, in fact, genetic relatives. As has been shown in natural experiments in Israeli Kibbutzim (Shepher 1971), Taiwanese marriages (Wolf 1995), and U.S. families with adopted and step-siblings (Lieberman, Tooby, and Cosmides 2007), when two genetically unrelated individuals are reared together from childhood—a cue which typically signals genetic relatedness—reduced sexual attraction results. Categorizing someone as "close kin" when they are not, eliminates a potential mate from the mating pool through the activation of sexual disgust. Thus emotion programs may direct behavior and decision making processes in ways that do not have adaptive value in modern environments. Since "our modern skulls house a stone age mind" (Cosmides and Tooby 2005), there may be situations in which our decision making systems are ill-equipped to handle inputs that differ from those that existed in ancestral environments. But, to isolate those mechanisms that may not be performing adaptively, it is critical to catalog our evolved decision making processes, to investigate the circumstances under which they evolved (which is time stamped into their design), and to map out their architecture (for example, the nature of the inputs and systems that they regulate).

In conclusion, emotion *is* cognition. That is, emotion programs are cognitive programs that activate a suite of psychological and physiological programs in response to a recurring situation which impacted survival and reproduction in ancestral environments. Emotions can be investigated using an information-processing view of the mind, taking into consideration the kinds of systems that would have performed a specific function. This approach sidesteps misleading dichotomies which have infiltrated research on emotions for centuries. Breaking through our intuitions about thinking versus feeling and about passion versus reason will allow for accelerated progress in understanding how the mind works and the nature of our evolved cognitive architecture.

Notes

1. Levenson et al. (1991) failed to replicate this finding in very young and very old subjects. This discrepancy may be due to the methods used in the induction of disgust and the proximity of disgust items during temperature assessment.

References

Abelson, Robert 1963. "Computer Simulation of 'Hot' Cognition." In *Computer Simulation of Personality: Frontier of Psychological Theory,* edited by Silvan S. Tomkins and Samuel Messic. New York: Wiley.

Adolphs, Ralph 2004. "Emotion, Social Cognition, and the Human Brain." In *Essays in Social Neuroscience,* edited by John T. Cacioppo and Gary G. Berntson. Cambridge, Mass.: MIT.

Adolphs, Ralph, Daniel Tranel, and Antonio R. Damasio. 2003. "Dissociable Neural Systems for Recognizing Emotions." *Brain and Cognition* 52(1): 61–69.

Angyal, Andra 1941. "Disgust and Related Aversions." *Journal of Abnormal and Social Psychology* 36(4): 393–412.

Averill, James R. 1980. "A Social Constructivist View of Emotion." In *Emotion: Theory Research and Experience,* Volume 1, edited by Robert Plutchik and Henry Kellerman. New York: Academic Press.

Barrett, H. Clark. 2005. "Enzymatic Computation and Cognitive Modularity." *Mind and Language* 20(3): 259–87.

Calder, Andrew J. 2003. "Disgust Discussed." *Annals of Neurology* 53(4): 427–8.

Calder, Andrew J., Jill Keane, and Facundo Manes. 2000. "Impaired Recognition and Experience of Disgust Following Brain Injury." *Nature Neuroscience* 3(11): 1077–8.

Clore, Gerald 1994. "Why Emotions Are Felt." In *The Nature of Emotions: Fundamental Questions,* edited by Paul Ekman and Richard J. Davidson. New York: Oxford University Press.

Cosmides, Leda. 1989. "The Logic of Social Exchange: Has Natural Selection Shaped How Humans Reason? Studies with the Wason Selection Task." *Cognition* 31(3): 187–276.

Cosmides, Leda, and John Tooby. 1987. "From Evolution to Behavior: Evolutionary Psychology as the Missing Link." In *The Latest on the Best: Essays on Evolution and Optimality*, edited by John Dupre. Cambridge, Mass.: The MIT Press.

———. 2000. "Evolutionary Psychology and the Emotions." In *Handbook of Emotions*, edited by Michael Lewis and Jeannette M. Haviland-Jones. New York: Guilford Press.

———. 2005. *What Is Evolutionary Psychology?: Explaining the New Science of the Mind.* New York: Yale University Press.

Curtis, Valerie, and Adam Biran. 2001. "Dirt, Disgust, and Disease: Is Hygiene in our Genes?" *Perspectives in Biology and Medicine* 44(1): 17–31.

Davey, Graham C. 1992. "Classical Conditioning and the Acquisition of Human Fears and Phobias: A Review and Synthesis of the Literature." *Advances in Behavior Research and Therapy* 14(1): 29–66.

Ekman, Paul, and Wallace V. Friesen. 1971. "Constants Across Cultures in the Face and Emotion." *Journal of Personality and Social Psychology* 17(2): 124–9.

Frijda, Nico. 1986. *The Emotions: Studies in Emotion and Social Interaction.* New York: Cambridge University Press

———. 2000. "The Psychologists' Point of View." In *Handbook of Emotions*, edited by Michael Lewis and Jeannette M. Haviland-Jones. New York: Guilford Press.

Gazzaniga, Michael S. 2000. *The New Cognitive Neurosciences.* 2nd edition. Cambridge, Mass.: MIT.

Gigerenzer, Gerd, and Rheinhard Selten. 2002. *Bounded Rationality: The Adaptive Toolbox.* New York: MIT.

Hagen, Edward. 2002. "Depression as Bargaining: The Case Postpartum." *Evolution and Human Behavior* 23(5): 323–36.

Haidt, Jonathan, Clark McCauley, and Paul Rozin. 1994. "Individual Differences in Sensitivity to Disgust: A Scale Sampling Seven Domains of Disgust Elicitors." *Personality and Individual Differences* 16(5): 701–13.

Haidt, Jonathan, Paul Rozin, Clark McCauley, and Sumio Imada. 1997. "Body, Psyche, and Culture: The Relationship Between Disgust and Morality." *Psychology and Developing Societies* 9(1): 107–31.

Harré, Rom. 1986. *The Social Construction of Emotions.* New York: Blackwell Publishing.

Hume, David. 1739. *A Treatise of Human Nature: Being an Attempt to Introduce the Experimental Method of Reasoning into Moral Subjects.* Volume 2. London: John Noon.

Isen, Alice M. 2000. "Positive Affect and Decision Making." In *Handbook of Emotions*, edited by Michael Lewis and Jeannette M. Haviland-Jones. New York: Guilford Press.

Izard, Carroll E. 1977. *Human Emotions.* New York: Plenum Press.

———. 1994. "Cognition is One of Four Types of Emotion Activating Systems." In *The Nature of Emotion, Fundamental Questions*, edited by Paul Ekman and Richard J. Davidson. New York: Oxford University Press.

James, William. 1884. "What Is an Emotion?" *Mind* os-IX(34): 188–205.

Johnson-Laird, Phillip N., and Keith Oatley. 2000. "Cognitive and Social Construction in Emotions." In *Handbook of Emotions,* edited by Michael Lewis and Jeannette M. Haviland-Jones. New York: Guilford Press.

Ketelaar, Tim 2004. "Ancestral Emotions, Current Decisions: Using Evolutionary Game Theory to Explore the Role of Emotions in Decision-Making." In *Evolutionary Psychology, Public Policy and Personal Decisions,* edited by Charles Crawford and Catherine Salmon. Mahwah, N.J.: Lawrence Erlbaum Associates, Inc.

Ketelaar, Tim, and Gerald L. Clore. 1997. "Emotions and Reason: The Proximate Effects and Ultimate Functions of Emotions." In *Personality, Emotion, and Cognitive Science.* Advances in Psychology Series, edited by Gerald Matthews. Amsterdam: Elsevier.

Kluger, Matthew J. 1979. "Temperature Regulation, Fever, and Disease." *International Review of Physiology* 20: 209–51.

Koukounas, Eric, and Marita McCabe. 1997. "Sexual and Emotional Variables Influencing Sexual Response to Erotica." *Behaviour Research and Therapy* 35(3): 221–30.

Lange, Carl G. 1885. "The Mechanism of the Emotions." Translated by Benjamin Rand. In *The Classical Psychologists,* edited by Benjamin Rand. Boston, Mass.: Houghton Mifflin, 1912.

Lawrence, Andrew D., Fionnuala C. Murphy, and Andrew J. Calder. 2004. "Dissociating Fear and Disgust: Implications for the Structure of Emotions." In *Cognition, Emotion and Psychopathology: Theoretical, Empirical and Clinical Directions,* edited by Jennifer Yiend. New York: Cambridge University Press.

Lazarus, Richard S. 1991. *Emotion and Adaptation.* New York: Oxford University Press.

Lerner, Jennifer S., Deborah A. Small, and George Loewenstein. 2004. "Heart Strings and Purse Strings: Carryover Effects of Emotions on Economic Decisions." *Psychological Science* 15(5): 337–41.

Levenson, Robert W., Laura L. Carstensen, Wallace V. Friesen, and Paul Ekman. 1991. "Emotion, Physiology and Expression in Old Age." *Psychology and Aging* 6(1): 28–35.

Lewis, Michael, and Jeannette M. Haviland-Jones. 2000. *Handbook of Emotions.* New York: Guilford Press.

Lieberman, Debra L. 2004. "Mapping the Cognitive Architecture of Systems for Kin Detection and Inbreeding Avoidance: The Westermarck Hypothesis and the Development of Sexual Aversions Between Siblings." 2004. *Dissertation Abstracts International: Section B: The Sciences and Engineering* 64(8-B): 4110.

Lieberman, Debra, John Tooby, and Leda Cosmides. 2007. "The Architecture of Human Kin Detection." *Nature* 445(7129): 727–31.

Marr, David. 1982. *Vision.* New York: W. H. Freeman and Company.

Miller, Susan B. 1993. "Disgust Reactions: Their Determinants and Manifestations in Treatment." *Contemporary Psychoanalysis* 29(4): 711–35.

Nesse, Randolph M., and George C. Williams. 1994. *Why We Get Sick: The New Science of Darwinian Medicine.* New York: Times Books.

Panksepp, Jaak. 1994. "A Proper Distinction Between Affective and Cognitive Process Is Essential for Neuro-Scientific Progress." In *The Nature of Emotion,*

Fundamental Questions, edited by Paul Ekman and Richard J. Davidson. New York: Oxford University Press.

Phillips, Mary L., and Maike Heining. 2002. "Neural Correlates of Emotion Perception: From Faces to Taste." In *Olfaction, Taste, and Cognition,* edited by C. Rouby and B. Schaal. New York: Cambridge University Press.

Phillips, Mary L., Isaac M. Marks, and Carl Senior. 2000. "A Differential Neural Response in Obsessive-Compulsive Disorder Patients with Washing Compared with Checking Symptoms to Disgust." *Psychological Medicine* 30(5): 1037–50.

Phillips, Mary L., Andrew W. Young, and Carl Senior. 1997. "A Specific Neural Substrate for Perceiving Facial Expressions of Disgust." *Nature* 389(6650): 495–8.

Pinker, Steven 1997. *How the Mind Works.* New York: W. W. Norton and Company.

Plutchik, Robert 1980. *Emotion: A Psychoevolutionary Synthesis.* New York: Harper and Row.

Rempel, John K., and Barbara Baumgartner. 2003. "The Relationship Between Attitudes Towards Menstruation and Sexual Attitudes, Desires, and Behavior in Women." *Archives of Sexual Behavior* 32(2): 155–63.

Roseman, Ira J., Cynthia Wiest, and Tamara S. Swartz. 1994. "Phenomenology, Behaviors, and Goals Differentiate Discrete Emotions." *Journal of Personality and Social Psychology* 67(2): 206–21.

Rozin, Paul, and April E. Fallon. 1987. "A Perspective on Disgust." *Psychological Review* 94(1): 23–41.

Rozin, Paul, Linda Millman, and Carol Nemeroff. 1986. "Operation of the Laws of Sympathetic Magic in Disgust and Other Domains." *Journal of Personality and Social Psychology* 50(4): 703–12.

Salovey, Peter, Brian T. Bedell, Jerusha B. Detweiler, and John D. Mayer. 2000. "Current Directions in Emotional Intelligence Research." In *Handbook of Emotions,* edited by Michael Lewis and Jeannette M. Haviland-Jones. New York: Guilford Press.

Schachter, Stanley. 1964. "The Interaction of Cognitive and Physiological Determinants of Emotional State." In *Advances in Experimental Social Psychology,* Volume 1, edited by Leonard Berkowitz. New York: Academic Press.

Schachter, Stanley, and Jerome E. Singer. 1962. "Cognitive, Social and Physiological Determinants of Emotional States." *Psychological Review* 69(5): 379–99

Seligman, Martin E. P., and Joanne L. Hager. 1972. *Biological Boundaries of Learning.* New York: Meredith.

Shatz, Carla J. 2002. "Emergence of Order in Visual System Development." In *Brain Development and Cognition: A Reader,* edited by Mark H. Johnson and Yuko Munakata. 2nd edition. Malden, Mass.: Blackwell Publishing.

Shepher, Joseph 1971. "Mate Selection Among Second-Generation Kibbutz Adolescents: Incest Avoidance and Negative Imprinting." *Archives of Sexual Behavior* 1(4): 293–307.

Shweder, Richard, and Robert LeVine. 1984. *Culture Theory: Essays on Mind, Self, and Emotion.* New York: Cambridge University Press.

Solomon, Robert C. 2000. "The Philosophy of Emotions." In *Handbook of Emotions,* edited by Michael Lewis and Jeannette M. Haviland-Jones. New York: Guilford Press.

Sprengelmeyer, Reiner, Andrew W. Young, Anke Sprengelmeyer, Andrew J. Calder, Duncan Rowland, David Perrett, Volker Homberg, and Herwig Lange. 1997. "Recognition of Facial Expressions: Selective Impairment of Specific Emotions in Huntington's Disease." *Cognitive Neuropsychology* 14(6): 839–79.

Stone, Valerie E., Leda Cosmides, John Tooby, Neal Kroll, and Robert T. Knight. 2002. "Selective Impairment of Reasoning About Social Exchange in a Patient with Bilateral Limbic System Damage." *Proceedings of the National Academy of Science* 99(17): 11531–6.

Tomkins, Silvan S. 1963. *The Negative Affects.* Volume 2 of *Affect, Imagery, Consciousness.* New York: Springer-Verlag.

Tooby, John, and Leda Cosmides. 1990. "The Past Explains the Present: Emotional Adaptations and the Structure of Ancestral Environments." *Ethology and Sociobiology* 11(3/4): 375–424.

———. 1992. "The Psychological Foundations of Culture." In *The Adapted Mind,* edited by Jerome H. Barkow, Leda Cosmides, and John Tooby. New York: Oxford University Press.

Trivers, Robert. 1971. "The Evolution of Reciprocal Altruism." *Quarterly Review of Biology* 46(1): 35–57.

Vaitl, Dieter, Anne Schienle, and Rudolf Stark. 2005. "Neurobiology of Fear and Disgust." *International Journal of Psychophysiology* 57(1): 1–4.

Vonderheide, Susan G., and Donald L. Mosher. 1988. "Should I Put in My Diaphragm? Sex-Guilt and Turn-Offs." *Journal of Psychology and Human Sexuality* 1(1): 97–111.

White, Geoffrey M. 2000. "Representing Emotional Meaning: Category, Metaphor, Schema, Discourse." In *Handbook of Emotions,* edited by Michael Lewis and Jeannette M. Haviland-Jones. New York: Guilford Press.

Wolf, Arthur P. 1995. *Sexual Attraction and Childhood Association: A Chinese Brief for Edward Westermarck.* Stanford, Calif.: Stanford University Press.

Wright, Paul, Guojun He, and Nathan A. Shapira. 2004. "Disgust and the Insula: fMRI Responses to Pictures of Mutilation and Contamination." *Neuroreport: For Rapid Communication of Neuroscience Research* 15(15): 2347–51.

Zajonc, Robert B., and Daniel N. McIntosh. 1992. "Emotions Research: Some Promising Questions and Some Questionable Promises." *Psychological Science* 3(1): 70–74.

Specific Mechanisms

· 7 ·

The Effects of Self-Esteem and Ego Threat on Decision Making

Catherine D. Rawn, Nicole L. Mead,
Peter Kerkhof, and Kathleen D. Vohs

I~~T TAKES~~ a constant stream of interpersonal decision making for people to be liked by others and to like themselves at the same time. Although often being liked and liking oneself go hand in hand, at times people make choices to give up on being liked in order to restore a positive self-image or to temporarily have a less positive self-image to prevent social exclusion. Ego threat and concomitant emotions play a role in interpersonal decision making among people who are low and high in self-esteem. The literature on threats to the self, feelings about the self, and interpersonal perceptions offers theoretical and empirical evidence in support of the nonintuitive conclusion that people with high self-esteem do not fare any better than people with low self-esteem in terms of how others feel about them. In fact, high self-esteem people become less likeable when they feel threatened. If changes in decision making underlie changes in behavior, decision making patterns among high and low self-esteem people under conditions of threat or nonthreat may be important.

Of the studies that have tested the effects of self-esteem, ego threat (and attendant emotions), and decision making, there is a subset that have tested directly the interrelation between threat and self-esteem. This literature demonstrates that low self-esteem people think first about how to satisfy relationship concerns and second about how to take care of the self, whereas high self-esteem people think first about how to satisfy their own wishes and desires and second about others' needs. These trends are excaberated by negative emotions that follow from ego threat. Following recent work (Baumeister, Vohs, DeWall, and Zhang 2007), we propose that securing future positive emotional states underlies the interpersonal decisions both low and high self-esteem people make. Differences in the degree to which people experience self-conscious emotions in situations of ego threat shape expectations of future emotional states. These expectations in turn shape decisions relating to interpersonal behavior in a direction that helps to either be liked by oneself or by others.

Differential Self-Perceptions as a Function of Self-Esteem

We define *self-esteem* as a subjective attitude towards oneself (Baumeister et al. 2003; Coopersmith 1967; Rosenberg 1965). Essentially, it is an evaluation or perception of one's self-worth (Leary et al. 1995). Accordingly, it is not a surprise that people with high self-esteem rate themselves more positively than do people with low self-esteem. For example, people with high self-esteem rate themselves as attractive (Diener, Wolsic, and Fujita 1995), intelligent (Gabriel, Critelli, and Ee 1994), popular (Battistich, Solomon, and Delucchi 1993), interpersonally competent (Buhrmester et al. 1988), and efficacious about their relationship skills (Chemers, Watson, and May 2000; Baumeister et al. 2003). Conversely, low self-esteem people are unconvinced that they are good short-term interaction partners (Campbell and Fehr 1990) or longer-term relationship partners (Murray, Holmes, and Griffin 2000; Murray et al. 2001) and, moreover, rate themselves as less attractive and intelligent relative to self-ratings among people with high self-esteem (Gabriel, Critelli, and Ee 1994). As is evident, the positive self-views held by people with high self-esteem means that they generally like and believe positive things about themselves (Brown 1993); this attitude extends to their self-beliefs about their social skills and interpersonal inclusion. Compared with low self-esteem people, high self-esteem people are more likely to believe that they are well liked (Brockner and Lloyd 1986).

Self-Reports as Disconnected from External Views

Researchers have found only scant relations in the association between self-ratings (by both high and low self-esteem people) and others' reports or objective measures. For instance, despite the finding that high self-esteem people rate themselves as highly attractive, there is only a small correlation between people's self-esteem and others' ratings of their attractiveness (Diener, Wolsic, and Fujita 1995; Gabriel, Critelli, and Ee 1994). Similarly, self-reports reveal a strong relationship between self-esteem and self-ratings of intelligence, but an external measure of intelligence showed no relation to the target's self-esteem (Gabriel, Critelli, and Ee 1994). Additionally, leadership ratings of military cadets, both in terms of a test of leadership and supervisors' ratings, are not predicted by cadets' self-reported self-esteem (Chemers, Watson, and May 2000). Hence, there is a rather large discrepancy between self-reports (by both high and low self-esteem people) and external reports. Despite the highly favorable self-views of a person with high self-esteem and the rather dysphoric self-views of a person with low self-esteem, there is little evidence that third-party assessments correspond to these self-reports.

A similar pattern exists in the interpersonal realm. In a study involving college roommates, Duane Buhrmester and his colleagues (1988) also found minimal correlations between self-reports of social skills (by both high and low self-esteem people) and roommate reports of the targets' social skills. In this study, ratings were made on five domains of interpersonal competence: initiation of interactions and relationships, assertion of personal rights, self-disclosure of personal info, emotional support of others, and management of interpersonal conflicts that arise in close relationships. Although significant (positive) correlations were found between the targets' self-esteem and self-ratings on the five domains of interpersonal competence—meaning that as self-esteem of the target went up, so did their positive appraisals of their own social skills—roommates' appraisals of the targets revealed that all but one of the five correlations were nonsignificant.

The one correlation in this study that was statistically significant pertained to targets' ability to initiate new interactions and relationships, on which high self-esteem targets were rated higher by their roommates on the ability to initiate new interactions (Buhrmester et al. 1988). This result suggests that people with high self-esteem are more comfortable seeking out interactions with new people than are those with low self-esteem, as reported by both targets and roommates. To extend this result to interpersonal decision making, it suggests that high self-esteem people may be willing to take more interpersonal risks, insofar as initiating a new interaction involves some chance of rejection.

The weak correlation between the targets' self-esteem and ratings by others was also obtained in an adolescent sample involving interpersonal relations. Julia Bishop and Heidi Inderbitzen's (1995) results paralleled these studies using peer reports: There was no association between peer acceptance and the targets' self-esteem. Popularity, as evaluated by peers, it seems, is not predicted by self-esteem.

Laboratory settings with unacquainted peers also converge on the same idea. In one study, college students participated in a fifteen-minute dyadic interaction (Campbell and Fehr 1990). Participants then rated their own behavior during the conversation on ten positive and ten negative domains. They also rated their partner's behavior on these same traits, and estimated what their partner thought of them (which is called the targets' *metaperception*). Whereas high self-esteem people accurately estimated how their partner viewed them during the interaction, low self-esteem participants rated themselves less positively than their high self-esteem counterparts, and therefore underestimated how positively they were regarded by their partners. That is, there was no difference in partner's ratings of the low and high self-esteem participants, yet there was a significant difference in metaperceptions, with low self-esteem participants underestimating how positively their partners viewed them.

Thus, the extant literature suggests only a weak correlation between informant- and self-report accounts given by high and low self-esteem people (Diener, Wolsic, and Fujita 1995; Jovanovic, Lerner, and Lerner 1989; Swann 1996). Evidence from both laboratory and naturalistic studies that have examined both adolescent and college samples does not support the notion that people with high self-esteem actually are more attractive, more intelligent, more popular, and better interaction partners than are people with low self-esteem, despite self-reports from these two groups stating that this is the case (Bishop and Inderbitzen 1995; Brockner and Lloyd 1986; Campbell and Fehr 1990; Heatherton and Vohs 2000; Vohs and Heatherton 2001, 2004). Regardless of others' views, such vastly differing self-views affect high and low self-esteem people's perception of their social inclusion and exclusion. In turn, these perceptions, and the potential threat and emotions that accompany them, affect interpersonal behavior and decisions in a way that may not correspond to others' perceptions.

Sociometer Theory: Self-Esteem and Perceptions of Social Inclusion Versus Exclusion

Despite the finding that peer and short-term-partner appraisals are no different for high self-esteem and low self-esteem people, the finding that low self-esteem people underestimate their social success and likeability suggests that they are particularly sensitive to rejection. When confronted with signs of rejection, high self-esteem people could maintain a sense of belongingness and acceptance due to their elevated perceptions of social acceptance, whereas low self-esteem people could be more sensitive to signs of social rejection because of their weak perceptions of acceptance.

According to the sociometer theory of self-esteem (Leary et al. 1995), self-esteem acts as a monitor of social acceptance. A high level of self-esteem means that the person perceives social inclusion and is not at risk for interpersonal rejection. Conversely, low self-esteem means that the person perceives a low potential for inclusion. Rejection does negatively affect people with high self-esteem, but their overarching belief that they are highly likeable signals to them that they are not in imminent danger of being totally ostracized. Low self-esteem indicates a perception that one has a low probability of social acceptance as well as a chronic inclusion deficit (that is, they consistently feel a lack of social acceptance).

Myriad evidence supports the sociometer theory of self-esteem. For example, Mark Baldwin and Lisa Sinclair (1996) demonstrated that low self-esteem people hold cognitive acceptance contingencies, which means that they have automatic cognitive links between failure (even performance failure) and rejection. High self-esteem people, conversely, do not show this acceptance contingency. Likewise, high self-esteem people perceive acceptance even when confronted with signs of rejection, whereas low self-esteem people perceived rejection despite signs of acceptance (Nezlek, Kowalski, and Leary 1997).

Implications of Self-Esteem and Perception of Inclusion for Interpersonal Decisions

Given that high self-esteem people are less concerned with how others view them, it follows that they may not feel bound to tailor their behaviors to gain social inclusion much of the time. Indirect evidence comes from research showing that self-esteem is a significant predictor of voice behavior in organizations (LePine and Van Dyne 1998). Specifically, those reporting high self-esteem were more likely to engage in discussions challenging the status quo with the intent of making positive improvements. Although voice is considered a proactive response to discontent, speaking out against one's colleagues is risky because it carries the possibility of disrupting relationships. Voice behavior therefore suggests that high self-esteem people are willing to challenge the status quo for the long-term good of themselves and others, even at the potential expense of upsetting current relationship harmony.

People with high self-esteem are not always models of exemplary interaction partners. In some research, high self-esteem participants were more likely than low self-esteem participants to use downward social comparisons when describing the relative difference between themselves and their partners. Low self-esteem people, in contrast, described their partner more positively than themselves (Schütz and Tice 1997). As opposed to the voice behavior described above, making downward social comparisons cannot be construed as intended for the good of others. However, what this behavior does have in common with voice behavior is that both are risky interpersonal behaviors. It appears that high self-esteem people are willing to sacrifice their current relationships to achieve other goals, including self-enhancement.

Research has also demonstrated that self-esteem influences the choice of interaction partners. A series of four experiments showed that high and low self-esteem participants based their choice of potential partners on a need for positive self-evaluation or the need to belong, respectively (Rudich and Vallacher 1999). In a series of studies, they demonstrated that high self-esteem participants chose partners based on their desire to interact with people who confirmed their positive self-view, even if that meant selecting an interaction partner who was not interested in forming a relationship with them. Low self-esteem participants demonstrated the opposite pattern, choosing partners primarily based on acceptance needs. They typically chose partners based on whether there was an opportunity to establish a relationship, even if the interaction partner did not rate them positively. Thus, the need for high self-esteem people to maintain positive self-views and the need for low self-esteem people to garner interpersonal acceptance have implications for the way people in each group choose to interact with others.

Differential Self-Presentation as a Function of Self-Esteem

Self-presentation strategies (Jones and Wortman 1973; Leary and Kowalski 1990) have also been linked to self-esteem in a manner which supports our argument that high self-esteem people are concerned with the self, whereas low self-esteem people are concerned with social relationships. Given the highly positive self-views of people with high self-esteem and the deflated self-views of people with low self-esteem, it is likely that they would differ in the way they present themselves to others. From a sociometer theory perspective (Leary et al. 1995), a person who chronically feels a lack of social acceptance would be predicted to self-present in a positive manner with the hopes of gaining acceptance. However, if a person has high self-esteem and feels comfortably included, he or she may not be as concerned with others' impressions, because inclusion concerns are less pronounced.

Research has confirmed that there exist differences in self-presentation as a function of self-esteem. Astrid Schütz and Dianne Tice (1997) found differences in the positivity of self-views as a function of self-esteem and the public (versus private) nature of self-descriptions. Replicating other findings that use self-report methods, people with high self-esteem mentioned fewer negative aspects about themselves when giving private reports than their low self-esteem counterparts. Furthermore, in private, high self-esteem participants rarely described themselves in altruistic or social terms, whereas people with low self-esteem minimized competency attributes and instead described themselves as social and altruistic (for example, sensitive or emotional).

No significant differences, however, were found between the number of negative aspects mentioned by low and high self-esteem participants when giving public reports. Both groups mentioned fewer negative aspects in public than private. High self-esteem participants qualified negative statements more than did participants with low self-esteem (for example, they used statements such as "as does everyone"). Thus, high self-esteem people do think of themselves in more positive terms, in private, than do low self-esteem people; however, they seem sensitive to self-presentation norms which discourage uniformly positive boasting about oneself. In public they reveal just as many negative items about themselves as do people with low self-esteem. This public modesty may be one reason why researchers fail to find likeability differences as rated by short-term interaction partners between people with low self-esteem and high self-esteem (for example, Vohs and Heatherton 2001, 2003, 2004). One exception is when participants are experiencing a threat to the self.

Examinations of in-group and out-group biases have also revealed differences between those with high versus low self-esteem in self-enhancement strategies consistent with our position in this chapter. Jonathan Brown, Rebecca Collins, and Greg Schmidt (1988) argued that high self-esteem people choose to use direct self-enhancement (that is, biases explicitly about oneself) by displaying own-group favoritism (that is, evaluating their group more favorably than the outgroup). People with low self-esteem did not use direct self-enhancement (that is, they did not display superior positive ratings of their own group). They did however use indirect self-enhancement (that is, biases through other people) by derogating the out-group rather than boosting the in-group.

Confirming these results, a recent meta-analysis demonstrated that high self-esteem people display more in-group bias than do low self-esteem people (Aberson, Healy, and Romero 2000). However, self-esteem and self-enhancement strategies moderated this relationship. High self-esteem people used more direct in-group bias, but the two groups showed comparable bias when using indirect group bias strategies. Furthermore, previous research has also found that low self-esteem people use indirect self-enhancement by basking in the reflected glory of others (which is known as BIRGing), whereas people with high self-esteem emphasize their own abilities and competencies (for example, Aberson 1999; Cialdini, Finch, and De Nicholas 1990; Schütz and Tice 1997; Vohs and Heatherton 2001, 2003, 2004). These results corroborate the idea that low self-esteem people do not use direct self-enhancement strategies (perhaps due to the social risk that accompanies them), but high self-esteem people are not shy about using direct self-enhancement (perhaps due to their need to maintain positive self-views).

Risky Decision Making as a Function of Self-Esteem

Recall that Jeffrey LePine and Linn Van Dyne (1998) found that high self-esteem predicted risky interpersonal behavior, in the form of voice behavior that could potentially disrupt collegial relationships in organizations. In contrast, research shows that low self-esteem people appear to make risky decisions for the self when social inclusion is at stake. Thomas Abernathy, Lisa Massad, and Lisa Romano-Dwyer (1995) reported that, in both longitudinal and cross-sectional research, self-esteem was negatively correlated with smoking behavior among adolescent girls. The researchers measured self-esteem and self-reported smoking behavior in a large group of adolescents from grades six through nine. Girls with low self-esteem during grade six were approximately three times more likely to smoke during this three-year period than were their high self-esteem counterparts. Since self-esteem is notably unstable during adolescent years, the researchers also computed analyses using self-esteem to predict smoking behavior cross-sectionally during any one year. Here again, girls with low self-esteem from grades six through eight were three times more likely to smoke than girls with high self-esteem. Given that the decision to smoke poses severe health risks for the self but may lead to social inclusion, this finding suggests that low self-esteem people may be more likely to take on risks to the self if it has the potential to lead to social inclusion.

Summary of Differential Self-Perceptions as a Function of Self-Esteem

Despite differences between high self-esteem people and low self-esteem people on self-reported attributes, there is no difference in popularity or likeability as a function of self-esteem as rated by others. Thus, it is perceived social inclusion that drives the behavior of low and high self-esteem people. They differ in their perceptions of social inclusion: high self-esteem people believe that they are included in social relationships and will be included in relationships in the future, whereas low self-esteem people are not as sure of their interpersonal-inclusion potential.

Many findings suggest that this difference in felt social inclusion has implications for the way the self is viewed in relation to others, and for interpersonal decisions, particularly in the form of risky interpersonal behavior. High self-esteem people use more downward social comparisons and more frequent voice behavior in organizational situations than do low self-esteem people. Both high and low self-esteem people want to present a positive image of themselves to others; however, high self-esteem people tend to emphasize their personal attributes, whereas low self-esteem people tend to emphasize qualities that strengthen their relationships with others. Examining the consequences of this pattern among high self-esteem people, Roy Baumeister and his colleagues (2003) have argued that people with high self-esteem reap most of the benefits of having high self-esteem, whereas most of the costs of high self-esteem are conferred on the people around them. Other research corroborates this idea and also its converse: the costs of low self-esteem weigh heavily on the self, yet there are some interpersonal benefits of low self-esteem. There is evidence that ego threat differentially influences both self-oriented and interpersonal decisions as a function of self-esteem. Following Roy Baumeister and colleagues (Baumeister et al. 2007; Baumeister, DeWall, and Zhang, chapter 1, this volume), we believe that the learning process that results from experiencing self-conscious emotions plays an important role in this decision making process.

Combined Effects of Ego Threat and Self-Esteem on Interpersonal Decisions

Ego threat differentially affects how people with high and low self-esteem view themselves and others (Heatherton and Vohs 2000; Vohs and Heatherton 2001, 2003, 2004), which in turn influences decision making. Typically, ego threat is induced by providing people with negative feedback about the self. A meta-analysis on ego-threat research confirms that people experience negative emotions after failure feedback and positive emotions after success feedback (Nummenmaa and Niemi 2004). However, interpersonal responses to ego threats differ as a function of self-esteem. A series of studies on the roles of ego threat and self-esteem on behavior suggests that after ego threat people trade off between focusing on the self and on relationships, such that ego threat exacerbates the demonstrated tendencies of high and low self-esteem people. Overall, research shows that high self-esteem people respond to threat by bolstering their self-views at the expense of their interpersonal relations, whereas low self-esteem people emphasize behaviors that lead to interpersonal success at the cost of repairing their damaged self-views (Heatherton and Vohs 2000; Vohs and Heatherton 2001, 2003, 2004).

Effects of Ego Threat on the Self

Much research shows that people with high self-esteem seek to enhance the self following ego threat. High self-esteem people respond to self-threats with increased conviction about their identity (McGregor and Marigold 2003), by persisting on a subsequent task in an attempt to improve performance on the failed task (McFarlin, Baumeister, and Blascovich 1984), and by increasing the positivity of their self-appraisals (Sommer and Baumeister 2002; Dodgson and Wood 1998). Additionally, high self-esteem people make more downward social comparisons after ego threat, which serves to ameliorate the negative effects of the threat on the ego (Vohs and Heatherton 2004).

People who have low self-esteem respond to ego threat differently than do those with high self-esteem. Low self-esteem people respond to ego threat by downgrading their self-appraisals (Sommer and Baumeister 2002; Dodgson and Wood 1998), by overgeneralizing the threat to domains in which the threat was not given (Baldwin and Sinclair 1996), and by focusing on others' superiority by making upward social comparisons (Vohs and Heatherton 2004). These processes further deflate the self-views of low self-esteem people.

Thus, it appears that ego threat exacerbates trait-level tendencies to view the self in a particular way: high self-esteem people take steps to restore their high self-esteem, and low self-esteem people seem to feel worse about the self in more ways than before the threat. In one set of studies, high and low self-esteem people received failure or success feedback on an anagram-solving task purportedly indicative of future university success (Dodgson and Wood 1998). Participants then identified which traits were descriptive of the self. After receiving failure feedback, high self-esteem people showed greater accessibility of positive traits and less accessibility of negative traits (relative to their counterparts who received success feedback). In contrast, negative traits were more accessible among low self-esteem people after they received failure feedback (relative to those who were told they had succeeded). These results demonstrate that high self-esteem people react to failure by emphasizing what is good about themselves, whereas low self-esteem people seem to recruit and endorse negative self-perceptions.

Effects of Ego Threat on Self-Conscious Emotions

When facing ego threat, people experience self-conscious emotions. Self-conscious emotions, such as shame, pride, guilt, and embarrassment, promote positive social functioning (Beer et al. 2003; Tracy and Robins 2004). For example, in one recent study, participants' ability to experience self-conscious emotions predicted socially appropriate regulation of self-disclosure and teasing (Beer et al. 2003). Recent work by Baumeister et al. (2007) advances a theory that explains how the events that trigger emotions come to shape subsequent behavior. In this model, full-blown conscious emotions (such as hatred, pride, shame, and joy) serve as feedback, which prompts people to reflect upon and learn from their previous actions. Furthermore, the experience of self-conscious emotions leaves an affective residue that forms the link from the emotion (as a feedback signal from the situations that brought about the emotions) to the current situation. This affective residue serves as a warning system: it becomes activated automatically when people enter a situation that perceptually resembles the situation which elicited the emotion previously; then, this affective residue guides behavior in the current situation so as to obtain or avoid the emotion that resulted from the previous situation. If the emotion experienced previously was positive, then the affective residue will serve an approach signal; however, in the current context of experiencing ego threat, the emotion will undoubtedly be negative, which will trigger avoidance. Rather than directly driving behavior, the main function of conscious emotions in this model is to enable people to learn from past experiences and, through affective traces, anticipate the possible emotional outcomes that may result from one's current behavioral options. Decisions can then be made to help secure future positive emotional states and prevent negative ones.

A learning process like the one advanced by Roy Baumeister et al. (2007) explains how self-conscious emotions promote positive social functioning. Repeated episodes of ego threat and concomitant negative self-conscious emotions (for example, humiliation) link certain situations to certain adverse feelings. The experience of such emotions may prompt reflection as to why one's behaviors led to, for example, humiliation, and how one's behavior added to that situation. The next time such a situation occurs, the affective warning system will signal that certain behaviors, such as those that may render a person unlikeable, should be avoided.

With respect to the behaviors of low self-esteem people, feeling guilty or embarrassed will likely shape interpersonal behavior (Beer et al. 2003) such that future guilt or embarrassment will be less likely. There is an inverse relationship between self-esteem and reports of embarrassment (Keltner and Buswell 1997) as well as various other self-conscious emotions (Brown and Marshall 2001). Ego threat intensifies this relationship, as low self-esteem people experience stronger self-conscious emotions after threat than do high self-esteem people (Brown and Dutton 1995; Brown and Marshall 2001). Specifically, people with low self-esteem, but not those with high self-esteem, experience a drop in pride and an increase in embarrassment and humiliation after threat (Dutton and Brown 1997).

How do self-conscious emotions shape the behavior of high self-esteem people? Research has revealed differences in the degree to which high self-esteem people, as compared to low self-esteem people, experience self-conscious emotions, particularly after ego threat. Moreover, these differences suggest that ego threat may differentially affect the social success of high and low self-esteem people. High self-esteem people may experience less intense self-conscious emotions following threat than they do without threat. Research shows that self-serving attributions, which are more frequent after threat for high self-esteem people (Campbell and Sedikides 1999), lead to a reduction in the experience of shame (Niedenthal, Tangney, and Gavanski 1994). Self-serving attributions may be part of the process that high self-esteem people use to suppress self-conscious emotions and consequently reaffirm the self (Dodgson and Wood 1998). Instead of self-conscious emotions, high self-esteem people are more likely to experience emotions aimed at the source of the negative feedback (for example, anger or resentment).

Therefore, a focus on recovering the self after threat may block high self-esteem people from experiencing self-conscious emotions, potentially hindering the learning process and the social skills that are built on these emotions (Beer et al. 2003; Tracy and Robins 2004). Conversely, the increase in self-conscious emotions experienced by low self-esteem people after threat suggests that they may make better interpersonal decisions than their nonthreatened counterparts with either low or high self-esteem.

Effects of Ego Threat and Self-Esteem on Decisions

Research suggests that ego threat further affects decisions involving risk as a function of self-esteem. It shows that high self-esteem people risk overconfidence in their own abilities, yet threatened low self-esteem people avoided risk when it could reflect poorly on themselves (that is, when the accuracy of their decision would be baldly exposed). Further data suggest that the negative affect experienced by low self-esteem people after threat may lead them to favor risks to the self (for example, they might risk physical health by having unprotected sex) rather than choose risks that would be potentially damaging to social relationships (for example, the risk of offending the other person by suggesting they use a condom). Also recall that girls with low self-esteem in grade six were 2.5 to 3.5 times more likely to smoke in grades six through nine than their high self-esteem counterparts (Abernathy, Massad, and Romano-Dwyer 1995). These findings point to a consistent pattern in line with the thesis of this chapter: After threat, low self-esteem people are risk averse when the outcome may reflect poorly on them but are willing to accept some risks to avoid damaging interpersonal relationships. Threatened high self-esteem people portray themselves as feeling better than they do, but at the possible expense of their social success. Anticipated future emotions lead low self-esteem people to attempt to prevent rejection, as the possibility of social rejection is hinted at by their affective warning system (Baumeister et al. 2007). In contrast, high self-esteem people aim to avoid future negative self-views and do so in a way that puts them at risk of being liked by others (Vohs and Heatherton 2001, 2003, 2004).

Self-Esteem, Threat, and Self-Oriented Decisions

The highly positive self-views that high self-esteem people summon after ego threat can lead to overconfidence in decision making. In one study, ego threat was induced in participants by suggesting that they may not "have what it takes" and may "choke under pressure" when making a bet on their future performance in a video game (Baumeister, Heatherton, and Tice 1993, 145). When threatened this way, high self-esteem participants made riskier bets than their counterparts who were not threatened, as well as relative to low self-esteem participants who were threatened or not threatened. Riskier bets meant less money was earned by the participant at the end of the game. Thus, it appears that ego threat inflates the self-perceptions of high self-esteem people beyond their actual capabilities, which leads to poorer decisions about their abilities and, consequently, to worse outcomes.

A study exploring anticipated regret supports the idea that threat leads to risk aversion among low self-esteem people. In this study, participants made a series of choices between "sure bets" and bets that were riskier but potentially more lucrative (Josephs et al. 1992). Participants were told that they could win up to one hundred dollars in the study, but that the exact amount would be determined by the average winnings of all participants, so it was in their best interest to attempt to increase this average. Ego threat was induced by informing participants that they would be made aware of the outcome of each choice at the end of the experiment, which served to heighten anticipated regret (Josephs et al. 1992, study 2). In the nonthreat condition, participants were told they would not know the outcome of their individual choices. Compared to high self-esteem participants in both the threat and nonthreat conditions, as well as to low self-esteem participants who did not anticipate knowing their choice outcomes, low self-esteem participants threatened by anticipatory regret made less risky decisions. Knowing that they would have to face the potentially bad outcomes of their choices led low self-esteem people to become risk averse in gain-framed decisions, selecting a certain low payment over a potentially more lucrative but uncertain option.

Taken together, these results suggest that relative to their nonthreatened counterparts, low self-esteem people become risk averse in financial decisions when threatened with the anticipation that the outcome may reflect poorly on the self. Threatened high self-esteem people are more willing to make financially risky bets as compared with nonthreatened high self-esteem people and to low self-esteem people in general. Threatened high self-esteem people compensate for threat by overestimating how good they are and becoming more risk seeking when the outcome has the potential to make them look good. Following Roy Baumeister et al. (2007), these behaviors may result from an attempt to secure future positive emotional states. In contrast, low self-esteem people receive a signal that future hurt is on its way and try to prevent this by making safe choices, whereas high self esteem people aim to regain their positive self-view by choosing potentially risky behaviors that may show to others how good they really are (Vohs and Heatherton 2004).

Implications for Interpersonal Decisions

This research regarding decision making after threat connects to research on decisions concerning the self versus others. The conclusion we draw from this research is that after threat, high self-esteem people prioritize the self at the expense of interpersonal concerns, whereas low self-esteem people may emphasize interpersonal relationships while neglecting their self-evaluations.

For example, high self-esteem participants derogated out-groups after receiving failure feedback on a test, whereas low self-esteem participants chose not to engage in this demeaning behavior (Crocker et al. 1987). In another set of studies, failure feedback was used to induce ego threat in half of the participants, and then participants' behavior was rated by a subsequent interaction partner (Heatherton and Vohs 2000; Vohs and Heatherton 2004). High self-esteem people who had been threatened were perceived as less likeable and as more antagonistic by their partners, compared to their nonthreatened counterparts and to low self-esteem people in both threat and nonthreat conditions. This may be partly due to the high self-esteem people's failure to acquire the social skills that result from experiencing self-conscious emotions. Additional research demonstrated that this effect was also due to a shift toward greater independence and less interdependence among threatened high self-esteem people (Vohs and Heatherton 2001). Low self-esteem people became more interdependent and less independent following threat, and were therefore perceived as more likeable by their partners. These results are consistent with the sociometer theory of self-esteem (Leary et al. 1995). After threat, low self-esteem people make efforts to foster social relationships and restore their low and threatened level of self-esteem through social connection. Conversely, high self-esteem people respond to threat by feeling badly, but not badly enough to warrant a concern over rejection. Not coincidentally, interaction partners responded to members of both groups in a manner opposite to the internal beliefs of those threatened individuals.

Recent research points to another change in the way that high and low self-esteem people perceive social interactions when they are threatened. Lora Park and Jennifer Crocker (2005) used threat and interaction procedures similar to those used by Kathleen Vohs and Todd Heatherton (2001, 2003, 2004). After a ten-minute interaction, partners rated target participants and the targets rated themselves on a number of interpersonal dimensions including likeability. Replicating Vohs and Heatherton's finding, interaction partners reported that ego-threatened high self-esteem targets were less supportive and less likeable than nonthreatened high self-esteem targets as well as low self-esteem targets in both the threat and nonthreat conditions. Notably, self-reports of threatened high self-esteem targets corroborated their partners' reports. Threatened high self-esteem targets reported liking the interaction partners less and felt less supportive of their partners during the interaction as compared to nonthreatened high self-esteem people as well as to low self-esteem people in general. Paradoxically, high self-esteem people seek to enhance the self after ego threat, yet they seem able to admit to being poor relationship partners.

There are multiple reasons why ego threat may make more extreme the behavior of high self-esteem people: Threat serves to make the independent aspects of the self especially salient (Vohs and Heatherton 2001). Whether it is because they experience less intense self-conscious emotions (Dutton and Brown 1997) or because rejection does not appear imminent (Leary et al. 1995), threatened high self-esteem people may decide that cultivating relationships is not important for repairing their damaged views of the self. Instead, their focus is on more purely self-enhancing pursuits. In this way, high self-esteem people, at some level, choose to sacrifice their interpersonal success in order to make themselves feel better after threat.

The Interpersonal Success of Threatened Low Self-Esteem People

The self-worth of people with low self-esteem appears to be closely tied to interpersonal relationships (Brockner and Lloyd 1986; Leary et al.

1995). When threatened, low self-esteem people perceive a lack of social acceptance, which then leads to concern with fostering social relationships and interpersonal success. In fact, some research suggests that low self-esteem people's concern for social connection after threat may lead to decisions which jeopardize their personal safety.

Ego threat, and the self-conscious emotions it induces, serves to increase the interdependence of low self-esteem people's self-construals, which mediates the relationship between self-esteem and positive social functioning after threat (Vohs and Heatherton 2001). In other words, threat increases the interdependence of low self-esteem people, which subsequently causes them to seek social acceptance and become more pleasant interaction partners, relative to nonthreatened low self-esteem people as well as to high self-esteem people in general (Heatherton and Vohs, 2000; Vohs and Heatherton, 2003, 2004).

Research on risky decision making has important implications given Vohs and Heatherton's (2001) findings. In two studies, people primed with interdependence were subsequently more likely to take financial risks (for example, to buy lottery tickets) but were less likely to take social risks (for example, to play truth or dare), compared to those primed with independence (Mandel 2003). Interdependence served to make people's social networks particularly salient, which then reminded people when they were making financial decisions of their financial safety net and the potential for embarrassment if they erred in social decisions.

Although the studies by Naomi Mandel (2003) did not examine the effect of self-esteem, these results provide a clue to understanding the effects of threat on low self-esteem people. We know that low self-esteem people are particularly likely to experience emotions such as embarrassment and that these emotions help rather than hinder social interaction (Beer et al. 2003). Moreover, the shift toward interdependence, which accompanies threat among low self-esteem people (Vohs and Heatherton 2001), in conjunction with the heightened experience of self-conscious emotions, may explain why threatened low self-esteem people are especially likely to behave in prosocial ways (for example, taking financial risks, such as sharing lottery winnings, that might hurt them personally but also might help their social group). These emotions need not have their most important effect at the moment they are experienced strongest. Rather, the repeated experience of strong self-conscious emotions may install an early warning system so that only a small hinge of self-conscious emotion suffices to produce the expectation that more of it will come. This expectation may lead low self-esteem people to change their behavior in order to avoid being rejected in the future.

Important research on risky health behaviors corroborates this idea. Low self-esteem people in a negative mood, similar to that induced by ego threat, are more likely to report intentions to engage in sexual intercourse without using a condom than are those who experienced a positive mood induction, as well as compared to high self-esteem people in general (MacDonald and Martineau 2002).

Recall that ego threat causes people to experience negative affect (Nummenmaa and Niemi 2004). Research has also shown that people with low self-esteem are not equipped nor motivated to repair the negative affect which occurs after ego threat (Heimpel et al. 2002) but instead seek to avoid feeling threatened (Vohs and Heatherton 2004; Wood et al. 1994). Two of the reasons participants gave for maintaining their negative moods were feeling overwhelmed with negative thoughts about themselves and feeling that they do not deserve to feel better (Heimpel et al. 2002, study 4).

These patterns mean that the negative affect induced by ego threat among low self-esteem people may have severe consequences for subsequent decisions regarding condom use (MacDonald and Martineau 2002). Research shows that intentions to use condoms positively predict behavior (Fisher, Fisher, and Rye 1995; Halpern-Felsher et al. 2004). Because we also know that ego threat increases interdependence among low self-esteem people (Vohs and Heatherton 2001), it follows that threatened low self-esteem people would seek to increase sexual connection and avoid risking rejection by insisting on condom use. Thus, it appears that threatened low self-esteem people are willing to risk their personal health in order to avoid potentially disrupting social intimacy and the negative emotions that follow from insisting on condom use.

Threat in Interracial Interactions

Studies examining interracial interactions further support the view that low self-esteem people are concerned with their social relationships whereas high self-esteem people are concerned with protecting their self-views, and that these tendencies are exacerbated under conditions of ego threat.

In general, African Americans score higher on self-report measures of self-esteem than do whites (Twenge and Crocker 2002). Nonetheless, some interracial interactions make salient for black people the possibility of social rejection (Shelton and Richeson 2005). Based on sociometer theory (Leary et al. 1995) and other research discussed earlier (Vohs and Heatherton 2001), we would then expect black people to become more likeable in an effort to reduce the likelihood of rejection. Research has confirmed this prediction. In black-white interracial interactions, black people respond to threats of prejudice in prosocial ways (Twenge and Crocker 2002). It is reasonable to consider a situation threatening in which social rejection is expected. Therefore, we view the prosocial response of black people in this study as parallel to the response of low self-esteem people under threat.

Additional investigations of interracial interactions further corroborate this interpretation. Black people enjoyed interacting with a white partner more when they were led to believe that their partner was prejudiced against blacks, which represents a heightened threat condition, relative to when they were led to believe the white partner was not prejudiced, that is, when threat was not as salient (Shelton 2003). Moreover, blacks liked interacting with whites more when they were actually interacting with someone who was trying very hard not to appear prejudiced (Shelton, Richeson, and Salvatore 2005).

Following from the logic of the sociometer theory, interracial interactions that involve the threat of prejudice may lower the perceived social acceptance of black people, thereby reducing their previously high self-esteem. Therefore, black people respond to this threat in the same way that low self-esteem people respond to ego threat. The anticipation of negative affect induces a desire for interpersonal acceptance, which appears to drive behaviors and attitudes that foster social relationships with others, including others who may be prejudiced against them but are showing some attempt to curb their behavior. It may be that the white person must show some attempt to appear not prejudiced in the interaction in order for the black person to respond to the threat of prejudice in prosocial ways. Outright discriminatory behavior toward black people may override the prosocial response. Further research should test the nuances of interracial interactions to understand the conditions under which ego threat interacts with self-esteem to produce prosocial attitudes and behavior.

Effects of Threat on Close Relationships

A close relationship, as opposed to the relatively brief encounters that are employed in many studies (Heatherton and Vohs 2000), provides a unique context for threat and self-esteem to affect decisions and behavior. Threats to a longer-term relationship may be understood as a type of threat to self, inasmuch as the self expands to include the relationship over time (Aron, Paris, and Aron 1995). Thus, threats to the relationship should affect people with high and low self-esteem differentially. From other research, we might predict that threat leads low self-esteem people to become better partners after threat, whereas high self-esteem people may come to ignore the relationship and focus on restoring their positive self-view. However, we also expect low self-esteem people to be more vigilant than high self-esteem people with regard to possible rejection (Leary et al. 1995). Therefore when a threat to a long-term relationship occurs, low self-esteem people may perceive the problem to be a larger threat than it actually is and may strategically decide to devalue the relationship and seek acceptance elsewhere. High self-esteem people, already confident in their partner's acceptance, may instead recruit their extremely positive view of the self and reaffirm the relationship in the face of threat.

Research shows that when threatened with rejection from a romantic partner, low self-esteem people (but not those with high self-esteem) felt less accepted by their partners, less close to their partners, and subsequently derogated their partners when given the opportunity to do so (Murray et al. 2002). When low self-esteem people were led to believe a problem existed in their romantic relationships, they read more into problems than was objectively warranted. This research suggests that when under threat, people love their partner like they love themselves. Feelings of rejection were exaggerated among low self-esteem people who were threatened with relationship difficulties. In contrast, high self-esteem people viewed their partners positively after a relationship threat—equally positively as nonthreatened people at any level of self-esteem.

Further research by Sandra Murray et al. (2003) suggests that the negative reactions to threat among low self-esteem people lead to a reduction in relationship satisfaction. People who felt less valued by their partners felt more hurt after day-to-day fluctuations in their partner's behavior (for example, their partner's moodiness). This hurt led to a greater likelihood of responding destructively rather than constructively to the partner's behavior fluctuations. That is, people who felt less valued responded to partners' transgressions with insults or yelling instead of forgiveness or a change in their own behavior. After a year, such destructive responses decreased relationship satisfaction.

Taken together, studies of close relationships suggest that low self-esteem people may perceive minor transgressions as especially threatening. This then leads them to respond destructively to a partner's behavior, causing a long-term reduction in relationship satisfaction. Again, a small hint of what may be to come is enough to set off behavior that, in this situation, is not beneficial for interpersonal relationships. It is possible that the spiral of reduced relationship satisfaction could be circumvented by helping low self-esteem people view themselves in a more positive—and more accurate—way. Indeed, research shows that highlighting strengths of the self or the failures in the partner reduces the felt insecurity of low self-esteem people by putting their partners "within psychological reach" (Murray et al. 2005, 327).

Summary of the Combined Effects of Ego Threat and Self-Esteem

Responses to ego threat appear to involve a trade-off between repairing oneself and repairing one's social standing, and the route chosen depends on one's self-esteem. High self-esteem people emphasize the self after threat, as evidenced by inflated perceptions of their own abilities. This leads them to make riskier bets regarding their own future performance. This self-focused perspective among high self-esteem people after threat appears to occur at the expense of their interpersonal success.

Conversely, threatened low self-esteem people avoid risk in domains that may further reflect poorly on their already deflated self-views but seek risk when it may enhance their social connections. People with low self-esteem respond to ego threat by seeking interpersonal closeness, potentially risking their physical health in the process (for example, by forgoing condom use in sexual activity). Part of the social success experienced by low self-esteem people after ego threat is due to a shift toward an interdependent self-concept and the heightened experience of self-conscious emotions. However, rejection sensitivity and misperceptions of their own likeability may undermine these efforts to avoid rejection in close relationships among low self-esteem people.

Conclusion

Based on the theoretical perspectives and empirical findings pertaining to the effects of self-esteem and ego threat on emotions and decision making, we conclude that links among self-esteem, ego threat, and emotion have implications for decision making. In brief, high self-esteem leads people to risk social success and financial gain in favor of boosting their self-evaluations. Low self-esteem leads people to risk themselves and their physical health in order to gain social inclusion. Ego threat intensifies these reactions by inducing negative emotions. Ego threat also intensifies socially adaptive emotions (for example, embarrassment) among low self-esteem people and inhibits them among high self-esteem people, further contributing to the relative other- and self-focus of these two groups, respectively.

Low self-esteem people seek to make choices that will protect (or avoid damaging) their social standing, especially under conditions of threat. Conversely, high self-esteem people already feel socially accepted, so they have little need to focus on interpersonal concerns. Instead, they seek to maintain or enhance their already positive self-views, leading to risky choices that can have social costs.

We have integrated a number of different lines of research to reach these conclusions. To our knowledge, a unified research program examining the effects of all three factors on decision making has yet to emerge. It would be useful for future research to test the effects of self-esteem and threat on risky decisions, as our literature review suggests there are important consequences (for example, condom use). Specifically, it would be interesting from both applied and theoretical perspectives to directly investigate our position that threatened low self-esteem people avoid risk when there is potential for further diminution of their self-views but approach risk when interpersonal gains are at stake; meanwhile, threatened high self-esteem people only approach risk that may improve their self-image but respond indifferently to choices involving interpersonal gain.

We argue that self-esteem differences in self-conscious emotions invoked by ego threat mediate these effects on decision making. However, existing research suggests that shifts in self-construal (that is, independence and interdependence), and not emotion alone, mediates the effects of ego threat and self-esteem on interpersonal success (Vohs and Heatherton 2001). Nonetheless, other research suggests there is a link between self-esteem, ego threat, and self-conscious emotions that is consistent with the sociometer approach. Future research should explicitly test the relationships among self-esteem, ego threat, and self-conscious emotions, as well as their combined effect on decision making.

A particularly intriguing research question is how self-conscious emotions shape the interpersonal decisions of low and high self-esteem people. Experiencing ego threat induces self-conscious emotions, and these emotions may directly affect subsequent behavior. However, focusing on the direct effect of emotions may distract us from the indirect, but perhaps more powerful, effect on behavior that emotions have. Experiencing emotions instigates learning and leaves affective traces which in future situations may give us a hint of expected consequences of given behaviors (Baumeister et al. 2007). In many instances, these expected emotions, rather than the consciously felt emotions, may be what drive much interpersonal decision making: they lead low self-esteem people to become more prosocial, whereas high self-esteem people change their behavior in a way that may help them restore their self-liking.

More broadly, we consider examining the effects of self-esteem on decision making as an important and practical contribution to the literature on this key construct in social psychology. By understanding the effects that self-esteem has on the choices and risks people take in everyday life, researchers in other areas, such as marketing, behavioral economics, and health psychology, may be able to take advantage of our vast knowledge of self-esteem. We are encouraged by the research discussed in this chapter that has made this connection and that the future will bring an even deeper appreciation of the impact of self-esteem and feelings of threat on decision making.

References

Abernathy, Thomas J., Lisa Massad, and Lisa Romano-Dwyer. 1995. "The Relationship Between Smoking and Self-Esteem." *Adolescence* 30(120): 899–907.

Aberson, Christopher L. 1999. "Low Self-Esteem and Ingroup Bias." *Social Behavior and Personality* 27(1): 17–27.

Aberson, Christopher L., Michael Healy, and Victoria Romero. 2000. "Ingroup Bias and Self-Esteem: A Meta-Analysis." *Personality and Social Psychology Review* 4(2): 157–73.

Aron, Arthur, Meg Paris, and Elaine N. Aron. 1995. "Falling in Love: Prospective Studies of Self-Concept Change." *Journal of Personality and Social Psychology* 69(6): 1102–12.

Baldwin, Mark W., and Lisa Sinclair. 1996. "Self-Esteem and 'If . . . Then' Contingencies of Interpersonal Acceptance." *Journal of Personality and Social Psychology* 71(6): 1130–41.

Battistich, Victor, Daniel Solomon, and Kevin Delucchi. 1993. "Interaction Processes and Student Outcomes in Cooperative Learning Groups." *Elementary School Journal* 94(1): 19–32.

Baumeister, Roy F., Todd F. Heatherton, and Dianne M. Tice. 1993. "When Ego Threats Lead to Self-Regulation Failure: Negative Consequences of High Self-Esteem." *Journal of Personality and Social Psychology* 64(1): 141–56.

Baumeister, Roy F., Jennifer D. Campbell, Joachim I. Krueger, and Kathleen D. Vohs. 2003. "Does High Self-Esteem Cause Better Performance, Interpersonal Success, Happiness, or Healthier Lifestyles?" *Psychological Science in the Public Interest* 4(1): 1–44.

Baumeister, Roy F., Kathleen D. Vohs, C. Nathan DeWall, and Liqing Zhang. 2007. "How Emotion Shapes Behavior: Feedback, Anticipation, and Reflection, Rather Than Direct Causation." *Personality and Social Psychology Review* 11(2): 167–203.

Beer, Jennifer S., Erin A. Heerey, Dacher Keltner, Donatella Scabini, and Robert T. Knight. 2003. "The Regulatory Function of Self-Conscious Emotion: Insights from Patients with Orbitofrontal Damage." *Journal of Personality and Social Psychology* 85(4): 594–604.

Bishop, Julia A., and Heidi M. Inderbitzen. 1995. "Peer Acceptance and Friendship: An Investigation of Their Relation to Self-Esteem." *Adolescence* 15(4): 476–89.

Brockner, Joel, and Kathy Lloyd. 1986. "Self-Esteem and Likeability: Separating Fact from Fantasy." *Journal of Research in Personality* 20(4): 496–508.

Brown, Jonathan D. 1993. "Motivational Conflict and the Self: The Double-Bind of Low Self-Esteem." In *Self-Esteem: The Puzzle of Low Self-Regard*, edited by Roy F. Baumeister. New York: Plenum Press.

Brown, Jonathan D., and Keith A. Dutton. 1995. "The Thrill of Victory, the Complexity of Defeat: Self-Esteem and People's Emotional Reactions to Success and Failure." *Journal of Personality and Social Psychology* 68(4): 712–22.

Brown, Jonathan D., and Margaret A. Marshall. 2001. "Self-Esteem and Emotion: Some Thoughts About Feelings." *Personality and Social Psychology Bulletin* 27(5): 575–84.

Brown, Jonathan D., Rebecca L. Collins, and Greg W. Schmidt. 1988. "Self-Esteem and Direct Versus Indirect Forms of Self-Enhancement." *Journal of Personality and Social Psychology* 55(3): 445–53.

Buhrmester, Duane, Wyndol Furman, Mitchell T. Wittenberg, and Harry T. Reis. 1988. "Five Domains of Interpersonal Competence in Peer Relationships." *Journal of Personality and Social Psychology* 55(6): 991–1008.

Campbell, Jennifer D., and Beverly Fehr. 1990. "Self-Esteem and Perceptions of Conveyed Impressions: Is Negative Affectivity Associated with Greater Realism?" *Journal of Personality and Social Psychology* 58(1): 122–33.

Campbell, W. Keith, and Constantine Sedikides. 1999. "Self-Threat Magnifies the Self-Serving Bias: A Meta-Analytic Integration." *Review of General Psychology* 3(1): 23–43.

Chemers, Martin M., Carl B. Watson, and Stephen T. May. 2000. "Dispositional Affect and Leadership Effectiveness: A Comparison of Self-Esteem, Optimism, and Efficacy." *Personality and Social Psychology Bulletin* 26(3): 267–77.

Cialdini, Robert B., John F. Finch, and Maralou E. De Nicholas. 1990. "Strategic Self-Presentation: The Indirect Route." In *Psychology of Tactical Communication,* edited by Michael J. Cody and Margaret L. McLaughlin. Clevedon, England: Multilingual Matters, Ltd.

Coopersmith, Stanley. 1967. *The Antecedents of Self-Esteem.* San Francisco, Calif.: W. H. Freeman and Company.

Crocker, Jennifer, Leigh L. Thompson, Kathleen M. McGraw, and Cindy Ingerman. 1987. "Downward Comparison, Prejudice, and Evaluations of Others: Effects of Self-Esteem and Threat." *Journal of Personality and Social Psychology* 52(5): 907–16.

Diener, Ed, Brian Wolsic, and Frank Fujita. 1995. "Physical Attractiveness and Subjective Well-Being." *Journal of Personality and Social Psychology* 69(1): 120–9.

Dodgson, Philip G., and Joanne V. Wood. 1998. "Self-Esteem and the Cognitive Accessibility of Strengths and Weaknesses After Failure." *Journal of Personality and Social Psychology* 75(1): 178–97.

Dutton, Keith A., and Jonathan D. Brown. 1997. "Global Self-Esteem and Specific Self-Views as Determinants of People's Reactions to Success and Failure." *Journal of Personality and Social Psychology* 73(1): 139–48.

Fisher, William A., Jeffrey D. Fisher, and Barbara J. Rye. 1995. "Understanding and Promoting AIDS-Preventive Behavior: Insights from the Theory of Reasoned Action." *Health Psychology* 14(3): 255–64.

Gabriel, Marsha T., Joseph W. Critelli, and Juliana S. Ee. 1994. "Narcissistic Illusions in Self-Evaluations of Intelligence and Attractiveness." *Journal of Personality* 62(1): 143–55.

Halpern-Felsher, Bonnie L., Rhonda Y. Kropp, Cherrie B. Boyer, Jeanne M. Tschann, and Jonathan M. Ellen. 2004. "Adolescents' Self-Efficacy to Communicate About Sex: Its Role in Condom Attitudes, Commitment and Use." *Adolescence* 39(155): 443–56.

Heatherton, Todd F., and Kathleen D. Vohs. 2000. "Interpersonal Evaluations Following Threats to Self: Role of Self-Esteem." *Journal of Personality and Social Psychology* 78(4): 725–36.

Heimpel, Sara A., Joanne V. Wood, Margaret A. Marshall, and Jonathan D. Brown. 2002. "Do People with Low Self-Esteem Really Want to Feel Better? Self-Esteem Differences in Motivation to Repair Negative Moods." *Journal of Personality and Social Psychology* 82(1): 128–47.

Jones, Edward E., and Camille Wortman. 1973. *Ingratiation: An Attributional Approach.* Morristown, N.J.: General Learning Press.

Josephs, Robert A., Richard P. Larrick, Claude M. Steele, and Richard E. Nisbett. 1992. "Protecting the Self from the Negative Consequences of Risky Decisions." *Journal of Personality and Social Psychology* 62(1): 26–37.

Jovanovic, Jasna, Richard M. Lerner, and Jacqueline V. Lerner. 1989. "Objective and Subjective Attractiveness and Early Adolescent Adjustment." *Journal of Adolescence* 12(2): 225–9.

Keltner, Dacher, and Brenda N. Buswell. 1997. "Embarrassment: Its Distinct Form and Appeasement Functions." *Psychological Bulletin* 122(3): 250–70.

Leary, Mark R., and Robin M. Kowalski. 1990. "Impression Management: A Literature Review and Two-Component Model." *Psychological Bulletin* 107(1): 34–47.

Leary, Mark R., Ellen S. Tambor, Sonja K. Terdal, and Deborah L. Downs. 1995. "Self-Esteem as an Interpersonal Monitor: The Sociometer Hypothesis." *Journal of Personality and Social Psychology* 68(3): 518–30.

LePine, Jeffrey A., and Linn Van Dyne. 1998. "Predicting Voice Behavior in Work Groups." *Journal of Applied Psychology* 83(6): 853–68.

MacDonald, Tara K., and Alanna M. Martineau. 2002. "Self-Esteem, Mood, and Intentions to Use Condoms: When Does Low Self-Esteem Lead to Risky Health Behaviors?" *Journal of Experimental Social Psychology* 38(3): 299–306.

Mandel, Naomi. 2003. "Shifting Selves and Decision Making: The Effects of Self-Construal Priming on Consumer Risk-Taking." *Journal of Consumer Research* 30(1): 30–40.

McFarlin, Dean B., Roy F. Baumeister, and Jim Blascovich. 1984. "On Knowing When to Quit: Task Failure, Self-Esteem, Advice, and Nonproductive Persistence." *Journal of Personality* 52(2): 138–55.

McGregor, Ian, and Denise C. Marigold. 2003. "Defensive Zeal and the Uncertain Self: What Makes You So Sure?" *Journal of Personality and Social Psychology* 85(5): 838–52.

Murray, Sandra L., John G. Holmes, and Dale W. Griffin. 2000. "Self-Esteem and the Quest For Felt Security: How Perceived Regard Regulates Attachment Processes." *Journal of Personality and Social Psychology* 78(3): 478–98.

Murray, Sandra L., Gina M. Bellavia, Paul Rose, and Dale W. Griffin. 2003. "Once Hurt, Twice Hurtful: How Perceived Regard Regulates Daily Marital Interactions." *Journal of Personality and Social Psychology* 84(1): 126–47.

Murray, Sandra L., John G. Holmes, Dale W. Griffin, Gina Bellavia, and Paul Rose. 2001. "The Mismeasure of Love: How Self-Doubt Contaminates Relationship Beliefs." *Personality and Social Psychology Bulletin* 27(4): 423–36.

Murray, Sandra L., Paul Rose, Gina M. Bellavia, John G. Holmes, and Anna G. Kusche. 2002. "When Rejection Stings: How Self-Esteem Constrains Relationship-Enhancement Processes." *Journal of Personality and Social Psychology* 83(3): 556–73.

Murray, Sandra L., Paul Rose, John G. Holmes, Jaye Derrick, Eric J. Podchaski, Gina Bellavia, and Dale W. Griffin. 2005. "Putting the Partner Within Reach: A Dyadic Perspective on Felt Security in Close Relationships." *Journal of Personality and Social Psychology* 88(12): 327–47.

Nezlek, John B., Robin M. Kowalski, and Mark R. Leary. 1997. "Personality Moderators of Reactions to Interpersonal Rejection: Depression and Trait Self-Esteem." *Personality and Social Psychology Bulletin* 23(12): 1235–44.

Niedenthal, Paula M., June P. Tangney, and Igor Gavanski. 1994. " 'If Only I Weren't' Versus 'If Only I Hadn't': Distinguishing Shame and Guilt in Counterfactual Thinking." *Journal of Personality and Social Psychology* 67(4): 585–95.

Nummenmaa, Lauri, and Pekka Niemi. 2004. "Inducing Affective States with Success—Failure Manipulations: A Meta-Analysis." *Emotion* 4(2): 207–14.

Park, Lora E., and Jennifer Crocker. 2005. "Interpersonal Consequences of Seeking Self-Esteem." *Personality and Social Psychology Bulletin* 31(11): 1587–98.

Rosenberg, Morris. 1965. *Society and the Adolescent Self-Image.* Princeton, N.J.: Princeton University Press.

Rudich, Eric A., and Robin R. Vallacher. 1999. "To Belong or to Self-Enhance? Motivational Bases for Choosing Interaction Partners." *Personality and Social Psychology Bulletin* 25(11): 1387–404.

Schütz, Astrid, and Dianne M. Tice. 1997. "Associative and Competitive Indirect Self-Enhancement in Close Relationships Moderated by Trait Self-Esteem." *European Journal of Social Psychology* 27(3): 257–73.

Shelton, J. Nicole. 2003. "Interpersonal Concerns in Social Encounters Between Majority and Minority Group Members." *Group Processes and Intergroup Relations* 6(2): 171–85.

Shelton, J. Nicole, and Jennifer A. Richeson. 2005. "Intergroup Contact and Pluralistic Ignorance." *Journal of Personality and Social Psychology* 88(1): 91–107.

Shelton, J. Nicole, Jennifer A. Richeson, and Jessica Salvatore. 2005. "Ironic Effects of Racial Bias During Interracial Interactions." *Psychological Science* 16(5): 397–402.

Sommer, Kristin L., and Roy F. Baumeister. 2002. "Self-Evaluation, Persistence, and Performance Following Implicit Rejection: The Role of Trait Self-Esteem." *Personality and Social Psychology Bulletin* 28(7): 926–38.

Swann, William B. 1996. *Self-Traps: The Elusive Quest for Higher Self-Esteem.* New York: Freeman.

Tracy, Jessica L., and Richard W. Robins. 2004. "Putting the Self into Self-Conscious Emotions: A Theoretical Model." *Psychological Inquiry* 15(2): 103–25.

Twenge, Jean M., and Jennifer Crocker. 2002. "Race and Self-Esteem: Meta-Analyses Comparing Whites, Blacks, Hispanics, Asians, and American Indians and Comment on Gray-Little and Hafdahl (2000)." *Psychological Bulletin* 128(3): 371–408.

Vohs, Kathleen D., and Todd F. Heatherton. 2001. "Self-Esteem and Threats to Self: Implications for Self-Construals and Interpersonal Perceptions." *Journal of Personality and Social Psychology* 81(6): 1103–18.

———. 2003. "The Effects of Self-Esteem and Ego Threat on Interpersonal Appraisals of Men and Women: A Naturalistic Study." *Personality and Social Psychology Bulletin* 29(11): 1407–20.

———. 2004. "Ego Threats Elicits Different Social Comparison Process Among High and Low Self-Esteem People: Implications for Interpersonal Perceptions." *Social Cognition* 22(1): 168–91.

Wood, Joanne V., Maria Giordano-Beech, Kathryn L. Taylor, John L. Michela, and Valeria Gaus. 1994. "Strategies of Social Comparison Among People with Low Self-Esteem: Self-Protection and Self-Enhancement." *Journal of Personality and Social Psychology* 67(4): 713–31.

· 8 ·

The Functions of Emotion in Decision Making and Decision Avoidance

CHRISTOPHER J. ANDERSON

Decisions have long been thought to suffer from the irrational influence of emotions. Emotions have been portrayed as an illegitimate factor in legal decisions (Dworkin 1977). Greek and Roman philosophers suggested that people would make better decisions if they minimized the emotional aspect of their inner lives. Most of these views portray "pure cognition" (that is, reason) as the primary, normative factor in decision making. Cognition is seen as constructing goals and decisions, and emotion is seen as playing a secondary role, perturbing the processes of reason.

In considering the interplay between decision, action, and emotion, some alternative roles emerge. When considering the question of whether emotions are harmful or helpful to decisions, we tend to make similar assumptions regarding the interplay of emotion and decision. The fundamental assumption is that a decision has primacy in time; the perception of a need for decision is taken as a given, as if it were a property of the environment. That is, when considering the role of the emotions, we often assume implicitly that the need for a decision is perceived first, and then emotions may enter into the decision process at any point after which it has begun. In this view, emotions may perhaps alter the decision from what it might have been had the decision maker avoided emotions during the decision process. In this case, the helpfulness and harmfulness of the emotions would be solely evaluated based on how emotions changed a decision from an emotionless benchmark.

This view of the interplay of emotions and decision, *emotion-mediated decision making*, has some merit, but conceals more than it reveals about emotions and decision making. Emotions have several additional critical roles in the decision process which are unrecognized in the emotion-mediated decision making perspective. A more encompassing view of the role of emotions in decisions, *emotion-constructed decision making*, includes the following roles:

1. Emotions constitute decisions; decisions are not a given but are shaped and created by emotions.
2. Emotions do affect the decision process once it is begun, though it is more effective to consider this as a question of *which* emotions affect the process, and the weight given them, than to attempt to compare emotional to emotionless decision making.
3. Emotions do not necessarily only lead to bad or good decisions, but can also lead to decision avoidance or decision seeking. Emotions influence metadecisions.
4. Emotions are involved in the implementation of decisions; once a decision has (apparently) been made, emotional factors may lead either to stalling or to swiftness in the implementation of the option chosen.
5. Emotions are part of the consequences of the outcomes of decisions, which in turn shapes their role in all phases of future decisions for that individual.

When considering whether emotions are helpful or harmful to decisions, it is necessary to consider all five roles that emotions play in the decision making process. The emotion-constructed decision making perspective is useful for expanding the focus from emotion's mediating role in decision making. Figure 8.1 summarizes the differences between the two perspectives. This chapter elaborates on each role of emotion in order to broaden the basic framework for how we construe the emotion-decision interface. As understanding the failure to decide is particularly relevant when considering emotions and decisions, we will also consider how each role of emotion contributes to decision avoidance.

Emotions Constitute Decisions: An Emotion-Constructed Decision Making Perspective

Scant work in any field of study has addressed the question of how decisions are perceived (Chapman and Niedermayer 2001). When do individuals perceive that they are facing a decision? What prompts that

Figure 8.1   Emotion-Mediated Decision Making Contrasted with Emotion-Constructed Decision Making

Emotion-Mediated Decision Making

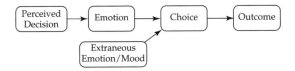

Emotion-Constructed Decision Making

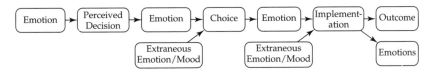

Source: Author's compilation.

event, and how are the perceptions shaped? Traditionally, the field has taken decisions for granted as something that the environment provides opportunities for. This is seen in the tendency for researchers to explicitly provide opportunities for decisions to research participants and to structure the options for them. In doing so, researchers do not ask questions regarding where decisions come from in a participant's ecology, nor what role emotions may play in choosing among decisions and in structuring those decisions.

To illustrate the ambiguities this approach creates, consider the original work documenting the status quo bias, a potentially general bias that humans have towards making decisions which preserve their current state of affairs (Samuelson and Zeckhauser 1988). William Samuelson and Richard Zeckhauser conducted a field study of faculty-retirement allocations and found that faculty did not make many changes to their portfolios, even when new faculty members of the same age selected substantially different allocations than the existing faculty's status quo, suggesting that market changes favored new allocations. However, presuming the status quo bias is intended to concern decision making per se, we cannot tell from this study whether or how the data reflect on any actual decision process. Perhaps many of the established faculty never considered making any decision about their retirement portfolio. This example of status quo bias might then indicate a general preference for status quo options, as the researchers argued, or it might only show that in general we do not perceive there to be a need for a decision unless something happens to bring a decision about.

In general we know little scientifically about why people consider making decisions at all. However, several hypotheses can help us generate a theory of decision perception, and thus help focus some attention on this area.

Within the context of emotion-constructed decision making, emotions are the primary shaper of decisions. Without emotions, and perhaps without negative emotions in particular, individuals would not make many decisions at all. A finding consistent with this perspective is that as adults age they exhibit more decision avoidance, which coincides with a trend in the reduction of experienced negative affect (Kennedy and Mather, chapter 11, this volume).

Researchers are currently formulating a theory of decision perception (Anderson 2007b; Huang and Anderson 2007). The foundation of this theory is the recognition that there are many more possible decisions to be made than the decision maker has resources to address. Resources for decision making (and for regulatory activity in general) are limited and can be depleted by behavioral control; the act of elevating a matter to a decision can deplete the resource further, leading to decision fatigue (Vohs et al. 2005). Making a choice, even when one prefers to make a choice, limits one's ability to perform other self-regulation tasks (Vohs et al. 2005; Baumeister et al. 1998).

Kenneth Arrow (1974) separates decision areas into *active, monitored,* and *passive,* providing a useful initial framework for how people deal with the abundance of possible decisions while considering their resources to make them. As for how potential decisions are sorted into these categories, it is unlikely that this sorting is a matter of explicit decision making; instead, the decision is implicitly made as resources are depleted on the items that appear to be most urgent to the decision maker's priorities. These priorities, however, are not consciously recognized, but rather they refer to the underlying priorities that drive behavior and are frequently not conscious. Supporting the nonconscious nature of many true priorities, decisions made using automatic thinking appear to be more effective (Dijksterhuis 2004).

Another framework which can be used to gain insight into the origin of decisions is the problem recognition framework, which suggests that decisions may originate via a perception of a discrepancy between the actual and ideal state of affairs (Workman and Studak 2006). Again, this begs the question of the origin of ideal states or actively monitored areas. These priorities, which arguably drive attention and action for particular decisions, are always fundamentally emotional, as they embody value judgments as well as concerns about minimizing vulnerability or striving to obtain a more valued experience. Thus, instead of constituting an interfering, perturbing force in decisions, emotions are a necessary component of noticing, prioritizing, and construing a decision in the first place.

Interestingly, this suggests that affect-minimizing forms of cognition, such as pure reason (which is often promoted as a normative standard), could interfere with optimal decision making. Reason could interfere, for example, by leading one to misperceive a decision or to undervalue the importance of a particular decision, relegating it to a passive or monitored area as opposed to the active decision area. It is not entirely resolved whether cognition generally plays a perturbing role and leads to less satisfying outcomes by prioritizing less important decisions. As noted, most work in this area takes the decision itself for granted and directly studies the perception and prioritization of decisions. Some recent research is consistent with the idea that emotions play a necessary and beneficial role in decision making which can be undermined by conscious reasoning. Researchers have found that normal individuals who deliberately attempt to make less emotional decisions fare worse (Carmon, Wertenbroch, and Zeelenberg 2003). Participants were given a choice of prizes after a study and were instructed either to make an immediate "gut" decision, or to pause and calculatedly consider the pros and cons of their prize options rationally. The individuals who made the "cognitive" decision enjoyed their prize item less later, and thus tended to regret their choice compared to those who made "gut" decisions.

Emotions Affect Decisions

The classical role considered for emotions in decision making is as a force that mediates between a perceived decision situation and a final decision. Decisions imply a cleavage, or a breaking off of many alternative possible futures, in favor of one route into our fortune. It is natural that a process that frequently involves choosing among such weighty, irreversible factors regarding how to make the best of our limited freedom would involve emotion. It has not always been felt that the emotion influence is deserved, or helpful, however.

The first factor one should recognize is that emotions mediate between a decision situation and the decision to be made more narrowly than many believe it to. Often, a hypothetical emotion-mediated decision is compared to a hypothetical emotionless decision. However, the emotionless comparison point is now recognized as a fallacy. Persons who cannot connect emotions to planning are impaired, such that their decisions do not form a good normative standard against which to judge decision making. Individuals who have difficulty connecting their emotions with decisions make very poor decisions in some contexts (Bechara et al. 1997; Shiv et al. 2005). Monkeys who have damage to the amygdala, an emotion center, become passive regarding important choices. They display a lack of preference for their caretaker as well as a lack of avoidance of snakes and potentially hostile primates (Bauman et al. 2004; Kalin, Shelton, and Davidson 2004). Individuals with normally functioning emotion systems can attempt to suppress their emotions, but this often impairs their thinking in multiple ways (Butler and Gross 2004; Richards, Butler, and Gross 2003). One more potential emotionless benchmark comes from philosophy. One may attempt a Stoicism in which one redefines priorities such that many emotions are circumvented, but there is scant evidence that this philosophical approach eliminates emotions; more plausibly, it alters the conditions under which they occur.

Furthermore, it is likely that without emotions, we would feel no need for decisions. Given the contention that emotions are the primary constituent of the perception of a decision, any plausibly emotion-free situation that involves a decision is likely to be neglected. If no emotionally oriented value motivates the decision, it will simply appear as if a decision does not need to be made. Emotions focus on areas of strategic importance to individuals (Higgins, Grant, and Shah 1999). Without emotions to alert us to situations and opportunities that affect these areas of strategic importance, all possible decisions would appear equal, and we would lack a principle, or any reason, on which to elevate a matter to an active decision area.

So, the mediating influence of emotions is somewhat narrower than it is often conceived: eliminating emotions from decisions seems to be a practical impossibility and would likely be ill-advised were it possible. However, emotions also have a broader role: specific emotions have different effects, and emotions not only mediate in the choice among alternatives, but also mediate in the frequent decision to make no decision at all (Anderson 2003; Luce, Bettman, and Payne 2001).

Nico Frijda (1986) influentially argued that emotions are states of "action readiness." Recent research has challenged this view. Emotions can also interfere with states of action readiness or can preclude a state of action readiness. The rational-emotional model, which incorporates a large amount of current research on decision avoidance, hypothesizes that emotions of anticipated regret and the unpleasantness of difficult decisions can lead an individual to adopt an aversive stance toward a decision and ultimately to avoid making the decision via one of several avoidant routes (Anderson 2003). Also consistent with this general concept of emotions precluding action readiness, Van Hook and Higgins (1988) reported that emotions produced by conflict between goals produce confusion and ultimately indecision. Another emotional route to indecision can come through perceiving chronic discrepancies between the ideal self and the self that one is becoming (Higgins, Vookles, and Tykocinski 1992). Instead of being states of action readiness, emotions are better conceived as reactions to human vulnerability (Nussbaum 2004). Nussbaum suggests that humans are inherently vulnerable because they are mortal, have limited control, and are social creatures, and that without these vulnerabilities, emotions would serve no purpose. To illustrate that point, consider the subject of Simone de Beauvoir's *All Men Are Mortal* (1946): a human who is immortal. The concept of an immortal person, considered by a stark realist with a grasp of human psychology, supports the connection between vulnerability, emotions, and what it means to be human. The immortal human is not recognizably human; it does not experience ordinary human emotions and instead tends to experience something like metaemotions. This is a sense that his endless existence lacks meaning without the vulnerabilities that cause emotions, which make life interesting and exciting when we succeed and fearsome when we fail. For this being, particulars are irrelevant, and sixty years is as meaningless a unit of time as sixty seconds.

Vulnerabilities are necessary for emotions; philosophers who advocate minimizing emotions, such as the Stoics, suggest that we minimize them by not valuing that which we cannot control—in effect, not valuing those things which cause vulnerability and reflect aspects of our vulnerability. Emotions can produce either action readiness or action inhibition, depending on the perceived vulnerability that the emotion is responding to, the perceived options, and the perceived efficacy of the individual at implementing those options. Emotions often precede inaction, so while it is tempting to think of emotions as action prompts, we do so at the risk of forgetting they are also action stops. Herbert Simon's (1967) conceptualization of emotion also supports this broader role; he thought of emotions as signals that something is wrong in our self-regulatory system. Thus while they could prompt new actions, they can also serve as signals to stop what we are doing or to consider alternatives to the actions we were planning. The recent renewed attention to the phenomenon of decision avoidance reflects this broader role of emotions during the decision process.

One aspect of the renewed recent attention to decision avoidance that has persistently presented a concern is the conceptualization of what constitutes an occurrence of decision avoidance (Anderson 2007a). In presenting the rational-emotional model of decision avoidance, I conservatively limited my treatment of forms or types of decision avoidance to those that had been actively researched in the literature. In attempting to apply this theory to naturally occurring behaviors, however, ambiguities become prevalent. Many situations seem to overlap multiple forms of decision avoidance, whereas some seem to fit types that have not been described. The most persistent concern is that many behaviors that appear on the surface to be decision avoidance actually might never have been decisions at all. (Again, the need to understand why and when a person perceives themselves to be facing a decision is salient in this case.) There are several forms that decision avoidance can take, and emotions may play a different role in each form.

One of the major difficulties in adapting decision avoidance to a framework is its apparent negative definition. Decision avoidance could be occurring at any given time that person is "doing nothing." Thus, what counts as decision avoidance? Is a person who is ill-informed about alternatives, or who avoids learning about possible alternatives, decision avoidant? How can we judge something that is nothing? If we were to define harmful decision avoidance by a utilitarianist standard, as any occasion on which a person fails to recognize or take an active decision that could improve their own well-being, the well-being of other humans, of other living things, or of the environment that sustains these beings, most people would make bad nondecisions all of the time. There are so many choices people could make to advance their well-being and the common well-being that even people who consciously have those goals do not always take the actions to which they aspire. It seems that very few people live up to their potential to do as well for themselves and others as they could. However, defining decision avoidance in terms of *all* decisions that are not made would broaden the scope beyond the domain of psychology, since we would not be considering anything that an individual is processing or doing.

As it is possible to define decision avoidance in a more positive way, we focus attention on these for the purpose of investigating the psychology of decision avoidance. Nonetheless, most broad decision avoidance would include the fact that people do not recognize important, valuable decisions they could make to benefit themselves and others in the first place. This ties back to the important point about the role of emotions in perceiving decisions. One way in which emotions can fail as guides to decision making is that they can focus individuals on too narrow a set of priorities. Emotions tend to be present bound; values for outcomes occurring far in the future are discounted at a hyperbolic rate (for discussions of this and other relationships between time, outcomes, values, and decisions, see Loewenstein, Read, and Baumeister 2003). Many decisions that can improve a person's well-being far in the future will not be made or even considered because the stakes will seem much lower than for more current, but actually less trivial, matters. Likewise, from a utilitarian perspective, which is a moral point of view, emotions are too narrow in that they are relatively egocentric. Humans are almost exclusively egocentric until about age four, when a theory of mind develops. A theory of mind diminishes, but does not undo, our fundamental concern with our self and our own personal circumstances. Emotions are related to this priority and are more concerned, for most people, with the vulnerability of the self than with other party. This may seem natural and understandable; however, when evaluating decisions from a moral utilitarian perspective, this fact about emotions will impoverish decisions, in that decisions that could enrich the general well-being more greatly will be considered (if at all) after decisions that can enrich the self's well-being to a lesser extent. While these points are important, and are worth further scrutiny, we focus on aspects of decision avoidance that can be identified in a more positive fashion and are thus amenable to traditional psychological investigation.

The initial definition of decision avoidance identified it closely with four empirically observed phenomena: status quo bias, omission bias, inaction inertia, and choice deferral. This definition compared it with related, but in practice separated, concepts of procrastination, unconflicted adherence, and defensive avoidance (Anderson 2003). The definition of decision avoidance needs sharpening that can be best obtained through classification which is not driven solely by reported phenomena. Too many behaviors, judging strictly from the observables, might be characterized as decision avoidance, and the definition places more emphasis on the commonalities between forms of decision avoidance. A proposal that sufficiently specifies the important differences between forms of decision avoidance is needed. In the process, we may also identify forms of decision avoidance for which there is no literature.

There are a number of dimensions on which we need to classify examples of decision avoidance in order to facilitate evaluation of it. It is assumed that the aim of classification is a completed decision-related behavior (or set of behaviors) which may reflect avoidance of decision.

The factors of classification considered here are divided into three factors: one factor pertains to the internal processes of the decision maker, and two factors relate to the nature of the output behavior. The internal processes that divide forms of decision avoidance are the awareness of alternatives and the intention to make a decision. The external factors are the alternatives that are actually available to the decision maker (apart from their perception of alternatives or lack of alternatives), and the overt route by which the decision avoidance occurs (that is, whether it is a passive or active behavior).[1]

Factors for Identifying Forms
of Decision Avoidance

A basic issue in trying to construct categories of decision avoidance concerns whether the individual acknowledges the presence of viable options, and therefore acknowledges a decision process in which to potentially engage. The presence of alternatives is a basic condition of scholarly definitions of a decision. However, there has been little research on how people perceive alternatives and delimit areas of decision in which to find alternatives. There has been some research on perceptions of decision showing both similarities and differences between lay and scholarly conceptions of what constitutes a decision (Chapman and Niedermayer 2001).

Alternatives: Awareness of a Decision

In my original analysis of decision avoidance, I posited as a first principle that organisms tend to conserve energy when they are not aware of options that could meet a need or desire, and I suggested caution in interpreting inactive behaviors as decision avoidance for this reason.

Questioning the normative status of decision avoidance brings to light a major ambiguity that this principle does not adequately handle: when an outside observer can identify options present that, in their perception, can fulfill the goals ascribed to the decision maker, can one argue that decision avoidance is occurring even though the decision maker acknowledges no options?

This possibility has to be left open because, otherwise, some instances of harmful decision avoidance will be misclassified as normal, adequate behaviors. However, there is no specific normative standard for how actively an individual should pursue awareness of options. One might suggest that it should depend on basic cost-benefit factors such as the importance of the goal and the difficulty of obtaining information about alternatives. Therefore, while decision avoidance in the absence of acknowledged options is different, it still may be justifiably called avoidance and evaluated as normatively inadequate decision making if options did in fact exist. Inaction without acknowledged options may still be "irrational" if the importance of the goal, ease of obtaining alternatives, and presence of unacknowledged options combine in such a way that the decision maker should have identified the options and made a decision. When a decision maker fails to act and it is unjustifiable to cite the lack of options, we may term this *neglect of options.*

Acknowledged options are the default in most decision making studies, which tend to explicitly present alternatives and do not ask participants to search for or generate alternatives as they often may have to in their own decision making ecology.

In any case, the decision maker's perception of alternatives or the lack of alternatives may be accurate or inaccurate, which has implications for the normative evaluation, and will be included in the analysis.

Intention: Decision Avoidant or Decision Seeking

Intentions regarding decisions constitute the individual's attitude toward making a decision: whether they are actively interested in making a decision or whether they would prefer to not make a decision. For instance, procrastination also might be plausibly considered a type of decision avoidance if we consider intentions to be a factor, because one possesses an intention to choose but fails to pursue it. This seems fundamentally different than the case in which a decision is not made but the individual did not intend to address the decision unless forced.

Route: Passive Versus Active Avoidance

Decision avoidance can be obtained without any overt behavior on the part of the decision maker. Failure or refusal to do anything represents the passive pole of the route by which decision avoidance occurs. However, decision avoidance need not be inactive and passive. One can also be decision avoidant through active means; this can happen by deliberately arranging matters so that the status quo will stay in place, or by deliberately seeking a deferral of the decision. While the concept of indecisiveness generally brings to mind passivity and inaction, we must remember that actions can be decision avoidant as well when they do not take advantage of alternatives.

Types of Decision Avoidance

With these factors for classification, we can identify a number of different types of decision avoidance. The processes behind some of these types have traditionally been studied separate from decision making or not studied at all.

For purposes of this classification, I will consider the following factors: awareness of alternatives, intention, and route. Although they may be best thought of as continua, I treat them as binary here in order to simplify the discussion. Refer to figures 8.2 (for forms of unawareness of alternatives) and 8.3 (for forms of awareness of alternatives) to follow the classification factors and their connection to the resulting decision labels.

Figure 8.2   Forms of Decision Avoidance Subsumed Within "Unaware of Alternatives"

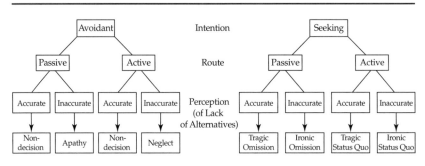

Source: Author's compilation.

Type 1: Unaware (of Alternatives), Avoidant Intention, and Passive

If the decision maker is passively doing nothing, is intending to do nothing, and is not aware of alternatives, this may reflect several things. This may be a reasonable response to the perceived lack of alternatives. It is more likely, however, that the decision maker is apathetic. No alternatives may be present because the decision maker remained passive and did not seek alternatives.

Thus, the accuracy of the perception of alternatives is critical to the evaluation; if no alternatives are present, it is impossible to negatively evaluate the decision because a true decision is not present (that is, *nondecision*). This applies in all cases in which no true alternatives were present. If, however, the decision maker is inaccurate in their perception of no options, this form of decision avoidance can be labeled *apathy*, because the individual does not know there were options, and is not actively seeking options.

Type 2: Unaware, Avoidant Intention, and Active

This case is somewhat paradoxical because it is hard to fathom an active route to decision avoidance when the decision maker is unaware of alternatives. Since the intention to avoid matches the lack of awareness of alternatives, we can come to one of two conclusions about behavior in this category: If the perception of no alternatives is accurate, then there are no identifiable alternatives to act upon; this is a nondecision. If the perception of no alternatives is inaccurate, the "activeness" may represent what can be labeled *willful neglect* of the alternatives. For exam-

Figure 8.3   Forms of Decision Avoidance Subsumed Within "Aware of Alternatives"

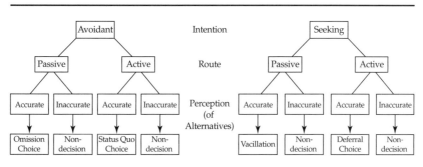

Source: Author's compilation.

ple, an individual may take deliberate actions that inhibit awareness of alternatives, such as self-distraction or self-escape.

Type 3: Unaware, Seeking Intention, and Passive

The cases in which the decision maker intends to act on an alternative but remains unaware of any alternatives also seem confusing initially. They can best be understood as "ironic" because the perceived lack of alternatives and resulting mismatch between intention and decision does not reflect the preferences of the decision maker. If the perception of having no alternatives is inaccurate, passive decision avoidance by someone who is decision seeking and unaware of alternatives is labeled *ironic omission.* It is called this because the individual may have made a decision to do nothing, believing this was the only option.

However, in the case of an individual with a preference to make a legitimate decision, it is more likely than in other categories that the perceived lack of alternatives is accurate, such that we can call an omission choice in this category a *tragic omission,* because the individual wished to take a more active decision but had no options. (Similar to the other cases of having no true alternatives, the tragic omission and status quo cases also count as nondecisions.)

Type 4: Unaware, Seeking Intention, and Active

As above, this also represents either a true lack of alternatives, and thus is labeled a *tragic status quo choice;* alternatively, it represents an *ironic status quo choice,* in which the status quo seems to be the only option but is not.

Type 5: Aware, Avoidant Intention, and Passive

If the awareness of alternatives is accurate, this reflects a deliberate choice to do nothing, and it is classified as an *omission selection.*

Type 6: Aware, Avoidant Intention, and Active

If the awareness of alternatives is accurate, this reflects a deliberate choice to take action that results in no change, and it is thus labeled a *status quo selection.*

Type 7: Aware, Seeking Intention, and Passive

In this case, one engages in decision avoidance in spite of an awareness of alternatives and an intention to act on an alternative. It is therefore classified as an omission, but instead of being deliberate, it reflects a difficulty in committing to the choice. This is often observed as *vacillation,* which may also be thought of as hesitation or implicit procrastination.

Type 8: Aware, Seeking Intention, and Active

This case is similar to the immediately preceding category; however, instead of omission, an action leads to decision avoidance, counter to intentions and awareness of alternatives. This is best reflected as a *choice deferral,* or explicit, deliberate procrastination in committing to a decision.

Emotions Affect Decision Implementation

The stage between making a choice and implementing it is nearly universally neglected within the area of judgment and decision making. Having a clear preference for one option and taking actions to commit to that option are generally treated as the same thing. However, we could profitably draw a distinction between indicating a preference for or intention to make a certain choice, and a person actually making a choice. In the human ecology, there is also often a period of time between those two events, lending further credence to the need to make such a distinction.

Distinctions between the preference to do something (that is, intention) and actions are partly within the purview of the procrastination literature (Ferrari, Johnson, and McCown 1995). This literature is often not considered in conjunction with the judgment and decision making literature (Konig and Kleinmann 2004). There is a small literature on decisional procrastination (Milgram and Tenne 2000, Orellana-Damacela, Tindale, and Suarez-Balcazar 2000), which refers to putting off a decision that one intends to make. However, we are concerned here with procrastination in general; decisional procrastination is only particularly relevant if the decision being analyzed is a decision about whether or not to make a decision. The procrastination literature cited above includes a host of predictors that are emotional or have close links to emotion: neuroticism, self-discrepancies, learned helplessness, anxiety, depression, fear of failure, low self-esteem, and steeper time discounting.

Procrastination is by no means the only manner in which the distinction between a decision and its implementation is relevant to the discussion of the function of emotions in the decision sequence. It just happens to be the one type of effect that has a literature. Procrastination may be conceived of as one pole of a single factor pertaining to decision implementation: the length of delay between determination of a preference and implementation. An emphasis that does not revolve around dysfunction (such as that which positive psychology provides) might lead to an interest in what factors lead to short delays between determination of a choice and its implementation. Also of interest is the potential phenomenon of decision switching, which would be related to vacillation but involves a more explicit original commitment that is altered before implementation. When do people implement a decision different than what they originally indicated they would prefer? Do emotional factors play a role in decision switching, as the emotion-constructed decision making perspective might presume they would? To the best of my knowledge, no literature considers cases of decision switching, which is not so much an oversight of the field as a natural result of the dominant methodologies, which equate determining a choice with implementation.

Emotion Is a Prominent Outcome of Decision; Shaping Its Role in Other Phases

Finally, emotions are obviously a part of the outcomes that one experiences as a result of making a particular decision. Recent research has paid more attention to this role, with distinctions being made between anticipated and experienced regret (Zeelenberg and Beattie 1997); however, substantially more research has focused on the former. Within the emotion-constructed decision making perspective, however, emotions are prominent throughout the entire decision making process, and much of decision making can be more generally characterized as self-regulation in respect to emotional goals and values.

Because emotions are thus going to be one of the most prominent outcomes of a decision, it should also be the case that experienced emotions alter the role that emotions play in subsequent decisions. When experienced emotions are discrepant with predicted emotions, not only should future predictions be updated to reflect this, thus altering future choices, but priorities for different decision areas (active, monitored, and passive areas) may change also. Thus, when individuals notice a number of outcomes wherein they ultimately enjoy experiential purchases more than material ones (Van Boven 2005), they should elevate decisions about experiences to an active area and relegate decisions about which material purchases to make to a lower rung (perhaps monitored or passive areas). However, as much research demonstrates that individuals systematically mispredict the occurrence, or at least the intensity and duration of emotions, implying that learning from or about emotional outcomes frequently does not work (Wilson and Gilbert 2003). However, this misprediction may itself play a functional role which helps maximize the useful role of emotions and minimize their wasteful role (Anderson 2005).

Conclusion

The emotion-constituted decision making perspective suggests several novel, and hopefully stimulating, hypotheses about the roles of emotion in choice. It also suggests that the question of whether emotions help or hurt decisions is misleading in the sense that emotions are a necessary component of decision making; they cannot altogether be done away with without either eliminating decision making entirely or depriving it extensively. Emotions are necessary for decision making, and from that point they can both help or harm it. However, without emotions at some point in the chain, there would be no decision of which to speak. The questions we ought to be asking, according to this new framework, are which emotions are helpful or harmful, and in which contexts they play that role. This framework also suggests that in evaluating the emotions, we need to consider how they structure the perception of decisions to be made at the outset and how they can influence both toward action and inhibition.

Notes

1. Another factor one might consider is the frequency of avoidance, and whether it is an acute occurrence, a chronic recurrence, or is in between.

Chronic decision avoidance seems likely to include precipitating factors that are not part of more episodic, acute avoidance.

References

Anderson, Christopher J. 2003. "The Psychology of Doing Nothing: Forms of Decision Avoidance Result from Reason and Emotion." *Psychological Bulletin* 129(1): 139–67.

———. 2005. "Alternative Perspectives on Omission Bias." *Behavioral and Brain Sciences* 28(4): 544.

———. 2007a. "Developmental Shifts in the Misprediction of Regret: Evidence for a Functional Role of Inaccurate Affective Forecasting." Manuscript in preparation, Temple University.

———. 2007b. "The Source of Decisions." Manuscript in preparation, Temple University.

Arrow, Kenneth J. 1974. *The Limits of Organization.* New York: W. W. Norton and Company.

Bauman, M. D., P. Lavanex, W. A. Mason, J. P. Capitanio, and D. G. Amaral. 2004. "The Development of Social Behavior Following Neonatal Amygdala Lesions in Rhesus Monkeys." *Journal of Cognitive Neuroscience* 16: 1388–411.

Baumeister, Roy F., Ellen Bratslavsky, Mark Muraven, and Dianne M. Tice. 1998. "Ego Depletion: Is the Active Self a Limited Resource?" *Journal of Personality and Social Psychology* 74(5): 1252–65.

Bechara, Antoine, Hanna Damasio, Daniel Tranel, and Antonio R. Damasio. 1997. "Deciding Advantageously Before Knowing the Advantageous Strategy." *Science* 275(5304): 1293–5.

Butler, Emily A., and James J. Gross. 2004. "Hiding Feelings in Social Contexts: Out of Sight Is Not Out of Mind." In *Regulation of Emotion,* edited by Pierre Phillipot and Robert S. Feldman. Mahwah, N.J.: Lawrence Erlbaum Associates, Inc.

Carmon, Ziv, Klaus Wertenbroch, and Marcel Zeelenberg. 2003. "Option Attachment: When Choosing Feels Like Losing." *Journal of Consumer Research* 30(1): 15–29.

Chapman, G., and L. Niedermayer. 2001. "What Counts as a Decision? Predictors of Perceived Decision Making." *Psychonomic Bulletin and Review* 8: 615–21.

de Beauvoir, Simone. 1946. *All Men Are Mortal.* New York: W. W. Norton and Company.

Dijksterhuis, Ap. 2004. "Think Different: The Merits of Unconscious Thought in Preference Development and Decision Making." *Journal of Personality and Social Psychology* 87(5): 568–98.

Dworkin, Ronald. 1977. *Taking Rights Seriously.* Cambridge: Cambridge University Press.

Ferrari, Joseph R., Judith L. Johnson, and William G. McCown. 1995. *Procrastination and Task Avoidance: Theory, Research, and Treatment.* New York: Plenum Press.

Frijda, Nico H. 1986. *The Emotions.* Cambridge: Cambridge University Press.

Higgins, E. Tory, Heidi Grant, and James Shah. 1999. "Self-Regulation and Quality of Life: Emotional and Non-Emotional Life Experiences." In *Well-Being: The Foundations of Hedonic Psychology*, edited by Daniel Kahneman, Ed Diener, and Norbert Schwarz. New York: Russell Sage Foundation.

Higgins, E. Tory, J. Vookles, O. Tykocinski. 1992. "Self and Health: How 'Patterns' of Self-Beliefs Predict Types of Emotional and Physical Problems." *Social Cognition* 10: 125–50.

Huang, P., and Christopher J. Anderson. 2007. "Agendas and Non-Agendas of Organizations." Working paper. Philadelphia, Penn.: Temple University.

Kalin, Ned H., Steven E. Shelton, and Richard J. Davidson. 2004. "The Role of the Central Nucleus of the Amygdala in Mediating Fear and Anxiety in the Primate." *Journal of Neuroscience* 24: 5506–15.

Konig, C. J., and M. Kleinmann. 2004. "Business Before Pleasure: No Strategy for Procrastinators?" *Personality and Individual Differences* 37: 1045–57.

Loewenstein, George, Daniel Read, and Roy F. Baumeister. 2003. *Time and Decision: Economic and Psychological Perspectives on Intertemporal Choice*. New York: Russell Sage Foundation.

Luce, Mary Frances, James R. Bettman, and John W. Payne. 2001. "Tradeoff Difficulty: Determinants and Consequences for Consumer Decisions." *Monographs of the Journal of Consumer Research* 1.

Milgram, Norman, and Rachel Tenne. 2000. "Personality Correlates of Decisional Task Avoidant Procrastination." *European Journal of Personality* 14(2): 141–56.

Muraven, Mark, and Roy F. Baumeister. 2000. "Self-Regulation and Depletion of Limited Resources: Does Self-Control Resemble a Muscle?" *Psychological Bulletin* 126(2): 247–59.

Nussbaum, Martha C. 2004. *Hiding from Humanity: Disgust, Shame, and the Law*. Princeton, N.J.: Princeton University Press.

Orellana-Damacela, Lucia E., R. Scott Tindale, and Yolanda Suarez-Balcazar. 2000. "Decisional and Behavioral Procrastination: How They Relate to Self-Discrepancies." *Journal of Social Behavior and Personality* 15: 225–38.

Richards, Jane M., Emily A. Butler, and James J. Gross. 2003. "Emotion Regulation in Romantic Relationships: The Cognitive Consequences of Concealing Feelings." *Journal of Social and Personal Relationships* 20(5): 599–620.

Samuelson, William, and Richard Zeckhauser. 1988. "Status Quo Bias in Decision Making." *Journal of Risk and Uncertainty* 1(1): 7–59.

Shiv, Baba, George Loewenstein, Antoine Bechara, Hanna Damasio, and Antonio R. Damasio. 2005. "Investment Behavior and the Negative Side of Emotion." *Psychological Science* 16(6): 435–9.

Simon, Herbert A. 1967. "Motivational and Emotional Controls of Cognition." *Psychological Review* 74(1): 29–39.

Van Boven, Leaf. 2005. "Experientialism, Materialism, and the Pursuit of Happiness." *Review of General Psychology* 9(2): 132–42.

Van Hook, Elizabeth, and E. Tory Higgins. 1988. "Self-Related Problems Beyond the Self-Concept: The Motivational Consequences of Discrepant Self-Guides." *Journal of Personality and Social Psychology* 55(4): 625–33.

Vohs, Kathleen D., Roy F. Baumeister, J. M. Twenge, B. J. Schmeichel, and Dianne M. Tice. 2005. "Decision Fatigue Exhausts Self-Regulatory Resources." Manuscript under review.

Wilson, T. D., and D. T. Gilbert. 2003. "Affective Forecasting." In *Advances in Experimental Social Psychology,* edited by Mark P. Zanna. New York: Elsevier.

Workman, Jane E., and Cathryn M. Studak. 2006. "Fashion Consumers and Problem Recognition Style." *International Journal of Consumer Studies* 30(1): 75–84.

Zeelenberg, Marcel, and Jane Beattie. 1997. "Consequences of Regret Aversion 2: Additional Evidence for Effects of Feedback on Decision Making." *Organizational Behavior and Human Decision Processes* 72(1): 63–78.

· 9 ·

Emotion Regulation and Impulse Control: People Succumb to Their Impulses In Order to Feel Better

MATTHEW T. GAILLIOT AND DIANNE M. TICE

ONE WAY in which emotions can affect decisions is by making people think and behave irrationally. In this view, emotion is the direct opposite of reason, causing people to make all sorts of bad decisions. For example, when people are jealous, they may commit crimes of passion, and when they are angry, they express road rage (Loewenstein 1996). Hence, in this view, emotion may lead directly to maladaptive decision making.

Another view is that emotions are beneficial to decision making. In this view, people make better, more adaptive decisions because of their emotions. For example, after losing one's money while gambling, a person may feel sad or upset and choose to quit gambling as a result (Damasio 1994). Thus, emotions may sometimes cause people to behave more rationally.

Though emotions can influence decision making directly (for example, fear might make a person decide to run away from danger), they might also influence decision making indirectly (see also Baumeister, DeWall, and Zhang, chapter 1, this volume; Andrade and Cohen, chapter 2, this volume). For example, efforts to change one's mood may influence decision making, and thus emotion regulation, rather than emotions, might sometimes affect decisions (see also Rawn et al., chapter 7, this volume). Considering research on self-regulation, goal pursuit, and impulse control, evidence shows that people sometimes make decisions which undermine their long-term goals in an effort to make themselves feel better in the short term. In other words, people sometimes give priority to regulating their emotions and feeling better in the short term rather than pursuing their long term goals.

The Importance and Difficulty of Impulse Control

The ability to control one's impulses and delay gratification in the pursuit of long-term goals is a vital capacity. To succeed, people must often exert self-control. For example, to succeed academically, one must study and refrain from partying. To maintain a healthy marriage, spouses must refrain from yelling at each other and must instead treat each other kindly. To avoid breaking the law or being incarcerated, one must resist speeding and must obey the speed limit, and one must resist aggressing against others—even idiots—and instead must keep one's temper in check. Likewise, a variety of evidence demonstrates numerous benefits experienced by those who capably exert self-control and control their impulses. Compared to people less able to exert self-control, people who are good at self-control experience greater interpersonal popularity, healthier relationships, perform better at school, cope better with stress, and maintain better mental health (Finkel and Campbell 2001; Mischel, Shoda, and Peake 1988; Shoda, Mischel, and Peake 1990). They more capably avoid such self-indulgent behaviors as overspending, overeating, drinking too much alcohol, and abusing drugs (Kahan, Polivy, and Herman 2003; Muraven, Collins, and Neinhaus 2002; Tangney, Baumeister, and Boone 2004; Vohs and Faber 2004; Vohs and Heatherton 2000). They also more effectively resist impulses to aggress, break the law, and engage in inappropriate or harmful sexual behaviors (DeWall et al. forthcoming; Gailliot and Baumeister 2007; Gottfredson and Hirschi 1990; Pratt and Cullen 2000). Thus the ability to control one's impulses is highly adaptive and beneficial.

Emotional Distress and Failures in Impulse Control

Despite the importance of impulse control, people oftentimes fail to control their impulses (Baumeister, Heatherton, and Tice 1994). Failures in dieting, smoking cessation, sexual restraint, money management, and alcohol and substance abuse are relatively frequent. If impulse control is so important, why are failures in impulse control so common? One reason is that people's goals are often in conflict. In particular, short-term goals often conflict with long-term goals. A compulsive shopper may strongly desire to purchase a new outfit, and such a short-term goal may very well provide temporary enjoyment. Yet the compulsive shopper may be in debt and cannot afford to purchase the outfit, and so his or her long-term goals require resisting such a purchase. In this instance, the short-term goal (that is, purchasing the outfit) conflicts directly with the long-term goal (that is, saving money and getting out of debt). To achieve long-term goals, one must forgo immediate gratification and deny oneself the pleasure obtained via satisfying short-term goals. Impulse control might therefore fail sometimes because people focus on the present to satisfy their short-term goals, thereby failing to achieve their long-term goals.

Emotional distress seems to be a prominent factor in impulse control which causes short-term goals to take precedence over long-term goals. When people are distressed emotionally, they oftentimes focus on the present and disregard their long-term plans. A person who is upset wants to feel better immediately, and the future seems less important to them. Thus, emotional distress leads to failures at delaying gratification (Mischel, Coates, and Raskoff 1968; Schwartz and Pollack 1977; Fry 1975).

Indeed, a variety of evidence is consistent with the idea that failures in impulse control are caused by attempts to regulate one's mood. Impulse control often fails during times of emotional distress. For instance, people are more likely to break their diets when they are emotionally distressed than when they are not (for example, Logue 1993; Greeno and Wing 1994; Heatherton and Polivy 1992). Emotional distress also has been linked with failures in smoking cessation (Ashton and Stepney 1982; Brownell et al. 1986; Schacter et al. 1977). People are also much more likely to fail at restraining themselves from drinking alcohol when they are in a negative mood than when they are in a positive mood (Hull, Young, and Jouriles 1986; Pickens et al. 1985). Gamblers and compulsive shoppers show a similar pattern of behavior, such that they are more likely to fail at controlling their gambling and shopping when emotionally distressed (O'Guinn and Faber 1987; Peck 1986). Emotional distress also leads to aggressive behavior (Berkowitz 1989). For social and other reasons, people must refrain from acting aggressively; yet when they are emotionally upset, people appear more likely to fail at controlling their aggressive impulses.

Thus a wide body of evidence links emotional distress with poor impulse control, because people make decisions that undermine their long-term goals when they are in a negative mood. Negative mood states make it less likely that people will successfully delay gratification. When emotionally distressed, people are more likely overeat, smoke, drink, gamble, overspend, and behave aggressively.

Although the mechanism by which emotional distress undermines impulse control is unknown, it is plausible that changes in glucose levels might play an important role. Specifically, if emotional distress is coupled with self-regulatory attempts to control the distress, then glucose might decrease. This happens because self-regulation consumes a relatively large amount of glucose and can deplete glucose in the bloodstream faster than it can be replenished (Gailliot et al. 2007). The reduced availability of glucose might then undermine impulse control later on.

Impulse Control and Emotion Regulation

For the most part, people want to be in a good mood. Thus, when in a bad mood, they oftentimes attempt to feel better by regulating or changing their mood. One common strategy for feeling better is self-indulgence, such as overeating, smoking, drinking alcohol, or simply lounging around. Such self-indulgence often conflicts with one's long-term goals, such as trying to diet, quit smoking or drinking, or maintain self-discipline (Baumeister, Heatherton, and Tice 1994). Nonetheless, people seem to readily break such long-term goals in hopes of feeling better immediately.

Bad moods seem to undermine impulse control, and many kinds of self-control failures happen when people are in bad moods (Baumeister, Heatherton, and Tice 1994). There are a number of different explanations as to why bad moods should undermine self-regulation. For instance, it is plausible that when in a bad mood, people might become self-destructive and seek to punish themselves. They might intentionally violate their long-term goals because they want to suffer when they are feeling bad. Alternatively, it is possible that negative mood states might simply impair good judgment and self-control. When they feel bad, people cannot choose wisely and can no longer control themselves. Or, perhaps being in a bad mood dampens motivation. When feeling bad, people no longer care to improve themselves or pursue meaningful long-term goals. Finally, emotion regulation may lead to decisions that ultimately interfere with long-term goals. A series of studies by Dianne Tice, Elaine Bratslavsky, and Roy Baumeister (2001) focus on this last explanation for why impulse control fails when people feel poorly. Three studies explicitly tested the idea that emotion regulation takes precedence over impulse control. When people feel bad, they give in to their impulses if they believe that it will make them feel better.

Emotion Regulation and Mood Freezing

One way of testing whether a behavior is an emotion-regulation strategy is to eliminate the possibility of a change in emotion and see if the behavior still occurs. If a behavior occurred primarily to change a mood or emotion state, then the behavior should be eliminated when the emotion state cannot change. Gloria Manucia, Donald Baumann, and Robert Cialdini (1984) developed a mood-freezing procedure to test whether a given behavior (in this case, helping behavior) was an emotion-regulation strategy or whether the behavior occurred for other reasons. The researchers reasoned that if a person's mood was frozen and not able to be changed, then the person would not engage in emotion-regulation strategies. Behaviors that occurred when people thought their moods were changeable, but not when they thought their moods were frozen, could therefore be attributable to emotion regulation. In their study, they convinced some participants that their mood was frozen by giving them a "mood-freezing pill," and then they checked to see if the helping behavior still occurred. To examine the effects of emotion regulation, one can compare the behavior of participants who take a "mood-freezing pill" to the behavior of those who do not take the pill. When people no longer believe that they can change their moods, they would be expected to stop engaging in behaviors that improve their moods. The researchers found that people helped when they felt bad and believed that their moods were changeable, but they did not help when they felt bad and believed that their moods were frozen. This demonstrated that emotion regulation mediated the link between distress and helping, because distressed people only helped if they believed that their moods could be improved by helping.

Tice, Bratslavsky, and Baumeister (2001) adopted Manucia, Baumann, and Cialdini's (1984) concept of mood freezing as a test of whether emotion regulation mediates the link between bad mood and loss of impulse control. Specifically, Tice, Bratslavsky, and Baumeister examined whether emotional distress would cause people to eat unhealthy foods, procrastinate, and fail to delay gratification, and whether emotionally distressed people would engage in these impulsive behaviors only when they believed that their moods could change. If people indulged their impulses when distressed and when their moods were changeable, but not when they were not distressed or when their believed that their moods were frozen, then the impulsive behavior can be attributed to attempts to improve mood. This would suggest that emotion regulation, rather than negative emotion per se, led to impulsive decision making.

Experiment 1: Eating Restraint

The first study conducted by Tice, Bratslavsky, and Baumeister (2001) examined eating restraint. The purpose of the study was to determine whether people eat unhealthy foods in an attempt to make themselves feel better. To test this hypothesis, the researchers first manipulated mood such that participants were placed in either a happy or a distressed mood. After this manipulation, some participants were led to believe that eating does not change mood. Participants were then given the opportunity to eat unhealthy snack foods. Prior research has shown that emotional distress causes people to overeat. Therefore, participants who were distressed should have eaten more food than those who were happy. However, if distress causes people to eat because they eat in order to alleviate their negative mood, then distressed participants should only have eaten more when they believed that eating would change their mood. Since eating supposedly would not have improved their mood, they should not have eaten for the sake of emotion regulation.

In the experiment, participants first read stories intended to alter their moods. Participants assigned to the emotionally distressed condition read about an automobile accident in which a driver was in a hurry, ran a red light, and caused an accident. This accident caused a child to be killed. This story is fairly upsetting to most people, and likewise, participants who read the story reported afterwards that they were especially sad. Participants in the happy condition read a similar story with a much more pleasant outcome. Rather than reading about the death of child, they read about a protagonist saving a child's life. This story had been used previously to improve mood (Wenzlaff, Wegner, and Roper 1988), and indeed, participants rated themselves as being relatively happy after reading it. To increase the emotional impact of the stories, participants read the story two times and imagined that they were the protagonist. They were then asked to dwell on their emotions and to write an essay about how they felt.

After reading the stories, participants were then given the opportunity to indulge themselves by eating some tasty foods. This segment of the study was presented as being a separate study from the first segment to make sure that participants would not suspect that the story they read had been intended to influence their eating behavior. Participants were given three kinds of snack foods to eat. They were asked to try each of the foods and to rate them on various dimensions. The amount of food that participants ate was the final dependent measure. Most people try to refrain from eating large quantities of unhealthy foods, and indeed, participants indicated later that they had hoped to avoid eating such foods. However, the foods were rated as tasty and enjoyable. Thus, eating more food can be seen as greater self-indulgence.

Before they were allowed to eat, participants in the mood-freeze condition received instructions intended to make them believe that they could not change their moods. Specifically, they were told that scientific evidence showed that eating does not make people feel better. Whatever mood they were in at the present moment was the mood they were likely to stay in throughout the experiment. Participants in the changeable mood condition, however, received no such instructions. Hence, similar to pilot participants who had been asked about their beliefs about mood and eating, they should have believed that eating was an effective means of changing one's mood.

The results were consistent with the idea that people eat to escape a bad mood and to feel better. In the changeable-mood condition, participants who had read the sad story ate significantly more food than participants who had read the happy story. Thus, emotional distress increased the amount of food that participants ate.

In the mood-freeze condition, however, participants who read the sad story did not eat any more food than did those who read the happy story (and in fact, they actually ate less). Thus, participants who thought that their moods were frozen and could not be changed by eating did not eat more food when they were sad. In other words, they did not seem to use eating as a strategy to improve their mood.

In summary, participants in the changeable-mood condition showed the typical pattern of self-indulgence when they were distressed, eating more food than those in a happy mood. However, participants in a sad mood did not eat more food when they thought that eating would not change their mood. Presumably, participants in a sad mood and the changeable-mood condition ate more because they thought that eating would make them feel better. For the participants in the mood-freeze condition, eating was no longer a viable strategy to improve their moods and so they did not eat more food in an attempt to feel better.

These results suggest that during times of emotional distress, people place more importance on emotion regulation than impulse control. When distressed, people want to feel better. In the hopes of feeling better, they abandon their long-term goals, such as losing weight and staying healthy. When eating no longer carries the promise of improving one's mood, however, people no longer eat to feel better.

Experiment 2: Delaying Gratification

Though the first study showed that emotion regulation takes precedence over impulse control, it was necessary to demonstrate that this occurs in domains other than eating. Hence, a second study examined whether people would fail to delay gratification in order to improve their mood. To do so, Tice, Bratslavsky, and Baumeister (2001) used a procedure to put participants in bad mood and again led some participants to believe that their moods were frozen and could not be changed. Participants then played a "commons-dilemma game" (borrowed from Knapp and Clark 1991). For this game, participants had to harvest fish on the computer for money. If they harvested the fish immediately, they would receive less money, but if they delayed gratification and harvested the fish later, they would receive much more money. If people give in to their impulses to feel better, then distressed participants should harvest the fish immediately to feel better—but only when they believed that their moods could be changed.

Another aim of the second study was to examine individual differences in the belief that people can change their moods. Some people believe that they can successfully change the way they feel and presumably attempt to change the way they feel, whereas other people believe so to a lesser extent and probably do not attempt to change their moods. If people give in to their impulses to feel better, then it would be expected that only those who believe that they can change their moods would do so.

More specifically, upon arriving at the experiment, participants completed the negative mood regulation scale (NMR), a measure of the belief that one's mood can be regulated (Catanzaro and Mearns 1990). Higher scores on the NMR indicate that the participant believes to a greater extent that his or her mood can be regulated. Next, all participants read the sad story used in the first study, and then they thought and wrote about their feelings. Participants later indicated how they felt, and they were indeed sad.

Participants then were led to believe that their mood either was or was not frozen. They were told that the next part of the study was intended to investigate the relationship between aromatherapy and problem solving skills. In actuality, this was only a cover story so that participants would not realize that the procedure was related to the manipulation of mood. Participants then sat in front of a lit, scented candle and were asked to sit with their eyes closed while thinking about the sad story they had just read.

Participants in the mood-freeze condition were told that aromatherapy temporarily freezes mood. A person's current emotional state during aromatherapy will become frozen and be resistant to change afterwards. Participants in the changeable-mood condition received no instructions about aromatherapy and mood. Thus, these participants should not have believed that their moods were frozen by the aromatherapy.

Last, participants completed the resource-dilemma game of harvesting fish, which served as the dependent measure of delaying gratification. For this game, participants were instructed to role-play catching fish from a pool and were paid one cent for each fish that they caught (and could earn up to ten dollars in total). During this game, the fish replenished themselves at a natural rate. One could catch all of the fish immediately and reap all of the rewards immediately. Or, one could fish more slowly and catch more fish but at a slower rate. Thus the long-term strategy would have been to fish patiently and slowly, thereby accumulating many fish. The short-term, impulsive strategy would have been to catch all of the fish immediately and deplete the pool's reserves. The long-term strategy would thus have allowed participants to ultimately catch more fish and earn more money. Hence, harvesting all the fish immediately indicated that a participant failed to delay gratification by giving in to his or her immediate impulses.

The results of the study were consistent with the idea that people give in to their impulses to feel better. Specifically, among participants scoring high on the NMR (that is, those who believed that they could change their mood), those who believed that their moods were frozen by the aromatherapy more successfully delayed gratification than those whose moods were not frozen. They earned more money during the game and left more fish in the pool at its end. Thus, for people who believe that they can change their moods, it appears that rewarding oneself immediately is one strategy for escaping a bad mood. When feeling distressed, these individuals rewarded themselves immediately by harvesting the fish immediately, but they did this only when they believed that their moods could be changed.

Among participants scoring low on the NMR (that is, those who believed that they could not change their mood), the mood-freezing manipulation did not appear to influence the tendency to delay gratification. This too is consistent with the idea that people give in to their impulses to feel better. These individuals do not believe that their behavior can alter their moods, and so they do not engage in behaviors aimed at altering their moods. Thus, whether their moods were changeable or frozen did not influence how they harvested the fish.

Experiment 3: Procrastination

The third study conducted by Tice, Bratslavsky, and Baumeister (2001) examined procrastination as an impulse-control measure. When people procrastinate, they give in to their immediate desires to avoid a difficult or challenging task, and thus they fail to control their impulses. Indeed, procrastination is desirable and enjoyable in the short term, as one engages in pleasurable activities instead of challenging tasks. For instance, a student might put off studying for a test to enjoy being with friends at the beach and mall. Yet procrastination is counterproductive in the long term, impairing task performance and causing greater emotional distress and physical illness later on (Tice and Baumeister 1997). The procrastinating student performs more poorly on tests and experiences greater anxiety around the time of the test. If emotion regulation takes precedence over impulse control, however, people might procrastinate in order to experience its short-term benefits of feeling better immediately and forgo larger, long-term rewards.

To test this hypothesis, Tice, Bratslavsky, and Baumeister (2001) manipulated mood such that participants were in either a good or bad mood. As in the second study, participants then completed the aromatherapy manipulation and were told that their moods were either frozen or changeable.

Participants then were given the opportunity to prepare for an important upcoming test which was said to be diagnostic of intelligence and future success. Participants could choose to prepare for the test by studying or to procrastinate by playing with puzzles and games or reading magazines.

If emotional distress causes poor impulse control, then participants in a sad mood should have procrastinated more (that is, they would study less) than participants in a happy mood. If people procrastinate in order to improve their moods, then only participants in a sad mood who believed that their moods could have been changed should have procrastinated more. That is, these participants would use procrastination as a strategy to improve their mood. If procrastination does not offer the promise of improving one's mood, then sad participants should not have procrastinated.

As a further test of this rationale, Tice, Bratslavsky, and Baumeister (2001) also manipulated the appeal of the games and puzzles that could be used to procrastinate. If people procrastinate to improve their moods, then they should choose to procrastinate by engaging in exciting and pleasurable activities and not those that are dull and unpleasant. To test this, researchers presented some participants with fun puzzles and games and others with dull puzzles and games. The prediction was that sad participants would choose to procrastinate only when the alternative activities were appealing, because these activities would have been more likely to improve their moods.

The results of the study were consistent with the hypothesis that emotion regulation takes precedence over impulse control, and that emotion regulation mediates the relationship between distress and procrastination. When participants had fun distractors, they spent a relatively large amount of time playing with the distractors when they were in a bad mood versus when they were in a good mood. This effect, however, occurred only among participants who believed that their moods were changeable and not among those who believed that their moods were frozen. Those who were in a bad mood, thought that their moods were changeable, and had fun distractors played with the distractors (that is, procrastinated) for the most amount of time compared to the other participants. Among participants who were given boring distractors, however, there were no differences in the amount of time spent procrastinating as a function of participants' mood and whether they believed that their mood was frozen or changeable. These results indicate that procrastination was used as a means of emotion regulation for those who had fun alternatives and thought their mood was changeable.

Conclusion

A variety of evidence shows that people are more likely to give in to their impulses when they are emotionally distressed. Tice, Bratslavsky, and Baumeister (2001) conducted three studies to determine whether emotionally distressed people make impulsive decisions in hopes of improving their mood. The first study showed that people eat unhealthy foods when they are in a bad mood, but they only do this when eating holds a promise of improving mood. A second study showed that people succumb to immediate temptations if doing so might help them feel better emotionally. Participants who were in a sad mood and thought that their mood was frozen successfully delayed gratification in a simulated fishing game. When they thought that their mood could not be changed, participants did not seek immediate gratification. The last study showed that people put off doing work and procrastinate if procrastination might improve mood. Participants in a sad mood chose to play with fun distractors (but not with boring distractors) rather than study if they thought that such procrastination could have changed their mood. If they thought that procrastination could not have changed their mood, then they were able to successfully resist the temptation to procrastinate.

In summary, these three studies conducted by Tice, Bratslavsky, and Baumeister (2001) provide converging evidence that emotion regulation often takes precedence over impulse control. Considerable research has shown a connection between negative moods and loss of impulse control, but these three studies suggest that, at least in some cases, emotion regulation mediates this relationship.

These studies also suggest that emotion and decision making may be linked by an indirect as well as direct relationships. In addition to examining the effects of specific emotions on decision making, it is also useful to examine the role that emotion regulation, rather than specific emotions per se, plays in decision making. Emotion regulation can take priority over long-term goals in some decision making contexts, particularly impulse-control contexts. When people are trying to escape from bad moods, they sometimes make decisions that undermine their long-term goals.

References

Ashton, Heather, and Ray Stepney. 1982. *Smoking: Psychology and Pharmacology.* London: Tavistock.

Baumeister, Roy F., Todd F. Heatherton, and Dianne M. Tice. 1994. *Losing Control: How and Why People Fail at Self-Regulation.* San Diego, Calif.: Academic Press.

Berkowitz, Leonard 1989. "Frustration-Aggression Hypothesis: Examination and Reformulation." *Psychological Bulletin* 106(1): 59–73.

Brownell, Kelly D., G. Alan Marlatt, Edward Lichtenstein, and G. Terence Wilson. 1986. "Understanding and Preventing Relapse." *American Psychologist* 41(7): 765–82.

Catanzaro, Salvatore J., and Jack Mearns. 1990. "Measuring Generalized Expectancies for Negative Mood Regulation: Initial Scale Development and Implications." *Journal of Personality Assessment* 54(3/4): 546–63.

Damasio, Antonio R. 1994. *Descartes' Error: Emotion, Reason, and the Human Brain.* New York: Grosset/Putnam.

DeWall, C. Nathan, Matthew T. Gailliot, Tyler Stillman, and Roy F. Baumeister. Forthcoming. *Low Self-Control Causes Aggressive Behavior.*

Finkel, Eli J., and William K. Campbell. 2001. "Self-Control and Accommodation in Close Relationships: An Interdependence Analysis." *Journal of Personality and Social Psychology* 81(2): 263–77.

Fry, P. S. 1975. "Affect and Resistance to Temptation." *Developmental Psychology* 11(4): 466–72.

Gailliot, Matthew T., and Roy F. Baumeister. 2007. "Self-Regulation and Sexual Restraint: Dispositionally and Temporarily Poor Self-Regulatory Abilities Contribute to Failures at Restraining Sexual Behavior." *Personality and Social Psychology Bulletin* 33(2): 173–86.

Gailliot, Matthew T., Roy F. Baumeister, C. Nathan DeWall, Jon K. Maner, E. Ashby Plant, Dianne M. Tice, Lauren E. Brewer, and Brandon J. Schmeichel. 2007. "Self-Control Relies on Glucose as a Limited Energy Source: Willpower is More Than a Metaphor." *Journal of Personality and Social Psychology* 92(2): 325–36.

Gottfredson, Michael R., and Travis Hirschi. 1990. *A General Theory of Crime.* Stanford, Calif.: Stanford University Press.

Greeno, Catherine G., and Rena R. Wing. 1994. "Stress-Induced Eating." *Psychological Bulletin* 115(3): 444–64.

Heatherton, Todd F., and Janet Polivy. 1992. "Chronic Dieting and Eating Disorders: A Spiral Model." In *The Etiology of Bulimia Nervosa: The Individual and Familial Context,* edited by Janis Crowther, Daniel L. Tennenbaum, Steven E. Hobfall, and Mary Ann Parris Stephens. Washington: Hemisphere.

Hull, Jay G., Richard D. Young, and Ernest Jouriles. 1986. "Applications of the Self-Awareness Model of Alcohol Consumption: Predicting Patterns of Use and Abuse." *Journal of Personality and Social Psychology* 51(4): 790–6.

Kahan, David, Janet Polivy, and C. Peter Herman. 2003. "Conformity and Dietary Disinhibition: A Test of the Ego-Strength Model of Self-Regulation." *International Journal of Eating Disorders* 33(2): 165–71.

Knapp, Andreas, and Margaret S. Clark. 1991. "Some Detrimental Effects of Negative Mood on Individuals' Ability to Solve Resource Dilemmas." *Personality and Social Psychology Bulletin* 17(6): 678–88.

Loewenstein, George. 1996. "Out of Control: Visceral Influences on Behavior." *Organizational Behavior and Human Decision Processes* 65(3): 272–92.

Logue, Alexandra W. 1993. *The Psychology of Eating and Drinking: An Introduction.* 2nd edition. New York: Freeman.

Manucia, Gloria K., Donald J. Baumann, and Robert B. Cialdini. 1984. "Mood Influences on Helping: Direct Effects or Side Effects?" *Journal of Personality and Social Psychology* 46(2): 357–64.

Mischel, Walter, Brian Coates, and Antonette Raskoff. 1968. "Effects of Success and Failure on Self-Gratification." *Journal of Personality and Social Psychology* 10(4): 381–90.

Mischel, Walter, Yuichi Shoda, and Philip K. Peake. 1988. "The Nature of Adolescent Competencies Predicted by Preschool Delay of Gratification." *Journal of Personality and Social Psychology* 54(4): 687–96.

Muraven, Mark, R. Lorraine Collins, and Kristen Neinhaus. 2002. "Self-Control and Alcohol Restraint: An Initial Application of the Self-Control Strength Model." *Psychology of Addictive Behaviors* 16(2): 113–20.

O'Guinn, Thomas C, and Ronald J. Faber. 1987. "Compulsive Buying: A Phenomenological Exploration." *Journal of Consumer Research* 16(2): 147–57.

Peck, C. P. 1986. "Risk-Taking Behavior and Compulsive Gambling." *American Psychologist* 41(4): 461–5.

Pickens, Roy W., Dorothy K. Hatsukami, J. W. Spicer, and D. S. Svikis. 1985. "Relapse by Alcohol Abusers." *Alcoholism: Clinical and Experimental Research* 9(3): 244–7.

Pratt, Travis C., and Francis T. Cullen. 2000. "The Empirical Status of Gottfredson and Hirschi's General Theory of Crime: A Meta-Analysis." *Criminology* 38(3): 931–64.

Schachter, Stanley, Brett Silverstein, Lynn T. Kozlowski, Deborah Perlick, C. Peter Herman, and Barry Liebling. 1977. "Studies of the Interaction of Psychological and Pharmacological Determinants of Smoking." *Journal of Experimental Psychology: General* 106(1): 3–40.

Schwartz, J. Conrad, and Pamela R. Pollack. 1977. "Affect and Delay of Gratification." *Journal of Research in Personality* 11(2): 141–64.

Shoda, Yuichi, Walter Mischel, and Philip K. Peake. 1990. "Predicting Adolescent Cognitive and Self-Regulatory Competencies from Preschool Delay of Gratification: Identifying Diagnostic Conditions." *Developmental Psychology* 26(6): 978–86.

Tangney, June P., Roy F. Baumeister, and Angie L. Boone. 2004. "High Self-Control Predicts Good Adjustment, Less Pathology, Better Grades, and Interpersonal Success." *Journal of Personality* 72(2): 271–322.

Tice, Dianne M., and Roy F. Baumeister. 1997. "Longitudinal Study of Procrastination, Performance, Stress, and Health: The Costs and Benefits of Dawdling." *Psychological Science* 8(6): 454–8.

Tice, Dianna M., Elaine Bratslavsky, and Roy F. Baumeister. 2001. "Emotional Distress Regulation Takes Precedence Over Impulse Control: If You Feel Bad, Do It!" *Journal of Personality and Social Psychology* 80(1): 53–67.

Vohs, Kathleen D., and Ronald J. Faber. 2004. "To Buy or Not To Buy?: Self-Control and Self-Regulatory Failure in Purchase Behavior." In *Handbook of Self-Regulation: Research, Theory, and Applications,* edited by Roy F. Baumeister and Kathleen D. Vohs. New York: Guilford Press.

Vohs, Kathleen D., and Todd F. Heatherton. 2000. "Self-Regulatory Failure: A Resource-Depletion Approach." *Psychological Science* 11(3): 249–54.

Wenzlaff, Richard M., Daniel M. Wegner, and David W. Roper. 1988. "Depression and Mental Control: The Resurgence of Unwanted Negative Thoughts." *Journal of Personality and Social Psychology* 55(6): 882–92.

Applications

· 10 ·

Reason and Emotion in Moral Judgment: Different Prototypes Lead to Different Theories

BENOÎT MONIN, DAVID A. PIZARRO,
AND JENNIFER S. BEER

O NE CAN not study the relationship between emotions and decisions without including an analysis of moral judgement, both because many significant decisions that individuals make every day involve morality, and because an increasingly influential school of thought stresses the importance of emotions in moral judgement. In fact, one of the major debates in the current study of morality in psychology pits emotion against reason—one side argues that moral judgment follows from emotional reactions, and the other side asserts the role of conscious reasoning in arriving at moral conclusions. The goal of this chapter is not to take sides in this debate. Instead, we hope to present the major issues involved, and attempt to reconcile competing accounts of moral judgment by proposing that they are potentially compatible. While it may sometimes seem that moral psychologists from opposing sides of the debate describe different species of "homo moralis," they are actually talking about the same being, albeit in varying prototypical situations. Those focusing on complex hypothetical dilemmas are likely to see moral judgment as the result of deliberative abstract reasoning, while those focusing on reacting to the transgressions of others are likely to see moral judgment as the result of quick emotions such as contempt, anger, or disgust. Both views might be correct, and both models represent judgment well as long as you restrain each to its indigenous situation. Favoring one view is ignoring the diversity of moral situations that people encounter in their everyday life. As evidence of this diversity, some authors have in mind yet other prototypical situations when investigating morality. Considering one of these as the modal moral situation yields yet another model of morality, and it is one that does not necessarily fit the reason-emotion dichotomy. For example, if the typical moral situation that researchers had in mind did not involve solving dilemmas or judging others but instead involved resisting temptation (which is admittedly an important part of our moral lives), then models of moral behavior would be less focused on reasoning or emotion and instead emphasize willpower and self-control.

Thus, disagreements about what empirical research tells us about moral judgment may unwittingly be the result of divergent assumptions about what constitutes the ideal-type situation of moral judgment in the first place. In a brief review of the history of the debate between the "emotionalist" and "rationalist" approaches to moral judgment, four examples of prototypical moral situations stand out: moral reactions, moral dilemmas, moral weakness, and moral fortitude. Each leads to a different perception of moral judgment. This framework can be used to inform the question of what it means to be a virtuous individual by considering four archetypes—the sheriff, the philosopher, the monk and the wrestler—which correspond to each of the prototypical situations.

A Short History of Emotion and Reason in Moral Judgment

One question that has troubled moral philosophers and psychologists for some time is whether moral judgments are primarily the fruits of reason or of emotion. One tradition holds that moral judgments are largely the output of our emotional system. A competing tradition holds that while emotions are often heavily involved in the process of moral judgment, our moral beliefs exist at heart because of the distinctly human ability to reason and to distinguish right from wrong. The tension between these two positions has a long history, in part because the truth of the matter was seen to have serious implications for the status of morality. This tension is best exemplified in the debate between the philosophers Immanuel Kant (1785/1957) and David Hume (1777/1969). If the moral notions that guide people's everyday moral pronouncements actually were the unreflective output of emotion, then the task of assessing the validity of such moral beliefs seemed problematic:

If a behavior shocks me but not my neighbor, who is to say if it is morally right or wrong? On the other hand, moral beliefs grounded in reason were, by virtue of the reliability of the reasoning process, more likely to be agreed upon by all as truth. The question of whether moral beliefs could be understood as objectively "true" (on par with, for instance, the law of gravity) is what kept the debate alive (Ayer 1952), until the descriptive facts of the matter—whether the moral judgments that we make on a daily basis are actually a product of emotional reactions or a product of reasoned deliberation—took center stage. And with this shift from what moral thinking *ought* to be to what it *actually* looks like, psychologists realized that they had a role to play in the question.

Rationalism in Moral Psychology

Interestingly, within moral psychology, the rationalist position emerged as an early winner. Developmental psychologists Jean Piaget (1932) and Lawrence Kohlberg (1969) fell squarely on the side of philosophers Immanuel Kant (1785/1959) and John Rawls (1999). The ability to reason was seen as the supreme path to distinguishing right from wrong. For example, in Kohlberg's view, moral judgment develops as a function of the developing cognitive abilities of the child; as reason develops, moral beliefs mature. Most modern rationalists hold reason to be at the helm of thought and behavior at least some of the time, even when the impact of reasoning on judgment is mediated through emotional mechanisms (Pizarro and Bloom 2003). They paint a picture in which reason can influence the emotional system. Evidence for this position often takes the form of demonstrating that reasoning can influence initial emotional reactions (for example, appraisal theory; Lazarus 1991), reason can regulate emotions in order to serve pre-existing, reasoned goals (Gross 1999), and reasoning processes can be readily observed when individuals are faced with moral dilemmas (Kohlberg 1969). Even in the face of evidence suggesting that moral judgments are *always* made with a large dose of accompanying emotions, the rationalist position can still claim that reasoning causally influences these emotions and the resulting judgments.

In the last few decades, however, other areas of psychology have increasingly called into question this dominant rationalist framework. Psychologists have become acutely aware of the limits of human reasoning (Kahneman and Frederick 2002; Simon 1967; Nisbett and Wilson 1977). For better or for worse, the human mind, while often making efficient use of limited processing power and information, can be shown to err in a reliable fashion. And the heuristics that are responsible for these errors, although perhaps rational in a broad sense, are characterized by a lack of rational deliberation. Adding insult to injury, we seem to make generous use of information that is not even consciously accessible; thus, our ability to utilize rational deliberation for many of our judgments is effectively preempted (Greenwald and Banaji 1995; Bargh 1994). These advances all contributed to weaken the grip of the strict rationalist framing on moral psychology.

Emotionalism in Moral Psychology

Besides cracks in the pedestal of rationalism, a second important factor in the emergence of the emotionalist perspective was the considerable rebirth of interest in emotional processes, which had historically been a fickle topic within psychology. This body of research points to the fact that emotions have a much more powerful influence on judgment than was previously believed. Emotions seem to pervade human judgment, and people are often unwittingly influenced by emotional responses that have nothing to do with the judgment at hand (Schwarz and Clore 1983; Bodenhausen, Sheppard, and Kramer 1994; Lerner and Keltner 2001). These insights have done serious damage to the view of humans as ideal rational creatures.

In contrast to rationalism, the emotionalist perspective (Kagan 1984; Haidt 2001; Prinz 2006) posits that emotions play a primary role as the causes of moral judgment and decision making. Evidence for the emotionalist approach often takes the form of demonstrating the thoughtless nature of many emotional reactions (Zajonc 1980), the strong emotional reactions observed when individuals make moral judgments (especially when judging the moral infractions of others; Haidt, Koller, and Dias 1993), the "dumbfounding" nature of many moral judgments (that is, the apparent inability to defend judgments rationally when asked; Haidt 2001), or the fact that many moral judgments seem to conflict with rational normative theories of morality (Baron 1993). While traditionally the underdog theory of moral judgment, emotionalism has emerged as an increasingly influential framework for understanding moral judgment in recent years (Haidt 2001).

While any psychologist working on these issues will likely respond that the truth is much more complex than a simple reason-emotion dichotomy, the debate between rationalism and emotionalism nonetheless lives on as one of theoretical emphasis (Haidt 2001; Pizarro and Bloom 2003).

Different Situations, Different Models of Morality

If the story ended here, it would be quite discouraging to the reader looking for a definitive model of "homo moralis." According to some accounts, morality is all about reasoning through a problem and working out the implications of various possible courses of action (Kohlberg 1969); according to others, morality is mostly a reaction to gut feelings which tell us something is right or wrong (Haidt 2001; Prinz 2006). Not only is there a fairly clean split on the emphasis that each model places on reason versus emotion, but also the types of experimental situations used to elicit moral judgments across experiments are even more variable. Some experimenters (most famously Kohlberg [1969], but also Jim Rest [1986] and other neo-Kohlbergians) ask participants to resolve dilemmas in which different moral principles collide. Others (Haidt, Koller, and Dias 1993) ask participants to act as observers and to approve or disapprove of the offending behavior of others. Still others locate themselves outside of the reason versus emotion debate, and yet study situations that would sound morally relevant to many readers, such as how humans succumb to temptation or resist immediate gratification for a greater future good (Giner-Sorolla 2001; Baumeister and Exline 1999).

In fact, these variations in methodology may offer an important clue as to why the models of moral judgment differ so radically in their emphasis on reason versus emotion. The different models of morality that have appeared in the literature over the years may be a direct consequence of the different moral situations considered by the researchers who have proposed them: If you observe humans as they try to solve complex moral dilemmas, you are likely to propose a model of morality that relies heavily on high-level reasoning. If you ask them how they feel about disgusting immoral acts, you are likely to conclude that morality is all about gut reactions that require little rational deliberation. Hence, the relative emphasis on reason versus emotion is largely determined by the prototypical moral situation under study. To the extent that people encounter all of these situations in the course of their daily lives (sometimes they have to make complex personal moral choices, and sometimes they witness the shocking behavior of others), the different models of moral judgment all approximate the truth of the matter. However, an understanding of the various situations that give rise to moral judgment becomes paramount.

In essence, the best way to get beyond the apparent clash between rationalists and emotionalists and to reconcile these competing traditions is to develop a typology of the moral situations that give rise to different judgmental processes. Although this may sound like a dichotomy between situations leading to emotionalism and situations leading to rationalism (thus replacing one dichotomy with another), this approach is broader. These two general situations are not the only ones used in the study of moral judgment. At least four such prototypical moral situations can be identified, each of which, when taken in isolation, paints a very different picture of what moral life is and of the relationship between reason and emotion (see also Monin, Pizarro, and Beer 2007).

Prototypes of Moral Situations

Moralists, like most scholars, love typologies, lists, and catalogues. From the Ten Commandments of the Pentateuch to the Seven Deadly Sins of the Christian tradition, from the six stages of moral development (Kohlberg 1969) to six links in the social intuitionist model (Haidt 2001), taxonomies provide helpful categories to decode the ambiguity of everyday life and to circumscribe the domain of morality. We do not pretend to provide such comfort here. Our categories are tentative, and are meant as an explanatory companion for the reader of moral psychology confused by the multiplicity of perspectives. At least four types of moral situations are evident in research conducted across various areas of the psychological literature on morality (see table 10.1). In the first prototypical situation—the *moral reaction* situation—an individual reacts to a moral infraction. A focus on this situation leads to a view that morality is governed by emotional impact and quick intuitions. The latter three moral situations place a greater emphasis on decision making and on predicting individual moral choices. In the *moral dilemma* situation, investigators ask participants to articulate how they might resolve the tension between two incompatible moral demands. These studies produce a view of morality based on verbalized reason. Traditionally outside of the morality literature, situations of *moral weakness* capture knowledge of the right thing to do but the lack willpower to carry it through. Focusing on these situations paints a view of morality centered on ego strength. Finally, in the *moral fortitude* situation we include all cases in which reason needs to override an initial moral opposition (for example, telling on a friend whom you have caught cheating despite your initial reluctance) or to call emotion to its aid (for example, bringing to mind outrageous cases of abuse to facilitate reporting a bully). It leads to a view of morality where emotion abounds but reason is firmly at the helm. The first prototypical situation (that is, moral reaction) predominantly focuses on the behavior of others, whereas the other three situations center more on one's own decisions. However, there are enough exceptions to this actor-observer pattern for us to avoid including it in our analysis.

Moral Reactions: Judging the Behavior of Others

One view of morality relates to judging others. The prototypical moral situation in this model is witnessing another individual commit a poten-

Table 10.1   Four Prototypical Moral Situations Found in Moral Psychology

Prototypical Moral Situation	Elements	Goal	Paragon of Virtue
Moral reactions	Emotions (morality)	To condemn or praise	Sheriff
Moral dilemmas	Reason (morality) Versus Reason (morality)	To know what should be done	Philosopher
Moral weakness	Reason (morality) Versus Emotion (immorality)	To resist temptation	Monk
Moral fortitude	Reason (morality) Versus Emotion (morality)	To carry out what you know ought to be done	Cognitive Wrestler

Source: Authors' compilation.

tially offensive behavior. The focus of morality is on how that behavior will be judged and what inference will be drawn about the perpetrator. This approach to morality is grounded in the social psychological tradition of person perception and causal attribution, and has most recently been defended in the social intuitionist model of moral judgment (Haidt 2001). Moral judgments, in this approach, are "evaluations (good versus bad) of the actions or character of a person that are made with respect to a set of virtues held to be obligatory by a culture or subculture" (Haidt 2001, 817). The social intuitionist model posits that moral judgments are primarily based on moral intuitions, which are, in turn, defined as "the sudden appearance in consciousness of a moral judgment, including an affective valence (good-bad, like-dislike), without any conscious awareness of having gone through steps of searching, weighing evidence, or inferring a conclusion" (Haidt 2001, 818). Like Justice Potter Stewart's definition of obscenity, a moral act is judged to be right or wrong because you just "know it when you see it" (Woodward and Armstrong 1979, 16). As mentioned above, this approach provides a valuable integration of the traditional study of moral judgment and recent advances in the study of emotion, implicit processes, and motivated cognition in social psychology.

We refer to this class of situations as *moral reactions* to retain the broader use of the term *moral judgment,* which is common in the literature.

Moral reaction approaches emphasize that emotions are squarely at the center of morality. For instance, despite the integration of reasoning into the social intuitionist model (Haidt 2001), the emphasis of the paper from its main title ("The emotional dog and it rational tail") to its last sentence (". . . moral emotions and intuitions drive moral reasoning, just as surely as a dog wags its tail") is that moral psychology has radically underestimated the primacy of emotion in moral judgment. Work stemming from this approach, which has examined such varying areas as cross-cultural judgments (Haidt, Koller, and Dias 1993; Rozin et al. 1999), moral emotions (Haidt 2002), and neurological processes (Greene and Haidt 2002), all converge on this same claim that "emotions are in fact in charge of the temple of morality" (Haidt 2002). The social intuitionist model is, at heart, squarely in the emotionalist camp. A similar perspective is reflected in the work using "moral outrage" as a predictor of condemnation (Tetlock et al. 2000) or punishment (Carlsmith, Darley, and Robinson 2002; Kahneman and Frederick 2002). Phil Tetlock and his colleagues(2000) explicitly describe the affective component of moral outrage as "anger, contempt, and even disgust toward violators" (855).

    This view of the moral agent as an observer lends itself well to the emerging methodology of neuroimaging, as researchers can record brain activity while participants are presented with vignettes or images. This is the approach taken by Jorge Moll and colleagues (Moll, Eslinger, and Oliveira-Souza 2001; Moll et al. 2002a, 2002b). For example, Moll et al. (2002b) scanned Brazilian subjects while they looked at "moral pictures portraying emotionally charged, unpleasant social scenes, representing moral violations (for example, physical assaults, poor children abandoned on the street, war scenes)" (2731). (These images were mostly derived from the international affective picture system [IAPS] [Lang, Bradley, and Cuthbert 1995]). When reactions to these moral pictures were contrasted to reactions to nonmoral, but unpleasant pictures (for example, body lesions, dangerous animals, or bodily products), the researchers found greater activation of "critical elements of a cortical-limbic network that enables humans to link emotional experience to moral appraisal" (2736) for the moral pictures than for the nonmoral ones.[1]

    One source of ambiguity in this literature is whether intuitions should be equated with emotions. Jonathan Haidt is often careful to distinguish the two, defining intuition sometimes as a form of cognition (Haidt 2001), and other times describing intuitions as "affect-laden" or as "quick, automatic affective reactions" (Greene and Haidt 2002, 517). A natural question, therefore, is whether there can be such a thing as a nonaffective intuition. In other words, are emotions (or at least is affect) necessary for moral judgment? Cass Sunstein (2005) provides an elegant review of the many mental shortcuts or "moral heuristics" that we rely on when making moral judgments, some of which have an affective component (for example, the outrage heuristic), while many others seem to rely more on basing moral reasoning on a number of simple schemas or maxims. Examples of such heuristics or maxims include "people should not be permitted to engage in moral wrongdoing for a fee" or "punish, and do not reward, betrayals of trust" (537). Sunstein argues that errors can occur as the result of the mindless application of these maxims. Indeed, this is what makes them moral heuristics: they work most of the time, but can lead one astray, as when the "wrongdoing for a fee" heuristic above erodes public support for emissions-trading policies (in which industries are allowed to buy out of reducing toxic emissions), which Sunstein argues is one of the best ways to reduce further ecological damage. Sunstein's moral heuristics are a rare example of nonemotional moral intuition in the literature, but his model shares with others their emphasis on quick, unreasoned reactions.

There is thus considerable evidence that when reacting to the behavior of others, we rarely rely on thoughtful deliberation. This is consistent with one understanding of how social emotions such as anger may have evolved. Economist Robert Frank (1988) describes emotions as serving a "pre-commitment" function. In this framework, the threat of an emotional reaction prevents wrongdoers from harming or cheating others in the first place, precisely because, being emotional, retaliation is supposed to be automatic and not appeasable by reason. Not unlike the "doomsday machine" theory developed by nuclear strategists during the cold war, the deterrent power of emotions is alleged to be their inexorability once set in motion. The emergence of an emotional system that guarantees a strong, swift emotional reaction, which in turn leads to the punishment of perpetrators (such as "cheaters"; Tooby and Cosmides 1990), is likely to be passed on to offspring because of the protection it provides.

This research provides a first consistent picture of moral judgment. However, this approach to morality is built around experimental evidence that gauges our reactions to the infractions of others. If we restrict the domain of morality to those instances in which we judge others, we are likely to conclude that morality is based on quick, affect-laden responses. But a very different view of moral judgment emerges when we consider other sorts of moral encounters. Most notably, if the perspective shifts away from the judgment of others to the analysis of an actor's own choices, one is likely to conclude something very different about the nature of moral judgment.

Moral Dilemmas: When Principles Clash

When we think about moral reasoning, what often comes to mind is the traditional moral dilemma: deciding between two morally right but incompatible courses of action. For example, reconciling conflicting demands on one's loyalties, "Sophie's choice" situations, and tragic trade-offs (Tetlock et al. 2000) are all instances in which no option is satisfactory because both alternatives have a moral justification. These moral dilemmas have captured the imagination of philosophers for centuries, and the most popular moral brainteasers rely precisely on the unresolved tension inherent in these examples. Perhaps unsurprisingly, Kohlberg's (1969) study of the cognitive development of morality started with exactly these types of dilemmas, refined over the years into the standard issue moral judgment interview (Colby, Kohlberg, and Kauffman 1987). His explicit goal was to discover how the development of reason influenced moral judgment and indeed "think-aloud" protocols and in-depth interviews soon revealed that people could engage in sophisticated reasoning about morality, weigh pros and cons, and reveal stable cognitive mindsets in the way they approached moral dilemmas. While some individuals took into account mostly fear of punishment or rejection (at preconventional stages), others embraced the rules of society as inherently worthy of respect (at conventional stages), and a few seemed to consider what they believed were universal principles and followed them even when they clashed with those of society (at postconventional stages). Despite possible differences in stages of reasoning, these individuals had one thing in common: their decision seemed based on conscious thought processes that could be articulated. In fact, the emphasis of this approach was not so much on the decision that participants eventually reached as it was on the accounts they gave of how they arrived at their particular decision.[2]

Rationalists enjoy the moral dilemma approach because of the reasoning that these ambiguous dilemmas elicit. Consider a metaphor from visual perception: With most straightforward images, our experience is one of immediate access to the world out there, and it is hard to believe much construction is involved. But with well-crafted ambiguous images, such as cartoonist W. E. Hill's 1915 oft-used "My Wife and My Mother-in-Law" (see figure 10.1; cited in Boring 1930), we catch ourselves going back and forth between the two perceptions, explicitly interpreting different parts of the picture ("there's the mouth, there's the nose . . .") in a process that is much more self-aware and apparently reasoned than

Figure 10.1   Visual Dilemma: My Wife or My Mother-in-Law

Source: Puck (1915), cited in Boring (1930).

ordinary perception. The elegant dilemmas designed by philosophers and used by moral psychologists of the cognitive tradition are not unlike these ambiguous pictures; they are designed to prevent the sort of swift judgment that occurs when we are judging others, instead eliciting deliberative reasoning.

Another orienting distinction (though not a rigid one) between the moral dilemma situation and the moral reaction situation is one of perspective. The dilemmas typically used in the moral dilemma situation (Kohlberg 1969; Colby, Kohlberg, and Kauffman 1987; Rest 1986), while sometimes third person at first glance (most famously the Heinz dilemma) are always designed to yield a fair amount of vacillation, and the participant must commit to a response by prescribing what should be done and justifying it. Respondents are therefore required to take the perspective of the actor in the situation, whereas dilemmas in the moral reaction tradition are really opportunities to condemn a behavior even when they are phrased as a first-person decision (see note 1). The complexity of scenarios in the moral dilemma situation not only stimulates reasoning, but also draws participants into the situation more than the typical social reaction scenarios. To contrast these two approaches, when judging the behavior of others, we often use knee-jerk reactions and gut feelings, whereas when deciding what the right course of action should be for our own life, we are more circumspect and mobilize our cognitive resources (if the stakes are high enough) to bring to bear the heavy machinery of moral reasoning.

Moral Weakness: Failures of Self-Control

One of the most perplexing puzzles for Greek philosophers was understanding how an individual could do something she did not want to do. For example, Why do I eat the fattening cookie when I do not want to break my diet? Why engage in an illicit affair despite my strong desire to stay faithful? These failures are common enough that the Greeks had a name for it: *akrasia,* which means incontinence or weakness of the will. In this tradition, emotions are conceptualized as passions, and to be human means to rise above these passions and to control them for the sake of higher moral goals. The role of cognition is to squash the passions in the service of reason. In the Christian tradition, the soul has to contend with an earthly body that sometimes makes inappropriate demands, in part because the devil knows how to use emotions to tempt humans into sin. A glance at the Seven Deadly Sins reveals that they are not acts, but impulses of the passions such as gluttony, lust, sloth and the like. And in the last century, Sigmund Freud's (1933) structural model depicted these passions as the primordial urges of the id, and posited that the primary role of the superego was to prevent the expression of all of the id's impulses.

Upon reflection, it seems that maybe more so than lofty moral dilemmas, challenges of self-control do constitute the stuff of our everyday moral life. These challenges could include resisting addictions, maintaining a diet, overcoming anger and staying calm with a rambunctious child, resisting the temptation to cut corners in our professional life, turning down extramarital sexual favors, or supporting a friend whose depression has become alienating. In a world that is seen as filled with passion and temptation, the primary moral goal is to resist them, and a moral psychologist focusing on these types of moral situations will come up with a model of homo moralis quite different from those related to moral dilemmas and moral reactions.

In fact, though not typically squarely within the realm of moral psychology, a fair amount of research on self-control within social psychology can illuminate this prototypical moral situation. For example, in these moral weakness examples, a self-interested, emotional first response has to be resisted in order for morality to prevail. How do people do it? Walter Mischel, in his seminal work on delay of gratification, asked children to sit in front of an attractive snack that they would be allowed to eat if they only waited for a few minutes. If waiting was too hard though, they could ring a bell and get half of the snack immediately, forgoing the other half in favor of instant gratification (Mischel and Ebbesen 1970; Mischel, Shoda, and Rodriguez 1989). Mischel and colleagues described the various cognitive techniques employed by children, most having to do with reallocating attention away from the reward (for example, looking away or singing). Although Mischel's findings reach beyond morality, the phenomenology of delay of gratification and the techniques used have great relevance in the case of moral control. Roger Giner-Sorolla (2001) emphasized the role of affect in dilemmas of self-control and showed that many of these dilemmas can be reduced to the "one in the hand versus two in the bush" logic captured by Mischel's paradigm. Giner-Sorolla describes guilty pleasures as situations that yield immediate reward and greater long-term cost (for example, sexual promiscuity); grim necessities are defined as situations requiring immediate cost for the promise of a later reward (for example, studying). Again, although some of Giner-Sorolla's examples go beyond the traditional domain of morality, there is much for moral psychologists to glean from this tradition when self-control is included within the realm of moral situations.

Sometimes it seems that it matters less whether we have the cognitive skills to overcome passions than whether we have the energy and motivation to do so. One may have every intention not to spank a child, but in the heat of the moment, with the stress of a demanding job and the exhaustion of a long week, a blow is dealt. Or a temptation is resisted effectively until an unexpected personal downturn lowers one's defenses, and one falls into relapse, corruption, or adultery. Thus the focus of dilemmas of self-control is once again the question of how reason can dominate emotions, with emotions pulling down and reason pulling up. One influential approach (Baumeister et al. 1998) has investigated the limits of self-control, demonstrating that self-control is not unlike a muscle: if it becomes depleted, subsequent self-control becomes much harder. Some of the most intriguing findings from this work on ego depletion suggest that when self-control is exerted in one domain, it becomes depleted such that later performance in an entirely different domain is likely to exhibit self-control failures. But, in keeping with the muscle metaphor, Baumeister and Exline (1999) contend that the will becomes stronger as it is exercised. Again, their model encompasses more than the moral domain, but their findings add an important element to our understanding of moral situations where individuals struggle to adhere to their moral beliefs because of the temptation of immediate satisfaction. This important and common moral predicament has, unfortunately, been underplayed by previous models of morality. As such, we know less about the role of self-control in everyday moral judgment than we probably should.

Moral Fortitude: Using Emotions in the Service of Reason

The fourth situation is called *moral fortitude* to capture the paradigmatic case in which individuals have the immediate knee-jerk reaction that a course of action is immoral but, upon reflection, realize that this action nevertheless needs to be taken in the service of a greater moral goal. An investigator of this type of situation would likely conclude that morality is best described as a struggle between various emotions, with reason acting as the ultimate arbiter. For instance, Joshua Greene and his colleagues (2004) recently posited the importance of cognitive conflict and control in moral judgment. The paradigmatic example that they present is one in which you have to smother your own baby to death to prevent enemy soldiers from discovering you and other villagers. In either case the child dies, but if you kill him before he cries, you and the villagers will live. They found that participants who took a long time to respond to dilemmas but ultimately gave the utilitarian response (that is, kill the baby) showed greater activation of areas typically associated with mental control. Greene et al. (2004) intentionally picked dilemmas that directly pitted consequentialism (which favors saving more lives) against deontology (in which pragmatic justifications are often irrelevant), and their finding that mental control is involved is of great import. The mistake would be to conclude from their work that this is how all morality works, and that reason is always in the business of moderating moral intuitions. What comes into play in these prototypical situations is most certainly an important part of the puzzle. However, we cannot rely on only one type of moral encounter to arrive at an accurate portrayal of homo moralis.

There is a long tradition of research in social psychology describing the processes people engage in to "quiet down" their moral intuitions (intuitions of this sort are typically referred to as "scruples" or "conscience"). Al Bandura et al.'s (1996) work on moral disengagement presents an elaborate model of the way people manage to do things that they would initially be uncomfortable doing, by either redefining the situation to remove morality from the equation, or by justifying the violation as a small one in the service of a greater good. Like a Frenchman learning to ignore his initial disgust for a smelly cheese or a surgeon learning to get over her inhibition for cutting the flesh of another human being, soldiers, executioners, and jurors all find ways to get over their initial moral intuitions in the service of a what they perceive as the greater good. Whereas moral reaction situations seemed to rely on "gut feeling" (that is, affect), here colloquial parlance would speak of "having the guts" (that is, overcoming affect) to do the right thing. (Other medical metaphors include "biting the bullet" or swallowing a "bitter pill.") Of course, research also depicts the darker side of this ability, in which moral disengagement leads to some of the worst horrors perpetrated by humankind. The insight here, however, is that if humans were guided solely by the sort of immediate intuitions described by emotionalist approaches, it is unlikely that we would have accomplished some of our best (and some of our worst) moral acts. Reason, by acting as arbiter, can put emotions at the service of the human imagination with all of its beautiful and dreadful consequences (Pizarro, Detweiler-Bedell, and Bloom 2006). Two processes in particular demonstrate the tools at the disposal of reason when it needs to override emotions: *appraisal* and *regulation*.

Appraisal.   Emotions most likely evolved as quick responses to solve specific environmental problems, but these responses depend greatly on our goals and the manner in which we appraise our current environment and situation (Lazarus 1991). For instance, when we perceive that events are consistent with the attainment of our goals, we tend to experience happiness. In contrast, if we perceive that a goal is threatened, we experience fear or anger. And when we perceive that a goal has failed irrevocably, we tend to experience sadness. Consistent with this approach, there is a large body of evidence demonstrating that emotions vary greatly depending on our appraisals of events (Ellsworth and Scherer 2003; Frijda 1987; Oatley and Johnson-Laird 1987; Ortony, Collins, and Clore 1988; Roseman, Antoniou, and Jose 1996; Scherer 1998, 2003; Smith and Lazarus 1993; Stein and Levine 1987, 1990; Stein, Trabasso, and Liwag 2000; Weiner 1985). Evidence from this appraisal approach lends support to the power of reason; that is, our emotions vary greatly depending on the sorts of thoughts that we bring to any given situation. So, while the presence of a bear may cause intense fear if we are out camping, it may only lead to mild amusement if we are at a circus. Alison Dandoy and Alvin Goldstein (1990) demonstrated that participants who adopted a detached, analytical attitude while viewing films of factory accidents experienced less physiological distress compared to participants who had received no such instructions. Thus our emotions are not purely at the mercy of our environment, and we can modulate our affective reactions by changing our outlook.

Such cognitive flexibility is also evident in the ease with which emotions can shift depending on the attributions we make about an individual's behavior. For example, our anger that a student failed to show up for an exam turns to sympathy if we discover that cause of the absence was a death in the family (Betancourt 1990). And one of the most robust findings from the study of empathy is that simply by shifting perspectives to take that of another, individuals become much more empathetic, and this in turn changes their moral judgments and behavior (Batson et al. 1988). Even simply shifting one's appraisal of another individual as being similar to oneself can change one's empathy towards the other (Batson et al. 1995).

While there is some disagreement over the contention that appraisals are necessarily conscious judgments (Lazarus 1991; Zajonc 1980), the fact that appraisals *can* be conscious is fairly noncontentious at this point. It is most likely also true that appraisals can be unconscious, and these nonconscious appraisals would certainly serve as a boundary condition for the power of reason.

Regulation.   The cognitive control that we have over our emotional responses is further evident in our ability to regulate our emotional reactions. While emotions were once seen as capricious influences that are passively experienced (hence the term *passion*), in many ways the biggest discovery in the modern science of emotion is the degree to which emotion and reason are interrelated. We are able to use our emotions to service our judgments or goals in a variety of manners. James Gross (1999) demonstrated that by reappraising stimuli or by selecting the situations we are exposed to, we are effectively able to preempt emotional responses that might otherwise have occurred. For instance, when individuals are viewing disgusting films, asking them to think of the films in unemotional terms can dramatically reduce their emotional response (Ochsner et al. 2002). And at a very basic level, if one is prone to getting mad at a certain person, one can avoid that person and thus avoid feeling anger. The various regulatory strategies that are available to us can be used in the service of previously decided goals, desires, and intentions.

This is true for our moral goals as well. Certain emotions seem to lend themselves nicely to the service of energizing moral goals. As an example, Paul Rozin and colleagues (1997) demonstrated the power of disgust in shaping moral opinions and attitudes. According to these researchers, issues that were previously nonmoral often come to possess moral status through the recruitment of disgust (a process Rozin labels *moralization*). In support of this view, Rozin, Markwith, and Stoess (1997) showed that vegetarians who abstain from meat for moral reasons are more likely to exhibit disgust in the presence of meat than vegetarians who do so for nonmoral (that is, health) reasons; Rozin and Leher Singh (1999) showed a similar pattern in the moralization of cigarette smoking. They present these findings as evidence of the power of disgust on our thinking about moral issues. It is likely that a cool-headed decision to avoid meat can be served by recruiting consistent emotions through a variety of tactics. A glance at the People for the Ethical Treatment of Animals (PETA) website illustrates how disgust is commonly used in the hope of strengthening an ethical argument.

The ability to override initial knee-jerk reactions and even to use emotion in the service of reason casts doubt on the strongest contentions of the emotionalist approach: that morality is mainly governed by quick affect-laden reactions. Our first reaction might be emotional (Zajonc 1980), but this response can be overcome. And if, as we have been arguing, investigators focus on such cases in which some emotions and intuitions need to be "quieted down," they are likely to conclude that morality is all about overcoming these initial reactions.

How Is One To Be Virtuous? The Philosopher, the Sheriff, the Monk, and the Cognitive Wrestler

Taking into account the sorts of moral encounters that are considered across different theoretical approaches not only elucidates the relative contribution of emotion and reason in moral judgment, but it also provides us with four very different models of what it means to be moral, suggesting different archetypes of the "virtuous person." While some models emphasize the virtues of reason and others emphasize emotions, others focus on the struggle between the two. Portraits of four ideals of the virtuous person (what would once have been called four "paragons" of virtue) are characterized by different relations between reason and emotion in moral judgment (see table 10.1).

The Philosopher

In the moral dilemma approach, to be virtuous is to think clearly about morality, and the ideal is *the philosopher*. The gray areas of life make it difficult to simply hold on to a set of predetermined abstract principles, so interpreting and applying them to everyday life is the challenge that must be met (Batson et al. 1997); the devil is in the details. In the way that the U.S. Supreme Court interprets the constitution, the virtuous person has the ability to live a decent, consistent life by utilizing reason when deciding upon her own actions as well as when judging the actions of others. Philosophical training is, in this view, the clear path to virtue. Kohlberg's (1969) view best exemplifies this; in the highest stages of moral development (that is, the postconventional stages 5 and 6), the virtuous individual engages in sophisticated moral reasoning about universal moral principles, and applies them to everyday judgment and decision making. Reason reigns supreme on this view, and emotions should be epiphenomenal at best, and intrusive at worst.

The Sheriff

According to emotionalist approaches such as the social intuitionist model, moral life (defined as judging others) is governed primarily by quick flashes of affect-laden approval or disapproval, and virtue would result from these flashes being timely and appropriate. "A virtuous person," write Jonathan Haidt and Craig Joseph (2004, 61), "is one who has the proper automatic reactions to ethically relevant events and states of affair." We call this model of virtue *the sheriff* in reference to the celebrated lawmakers of the old American west who would shoot first and ask questions later; these lawmakers, in a pinch, had to trust their instincts to make quick, accurate decisions. For the rest of us, these intuitions, according to Haidt (2001), are primarily of evolutionary (Oum and Lieberman, chapter 6, this volume) and cultural origin. However, intuitions can be shaped by reason, especially through social persuasion (link 4 in Haidt's 2001 model), reasoned judgment (link 5), and private reflection (link 6). Because the reasoned links are posited to occur much less frequently (and they primarily occur for philosophers), it would seem that the virtuous individual would be one who is attuned to her primal, gut feelings as well as to her culture's mores. Focusing on one's feelings of compassion can lead to overweighing the needs of those who are physically close at the expense of distant suffering others (Singer 1995). Cultural mores also have their pitfalls, as when moral emotions of disgust and contempt are put to the service of a racist ideology (Haidt and Joseph 2004). Given these problems, a normative theory of what should be the *proper* automatic reactions is still necessary; however, the emphasis of this view is that virtue is all about having the right intuitions.

The Monk

If one sees morality as a struggle to uphold principles (and to avoid being morally weak), the virtuous individual must fight the passions which would inevitably lead to his downfall. Asceticism, discipline, and self-control are the name of the moral game. By keeping in mind long-term lofty benefits over short-term gratifications (Giner-Sorolla 2001), the virtuous individual develops the ego control (Baumeister et al. 1998; Baumeister and Exline 1999) required to follow simple edicts and lead a virtuous life. The metaphor of *the monk* captures this and is exemplified by the strict rules of Christian monastic orders (for example, the Benedictines) which left few aspects of life unregulated. The monk's role in these orders was merely to obey and train himself to banish earthly passions. While this view is traditionally associated with the banishment of all emotions, a recent focus on positive emotions such as awe and elevation (Haidt 2002; Keltner and Haidt 2003) suggests that there may be emotional components associated with the virtuous life and that it may be simplistic to see monastic life as a rejection of all emotions.

The Cognitive Wrestler

The fourth view of the virtuous person is the most complex, as it takes elements from the previous views of virtue to form a composite of what the virtuous individual should be, especially in cases that we have defined as requiring moral fortitude. This view acknowledges the role of emotions but gives a primary role to reasoning in channeling, reshaping, or overriding these emotions. This is the view of the virtuous man embedded in Haidt's (2001) reasoning links, as well as defended by David Pizarro and Paul Bloom (2003). In this view, cognition should oversee emotions not only to resist "base" appeals (as is the case with the monk), but also to overcome the pitfalls and biases of knee-jerk moral reactions (such as those that plague the sheriff). Unlike the philosopher, this model of virtue can tame and juggle emotions, recognizing when an emotion is a valid input and when it should be kept in check. We call it the *cognitive wrestler* (in a jesting reference to Fiske and Taylor's [1984] "cognitive miser" and Bargh's [1999] "cognitive monster") to illustrate a cognitive system wrestling with emotions in order to put them to good use. The metaphor of a wrestler also contains the channeling of anger to serve the long-term goals of winning a fight. Greene et al. (2004) have offered a version of this view and present evidence in the form of reaction time or activation of areas associated with cognitive conflict to document the internal struggles between emotion and reason. This view acknowledges the role of emotions but, unlike with the monk, it does not conceptualize emotions as entirely polluting to the pursuit of a virtuous life. Rather, emotions can be recruited by reason to serve higher goals, and people can train themselves to eventually exhibit the proper automatic reactions that will ensure they remain on the straight path toward virtue.

Conclusion

The debate about the role of reason and emotion in moral judgment has a long history. Rather than declaring either side the victor, it is important to understand that the relationships between reason and emotion presented in this debate are shaped by the sorts of situations researchers have investigated in their experiments. Emotionalist approaches tend to favor one type of moral situation (that is, reactions to infractions), while rationalists favor another (that is, moral dilemmas). These investigations tend to yield answers consistent with the theoretical approach of the researcher. Considering the four different paradigmatic moral encounters, it becomes clear that focusing on only one encounter at the expense of others can lead to a radically different understanding of the relationship between emotion and reason. In turn, it leads to a different understanding of how moral judgment works.

Psychologists have disagreed on the role of emotions in moral judgment: some see emotions as irrelevant at best, intrusive at worst, and others see emotions as the root of all moral judgments. Providing an answer to the question of whether emotions help or hurt moral decision making requires that one understands the place of emotion in moral judgment. Our analysis of the different prototypical moral situations demonstrates that the answer is, as often, that it depends. Indeed, the answer appears to be more interesting than the question allows for. Emotions can help when they lead to quick and proper condemnation of a moral violation (in the case of moral reactions), when they orient us to the correct course of action (in the case of moral dilemmas), when they hold a promise that is worth working towards (in the case of moral weaknesses), or even when they trump another emotion in service of the greater good (in the case of moral fortitude). They can also hurt when they lead to excessive or inappropriate condemnation (in the case of moral reaction), when they cloud our ability to think clearly based on abstract values (in the case of moral dilemmas), when their lure prevents us from implementing higher goals (in the case of moral weakness), or even when they lead to a naïve moral impulse which prevents the implementation of a superior moral action (in the case of moral fortitude). As all of these examples reveal, the answer may not be straightforward, but ignoring emotions in the study of moral judgment would be a glaring oversight.

The four prototypes presented here, while meant to be merely descriptive, paint different portraits of what it might mean to be moral or virtuous and thus yield diverging prescriptive agendas. This last step of offer-ing different paragons of virtue might immediately arouse suspicion among moral psychologists who are always careful to avoid making nor-mative claims. What *is*, after all, has no bearing on what *ought* to be. But we agree with Alan Waterman (1988), who, in his piece on the uses of psy-chological theory and research in the process of ethical inquiry, delineated what might be within the reach of moral psychologists who are wary of making normative claims based on the descriptive tools of science. Waterman argued that while we have to leave the evaluation of the ulti-mate causes or consequences of behavior to our philosopher colleagues, this does not mean that we cannot test the various models of how these behaviors come about or the descriptive assumptions made by various philosophical approaches. *Ought*, after all, implies *can*. And a normative theory of morality must be informed about the constraints of human psy-chology. So, while evaluating such concepts as "proper automatic reac-tions" (Haidt and Joseph 2004), for example, we are poorly equipped to determine if they really are proper; however, we are superbly equipped to test whether they are automatic. This piece of empirical information can lead to very different accounts of what it means to be virtuous.

When taking these various approaches to the study of moral judgment into account, it seems that the best description of homo moralis is that of a cognitive wrestler. In the medieval world, morality was often associ-ated with resisting inner demons, and thus the virtuous monk reigned supreme. The Enlightenment, on the other hand, provided a rationalist view of sin as flawed, immature reasoning and held the virtuous philoso-pher as the moral exemplar. Recent advances in the study of moral judg-ment have painted morality as a scuffle between quick affect-laden intuitions and reasoned deliberation that can respond to these impulses intelligently and even shape them for the future. This balance can be characterized as a cognitive wrestler, taking each influence into account in a constant struggle to be virtuous. Wrestling, of course, can be a tag-team sport: the goal of the virtuous individual, then, is to stay in tune with the inner voices of emotion and intuition, trust intuitions like the sheriff, use reason like the philosopher to apply principles and guide action, and use willpower like the monk in the struggle to override intu-itions and emotions that may lead the individual astray.

Notes

1. Other neuroimaging studies that have asked participants to take the first-person perspective (Greene et al. 2001, 2004) have used scenarios so far removed from many respondents' own experiences (for example, "You are

a fifteen-year-old girl who has become pregnant.") that it is hard to believe that respondents truly abandoned an observer perspective. Furthermore, one behavioral option is often so despicable (for example, discarding an unwanted newborn into a dumpster) that it is unclear whether respondents' affective reaction results from imagining being in that situation, or, more credibly, from hearing that someone would even consider such a gruesome act. One interpretation of these data is that participants were taking a third-person approach to the dilemmas, and many of the "personal" dilemmas presented were gruesome enough (for example, a man hiring someone to rape his wife so she would turn back to him for comfort) to yield an immediate emotional reaction without any real hesitation between the options proposed. Thus, we see these studies as falling in the moral judgment category and yielding a view of morality based on emotion (Greene et al. 2001), although later findings in this program of research also fit into the moral fortitude situation (Greene et al. 2004).

2.   The fact that reasoning can be studied in these cases, of course, does not prove that reasoning is causal, as Haidt (2001) points out. This may simply be a case of post-hoc rationalization. Needless to say, many of the emotionalists' evidence for the primacy of emotion suffers from the same problem: demonstrating the presence of emotion during a judgment is hardly sufficient support for the claim that emotion is causal.

References

Ayer, Alfred J. 1952. *Language, Truth and Logic.* 1st edition. New York: Dover Publications.

Bandura, Albert, Claudio Barbaranelli, Glen V. Caprara, and Concetta Pastorelli. 1996. "Mechanisms of Moral Disengagement in the Exercise of Moral Agency." *Journal of Personality and Social Psychology* 71(2): 364–74.

Bargh, John A. 1994. "The Four Horsemen of Automaticity: Awareness, Intention, Efficiency, and Control in Social Cognition." In *Handbook of Social Cognition, Volume 1*, edited by Robert S. J. Wyer, Jr. and Thomas K. Srull. Hillsdale, N.J.: Lawrence Erlbaum Associates, Inc.

———. 1999. "The Cognitive Monster: The Case Against the Controllability of Automatic Stereotype Effects." In *Dual Process Theories in Social Psychology*, edited by Shelly Chaiken and Yaacov Trope. New York: Guilford Press.

Baron, Jonathan. 1993. *Morality and Rational Choice.* Boston, Mass.: Kluwer Academic Publishing.

Batson, C. Daniel, Cynthia L. Turk, Laura L. Shaw, and Tricia R. Klein. 1995. "Information Function of Empathic Emotion: Learning that We Value Other's Welfare." *Journal of Personality and Social Psychology* 68(2): 300–13.

Batson, C. Daniel, Diane Kobrynowicz, Jessica L. Dinnerstein, Hannah C. Kampf, and Angela D. Wilson. 1997. "In a Very Different Voice: Unmasking Moral Hypocrisy." *Journal of Personality and Social Psychology* 72(6): 1335–48.

Batson, C. Daniel, Janine L. Dyck, J. Randall Brandt, Judy G. Batson, Anne L. Powell, M. Rosalie McMaster, and Cari Griffitt. 1988. "Five Studies Testing

Two New Egoistic Alternatives to the Empathy-Altruism Hypothesis." *Journal of Personality and Social Psychology* 55(1): 52–77.

Baumeister, Roy F., and Julie J. Exline. 1999. "Virtue, Personality, and Social Relations: Self-Control as the Moral Muscle." *Journal of Personality* 67(6): 1165–94.

Baumeister, Roy F., Ellen Bratslavsky, Mark Muraven, and Diane M. Tice. 1998. "Ego Depletion: Is the Active Self a Limited Resource?" *Journal of Personality and Social Psychology* 74(5): 1252–65.

Betancourt, Hector. 1990. "An Attribution-Empathy Model of Helping Behavior: Behavioral Intentions and Judgments of Help-Giving." *Personality and Social Psychology Bulletin* 16(3): 573–91.

Bodenhausen, Galen V., Lori A. Sheppard, and Geoffrey P. Kramer. 1994. "Negative Affect and Social Perception: The Differential Impact of Anger and Sadness." *European Journal of Social Psychology* 24(1): 45–62.

Boring, Edwin G. 1930. "A New Ambiguous Figure." *American Journal of Psychology* 42(3): 444–5.

Carlsmith, Kevin M., John M. Darley, and Paul H. Robinson. 2002. "Why Do We Punish? Deterrence and Just Deserts as Motives for Punishment." *Journal of Personality and Social Psychology* 83(2): 284–99.

Colby, Anne, Lawrence Kohlberg, and Kelsey Kauffman. 1987. "Instructions for Moral Judgment Interviewing and Scoring." In *The Measurement of Moral Judgment*, Volume 1, edited by Anne Colby and Lawrence Kohlberg. Cambridge: Cambridge University Press.

Dandoy, Alison C., and Alvin G. Goldstein. 1990. "The Use of Cognitive Appraisal to Reduce Stress Reactions: A Replication." *Journal of Social Behavior and Personality* 5: 275–85.

Ellsworth, Phoebe C., and Klaus R. Scherer. 2003. "Appraisal Processes in Emotion." In *Handbook of Affective Sciences*, edited by R. J. Davidson, K. R. Scherer, and H. H. Goldsmith. New York: Oxford University Press.

Fiske, Susan T., and Shelly E. Taylor. 1984. *Social Cognition*. 1st edition. Reading, Mass.: Addison-Wesley.

Frank, Robert H. 1988. *Passions Within Reason*. New York: W. W. Norton and Company.

Freud, Sigmund. 1933. *New Introductory Lectures in Psychoanalysis*. New York: W. W. Norton and Company.

Frijda, Nico H. 1987. "Emotion, Cognitive Structure, and Action Tendency." *Cognition and Emotion* 1: 115–43.

Giner-Sorolla, Roger. 2001. "Guilty Pleasures and Grim Necessities: Affective Attitudes in Dilemmas of Self-Control." *Journal of Personality and Social Psychology* 80(2): 206–21.

Greene, Joshua, and Jonathan Haidt. 2002. "How (and Where) Does Moral Judgment Work?" *Trends in Cognitive Sciences* 6(12): 517–23.

Greene, Joshua D., Leigh E. Nystrom, Andrew D. Engell, John M. Darley, and Jonathan D. Cohen. 2004. "The Neural Bases of Cognitive Conflict and Control in Moral Judgment." *Neuron* 44: 389–400.

Greene, Joshua D., Brian R. Sommerville, Leigh E. Nystrom, John M. Darley, and Jonathan D. Cohen. 2001. "An fMRI Investigation of Emotional Engagement in Moral Judgment." *Science* 293(5537): 2105–8.

Greenwald, Anthony G., and Mahzarin R. Banaji. 1995. "Implicit Social Cognition: Attitudes, Self-Esteem, and Stereotypes." *Psychological Review* 102(1): 4–27.

Gross, James J. 1999. "Emotion Regulation: Past, Present, Future." *Cognition and Emotion* 13(5): 551–73.

Haidt, Jonathan. 2001. "The Emotional Dog and Its Rational Tail: A Social Intuitionist Approach to Moral Judgment." *Psychological Review* 108(4): 814–34.

———. 2002. "The Moral Emotions." In *Handbook of Affective Sciences*, edited by Richard J. Davidson, Klaus R. Scherer, and H. Hill Goldsmith. Oxford: Oxford University Press.

Haidt, Jonathan, and Craig Joseph. 2004. "Intuitive Ethics: How Innately Prepared Intuitions Generate Culturally Variable Virtues." *Dædalus* 133(4): 55–66.

Haidt, Jonathan, Silvia H. Koller, and Maria G. Dias. 1993. "Affect, Culture and Morality, or Is It Wrong to Eat Your Dog?" *Journal of Personality and Social Psychology* 65(4): 613–28.

Hume, David. 1777/1969. *An Enquiry Concerning the Principles of Morals.* La Salle, Ill.: Open Court.

Kagan, Jerome. 1984. *The Nature of the Child.* New York: Basic Books.

Kahneman, Daniel, and Shane Frederick. 2002. "Representativeness Revisited: Attribute Substitution in Intuitive Judgment." In *Heuristics and Biases: The Psychology of Intuitive Judgment*, edited by Thomas Gilovich, Dale Griffin, and Daniel Kahneman. New York: Cambridge University Press.

Kant, Immanuel. 1785/1959. *Foundation of the Metaphysics of Morals.* Translated by L. W. Beck. Indianapolis, Ind.: Bobbs-Merrill.

Keltner, Dacher, and Jonathan Haidt. 2003. "Approaching Awe, a Moral, Spiritual, and Aesthetic Emotion." *Cognition and Emotion* 17(2): 297–314.

Kohlberg, Lawrence. 1969. "Stage and Sequence: The Cognitive-Developmental Approach to Socialization." In *Handbook of Socialization Theory and Research*, edited by David A. Goslin. Chicago: Rand McNally.

Lang, Peter J., Margaret M. Bradley, and Bruce N. Cuthbert. 1995. "International Affective Picture System (IAPS)." Bethesda, Md.: National Institute of Mental Health Center for the Study of Emotion and Attention.

Lazarus, Richard S. 1991. *Emotion and Adaptation.* London: Oxford University Press.

Lerner, Jennifer S., and Dacher Keltner. 2001. "Fear, Anger, and Risk." *Journal of Personality and Social Psychology* 81(1): 146–59.

Mischel, Walter, and Ebbe B. Ebbesen. 1970. "Attention in Delay of Gratification." *Journal of Personality and Social Psychology* 16(2): 239–337.

Mischel, Walter, Yuichi Shoda, and Monica L. Rodriguez. 1989. "Delay of Gratification in Children." *Science* 244(4907): 933–8.

Moll, Jorge, Paul J. Eslinger, and Ricardo de Oliveira-Souza. 2001. "Frontopolar and Anterior Temporal Cortex Activation in a Moral Judgment Task: Preliminary Functional MRI Results in Normal Subjects." *Arq. Neuropsiquiatr.* 59(3-B): 657–64.

Moll, Jorge, Ricardo de Oliveira-Souza, Ivanei E. Bramati, and Jordan Grafman. 2002a. "Functional Networks in Emotional Moral and Nonmoral Social Judgments." *Neuroimage* 16(3A): 696–703.

Moll, Jorge, Ricardo de Oliveira-Souza, Paul J. Eslinger, Ivanei E. Bramati, Janaína Mourão-Miranda, Pedro Angelo Andreiuolo, and Luiz Pessoa. 2002b. "The Neural Correlates of Moral Sensitivity: A Functional Magnetic Resonance Imaging Investigation of Basic and Moral Emotions." *The Journal of Neuroscience* 22(7): 2730–6.

Monin, Benoît, David A. Pizarro, and Jennifer S. Beer. 2007. "Deciding vs. Reacting: Conceptions of Moral Judgment and the Reason-Affect Debate." *Review of General Psychology* 11(2): 99–111.

Nisbett, Richard, and Tim D. Wilson. 1977. "Telling More Than We Know: Verbal Reports on Mental Processes." *Psychological Review* 84(3): 231–95.

Oatley, Keith, and Philip N. Johnson-Laird. 1987. "Toward a Cognitive Theory of Emotions." *Cognition and Emotion* 1: 29–50.

Ochsner, Kevin N., Silvia A. Bunge, James J. Gross, and John D. E. Gabrieli. 2002. "Rethinking Feelings: An fMRI Study of the Cognitive Regulation of Emotion." *Journal of Cognitive Neuroscience* 14(8): 1215–29.

Ortony, Andrew, Allan Collins, and Gerald L. Clore. 1988. *The Cognitive Structure of Emotions.* Cambridge: Cambridge University Press.

Piaget, Jean. 1932. *The Moral Judgment of the Child.* New York: Harcourt, Brace Jovanovich.

Pizarro, David A., and Paul Bloom. 2003. "The Intelligence of the Moral Intuitions: A Comment on Haidt (2001)." *Psychological Review* 110(1): 193–6.

Pizarro, David A., Brian Detweiler-Bedell, and Paul Bloom. 2006. "The Creativity of Everyday Moral Reasoning: Empathy, Disgust and Moral Persuasion." In *Creativity and Reason in Cognitive Development,* edited by James C. Kaufman and John Baer. New York: Cambridge University Press.

Prinz, Jesse J. 2006. *The Emotional Construction of Morals.* Oxford: Oxford University Press.

Rawls, John. 1999. *A Theory of Justice.* Cambridge, Mass.: Harvard University Press.

Rest, James R. 1986. *Moral Development: Advances in Research and Theory.* New York: Greenwood Publishing Group.

Roseman, Ira J., Ann Aliki Antoniou, and Paul E. Jose. 1996. "Appraisal Determinants of Emotions: Constructing a More Accurate and Comprehensive Theory." *Cognition and Emotion* 10(3): 241–78.

Rozin, Paul. 1999. "The Process of Moralization." *Psychological Science* 10(3): 218–21.

Rozin, Paul, and Leher Singh. 1999. "The Moralization of Cigarette Smoking in the United States." *Journal of Consumer Psychology* 8(3): 339–42.

Rozin, Paul, Maureen Markwith, and Caryn Stoess. 1997. "Moralization and Becoming a Vegetarian: The Transformation of Preferences into Values and the Recruitment of Disgust." *Psychological Science* 8(2): 67–73.

Rozin, Paul, Laura Lowery, Sumid Imada, and Jonathan Haidt. 1999. "The CAD Triad Hypothesis: A Mapping Between the Three Moral Emotions (Contempt, Anger, Disgust) and the Three Moral Codes (Community, Autonomy, Divinity)." *Journal of Personality and Social Psychology* 76(4): 574–86.

Scherer, Klaus R. 1998. "Appraisal Theory." In *Handbook of Cognition and Emotion,* edited by Tim Dalgleish and Mick Power. Chichester, England: Wiley.

————. 2003. "Introduction: Cognitive Components of Emotion." In *Handbook of the Affective Sciences,* edited by Richard J. Davidson, Klaus R. Scherer, and H. Hill Goldsmith. New York: Oxford University Press.

Schwarz, Norbert, and Gerald L. Clore. 1983. "Mood, Misattribution, and Judgments of Well-Being: Informative and Directive Functions of Affective States." *Journal of Personality and Social Psychology* 45(3): 513–23

Simon, Herbert A. 1967. "Motivational and Emotional Controls of Cognition." In *Models of Thought,* edited by Herbert A. Simon. New Haven, Conn.: Yale University Press.

Singer, Peter. 1995. *How Are We to Live?* Amherst, N.Y.: Prometheus Books.

Smith, Craig A., and Richard S. Lazarus. 1993. "Appraisal Components, Core Relational Themes, and the Emotions." *Cognition and Emotion* 7(3–4): 233–69.

Stein, Nancy L., and Linda J. Levine. 1987. "Thinking About Feelings: The Development and Organization of Emotional Knowledge." In *Cognition, Conation and Affect.* Vol. 3 of *Aptitude, Learning, and Instruction,* edited by Richard E. Snow and Marshall J. Farr. Hillsdale, N.J.: Lawrence Erlbaum Associates, Inc.

————. 1990. "Making Sense Out of Emotion: The Representation and Use of Goal-Structured Knowledge." In *Psychological and Biological Approaches to Emotion,* edited by Nancy L. Stein, Bennett Leventhal, and Thomas R. Trabasso. Hillsdale, N.J.: Lawrence Erlbaum Associates, Inc.

Stein, Nancy L., Thomas R. Trabasso, and Maria D. Liwag. 2000. "A Goal Appraisal Theory of Emotional Understanding: Implications for Development and Learning." In *Handbook of Emotions,* edited by Michael Lewis and Jeannette M. Haviland-Jones. 2nd edition. New York: Guilford Press.

Sunstein, Cass R. 2005. "Moral Heuristics." *Behavior and Brain Sciences* 28(4): 531–42.

Tetlock, Philip E., Orie V. Kristel, S. Beth Elson, Melanie C. Green, and Jennifer S. Lerner. 2000. "The Psychology of the Unthinkable: Taboo Trade-Offs, Forbidden Base-Rates, and Heretical Counterfactuals." *Journal of Personality and Social Psychology* 78(5): 853–70.

Tooby, John, and Leda Cosmides. 1990. "The Past Explains the Present: Emotional Adaptations and the Structure of Ancestral Environments." *Ethology and Sociobiology* 11: 375–424.

Waterman, Alan S. 1988. "On the Use of Psychological Theory and Research in the Process of Ethical Inquiry." *Psychological Bulletin* 103(3): 283–98.

Weiner, Bernard 1985. "An Attributional Theory of Achievement Motivation and Emotion." *Psychological Review* 92(4): 548–73.

Woodward, Bob, and Scott Armstrong. 1979. *The Brethren: Inside the Supreme Court.* New York: Simon & Schuster.

Zajonc, Robert B. 1980. "Feeling and Thinking: Preferences Need No Inferences." *American Psychologist* 35(2): 151–75.

· 11 ·

Aging, Affect, and Decision Making

QUINN KENNEDY AND MARA MATHER

O LDER ADULTS are faced with complex decisions, particularly medical and financial decisions, which can carry high levels of risk and have important consequences for their quality of life. Do older adults make decisions any differently than younger adults? Decision making involves cognitive and emotional processes that have been shown to change with age; for example, maintaining and manipulating information in working memory (MacPherson, Phillips, and Della Sala 2002), and dealing with the emotional aspects of a decision (Bechara et al. 1999; Blanchard-Fields, Jahnke, and Camp 1995).

Research shows that emotional goals, such as feeling good in the moment, become more salient as people get older (Carstensen, Isaacowitz, and Turk-Charles 1999). These changes have implications for older adults' decision making. Older adults are more likely to attend and remember positively valenced information than are younger adults (Carstensen and Mikels 2005; Carstensen, Mikels, and Mather 2006; Mather 2004; Mather and Carstensen 2005), which may lead older adults to focus on different aspects of information available during the decision making process than younger adults (Mather, Knight, and McCaffrey 2005) and remember their past decisions more positively than the decisions merit (Mather and Johnson 2000).

One area in which age affects decision making includes decisions involving assessments of risk. A risky choice is one in which there is a probability or chance of various outcomes occurring. The final outcome is not determined by the choice, but by the way that the chosen probabilistic situation turns out. In contrast, other choices are riskless in that the ultimate outcome for each option is known in advance and there is not uncertainty about how each option will turn out. The literature on emotion, decision making, and aging shows that age-related changes in emotion affect older adults' decision making about options with uncertain outcomes.

Affect and Decision Making

While emotion and cognition often work together in decision making, emotion overrides cognition under some circumstances. Emotional reactions occur more rapidly than cognitive responses (LeDoux 1993; Zajonc 1980), and therefore can direct cognitive assessments such as the perception of risk (Finucane et al. 2000). One example of directing cognitive assessments is that people often overweigh small probabilities or perceive a negative relationship between risks and benefits even when they are positively correlated; such judgments contradict rational thought (Finucane et al. 2000; Loewenstein et al. 2001). The tendency to erroneously perceive a negative relationship between perceived risk and perceived benefit seems to be the result of referring to one's affective response when judging both risk and benefit. For instance, people who feel more positively about cell phones rate the benefit of cell phones higher and the risk lower than those who feel more negatively about cell phones. This negative correlation increases when people are asked to make the judgments under time pressure and there is less time for analytic deliberation (Finucane et al. 2000).

In addition, several factors that influence risk taking behavior are mediated by affect rather than cognition; these include background mood, the time interval between decision and outcome, and vividness with which the outcome is represented mentally (Loewenstein et al. 2001). For example, emotional reactions are more sensitive to vivid possibilities than to the probability of an event occurring (Loewenstein et al. 2001). Thus, when an emotionally evocative outcome, such as winning a million dollars in a lottery, is involved in a risky decision, people are relatively insensitive to the probability of the outcome occurring. Whether the odds are one in one hundred million or one in one hundred thousand will make little difference in the decision to buy the lottery ticket.

Emotion plays an integral yet multifaceted role in decision making. Different emotions and even different aspects of the emotional experience affect decision making in distinct ways, and the effects of emotion on risky decision making depends on the nature of the risk, the level of risk involved, and whether potential losses are personally relevant or not (Isen 2000; Isen, Nygren, and Ashby 1988; Isen and Patrick 1983; Mann 1992). For example, people in a positive mood are less risk taking than people in a neutral mood when the potential loss is personally relevant, regardless of the level of risk (Nygren et al. 1996).

Positive Emotions

Work by the psychologist Alice Isen and her colleagues demonstrates that positive mood has a complex effect on risk perception and decision making for risk (Isen 2000; Isen and Labroo 2003; Isen, Nygren, and Ashby 1988; Isen and Patrick 1983; Isen, Rosenzweig, and Young 1991; Mann 1992). People may be aware of their positive mood and may try to maintain it, leading to more conservative risk taking when the task is personally relevant. For example, participants induced into a positive mood bet more on a low-risk bet but less on a high-risk bet (Isen and Patrick 1983). These studies typically have used mood-induction techniques in the laboratory. Consistent with this pattern of findings in which people in a positive mood are more optimistic in their perceptions of positive outcomes yet more conservative in their actual risk taking behavior, a naturalistic study that examined managers' risk perceptions and risk intentions for business decisions found that managers who reported high levels of positive affect reported significantly lower perceptions of risk and personal consequence but were not more likely to seek risk compared to managers who reported low levels of positive affect (Williams, Zainuba, and Jackson 2003). Thus, perception of risk and reward by itself does not necessarily predict risk taking behavior.

Negative Emotions

Negative emotions affect risk perceptions and behavior, as well as how and how much people process information when making a decision. In Steve Williams, Muhamed Zainuba, and Robert Jackson's (2003) study regarding managers' perceptions of risk, managers who reported high levels of negative affect perceived risk-related gains more pessimistically and were more risk avoidant than managers who reported low levels of negative affect. The decision itself can be negatively laden. Many decisions, such as medical and financial decisions, are emotionally difficult. In these situations, negative emotions can act as a motivator for avoidance of most of the negative aspects of the decision making process (Luce 1998). Participants with the highest decision-related negative affect were more likely to choose an avoidant option (that is, the status quo) when selecting which automobile to purchase; those who chose an avoidant option reported less intense negative emotions than those who chose other options (Luce 1998). Thus, negatively laden decisions can prompt the use of emotion-regulation strategies (in this case, avoidance).

Recently, researchers have begun to tease apart the effects of different negative emotions on decision making. Sadness, which is associated with the loss or absence of reward and a motivation to acquire reward, can lead to a preference for high-reward, high-risk options over low-reward, low-risk options (Raghunathan and Pham 1999). In contrast, anxiety is the feeling of high uncertainty over the outcome and low control over the situation, and can lead to risk avoidance (Raghunathan and Pham 1999). Depression, of which one symptom is the lack of energy, is associated with action aversion, leading to slower decision making and greater reluctance to make decisions (Loewenstein et al. 2001). In addition, anger and fear lead to different effects on risk estimates (Lerner et al. 2003). Anger also interacts with decision-related affect differently than sadness. Using the same paradigm as the automobile study described above (Luce 1998), participants induced into an angry mood were more likely to select the avoidant option (that is, the status quo) than participants in a neutral mood when the decision was emotionally difficult. In contrast, participants induced into a sad mood chose the avoidant option regardless of the level of negative emotion associated with the decision (Garg, Inman, and Mittal 2005).

In summary, emotions have direct and indirect effects on decision making for risk. Current mood, the emotional attributes of the decision, and emotional reactions all contribute to the decision making process and outcome. Of note are the findings that people often attempt to regulate their emotions during the decision making process: when in a positive mood, people attempt to maintain it by being more conservative for personally relevant risk (Isen 2000). Decision-related negative affect, particularly when coupled with current feelings of anger, can lead to decision avoidance (Anderson 2003; Garg, Inman, and Mittal 2005; Luce 1998; Mather 2006).

Aging and Affect

Despite physical and social losses, adults sixty-five years and older experience high levels of emotional well-being into advanced old age. Life satisfaction among older people increases or is comparable to levels among young adults in their twenties: the declines in life satisfaction that are seen in very old age are in part due to proximity to death, presumably because of declines in health (Agren 1998; Diener and Suh 1998; Mroczek and Spiro 2005). Emotional well-being typically is defined by high frequencies of positive and low frequencies of negative emotions. There appears to be a curvilinear relationship between age and frequency of positive and negative emotions, with the least optimal emotional experiences in young adulthood and the most optimal emotional experiences in early old age (Charles, Reynolds, and Gatz 2001; Stacy and Gatz 1991).[1]

As people approach their eighties, the quality of emotional experience declines from this peak somewhat (Charles, Reynolds, and Gatz 2001; Stacy and Gatz 1991). However, at no point do older adults experience greater frequencies of negative affect than do younger adults (Carstensen et al. 2000). Furthermore, older adults experience longer durations of positive emotions and shorter durations of negative emotions than younger adults do (Carstensen et al. 2000).

The Salience of Emotion in Old Age

According to socioemotional selectivity theory (Carstensen, Isaacowitz, and Turk-Charles 1999), as people age and perceive time as increasingly limited, they place greater importance on emotional goals, such as feeling good in the moment and creating emotional meaning from life, and more importance on the emotional aspects of their lives than on achieving knowledge related goals, such as acquiring information. The increased salience of emotion leads to emotional well-being and improved emotion regulation. Several lines of research now document that older adults place greater importance on emotional goals, experience high levels of emotional well-being, and regulate their emotions better than younger adults (Agren 1998; Carstensen et al. 2000; Charles, Reynolds, and Gatz 2001; Diener and Suh 1998; Gross et al. 1997).

The increased salience of emotion with age also occurs in the areas of preferences, attention, and memory (Mather and Carstensen 2005). Compared to younger adults, older adults attend to and remember a greater proportion of emotional information than neutral information and prefer and better remember advertisements with emotional slogans than those with knowledge-related slogans (Fung and Carstensen 2003). The increased salience of emotion appears to be driven by heightened attention and memory for positive information and de-emphasis on negative stimuli (Carstensen and Mikels 2005; Mather and Carstensen 2005). This positivity effect has been defined as a developmental pattern in which there is a shift from a disproportionate preference for negative information in young adulthood to a disproportionate preference for positive information in old age (Carstensen, Mikels, and Mather 2006). It is linked with improved emotional well-being, as studies have found that older adults show enhanced moods after recalling autobiographical events, especially among those who show the positivity effect in their memories (Kennedy, Mather, and Carstensen 2004; Pasupathi and Carstensen 2003).

Positivity Effects Among Older Adults

Remembering positive information is likely to benefit emotional well-being more than remembering negative information is likely to. Thus, older adults' focus on emotion may lead to selective increases in the potency of positive information relative to negative information. Below, we briefly review evidence of a positivity effect among older adults in the areas of attention, memory retrieval, memory-review strategies, and autobiographical memory.

Attention.   If older adults focus on emotional goals, this bias also should appear in earlier stages of the memory process, such as in the encoding phase. In one study, age differences in the encoding phase were examined by having younger and older adults view positive, negative, and neutral pictures while their brain activity was recorded using a functional magnetic resonance imaging (fMRI) scanner (Mather et al. 2004). Both older and younger adults showed greater activation in the amygdala for emotional pictures than for neutral pictures. However, for older adults, seeing positive pictures led to greater amygdala activation than seeing negative pictures, whereas younger adults showed similar levels of activation for positive and negative pictures. These findings indicate that younger and older adults show different patterns of attention during initial encoding depending on the emotional valence of the stimuli.

Age differences in attention also were found in a study in which older and younger adults completed a dot-probe task (Mather and Carstensen 2003). Participants first viewed a neutral and an emotional version of a face displayed on the left and right sides of the computer screen for one thousand milliseconds. The faces disappeared from the screen and a small gray dot appeared in the center of where one of the faces had been displayed. As soon as they saw the dot probe, participants pressed a key on the keyboard. Older adults were significantly slower in responding to the dot probe behind negative faces than behind neutral faces; this bias did not appear in younger adults' response rates. Although no significant age-group difference was found for the positive trials, older adults were significantly faster in responding to dot probes behind the positive faces than behind neutral faces. Similar age differences in attention to emotional stimuli have been found in eye-tracking studies (Isaacowitz et al. 2006a, 2006b; Rosler et al. 2005).

These age differences in attention occur during decision making as well. For instance, when making a choice between descriptions of two cars in which each option included both positive and negative features, older adults spent a larger proportion of their time reviewing the positive features than the younger adults did, whereas the younger adults spent more of their time reviewing the negative features than the older adults did (Mather, Knight, and McCaffrey 2005). Older adults also had more accurate memory for positive features than for negative features, whereas younger adults did not show this bias.

Memory Retrieval.   Recent findings indicate that older adults disproportionately forget negative information (Charles, Mather, and Carstensen 2003; Denburg et al. 2003; Leigland, Schulz, and Janowsky 2004; Mather and Knight 2005; Mather, Knight, and McCaffrey 2005). For example, after looking at a slide show of positive, negative, and neutral pictures, older adults recalled a greater proportion of positive pictures than negative pictures compared with younger adults (Charles, Mather, and Carstensen 2003). This diminishment of negative memory relative to positive memory among older adults was revealed both when participants listed all of the pictures they remembered and when, out of a series of pictures, they indicated which pictures they had seen before and which were new pictures. Furthermore, the age differences could not be accounted for by differences in mood in the two samples or in differences in the intensity level of the negative and positive pictures.

Memory Review Strategies.   These studies indicate that older adults attend more to emotional information than nonemotional information and more to positive than to negative information. Results from a study of memory for decisions provides evidence that older adults' emotionally gratifying memories go beyond just remembering relatively fewer negative elements of an event; they extend also to choice-supportive memory. Choice-supportive memory occurs when people attribute more positive features to the option they have chosen and more negative features to the option they have rejected (Benney and Henkel 2006; Henkel and Mather 2007; Mather, Shafir, and Johnson 2000, 2003). In a study comparing younger and older adults' memories of choices (Mather and Johnson 2000), participants chose between two options, each of which included positive and negative features. Older adults were more likely to attribute more positive and fewer negative features to options that they chose than to the options that they did not choose. These findings held even after controlling for age-related declines in memory. Although older adults were more choice supportive than younger adults in the control condition, younger adults displayed the same levels of choice-supportive memory as older adults when participants were instructed to think about how they felt about the options in each decision task. In contrast, older adults were significantly choice supportive in every condition, whether they were cued to focus on their emotions or not. The findings demonstrate that older and younger adults focus on the same information quite differently. Older adults spontaneously focus on the affective qualities of information, whereas younger adults do not. When younger adults do focus on the affective qualities of the information, they show the same choice-supportive bias as older adults. The findings indicate that affective processing of information contributes to choice-supportive behavior. In particular, older adults may use choice-supportive memory as a way to regulate their current emotional state.

Autobiographical Memory.   Longitudinal studies of distant personal memories find a positivity effect with age for many types of personal information, including parental care, emotionally charged personal experiences, physical and emotional well-being, and personality characteristics (Field 1981, 1997; Kennedy, Mather, and Carstensen 2004; Robbins 1963; Yarrow, Campbell, and Burton 1970). When given cues to retrieve autobiographical memories, older adults retrieve more positive memories than negative memories (Serrano, Latorre, and Gatz 2007) and are less likely to retrieve negative memories than are younger adults (Schlagman, Schulz, and Kvavilashvili 2006; Schulkind and Woldorf 2005).

Age-related forgetting of past traumatic personal experiences also occurs (Robins et al. 1985; Wagenaar and Groeneweg 1990), which should aid current emotional well-being. These findings are consistent with a study in which younger and older adults recalled memories from previous periods of life (Berntsen and Rubin 2002). Negative memories were longer-lasting for younger adults, whereas positive memories endured longer for older adults.

Positively recalling the distant past appears to aid emotional well-being. In a study of American nuns, older participants were more likely to distort autobiographical memories in a positive direction and end up in a better mood than before they recalled their memories compared to younger participants (Kennedy, Mather, and Carstensen 2004). In this study, all the sisters recalled personal information that they had originally reported fourteen years prior. Thus the findings are not due to older participants recalling more temporally distant information than younger participants. In addition, findings remained after controlling for scores on a short-term memory test and for current mood at the time of recollection.

In summary, older adults attend more to emotional information; in particular, they attend more than younger adults to positively valenced information relative to other types of information (Carstensen and Turk-Charles 1994; Fung and Carstensen 2003; Hashtroudi, Johnson, and Chrosniak 1990). Furthermore, several memory studies suggest that older adults regulate their emotions while recalling past decisions, public events, and personal experiences in ways that optimize current emotional states (Kennedy, Mather, and Carstensen 2004; Levine and Bluck 1997; Mather and Johnson 2000; Pasupathi and Carstensen 2003). As a whole, the literature on aging and emotion indicates that older adults place greater importance on emotion, leading to higher levels of emotional well-being and more effective emotion regulation than younger adults.

Aging and Decision Making

Most studies of decision making for risk that include older adults do not report age differences in risk attitude and risk behavior for financial decisions, health decisions, or games of risk (Bechara et al. 1994; Kovalchik et al. 2005; Mayhorn, Fisk, and Whittle 2002; Stout, Rodawalt, and Siemers 2001; Zwahr, Park, and Shifren 1999). Even when negative aging stereotypes were activated, older adults had equivalent levels of risk behavior in playing a computerized version of blackjack compared to younger adults (Ashman et al. 2003). Several other studies found no age differences in risk behavior when selecting cards from decks varying in their level of risk and rewards; indeed, some of these studies found that older and younger adults were equally likely to select cards from high-reward, high-risk decks (Bechara et al. 1994, 1998; Dror, Katona, and Mungur 1998; MacPherson, Phillips, and Della Sala 2002; Wilder, Weinberger, and Goldberg 1998; Wood et al. 2005). These studies primarily have used the Iowa gambling task, in which participants learn the contingencies of the payoffs through trial and error (Bechara et al. 1999). One study that displayed the probabilities of winning did find that older adults were less risk taking than younger adults (Deakin et al. 2004). The authors suggest that in experience-based tasks older adults may be slower in learning to avoid high-risk options than younger adults, leading older adults to make more risky decisions than they would otherwise (Deakin et al. 2004). If this is the case, then the amount of cognitive demand and memory demand required by the decision making task may affect older adults' risk behavior.

Evidence also indicates that older and younger adults perceive risk in comparable ways. Both younger and older adults tend to value immediate reward over longer-term, more profitable gain (Green et al. 1996; MacPherson, Phillips, and Della Sela 2002). When forced to make a decision in hypothetical scenarios, such as whether or not to begin cancer or estrogen-replacement therapy, no significant age differences emerged for participants' estimates of the risk of therapy (Zwahr, Park, and Shifren 1999). Furthermore, both younger and older adults are equally

susceptible to framing effects, in which changes in the wording of a decision option such that the option is viewed as either a gain (that is, positive
framing) or a loss (that is, negative framing) lead to changes in the perception of the expected utility of the decision option. Positive framing is
associated with risk aversion, whereas negative framing is associated
with risk taking (Mayhorn, Fisk, and Whittle 2002). An exception to the
above findings is that older adults who have disproportionate aging of the
ventromedial prefrontal cortex (vmPFC), an area associated with decision
making and reasoning, appear to make more risky and less advantageous
gambling decisions than younger adults and older adults with typical
aging of the vmPFC (Denburg, Tranel, and Bechara 2005). This finding is
consistent with research on decision making for risk among patients with
prefrontal cortex lesions (Bechara et al. 1994; Bechara et al. 1999), in which
the patients were more risk taking than healthy controls. Currently, it is
unknown whether damage to the prefrontal cortex is linked with greater
desire for risk taking or to ignorance of the level of risk involved (Sanfey
et al. 2003). Thus, some older adults who show advanced aging to their
vmPFC make more risky decisions than younger adults, but the motive is
unclear (Denberg, Tranel, and Bechara 2005).

Despite the general similarity across younger and older adults in
risk taking tendencies, older adults do deal with certain aspects of the
decision making process differently from younger adults. Compared
with younger adults, older adults forget early decisions on the Iowa gambling task more quickly and are more likely to make decisions based on
recently experienced outcomes rather than from more objective cognitive assessments which incorporate all experienced outcomes (Wood
et al. 2005). They also tend to generate fewer options, deliberate for less
time, and seek out and review less information—particularly negative
information—than younger adults in hypothetical and real-life situations
(Berg, Meegan, and Klaczynski 1999; Löckenhoff and Carstensen 2004;
Mather, Knight, and McCaffrey 2005). In fact, in a study of everyday decisions regarding medical adherence and nutrition, most of the errors made
by older adults' were due to incomplete reading of the provided information (Willis, Dolan, and Bertrand 1999). Finally, older adults also are
more likely than younger adults to avoid making a decision regarding
serious medical treatments; they do this by either putting off making a
decision or preferring that their physician make the decision for them
(Hudak et al. 2002; Mather 2006; Orsino et al. 2003).

In summary, laboratory studies indicate that the majority of older
adults and younger adults have comparable levels of risk aversion and
perceive comparable amounts of risk involved in making decisions. Older
adults, however, forget decisions more rapidly, deliberate for less time,
seek out less information, are more decision avoidant, and use less cogni-

tively demanding information-search strategies than younger adults; such activities could lead to more risky decisions. In particular, there are two factors that change with age—memory and emotional salience—which could influence older adults' decision making about alternatives with uncertain outcomes.

Age Differences in Memory that May Affect Decision Making

Decision making depends on working memory and long-term memory (Bechara et al. 1998). Compared to younger adults, older adults have a reduced capacity for working memory in terms of immediately available information, such as remembering telephone numbers (Light, Zelinski, and Moore 1982), as well as a worse long-term memory (Ahlberg and Sharps 2002). Little is currently known as to how age differences in memory affect decision making. A recent study suggests that memory decline affects decision making in old age. When asked to judge several hypothetical patients' diseases based on information provided, older adults made more conservative judgments than younger adults. However, when older adults were given more time to study the information, age differences in the level of conservatism disappeared (Spaniol and Bayen 2005). Findings from this study indicate that after controlling for memory encoding, no age differences occur for level of conservatism. More work is needed to understand whether the effect of memory on any particular task depends on the extent and type of memory that the task requires, and whether these particular memory demands mediate the effects of aging on risk taking.

One decision making strategy linked to memory which has been extensively studied is the use of heuristics. Older adults are more likely to rely on gist information or heuristics in recall (Bayen et al. 2000; Mather, Johnson, and De Leonardis 1999). Heuristic decisions are habitual, intuitive, nonanalytical, and require minimal processing speed (Ariely and Zakay 2001). A similar reliance on heuristic processing may occur in older adults' decision making as well (Peters et al. 2000; Yates and Patalano 1999). For example, older adults are more likely than younger adults to use personal experience in making judgments (Löckenhoff and Carstensen 2004) and to rely on stereotypes in source monitoring (Mather, Johnson, and De Leonardis 1999).

The reliance on heuristics under certain circumstances can be beneficial and, in other cases, detrimental. For example, it can be detrimental if older adults rely solely on general background knowledge in reviewing medical information and in giving advice to another medication user (Gould 1999). However, researchers have suggested that older adults do not show the "attraction effect"—an effect that occurs when adding an irrelevant option to an existing set of options increases the likelihood of people choosing the irrelevant option—because of their reliance on heuristics (Kim and Hasher 2005). The attraction effect leads to inconsistent decisions across similar problems, which can have deleterious effects. To date, little is known about the relationship between age-related changes in the reliance on heuristics and decision making for risk, but findings do suggest that older adults rely more on heuristics in their decision making as well as in their memory.

The Relationship Between Aging, Affect, and Decision Making

The increased salience of emotion with age may lead to age differences in decision making processes and behavior. This can happen in three ways: the effects of emotion on decision making found among young adults will be heightened among older adults, a focus on the emotional aspects of decision making will increase with age, or greater likelihood of showing a positivity effect in memory for past decisions among older adults than among younger adults.

Greater Effects of Emotion on Decision Making Due to the Increased Salience of Emotion with Age

Research shows that emotion regulation can occur during the decision making process. When faced with a decision, people try to maintain a positive mood; when in a negative mood, people try to mitigate negative feelings (Anderson 2003; Isen 2000; Luce 1998). Older adults are more adept at emotion regulation than younger adults, and therefore may be more likely to try to regulate their emotions during the decision making process. Older adults also are more likely to be in a positive mood at any given time compared to younger adults (Carstensen et al. 2000). According to theories about mood maintenance (Isen 2000), older adults should be more likely than younger adults to have low thresholds for risk when the decision is personally relevant. To our knowledge, this question has yet to be addressed experimentally.

Greater attention to maintaining positive mood and better emotion regulation may also explain why older adults are more likely to avoid making a serious medical decision compared to younger adults. Deciding whether or not to have a serious medical procedure, such as total joint arthroplasty, is a highly emotional, conflict-laden task, and thus one way to avoid negative affect is to postpone the decision (Hudak et al. 2002). Other research has demonstrated that people who feel decision-related negative affect are more likely to choose an avoidant option and to have a less negative affect after doing so (Luce 1998). We conjecture that attempting to mitigate decision-related affect may also lead older adults to deliberate for less time and seek out less information for negatively laden decisions than younger adults do.

Focus on Emotional Aspects of Decision Making

Research indicates that older adults are more attuned to the emotional aspects of everyday interpersonal problems and adjust their problem-solving strategies accordingly (Blanchard-Fields, Jahnke, and Camp 1995; Blanchard-Fields, Stein, and Watson 2004; Watson and Blanchard-Fields 1998). In solving everyday interpersonal problems, older adults show greater flexibility in their use of problem-solving strategies, are better able to place the problem in context, and are better able to adjust their problem-solving strategy accordingly (Blanchard-Fields, Stein, and Watson 2004). For example, younger adults reported using mostly problem-focused strategies regardless of problem type or the emotional consequences of the solution. In contrast, older adults reported changing their strategies based on the emotional salience of the problem. They used problem-focused strategies for problems that were not emotionally salient and emotion-focused strategies for emotionally salient problems.

Older adults utilize heuristics when making decisions, in part due to age-related changes in cognitive processes (Mather, Johnson, and De Leonardis 1999; Peters et al. 2000). They may rely more heavily on a particular type of heuristic—the affective heuristic—than younger adults. The affective heuristic is the reliance on the emotional labels associated with the decision or judgment (Slovic et al. 2002). The stronger the affective impression of a potential decision and the more clearly positive or negative the impression is, the more weight the affective impression has on decision making. For example, when people have a strong positive or negative affective reaction to a particular decision, the affective reaction overrides sensitivity to changes in probabilities. The increased salience of emotion coupled with declining memory in old age may lead to a greater reliance on the affective heuristic than on other types of heuristics. Time pressure leads to greater reliance on the affective heuristic and to poorer decision making (Finucane et al. 2000; Mann 1992). Because older adults process information more slowly than younger adults, they may feel more pressured by time and consequently rely more heavily on the affective heuristic.

Positive Memory Effect for Past Decisions

As research shows, older adults disproportionately attend to and remember positive information compared to negative information, showing a positivity effect. The positivity effect may lead older adults to disproportionately remember their good decisions over their bad decisions, or the positive aspects of past decisions over the negative aspects to a greater extent than younger adults. They also may forget bad decisions more rapidly than good decisions. This memory bias may then influence future decisions for risk. For example, older gamblers report that their largest win in the past year was a significantly larger amount than that reported by younger gamblers (Desai et al. 2004). There are several possible explanations for this age difference. It may be that because older adults gamble more frequently, their chances of "winning big" are better. It may also be that older adults bet more money. Or, it could be due to the positivity effect, in which the older gamblers recalled their biggest win as larger than it actually was, whereas younger adults are less optimistic in their recall. Indeed, older adults are more likely to attribute more positive and fewer negative attributes to options they chose than to options they did not choose, showing choice-supportive memory (Mather and Johnson 2000). Furthermore, research on the affective heuristic has demonstrated that the remembered affect associated with a product influences subsequent product choice (Slovic et al. 2002). Thus, if older adults remember more positive attributes than negative attributes of past decisions—even if the decision was poor—they may be likely to make the same decision in the future.

Conclusion

Older adults are faced with complex and difficult decisions, particularly in the areas of medical and financial decisions. Many of these decisions are risky, such as whether or not to have a serious medical procedure or deciding how much money to gamble at the casino. Yet little research to date has investigated how older adults make decisions and which factors may influence older adults' decision making. Linking the literatures on aging, emotion, and decision making, we suggest that age-related changes in emotion lead to age differences in the decision making process and memory for past decisions.

Compared to younger adults, older adults disproportionately attend to and remember emotional information more than nonemotional material; this age-related focus on emotion appears to be driven primarily by a focus on positive emotion. This positivity effect can affect older adults' decision making for risk in multiple ways, including greater reliance on the affective heuristic, greater effort to maintain positive mood during the decision making process, greater attention to the emotional aspects of the decision making process, and positively biased memory for past decisions. These emotional factors may hurt the effectiveness of older adults' decisions in some situations. For example, avoiding careful consideration of negative features of choice options may lead to poor choices. However, older adults' strategies should lead them to suffer less emotional pain as they make decisions as well as later when they recollect past decisions.

Notes

1. A similar curvilinear pattern is found for self-esteem, in which self-esteem gradually increases through adulthood with a peak in the late sixties, and then declines through very old age (Robins and Trzesniewski 2005).

References

Agren, Margareta. 1998. "Life at 85 and 92: A Qualitative Longitudinal Study of How the Oldest Old Experience and Adjust to the Increasing Uncertainty of Existence." *International Journal of Aging and Human Development* 47(2): 105–17.

Ahlberg, Shari W., and Mathew J. Sharps. 2002. "Bartlett Revisited: Reconfiguration of Long-Term Memory in Young and Older Adults." *Journal of Genetic Psychology* 163(2): 211–8.

Anderson, Christopher J. 2003. "The Psychology of Doing Nothing: Forms of Decision Avoidance Result from Reason and Emotion." *Psychological Bulletin* 129(1): 139–67.

Ariely, Dan, and Dan Zakay. 2001. "A Timely Account of the Role of Duration in Decision Making." *Acta Psychologica* 108(2): 187–207.

Ashman, Ori, Itiel E. Dror, Melissa A. Houlette, and Becca R. Levy. 2003. "Preserved Risk-Taking Skills in Old Age." *North American Journal of Psychology* 5(3): 397–407.

Bayen, Ute J., Glenn V. Nakamura, Susan E. Dupuis, and Chin-Lung L. Yang. 2000. "The Use of Schematic Knowledge About Sources in Source Monitoring." *Memory and Cognition* 28(3): 480–500.

Bechara, Antoine, Antonio R. Damasio, Hanna Damasio, and Steven W. Anderson. 1994. "Insensitivity to Future Consequences Following Damage to Human Prefrontal Cortex." *Cognition* 50(1–3): 7–15.

Bechara, Antoine, Hanna Damasio, Antonio R. Damasio, and Gregory P. Lee. 1999. "Different Contributions of the Human Amygdala and Ventromedial Prefrontal Cortex to Decision-Making." *Journal of Neuroscience* 19(13): 5473–81.

Bechara, Antoine, Hanna Damasio, Daniel Tranel, and Steven W. Anderson. 1998. "Dissociation of Working Memory from Decision Making Within the Human Prefrontal Cortex." *Journal of Neuroscience* 18(1): 428–37.

Benney, Kristen S., and Linda A. Henkel. 2006. "The Role of Free Choice in Memory for Past Decisions." *Memory* 14(8): 1001–11.

Berg, Cynthia A., Sean P. Meegan, and Paul Klaczynski. 1999. "Age and Experiential Differences in Strategy Generation and Information Requests for Solving Everyday Problems." *International Journal of Behavioral Development* 23(3): 615–39.

Berntsen, Durthe, and David C. Rubin. 2002. "Emotionally Charged Autobiographical Memories Across the Lifespan: The Recall of Happy, Sad, Traumatic, and Involuntary Memories." *Psychology and Aging* 17(4): 636–52.

Blanchard-Fields, Fredda, Heather C. Jahnke, and Cameron Camp. 1995. "Age Differences in Problem-Solving Style: The Role of Emotional Salience." *Psychology and Aging* 10(2): 173–80.

Blanchard-Fields, Fredda, Renee Stein, and Tanya L. Watson. 2004. "Age Differences in Emotion-Regulation Strategies in Handling Everyday Problems." *Journals of Gerontology: Series B: Psychological Sciences and Social Sciences* 59B(6): 261–9.

Carstensen, Laura L., and Joseph L. Mikels. 2005. "At the Intersection of Emotion and Cognition: Aging and the Positivity Effect." *Current Directions in Psychological Science* 14(3): 117–21.

Carstensen, Laura L., and Susan Turk-Charles. 1994. "The Salience of Emotion Across the Adult Life Span." *Psychology and Aging* 9(2): 259–64.

Carstensen, Laura L., Derek M. Isaacowitz, and Susan Turk-Charles. 1999. "Taking Time Seriously: A Theory of Socioemotional Selectivity Theory." *American Psychologist* 54(3): 165–81.

Carstensen, Laura L., Joseph L. Mikels, and Mara Mather. 2006. "Aging and the Intersection of Cognition, Motivation and Emotion." In *Handbook of the Psychology of Aging,* edited by James Birren and K. Warner Schaie. San Diego, Calif.: Academic Press.

Carstensen, Laura L., Monisha Pasupathi, Ulrich Mayr, and John R. Nesselroade. 2000. "Emotional Experience in Everyday Life Across the Adult Life Span." *Journal of Personality and Social Psychology* 79(4): 644–55.

Charles, Susan, Mara Mather, and Laura L. Carstensen. 2003. "Aging and Emotional Memory: The Forgettable Nature of Negative Images for Older Adults." *Journal of Experimental Psychology: General* 132(2): 310–24.

Charles, Susan, Chandra A. Reynolds, and Margaret Gatz. 2001. "Age-Related Differences and Changes in Positive and Negative Affect over 23 Years." *Journal of Personality and Social Psychology* 80(1): 136–51.

Deakin, Julia, Michael Aitken, Trevor Robbins, and Barbara J. Sahakian. 2004. "Risk Taking During Decision-Making in Normal Volunteers Changes with Age." *Journal of the International Neuropsychological Society* 10(4): 590–8.

Denburg, Natalie L., Daniel Tranel, and Antoine Bechara. 2005. "The Ability to Decide Advantageously Declines Prematurely in Some Normal Older Adults." *Neuropsychologia* 43(7): 1099–1106.

Denburg, Natalia L., Tony W. Buchanan, Daniel Tranel, and Ralph Adolphs. 2003. "Evidence for Preserved Emotional Memory in Normal Older Adults." *Emotion* 3(3): 239–53.

Desai, Rani A., Paul K. Maciejewksi, David J. Dausey, Barbara J. Caldarone, and Marc N. Potenza. 2004. "Health Correlates of Recreational Gambling in Older Adults." *American Journal of Psychiatry* 161(9): 1672–9.

Diener, Ed, and Eukook Suh. 1998. "Subjective Well-Being and Age: An International Analysis." *Annual Review of Gerontology and Geriatrics* 17: 304–24.

Dror, Itiel E., Michelle Katona, and Kruhna Mungur. 1998. "Age Differences in Decision Making: To Take a Risk or Not." *Gerontology (Experimental Section)* 44(2): 67–71.

Field, Dorothy. 1981. "Retrospective Reports by Healthy Intelligent Elderly People of Personal Events of Their Adult Lives." *International Journal of Behavioral Development* 4: 77–97.

———. 1997. "Looking Back, What Period of Your Life Brought You the Most Satisfaction?" *International Journal of Aging and Human Development* 45(3): 169–94.

Finucane, Melissa, Ali Alhakami, Paul Slovic, and Stephen M. Johnson. 2000. "The Affect Heuristic in Judgments of Risks and Benefits." *Journal of Behavioral Decision Making* 13(1): 1–17.

Fung, Helenett H., and Laura L. Carstensen. 2003. "Sending Memorable Messages: Age Differences in Preference and Memory for Advertisements." *Journal of Personality and Social Psychology* 85(1): 163–78.

Garg, Nitika, J. Jeffrey Inman, and Vikas Mittal. 2005. "Incidental and Task-Related Affect: A Re-Inquiry and Extension of the Influence of Affect on Choice." *Journal of Consumer Research* 32(1): 154–9.

Gould, Odette N. 1999. "Cognition and Affect in Medication Adherence." In *Processing of Medical Information in Aging Patients: Cognitive and Human Factors Perspectives,* edited by Denise C. Park and Roger W. Morrell. Mahwah, N.J.: Lawrence Erlbaum Associates, Inc.

Green, Lawrence, Joel Myerson, David Lichtman, Suzanne Rosen, and Astrid Fry. 1996. "Temporal Discounting in Choice Between Delayed Rewards: The Role of Age and Income." *Psychology and Aging* 11(1): 79–84.

Gross, James J., Laura L. Carstensen, Monisha Pasupathi, Jeanne Tsai, Carina Götestam Skorpen, and Angie Hsu. 1997. "Emotion and Aging: Experience, Expression, and Control." *Psychology and Aging* 12(4): 590–9.

Hashtroudi, Shahin, Marcia K. Johnson, and Linda D. Chrosniak. 1990. "Aging and Qualitative Characteristics of Memories for Perceived and Imagined Complex Events." *Psychology and Aging* 5(1): 119–26.

Henkel, Linda A., and Mara Mather. 2007. "Memory Attributions for Choices: How Beliefs Shape Our Memories." *Journal of Memory and Language* 57(2): 163–76.

Hudak, Pamela L., Jocalyn P. Clark, Gillian A. Hawker, Peter C. Coyte, Nizar N. Mahomed, Hans J. Kreder, and James G. Wright. 2002. " 'You're Perfect for the Procedure! Why Don't You Want It?' Elderly Arthritis Patients' Unwillingness to Consider Total Joint Arthroplasty Surgery: A Qualitative Study." *Medical Decision Making* 22(3): 272–8.

Isaacowitz, Derek M., Heather A. Wadlinger, Deborah Goren, and Hugh R. Wilson. 2006a. "Is There an Age-Related Positivity Effect in Visual Attention? A Comparison of Two Methodologies." *Emotion* 6(3): 511–56.

———. 2006b. "Selective Preference in Visual Fixation Away from Negative Images in Old Age? An Eye Tracking Study." *Psychology and Aging* 21(2): 40–48.

Isen, Alice. 2000. "Some Perspectives on Positive Affect and Self-Regulation." *Psychological Inquiry* 11(3): 184–7.

Isen, Alice, and Aparna A. Labroo. 2003. "Some Ways in Which Positive Affect Facilitates Decision Making and Judgment." In *Emerging Perspectives on Judgment and Decision Research,* edited by Sandra L. Schneider and James Shanteau. New York: Cambridge University Press.

Isen, Alice, and Robert Patrick. 1983. "The Effect of Positive Feelings on Risk Taking: When the Chips Are Down." *Organizational Behavior and Human Performance* 31(2): 194–202.

Isen, Alice, Thomas E. Nygren, and F. Gregory Ashby. 1988. "Influence of Positive Affect on the Subjective Utility of Gains and Losses: It Is Just Not Worth the Risk." *Journal of Personality and Social Psychology* 55(5): 710–7.

Isen, Alice, Andrew S. Rosenzweig, and Mark J. Young. 1991. "The Influence of Positive Affect on Clinical Problem Solving." *Medical Decision Making* 11(3): 221–7.

Kennedy, Quinn, Mara Mather, and Laura L. Carstensen. 2004. "The Role of Motivation in the Age-Related Positivity Effect in Autobiographical Memory." *Psychological Science* 15(3): 208–14.

Kim, Sunghan, and Lynn Hasher. 2005. "The Attraction Effect in Decision Making: Superior Performance by Older Adults." *The Quarterly Journal of Experimental Psychology* 58A(1): 120–33.

Kovalchik, Stephanie, Colin F. Camerer, David M. Grether, Charles R. Plott, and John M. Allman. 2005. "Aging and Decision Making: A Comparison Between Neurologically Healthy Elderly and Young Individuals." *Journal of Economic Behavior and Organization* 58(1): 79–94.

LeDoux, Joseph E. 1993. "Emotional Memory: In Search of Systems and Synapses." *Annual Academy of Sciences* 702(1): 149–57.

Leigland, Lindsey A., Laura E. Schulz, and Jeri S. Janowsky. 2004. "Age Related Changes in Emotional Memory." *Neurobiology of Aging* 2(8): 1117–24.

Lerner, Jennifer S., Roxana M. Gonzalez, Deborah A. Small, and Baruch Fischhoff. 2003. "Effects of Fear and Anger on Perceived Risks of Terrorism: A National Field Experiment." *Psychological Science* 14(2): 144–50.

Levine, Linda J., and Susan Bluck. 1997. "Experienced and Remembered Emotional Intensity in Older Adults." *Psychology and Aging* 12(3): 514–23.

Light, Leah L., Elizabeth M. Zelinski, and Martha Moore. 1982. "Adult Age Differences in Reasoning from New Information." *Journal of Experimental Psychology: Learning, Memory, and Cognition* 8(5): 435–47.

Löckenhoff, Corinna, and Laura L. Carstensen. 2004. "Socioemotional Selectivity Theory, Aging, and Health: The Increasingly Delicate Balance Between Regulating Emotions and Making Tough Choices." *Journal of Personality* 72(6): 1395–1424.

Loewenstein, George, Elke U. Weber, Christopher K. Hsee, and Ned Welch. 2001. "Risk as Feelings." *Psychological Bulletin* 127(2): 267–86.

Luce, Mary Frances. 1998. "Choosing to Avoid: Coping with Negatively Emotion-Laden Consumer Decisions." *The Journal of Consumer Research* 24(4): 409–33.

MacPherson, Sarah E., Louise H. Phillips, and Sergio Della Sala. 2002. "Age, Executive Function, and Social Decision Making: A Dorsolateral Prefrontal Theory of Cognitive Aging." *Psychology and Aging* 17(4): 598–609.

Mann, Leon. 1992. "Stress, Affect, and Risk Taking." In *Risk-Taking Behavior,* edited by J. F. Yates. Chichester, UK: John Wiley and Sons, Ltd.

Mather, Mara. 2004. "Aging and Emotional Memory." In *Memory and Emotion,* edited by D. Reisberg and P. Hertel. New York: Oxford University Press.

———. 2006. "A Review of Decision Making Processes: Weighing the Risks and Benefits of Aging." In *When I'm 64,* edited by Laura L. Carstensen and Christine R. Hartel. Washington: The National Academies Press.

Mather, Mara, and Laura L. Carstensen. 2003. "Aging and Attentional Biases for Emotional Faces." *Psychological Science* 14(5): 409–15.

———. 2005. "Aging and Motivated Cognition: The Positivity Effect in Attention and Memory." *Trends in Cognitive Sciences* 9(10): 496–502.

Mather, Mara, and Marcia K. Johnson. 2000. "Choice-Supportive Source Monitoring: Do Our Decisions Seem Better to Us as We Age?" *Psychology and Aging* 15(4): 596–606.

Mather, Mara, and Marisa Knight. 2005. "Goal-Directed Memory: The Role of Cognitive Control in Older Adults' Emotional Memory." *Psychology and Aging* 20(4): 554–70.

Mather, Mara, Marcia K. Johnson, and Doreen M. De Leonardis. 1999. "Stereotype Reliance in Source Monitoring: Age Differences and Neuropsychological Test Correlates." *Cognitive Neuropsychology* 16(3/4/5): 437–58.

Mather, Mara, Marisa Knight, and Michael McCaffrey. 2005. "The Allure of the Alignable: Younger and Older Adults' False Memories of Choice Features." *Journal of Experimental Psychology: General* 134(1): 38–51.

Mather, Mara, Eldar Shafir, and Marcia K. Johnson. 2000. "Misremembrance of Options Past: Source Monitoring and Choice." *Psychological Science* 11(2): 132–8.

———. 2003. "Remembering Chosen and Assigned Options." *Memory and Cognition* 31(3): 422–34.

Mather, Mara, Turhan Canli, Tammy English, Sue Whitfield, Peter Wais, Kevin Ochsner, and John D. E. Gabrieli. 2004. "Amygdala Responses to Emotionally Valenced Stimuli in Older and Younger Adults." *Psychological Science* 15(4): 259–63.

Mayhorn, Christopher B., Arthur D. Fisk, and Justin D. Whittle. 2002. "Decisions, Decisions: Analysis of Age, Cohort, and Time of Testing on Framing of Risky Decision Options." *Human Factors* 44(4): 515–21.

Mroczek, Daniel K., and Auron Spiro. 2005. "Change in Life Satisfaction During Adulthood: Findings from the Veterans Affairs Normative Aging Study." *Journal of Personality and Social Psychology* 88(1): 189–202.

Nygren, Thomas E., Alice Isen, Pamela J. Taylor, and Jessica Dulin. 1996. "The Influence of Positive Affect on the Decision Rule in Risk Situations: Focus on

Outcome (and Especially Avoidance of Loss) Rather than Probability." *Organizational Behavior and Human Decision Processes* 66(1): 59–72.

Orsino, Angela, Jill I. Cameron, Maja Seidl, David Medelssohn, and Donna E. Stewart. 2003. "Medical Decision-Making and Information Needs in End-Stage Renal Disease Patients." *General Hospital Psychiatry* 25(5): 324–31.

Pasupathi, Monisha, and Laura L. Carstensen. 2003. "Age and Emotional Experience During Mutual Reminiscing." *Psychology and Aging* 18(3): 430–42.

Peters, Ellen, Melissa Finucane, Donald G. MacGregor, and Paul Slovic. 2000. "The Bearable Lightness of Aging: Judgment and Decision Processes in Older Adults." In *The Aging Mind: Opportunities in Cognitive Research,* edited by Paul C. Stern and Laura L. Carstensen. Washington: National Academy.

Raghunathan, Rajagopal, and Michael Tuan Pham. 1999. "All Negative Moods Are Not Equal: Motivational Influences of Anxiety and Sadness on Decision Making." *Organizational Behavior and Human Decision Processes* 79(1): 56–77.

Robbins, Lillian C. T. 1963. "The Accuracy of Parental Recall of Aspects of Child Development and of Child Rearing Practices." *Journal of Abnormal and Social Psychology* 66(3): 261–70.

Robins, Lee N., Sandra P. Schoenberg, Sandra J. Holmes, Kathryn S. Ratcliff, Alexandra Benham, and Jane Works. 1985. "Early Home Environment and Retrospective Recall: A Test for Concordance Between Siblings With and Without Psychiatric Disorders." *American Journal of Orthopsychiatry* 55(1): 27–41.

Robins, Richard W., and Kali H. Trzesniewski. 2005. "Self-Esteem Development Across the Lifespan." *Current Directions in Psychological Science* 14(3): 158–62.

Rosler, Alexander, C. Ulrich, J. Billino, P. Sterzer, S. Weidauer, T. Bernhardt, H. Steinmetz, L. Frohich, and A. Kleinschmidt. 2005. "Effects of Arousing Emotional Scenes on the Distribution of Visuospatial Attention: Changes with Aging and Early Subcortical Vascular Dementia." *Journal of the Neurological Sciences* 229–30: 109–16.

Sanfey, Alan, Reid Hastie, Marc K. Colvin, and Jordan Grafman. 2003. "Phineas Gauged: Decision-Making and the Human Prefrontal Cortex." *Neuropsychologia* 41: 1218–29.

Schlagman, Suzanne, Joerg Schulz, and Lia Kvavilashvili. 2006. "A Content Analysis of Involuntary Autobiographical Memories: Examining the Positivity Effect in Old Age." *Memory* 14(2): 161–75.

Schulkind, Mathew D., and Gillian M. Woldorf. 2005. "Emotional Organization of Autobiographical Memory." *Memory and Cognition* 33(6): 1025–35.

Serrano, Juan P., Jose M. Latorre, and Margaret Gatz. 2007. "Autobiographical Memory in Older Adults With and Without Depressive Symptoms." *International Journal of Clinical and Health Psychology* 7(1): 41–57.

Slovic, Paul, Melissa Finucane, Ellen Peters, and Donald G. MacGregor. 2002. "The Affect Heuristic." In *Heuristics and Biases,* edited by Thomas Gilovich and Dale Griffin. New York: Cambridge University Press.

Spaniol, Julia, and Ute J. Bayen. 2005. "Aging and Conditional Probability Judgments: A Global Matching Approach." *Psychology and Aging* 20(1): 165–81.

Stacy, Candace A., and Margaret Gatz. 1991. "Cross-Sectional Age Differences and Longitudinal Change on the Bradburn Affect Balance Scale." *Journal of Gerontology: Psychological Sciences* 46(2): 76–78.

Stout, Julie C., William C. Rodawalt, and Eric R. Siemers. 2001. "Risky Decision Making in Huntington's Disease." *Journal of the International Neuropsychological Society* 7: 92–101.

Wagenaar, Willem A., and Jop Groeneweg. 1990. "The Memory of Concentration Camp Survivors." *Applied Cognitive Psychology* 4(2): 77–87.

Watson, Tonya L., and Fredda Blanchard-Fields. 1998. "Thinking with Your Head and Your Heart: Age Differences in Everyday Problem-Solving Strategy Preferences." *Aging, Neuropsychology, and Cognition* 5(3): 225–40.

Wilder, Kelly E., Daniel R. Weinberger, and Terry E. Goldberg. 1998. "Operant Conditioning and Orbitofrontal Cortez in Schizophrenic Patients: Unexpected Evidence for Intact Functioning." *Schizophrenia Research* 30(2): 169–74.

Williams, Steve, Mohamed Zainuba, and Robert Jackson. 2003. "Affective Influences on Risk Perceptions and Risk Intention." *Journal of Managerial Psychology* 18(2): 126–37.

Willis, Sherry L., Melissa Dolan, and Robert Bertrand. 1999. "Processing of Medical Information in Aging Patients: Cognitive and Human Factors Perspectives." In *Problem Solving on Health-Related Tasks of Daily Living,* edited by Denise C. Park and Roger W. Morrell. Mahwah, N.J.: Lawrence Erlbaum Associates, Inc.

Wood, Stacey, Jerome Busemeyer, Andreau Koling, Cathy R. Cox, and Haiker Davis. 2005. "Older Adults as Adaptive Decision Makers: Evidence from the Iowa Gambling Task." *Psychology and Aging* 20(2): 220–5.

Yarrow, Marian R., John D. Campbell, and Roger V. Burton. 1970. "Recollections of Childhood: A Study of the Retrospective Method." *Monographs of the Society for Research in Child Development* 35(5): 1–83.

Yates, J. Frank, and Andrea L. Patalano. 1999. "Decision Making and Aging." In *Processing of Medical Information in Aging Patients: Cognitive and Human Factors Perspectives,* edited by Denise C. Park and Roger W. Morrell. Mahwah, N.J.: Lawrence Erlbaum Associates, Inc.

Zajonc, Robert B. 1980. "Feeling and Thinking: Preferences Need No Inferences." *American Psychologist* 35(2): 151–75.

Zwahr, Melissas D., Denise C. Park, and Kim Shifren. 1999. "Judgments About Estrogen Replacement Therapy: The Role of Age, Cognitive Abilities, and Beliefs." *Psychology and Aging* 14(2): 179–91.

· 12 ·

Affect and Cognition as a Source of Motivation: A New Model and Evidence from Natural Experiments

LORENZ GOETTE AND DAVID HUFFMAN

WHEN WORKING toward completion of a long-term project, individuals make effort choices. Many important stages in life involve working on such long-term projects; examples include completing an education, working toward a promotion, working out to lose weight, or working to generate the necessary income to pay for an important future expense. All of these examples share the property that completion of the project requires effort exerted over a sustained period of time, sometimes for many years. Progress toward completion is steady, but each day's effort is only a small step towards completion of the overall project. Until recently, decision research assumed that the primary source of human motivation in these kinds of situations was cognitive. In the purely cognitive framework, motivation to exert effort is modeled as the outcome of a conscious calculation in which the individual chooses the course of action with the highest net benefit.

By contrast, new evidence points to the importance of affect as a source of motivation.[1] Experiments show that, at every instance, humans (and other animals) tend to evaluate performance on a task relative to narrowly defined goals or "mileposts" along the way. They experience affect as they make progress, or fail to make progress, toward these more narrowly defined goals. Narrowly defined goals seem to be pervasive for the types of long-term projects we consider; for instance, individuals might set a target on how much progress to make on a dissertation per day, how many calories to lose per workout, or how much money to earn per day in a piece-rate job.

The affective reaction triggered by progress relative to these narrow goals has an impact on behavior. In particular, affect apparently explains loss aversion, which refers to a strong preference for not falling short of a reference point or goal and acts as a psychological incentive to exert effort as long as the individual is below the goal. The tendency for affect to become increasingly intense as distance from a goal decreases can explain the so-called goal gradient effect, the tendency for humans, monkeys, and other animals to increase effort as a goal draws nearer. This is in contrast to what the standard economic model would predict: broadly speaking, the standard economic model says that exerting effort at a constant pace over every day is optimal when working on a long-term project. An exception is that effort should increase on days when a random change in the environment makes the marginal productivity of effort high, and less effort should be exerted on days when effort does not translate into significant progress on the project. But the model contends that variations in effort over time across or within days, unless they are a response to such external shocks, are not optimal.

Because the standard model in economics is purely cognitive, an alternative model is necessary to incorporate affect as an additional source of motivation. The key feature of this model is that affect is aroused by performance relative to one or more narrowly defined goals which must be passed in order to complete the long-term project (for example, daily page goals as part of working towards a dissertation). This affective motivation can override the priorities assigned by cognitive decision making and distort the individual's effort profile on the way to completion of the project. Affect is assumed to respond to the immediacy of a goal or reward, increasing in intensity and creating a stronger motivation to exert effort as one of the narrowly defined goal draws near. We formalize this tension between affect and cognition in similar way to George Loewenstein and Ted O'Donoghue (2005), assuming a two-part objective function for the individual; one part corresponds to the preferences of the forward-looking, cognitive self, and the other part to the more myopic process that drives affective impulses.

This alternative model generates a psychological incentive to not fall short of a goal, consistent with experimental evidence on loss aversion, and predicts an increasing effort profile leading up to a goal, consistent with experimental evidence on the goal gradient effect. The model also predicts that a temporary shock to productivity (for example, a day on which it is particularly easy for individuals to make progress on their long-term project) may lead to lower total effort on that day, because it causes the individuals to reach their daily goals more quickly and thus removes some of the motivation arising from affect earlier in the day. This finding is at odds with a central prediction of the standard economic model that individuals should work harder when a shock makes their productivity temporarily high. It is consistent, however, with a body of anecdotal evidence: students work particularly long hours on days when they have not been very productive, in order not to fall short of a page-per-day target; individuals extend their workout time on days when they feel lethargic, because by the end of their usual workout time they are still below a calories-per-workout goal; piece-rate workers knock off work early on a day when they earned more than usual and were able to sur-pass a daily income target particularly quickly.

In our view the best-developed source of evidence on these mechanisms is the literature examining day-to-day effort choices of workers paid on piece rates. This recent literature focuses on workers who are free to vary effort over the workday such as cab drivers, bicycle messengers, and man-ual workers. The key stylized fact from this literature is that a worker's total daily effort is typically unchanged, or even decreases, on days when the wage is temporarily high (Goette, Huffman, and Fehr 2004).

In support of this alternative model of affect and motivation, new empirical evidence using data from a real work setting where workers face strong financial incentives demonstrates the relevance of affect for motivation. Our data come from two bicycle messenger firms, and allow us to observe the within-day effort profiles of individual messengers. Bicycle messengers are attractive subjects for study because they have rel-ative freedom to choose their effort. It is also important that luck plays a significant role in determining their daily earnings: messengers are paid a piece rate and can earn substantially more or less than expected on a given day simply because they were lucky and obtained an attractive assignment.

Effort profiles throughout the day might be affected by good luck or bad luck (that is, windfall gains or losses) early in the day. The standard model predicts that within-day windfall gains should have no impact on effort, because they are trivial with respect to the long-term project of accumulating income. By contrast, the affect-based model predicts that windfall gains in the morning can have a significant impact on the effort profile over the afternoon. A lucky morning can position a mes-senger quite close to the narrowly defined daily goal by the first hours of the afternoon; as a result, the goal gradient takes effect earlier, and the messenger works harder compared to other messengers. Later in the afternoon, when other messengers are getting close to their goals, the lucky messenger has already achieved the goal and thus works less hard. In fact, we find exactly this pattern at both firms: early afternoon effort (that is, the first few hours of the afternoon) is positively correlated with a windfall gain in the morning, but late afternoon effort (that is, the final hours of the day) is negatively correlated with a windfall gain in the morning. We also conducted a complementary survey of bicycle messengers in which we asked directly about the importance of a daily earnings goal for motivation to exert effort, and we find additional evidence supporting the alternative model of labor supply.

These findings contribute to the recent empirical literature on labor supply and loss aversion and builds on the finding that total daily effort sometimes decreases in response to a wage increase. The seminal paper in this literature, Colin Camerer et al. (1997), studied New York City cab-drivers and argued that the tendency for cabbies to work short hours on high-wage days reflects loss aversion around a daily income target. More recently, Ernst Fehr and Lorenz Goette (2007) conducted a field experiment in which bicycle messengers were given a higher wage for one month and found that messengers decreased effort during shifts in this month. The decrease was strongest for messengers who were loss averse, as measured by a lottery experiment. This chapter extends the income-targeting hypothesis by emphasizing the affective underpinnings of loss aversion and by building a dynamic model of progress towards a daily goal that incorporates another aspect of affective evaluation: immediacy. The model can predict a decrease in daily effort due to an increase in the wage (that is, productivity), which is consistent with previous findings. It also generates a new prediction linking income targeting to affect (that is, the goal gradient) which is testable using our data on within-day effort profiles. Importantly, this strategy avoids some of the concerns raised about interpretation of the findings in Camerer et al. (1997) and provides new support for the income-targeting hypothesis.[2]

Working on Long-Term Projects: The Roles of Cognition and Affect

The standard economic model captures the deliberative side of human decision making and can be applied to the case of working on a long-term project. Such projects take effort over a prolonged period of time and have some threshold amount necessary to achieve completion. Progress toward completion of the long-term project is a function of effort as well as random occurrences that are beyond the individual's control. Our aim here is to examine how effort put into the project will vary over short time horizons after a random shock occurs. In particular, we examine how sensations of progress or lagging behind narrowly defined goals affect effort on the long-term project.

Formally, in order to complete the long-term project, cumulative effort has to exceed a threshold Q. That is,

$$\sum_{t=1,\dots T} w_t \left(e_{0t} + e_{1t} + e_{2t} \right) + z_t \geq Q \qquad (12.1)$$

The term e_{0t} is effort "in the morning" of date t, while e_{1t} and e_{2t} represent the effort put into the project in the early and late afternoon of date t. Not all days are equally productive: we model this with the factor q_t, which affects the rate at which effort increases output towards the goal. There is also an element of uncontrollable luck in progress toward the goal, reflected in the term z_t. We also assume that effort exerted in each episode is costly. In particular, we assume that as effort increases, it becomes increasingly painful. Formally, in each work episode, effort costs are given by a convex function of effort $c(e)$, with the property that the marginal costs of effort are increasing.

It can easily be shown that the optimal effort level in hour m is the amount of effort such that the extra benefit from exerting another unit of effort is just offset by the extra cost of that unit. Formally, the optimal level solves the following first order condition:

$$c'\left(e_{mt} \right) = \lambda w_t \qquad (12.2)$$

where $c'()$ is the cost of one additional unit of effort, and λw_t is the increase in utility from exerting an additional unit of effort. The term λ reflects how much the individual's utility is increased by a one-unit increase in output towards the long-term threshold Q, while w_t is the temporary productivity with which effort is translated into progress towards Q on day t.

There are two important implications from equation 12.2. The first is that an increase in w_t should lead to an increase in effort, limited by how quickly effort costs increase. Intuitively, in order to maximize utility, the individual should take advantage of temporarily high productivity and put in extra effort, because progress per unit of effort is higher than usual. The second important implication is that windfall gains in progress towards the goal, z_t, in equation 12.1 should not affect labor supply to a first approximation. These windfalls do affect the overall distance to completion, but the change is minimal for a long-term project.[3]

In analyzing effort choices (that is, labor supply) of piece-rate workers, it is natural to interpret w_t as the piece rate. This rate determines progress per unit of effort towards a long-term project of earning an income amount Q, which must be sufficient to meet future expenses. In this context, a windfall gain z_t could be a generous tip, or some other lucky burst of productivity on day t. The only channel through which this windfall could influence effort would be through λ. However, if the windfall z_t is small relative to the needed income Q, then λ should be expected to be constant with respect to small windfall gains.

Incorporating Affect and Cognition in Decision Making

Recent research in neuroscience provides groundwork for understanding the roles of cognition and affect in determining individual motivation. A prominent model in neuroscience is that cognition and affect are governed by distinct neural systems in the brain (Cohen 2005). The affective system, closely related to what Ajay Satpute and Matthew Lieberman (2004) define as the reflexive system, is thought to include older brain structures such as the basal ganglia, the amygdala, ventromedial prefrontal cortex, and parts of anterior cingulate cortex. The cognitive system, or the "reflective system" in Satpute and Lieberman (2004), includes the lateral prefrontal cortex, the ventral parts of anterior cingulate cortex, parts of the temporal lobes, and the posterior parietal cortex.

An important implication of the dual-process structure of the brain is the possibility for conflicting motivations. Conflict can occur because the affective system has a relatively "conservative" set of preprogrammed priorities, which may ignore some of the broader, long-term considerations that inform cognitive decision making.

One example of the affective system's conservatism is a tendency to prioritize immediate rewards and threats over longer-term considerations. A famous series of studies in psychology demonstrates the impact of immediacy on impulsive behavior by showing that subjects are more likely to choose a small immediate reward over a larger delayed reward if the immediate reward is visible at the time of the decision (Mischel, Ebbesen, and Zeiss 1972; Mischel, Shoda, and Rodriguez 1989; Mischel, Ayduk, and Mendoza-Denton 2003). More recently, Samuel McClure et al. (2004) find evidence suggesting that the cognitive system of the brain is involved in making intertemporal trade-offs in general, but that the affective system is activated only when the trade-off involves an immediate reward. The relative strength of activation of these two systems predicts whether the individual chooses an immediate reward or waits for the larger delayed reward.

The affective system is also conservative when it comes to the possibility of losses. Choice experiments reveal that many people exhibit reference-dependent valuation, defining outcomes in terms or gains or losses relative to a reference level. In these evaluations, people tend to be loss averse, disliking losses more than they like gains of the same amount (Tversky and Kahneman 2000). Loss aversion prevents an individual from gambling on options involving very high risk, which is a pattern that may be useful to avoid most harmful outcomes. Several studies show a clear involvement of brain networks associated with the affective (or, the reflexive) system when individuals make loss-averse choices. Sabrina Tom and her colleagues (2007) find that loss-averse behavior correlates with brain activity in ventromedial prefrontal cortex (vmPFC) and ventral striatum. Baba Shiv et al. (2005) conduct a choice experiment involving real-stakes lotteries, in which the subjects include individuals with damage to the vmPFC. The researchers in this study find that normal subjects display loss aversion, but the brain-damaged patients do not. This pattern points to the vmPFC as a brain region necessary for behavior to exhibit loss aversion. More indirectly, Keith Chen, Venkat Lakshminarayanan, and Laurie Santos (2005) provide evidence that loss aversion is seated in the structures of the brain that humans and monkeys have in common by showing that even capuchin monkeys exhibit loss aversion with respect to gambles.

Affect and Task Motivation

A number of studies provide direct evidence on the importance of affect for motivating task effort. Consistent with the myopic reference-dependent character of the affective system, affect is found to play a role in task effort mainly when an individual has a goal or reference point in mind and when the individual is close to achieving that goal. The resulting effort profile involves higher overall effort below a goal, with an increasing goal gradient in effort up until the point when the goal is achieved.

A study by Chip Heath, Richard Larrick, and George Wu (1999) finds evidence that goals act as reference points, and that affect provides a source of motivation to achieve goals in a way that is consistent with loss aversion and the goal gradient. The researchers posed subjects with the following hypothetical scenario:

> Sally and Trish both follow workout plans that usually involve doing 25 sit-ups. One day, Sally sets a goal of performing 31 sit-ups. She finds herself very tired after performing 35 sit-ups and stops. Trish sets a goal of performing 39 sit-ups. She finds herself very tired after performing 35 sit-ups and stops. Who is experiencing more emotion? (86)

Most subjects indicate that Trish, who is below her goal, is experiencing more emotion than Sally, who is above her goal by the same amount. This is consistent with the goal acting as a reference point and triggering the type of affective response that appears to play a role in explaining loss aversion. In another question, the researchers describe a similar situation, but ask participants who they think will exert more effort to do one more sit-up. Again, the question is careful to hold previous effort constant. Most subjects indicate that the individual below the goal will exert more effort than the individual who has surpassed the goal, consistent with loss aversion serving as a source of motivation. Finally, the researchers ask a question in which two individuals have completed the same number of sit-ups and are both below their goal, but they have different goals. Consistent with the goal gradient and an increasing role for affect as a goal draws near, subjects indicate that the individual with the closer goal will work harder to perform one additional sit-up.

The first behavioral evidence of a goal gradient was observed in studies using animals. The seminal empirical study on the goal gradient was conducted by Clark Hull (1934), which showed that rats run progressively faster in a straight runway as they approach a food reward. Other animal studies followed, documenting a similar pattern in effort towards a goal (Heilizer 1977).

More recently, some animal studies have found evidence at a neurological level suggesting that the affective system plays a role in generating the goal gradient in effort. Munetaka Shidara, Thomas Aigner, and Barry Richmond (1998), as well as Munetaka Shidara and Barry Richmond (2002), monitored the brain activity of monkeys as they exerted effort to reach a reward; they found selective response in the ventral striatum and anterior cingulate, as visual cues signaled increasing proximity to the reward. (Distance to the reward was varied randomly over time, so monkeys had to rely on cues to infer current proximity.) These structures are believed to be part of a loop between reward expectancy, affective response, and effort. At the same time that the monkeys exhibited increasing activation in these parts of the affective system, they also exhibited a goal gradient, increased effort, and fewer mistakes on the task as distance to the goal decreased.

Kelly See, Chip Heath, and Craig Fox (2003) provide evidence of a similar pattern of behavior in humans, in a study using college athletes. In this study, a goal was marked on a four-hundred-meter track, and a subject was positioned at one of two distances from the goal. The subject was then instructed to start running at a gradual pace, until hearing a loud noise generated by the experimenters, which could happen at any time. The subject was told that the noise signaled the beginning of a ten-second period during which they should try as hard as possible to reach the goal line. The treatment variable was the distance remaining to the goal when the noise was produced. Importantly, both groups of subjects heard the noise at a point when the goal was clearly unattainable in ten seconds; distances to the goal were clearly marked on the track, and all subjects were aware of relevant world-record times (indicating to them that the goal was impossible). The main finding of the study is that subjects who heard the noise at a closer distance to the goal ran harder than subjects who heard the noise when they were relatively far from the goal, consistent with the goal gradient effect. Notably, subjects were put in a position in which they had to make decisions very quickly, and were thus especially likely to be motivated by the fast-acting affective system of the brain.

Ran Kivetz, Oleg Urminsky, and Yuhuang Zheng (2005) also find behavioral evidence of a goal gradient among humans in the domain of consumer choice. In one experiment, people were offered cards allowing them to receive a free coffee after they had purchased nine previous coffees. Consistent with the goal gradient, participants increased the frequency of coffee purchases as distance from the reward decreased. A similar pattern was observed in an online experiment in which participants received a reward after rating a certain number of songs.

A New Model of Motivation to Work on a Long-Term Project

From these findings, we develop a new model of behavior which considers both the traditional cognitive model of working on a long-term project as well as the role of affect as a source of motivation. Building on evidence from psychology and neuroscience, this model allows for conflict between cognitive decision making and affective impulses, formalizing the affective system in a way that captures the key properties of affective evaluation. This model adopts the terminology of labor supply in the workplace, but it can still be interpreted as applying to long-term projects more generally.

In the spirit of Loewenstein and O'Donoghue (2005) and other dual-process models in economics (Thaler and Shefrin 1981; Bernheim and Rangel 2003, 2004; Benhabib and Bisin 2004; Fudenberg and Levine 2006), we assume a two-part objective function for the individual. The first part describes the preferences that inform the individual's cognitive decision making. As in the standard model of labor supply in economics, this portion of the objective function values progress towards the long-term project (that is, maximizing lifetime income) linearly over the course of work period t. More formally, net utility in period t, from a cognitive perspective, is given by:

$$U_t = w_t e_t + z_t - c(e_t) \tag{12.3}$$

where the utility from an additional unit of progress towards income threshold Q, λ is normalized to 1, w_t is the wage in period t, z_t is income from previous periods which is unrelated to current period effort, and $c()$ is a convex function capturing the cost of effort in utility terms. We denote the optimal level of effort from the perspective of the cognitive system as $e_t^c = \text{argmax } U_t$.

The second part of the worker's objective function corresponds to the preferences of the affective system. Consistent with reference dependence, the affective system's valuation of income over the day is assumed to vary with distance from a daily goal or income target, denoted r. Importantly, this valuation is assumed to be nonlinear; it reflects increasing motivation as distance to the goal decreases and dissipation of motivation once earnings have surpassed the narrowly defined daily goal. We formalize the net benefits of effort in period t, to the affective system, as:

$$v\left(w_t e_t + z_t - r\right) - c\left(e_t\right) \tag{12.4}$$

The function $v()$ captures the affective system's valuation of progress on the project. We assume that $v'()$, the additional value to the affective system of an additional unit of income, is increasing as total daily output approaches r from below, consistent with increasing motivation. Once total earnings have surpassed r, however, $v'()$ is assumed to decrease with further output, reflecting a dissipation of motivation. Furthermore, we assume that $v'(-x) > v'(x)$ for any $x > r$ (that is, the affective value of an additional dollar is always greater when the individual is below the goal, consistent with loss aversion).[4] We denote the optimal level of effort from the perspective of the affective system as $e_t^A = \text{argmax } V_t$.

Following Loewenstein and O'Donoghue (2005), we combine the cognitive and affective components into a single objective function, and assume that the worker tries to achieve the cognitive optimum, e^C, in each work period, subject to willpower costs involved in moving effort away from the affective optimum, e^A. Willpower costs are denoted h and are assumed to increase linearly in distance between the chosen effort level, e^*, and the effort level preferred by the affective system. We also assume that the worker does not take into account the impact of current effort on willpower costs in future periods.[5]

Having defined the objective function, we can write down the worker's decision problem. We will focus on a worker's effort decisions over the afternoon conditional on morning earnings. For simplicity, we assume that the afternoon has only two periods. In this case, the worker's decision problems in the first and second periods of the afternoon can be written as follows:

$$\underset{e_1}{\text{Max }} Q_t = w_1 e_1 + w_2 e_2 - c\left(e_1\right) - c\left(e_2\right) - -h\left[v\left(w_1 e_1^A + z_1 - r\right) - c\left(e_1^A\right)\right.$$

$$\left. - \left(v\left(w_1 e_1 + z_1 - r\right) - c\left(e_1\right)\right)\right] \tag{12.5}$$

and

$$\underset{e_2}{Max}\, Q_t = w_2 e_2 - c(e_2) - -h\Big[v\big(w_1 e_1^A + w_2 e_2^A + z_2 - r\big) - c\big(e_2^A\big)$$
$$- \big(v\big(w_1 e_1 + w_2 e_2 + z_2 - r\big) - c\big(e_2\big)\big)\Big] \tag{12.6}$$

Willpower costs are captured by the terms in brackets, which express the difference between the affective system's objective function evaluated at the affective optimum, e^A, and the affective system's objective function evaluated at the worker's chosen effort level. Willpower costs are thus equal to zero if the worker complies with the wishes of the affective system, increasing linearly in deviations from e^A.

The optimal effort levels in period-2 and period-1 are then given by the following first order conditions:

$$c'(e_1) = w\, \frac{\begin{aligned}&1 + hv'\big(w_1 e_1 + z_1 - r\big)\\[4pt] &+ \left[\frac{h\big(1 - v'\big(w_1 e_1 + w_2 \tilde{e}_2 + z_2 - r\big)\big)}{1+h}\frac{\partial \tilde{e}_2}{\partial e_1}\right]\end{aligned}}{1+h} \tag{12.7}$$

and

$$c'(e_2) = w\, \frac{1 + hv'\big(w_1 e_1 + w_2 e_2 + z_2 - r\big)}{1+h} \tag{12.8}$$

In these equations, $\tilde{e}_2$ is the effort that the period-one self expects to exert in period-2. A first observation is that affect can lead to either lower or higher effort levels compared to effort levels predicted by the standard model. One determining factor is quite intuitive and can be seen by comparing (equation 12.8) to the condition for optimal effort in the standard cognitive model. According to (equation 12.8), effort in period-2 is higher than in a purely cognitive model if the value that the affective system places on an additional dollar of income, $v'()$, is greater than one (which is the value that the cognitive system places on an additional dollar; recall that λ was assumed to be equal to one). Similarly, if the affective system cares less about income than the cognitive system (that is, $v'() < 1$), effort in period-2 is lower than in a purely cognitive model.

The condition for effort in period-1 is more complicated. The term in brackets in (equation 12.7) arises because the individual is assumed to be forward looking and "sophisticated" (that is, the individual takes into account the impact of current effort choices on behavior in period-2). Effort in period-1 has an impact on effort in period-2 by changing distance from the goal, and thus changing the affective system's valuation of income in the second period. Whether effort in period-1 is higher or lower than effort in the standard model thus depends on two factors: whether the affective system's valuation of income in period-1 is more or less than one, and whether the additional sophistication motives captured by the terms in brackets tend to increase or decrease effort in period-1.

Although in general the impact of affect on effort is ambiguous, two specific examples demonstrate how the affective system in the model leads to a goal gradient, consistent with experiments on task effort. In each case, a windfall gain in the morning, reflected in an increase in z_t, leads to greater effort in period-1 and lower effort in period-2. Thus, an increase in the daily wage could potentially lead to a decrease in total daily effort.

As a first example, suppose the individual is below the goal in both periods of the afternoon and reaches the target only at the very end of the day. Furthermore, assume that the individual is naïve (that is, the individual does not take into account the impact of current effort on future affective evaluations, so the bracketed terms in (equation 12.7) disappear). In this case, the model clearly predicts a goal gradient (that is, $e_1 < e_2$), because the individual is closer to the goal and $v'()$ is larger in period-2. Now suppose that the individual experiences a windfall gain in the morning, such that the individual is above the goal in period-2. Period-1 effort must be higher than before, because the individual is now relatively closer to the goal in period-1. In period-2, effort is lower than before, because the individual is beyond the goal and the affective valuation of income is lower. Thus, after a windfall gain in the morning, the model predicts a positive response of effort early in the afternoon and a negative response later in the afternoon.

The model makes the same prediction in the second example, in which the individual is now assumed to be "sophisticated," provided that the affective system places a relatively large value on income (that is, $v'() > 1$) in both periods. In this case, sophistication effects reinforce the goal gradient. Intuitively, $v'() > 1$ implies that the affective system cares "too much" about income in the second period. This gives the first-period self a motive to reduce effort in period-1 in order to increase distance from the goal in period-2, thus reducing the affective system's valuation of income in the second period. Formally, this result arises because the sign of the product in the brackets in (equation 12.7) is negative, leading to even lower effort in period-1 compared to period-2. To see this, note that the derivative of $\tilde{e}_2$ with respect to e_1 is positive because effort in period-1 moves the individual closer to the goal in period-2, which increases $\tilde{e}_2$. Given $v'() > 1$, the sign of the product is unambiguously negative. Turning to the case in which a windfall gain in the morning causes the individual to be above the goal in period-2, sophistication effects reinforce the tendency for effort to increase in period-1 and decrease in period-2. To see this, note that the product in brackets is now positive because the derivative of $\tilde{e}_2$ with respect to e_1 is positive: an increase in e_1 places the individual farther beyond the goal in period-2 and thus leads to a lower $\tilde{e}_2$.

A final noteworthy feature of the model is the predicted response to a wage increase. In line with empirical evidence showing that workers sometimes reduce total daily effort on high-wage days, the model can predict a decrease in total daily effort if the wage goes up. To see this, suppose that on a low-wage day the worker is below the goal for the whole day. On a high-wage day, in contrast, it is easier to reach the goal by the second period in the afternoon. Switching from being above the goal to below the goal in period-2 can decrease effort in period-2, because the affective system no longer places a high value on income once the goal is achieved. Although a wage increase tends to encourage higher effort (through the channel of purely financial incentives considered by the cognitive system, and due to the goal gradient in earlier periods of the day), a strong drop in effort during period-2 could result in a net drop in total daily effort. The model predicts that the drop in effort is more likely dominant if workers are allowed to quit early (that is, if they reduce effort in period-2 all the way to zero, consistent with findings in the empirical literature). For example, Ernst Fehr and Lorenz Goette (2007) find that a wage increase causes a relatively small decrease in daily effort at a Swiss bicycle-messenger firm in which messengers are able to reduce effort, but are not allowed to quit entirely, before the end of their daily shift. Camerer et al. (1997) find a larger decrease in effort among cabdrivers, potentially reflecting the greater freedom of cabdrivers to quit early.

Data Description and Empirical Design

In order to test the relevance of affect for labor-supply choices in a real-work setting, we analyze data from two bicycle-messenger firms operating in the same city, which we will call *Firm A* and *Firm B*. Bicycle-messenger firms offer same-day or same-hour delivery of packages in urban areas where traffic-congested streets make a bicycle the fastest method of delivery. At the firms we study, messengers are paid a simple piece rate, which is a fixed fraction of the price of each delivery (50 percent). Delivery prices vary based on the distance the messenger must carry the delivery, how quickly the customer needs the delivery, and the weight of the package.

Bicycle messengers are attractive subjects for the study of motivation and effort because they have substantial discretion over how hard they work, and when they work, during a workday. Deliveries are announced over the airwaves by a dispatcher and are heard by all of the company's messengers working that day. Messengers have several ways to vary effort in this setting: (1) they can work hard to finish deliveries quickly and lobby the dispatcher for more deliveries, or (2) they can make deliveries slowly and respond slowly to the dispatcher's calls on the radio.

We use the electronic delivery records of Firms A and B to study the effort decisions of individual messengers. These records span several years for each firm, and include all deliveries made by all workers. Crucially, the records include the date and time of day of each delivery made by a messenger, as well as the price of the delivery. With this information we are able to see the effort profile over the day of each messenger and study the impact of windfall gains in the morning on effort profiles in the afternoon.

We also conducted a survey with messengers in the same city.[6] A total of 119 messengers returned completed surveys, giving us a response rate of roughly 60 percent. The survey was administered in two ways: (1) we contacted messenger firms and arranged to leave the survey in the mailboxes of the messengers at these firms, and (2) during the working day, we handed out surveys to messengers waiting for deliveries at one of several well-known waiting spots. Messengers were paid for completing the survey and had a deadline of four weeks to return the survey. Most messengers returned the survey within a few days.

Descriptive Statistics

We begin our analysis with some simple descriptive statistics. These give a sense for the typical working day experienced by a bicycle messenger and point to the importance of luck for determining a messenger's daily earnings.

Table 12.1 describes the length of the workday for a bicycle messenger in terms of total hours on the job. At both firms, the majority of messengers are on the job for ten hours, but there appears to be some margin for quitting early or working late: roughly 20 percent work only nine hours, and 20 percent work eleven hours or more. Figure 12.1 shows the distributions of quitting and starting times at the two firms. The majority of messengers start work between eight o'clock and nine o'clock in the morning, and 80 percent start before ten o'clock in the morning. In the afternoon, only about 5 percent of messengers quit before four o'clock. Roughly 10 percent quit between four o'clock and five o'clock, 40 percent

Table 12.1   The Distribution of Hours on the Job

Firm A		Firm B	
6–	1.39	6–	0.94
7	3.30	7	1.45
8	8.73	8	4.55
9	24.39	9	20.34
10	40.34	10	53.63
11+	21.85	11+	19.00

Source: Authors' calculations.

quit between five o'clock and six o'clock, and 35 percent quit between six o'clock and seven o'clock.

Figure 12.2 shows the distributions of daily earnings for messengers at Firm A and Firm B. Two features of these distributions are noteworthy: First, they are quite similar across firms. Second, daily earnings are highly variable. The standard deviation of daily earnings is $46.27 at Firm A and $50.29 at Firm B. Morning earnings, which are not shown, are also similarly variable, with a standard deviation of roughly $30.00 at both firms.

There are several possible sources of the variation in messengers' earnings. We are particularly interested in the variation in morning earnings that represents windfall gains or luck. However, some of the variation in earnings is certainly due to day-to-day fluctuations in demand for messenger services or differences in messenger characteristics. Therefore, to assess the importance of windfall gains for determining a messenger's earnings, we must first remove the variation due to day and messenger effects. Table 12.2 shows an analysis of variance for morning earnings. The adjusted R-squared statistics indicate that day and messenger effects explain a significant portion of the variation in morning earnings at both firms. However, consistent with the prediction of an important role for luck in determining morning earnings, there remains substantial unexplained variation. This variation is economically meaningful to messengers, as shown by the fact that the standard deviation of unexplained variance is equivalent to roughly 30 percent of a messenger's average morning earnings.

There are two important sources of randomness in daily earnings for a bicycle messengers. First, earnings vary with the characteristics of a delivery (that is, the service type, and the pick-up and drop-off zones of the delivery) which are not necessarily correlated with the effort required to make the delivery. For example, two deliveries may involve the same effort, but because one happens to cross the border of a pric-

Figure 12.1   The Workday at Firms A and B

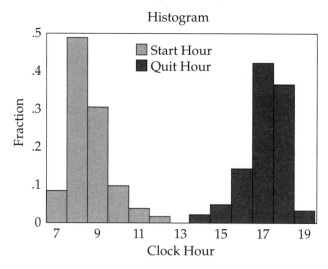

Start and Quit Hours, Firm A

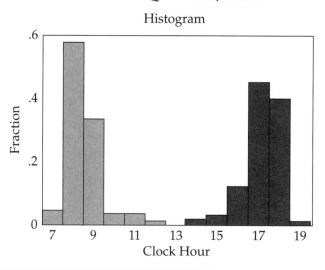

Start and Quit Hours, Firm B

Source: Authors' calculations.

Figure 12.2   Daily Earnings

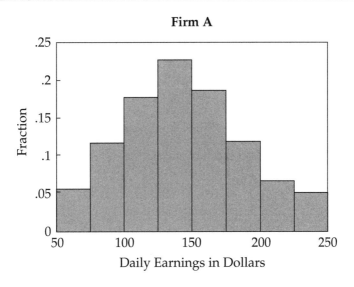

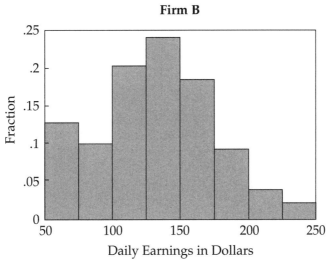

Source: Authors' calculations.

Table 12.2   ANOVA for Morning Earnings.

	Firm A	Firm B
	Adjusted R-squared	
Date Fixed Effects	.1238	.1000
Date and Messenger Fixed Effects	.3106	.5983
SD of Unexplained Variance (as percent of average morning earnings)	33.04	28.69
Observations	21,474	22,866

Source: Authors' calculations.

ing zone in the city, it may generate significantly higher earnings. Messengers also talk about the importance of luck in generating a collection of deliveries that "line up," allowing the messenger to deliver all packages along a roughly linear path rather than having to make significant detours for each one. The second important source of randomness comes from the fact that if one messenger gets a delivery due to fortunate timing in answering the dispatcher's call, another messenger is prevented from getting the delivery.

Empirical Design

Our empirical strategy is to test for an impact of windfall gains in the morning on effort in the afternoon. In the standard model, within-day windfall gains should have no impact on effort, because they are trivial relative to lifetime and thus cannot change the marginal valuation of income. On the other hand, if workers attach affective significance to the level of their daily earnings, windfall gains could have an impact on effort. The alternative model of effort that considers affect makes a distinct prediction regarding the impact of a windfall gain in the morning: workers who had lucky mornings are predicted to work harder than other messengers at the beginning of the afternoon because they are relatively closer to reaching their goals; the same workers are expected to work less hard than the others towards the end of the day because they have already surpassed their goals.

Our analysis focuses on the relationship between windfall gains in the morning and effort in the afternoon. Although we could measure windfall gains in terms of earnings, we instead use revenues, which are a simple function of earnings (earnings/0.50); revenues have the advantage that they yield a direct interpretation in terms of benefits for the firm. We calculate a messenger's morning revenues on a particular day by summing the value of all deliveries a messenger completed between the beginning of work and lunchtime.

We measure effort in the afternoon as follows: starting at one o'clock, we follow each messenger working on a particular afternoon for six hours (this is the maximum number of hours a messenger works in the afternoon at both firms) and use hourly revenues as an indicator of effort. This creates six measurements of hourly effort for a messenger working on a particular afternoon. If a messenger had zero revenues during an hour, we set effort equal to zero in that episode. This measure of work effort is the broadest possible and is precisely as standard economic theory suggests it should be. It captures how hard a messenger is working, whether he is taking breaks during the day, and when the messenger quits for the day (after the messenger quits, we set effort equal to zero for the remaining hours in the workday).

We then estimate equations of the form:

$$e_{ikt} = \gamma^1 Morning_{ikt}^1 + \gamma^2 Morning_{ikt}^2 + \cdots + \gamma^6 Morning_{ikt}^6$$
$$+ \beta x_{it} + a_i + d_t + \varepsilon_{ikt} \tag{12.9}$$

In this equation, e_{ikt} is the effort of messenger i at hour k on date t. Our coefficients of interest are the γ^k coefficients: the variable $Morning^k$ is the product of morning revenues for the individual and a dummy variable equal to one if it is the kth hour of the afternoon. We want the γ^k coefficients to reflect the impact of windfall gains on effort in work hour k. For the coefficients to have this interpretation, we control for factors besides luck that determine variation in morning revenues.

The vector x consists of time-variant individual control variables. These include the starting hour on day t, the number of days of experience at the firm, as well as dummy variables equal to one if the messenger worked the day before or the day after date t, to control for fatigue spillovers between days. We also include a messenger fixed effect, a_i, to control for time-invariant individual characteristics, such as ability, and a fixed effect, d_{ht}, which we estimate separately for each day at each firm to control for firm-specific, day-specific shocks, such as weather.

With these controls in place, γ^k indicates the amount that the messenger changed effort in work hour k in response to an increase in windfall gains in the morning. The model incorporating affect predicts positive values for γ^k early in the afternoon and potentially negative values for γ^k later in the day. The prediction of the standard model is that γ^k should be zero for all hours.

One caveat is that we might not eliminate all factors other than luck that could drive morning revenues. If a portion of the variation in morning earnings is still positively correlated with effort in the morning, and morning effort causes fatigue and makes it harder to work in the afternoon, then the standard model could predict negative γ^k's in the afternoon.[7] This is unlikely given our controls however, and given that messengers typically take a lunch break and have the opportunity to rest, which minimizes the relevance of fatigue effects from the morning. Also, this channel should not lead to the reversal in correlation predicted by the alternative model; if workers with high morning earnings are fatigued, they might work less hard in the afternoon, but the standard model does not predict a goal gradient effect (that is, γ^k's that are *increasing* over the first portion of the afternoon). Thus a goal gradient is an indication that affect, and not fatigue, explains the response to changes in morning earnings.

We estimated our baseline regression equation using ordinary least squares (OLS). An important issue is how one should calculate the standard errors of the estimated coefficients. Given the hourly frequency of our measures, there are various ways in which ε_{it}, the error term, departs from the OLS assumptions. First, the way that we construct our measure of labor supply makes the error term inherently heteroskedastic.[8] We correct for this by estimating robust standard errors. Second, there are two potential sources of correlation between the error terms. Within a given day, when one messenger is assigned a delivery, another messenger will have one fewer delivery. This leads to a negative correlation of the residuals within a day, rendering OLS standard errors too large. On the other hand, there could be a positive correlation in ε_{it} for observations coming from a given messenger, rendering OLS standard errors too small (Bertrand, Duflo, and Mullainathan 2004). As a consequence, we estimate two sets of standard errors. One set is adjusted for "clustering," or correlation, in the error term across days. Because this ignores the potentially positive correlation within individuals, we consider these standard errors to be the lower bounds. The other standard error is adjusted for clustering on messengers. We consider this to be the upper bound on the standard errors, because it ignores the potentially negative correlation within days. However, our basic conclusions do not depend on which adjustment of standard errors we use.

Results

Figure 12.3 summarizes the results from our regression analysis using the delivery records of Firms A and B. The figure plots the values of the γ^k regression coefficients, multiplied by fifty to illustrate the impact of a fifty dollar windfall gain. All coefficients are statistically significant at

Figure 12.3   Effort over Time: The Impact of a $50 Increase in Morning Revenues (+/−2* s.e. of Estimate)

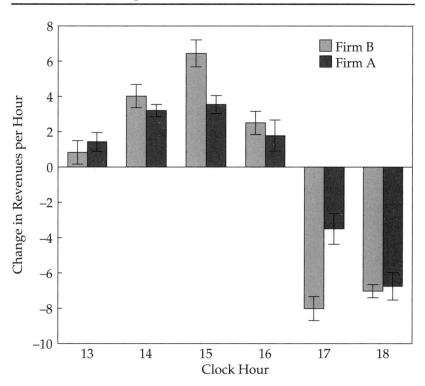

Source: Authors' calculations.
Note: Mean revenues appr. $16/hour. Controls for (i) Messenger fixed effects, (ii) Firm*day fixed effects, (iii) Start hour. Standard errors adjusted for clustering on messenger.

the 1 percent level, except for the coefficient for the first hour of the afternoon at Firm A, which is not significant.

Figure 12.3 shows that windfall gains in the morning have a statistically significant impact on the effort profile in the afternoon, which is contrary to the predictions of the standard cognitive model of labor supply. On the other hand, the response of effort to the windfall gain is consistent with the prediction that messengers attach affective significance to a daily earnings goal. As predicted by the alternative model of labor supply, a messenger with a windfall gain works harder than other messengers in the first part of the afternoon but less hard later in the day. Furthermore, the fact that the relative difference in effort increases over the first few hours is consistent with the goal gradient prediction of the model and not with an explanation based on fatigue from the morning.[9]

Our results are also consistent with previous studies, which conclude that daily earnings goals influence the effort decisions of piece-rate workers. These studies have focused on the impact of day-to-day variation in wages on total daily effort and have found that higher wages lead to lower daily effort; this is consistent with the prediction that workers achieve a daily earnings goal more quickly the higher their wage (Camerer et al. 1997; Chou 2002; Fehr and Goette 2007). With the exception of Lorenz Goette and David Huffman's (2005) study, however, these studies have not been able to observe within-day effort profiles and thus have not been able to test for the goal gradient effect. Goette and Huffman study the impact of exogenous increases in the piece rates at two bicycle messenger firms. They find that messengers paid at high piece rates work harder earlier in the day but less hard later in the day compared to messengers paid at low piece rates. This is consistent with other evidence on the goal gradient effect.

Survey Evidence

An advantage of conducting a survey is that we asked messengers directly whether they have earnings goals that are relevant during the workday. Accordingly, the survey included the following question: "After earning ___ dollars during the day, it feels less urgent to earn another dollar (if this question does not apply to you, answer with N.A.)." Of the messengers surveyed, 73 percent responded that they have a dollar amount in mind during the day. The survey also asked, "What is the minimum amount you need to earn in a day, to make it worthwhile to come to work?" With only a few exceptions, this minimum amount is below the amount reported in the first question; this indicates that the first question measures an earnings goal that is distinct from a daily minimum.

Another question in the survey presented respondents with a hypothetical scenario, which was designed to correspond to our analysis of the delivery records. The question describes two scenarios: in one scenario, the messenger has had a "good" morning, earning much more than average; in the other scenario, the messenger has had a "slow" morning, earning much less than average. The question states that the messenger worked equally hard in the two scenarios and that in either case the afternoon is expected to be good. This establishes a difference in earnings across the scenarios due to windfall gains and not due to effort. The question then asks the messenger to fill in the following statement, using a scale that ranges from "much less" to "much more":

"After the slow morning, I care ___ about earning another dollar, relative to after the good morning." In the survey responses, 18 percent of messengers say they care the same, 72 percent say they care more, and 10 percent say they care less about earning another dollar after the slow morning. This indicates that the majority of the messengers are loss averse around a daily income goal: a good morning puts a worker close to their daily target and leads to lower marginal utility of income in the afternoon. Because the question keeps morning effort constant across both scenarios, fatigue does not appear to explain why messengers say that they would work less hard after a good morning.

Conclusion

The standard economic model assumes that an individual working on a long-term project decides how hard to work and when to work based on a purely cognitive calculation of costs and benefits. By contrast, a new dual-process model of effort indicates that affect is an additional important source of motivation. This model builds on evidence from neuroscience. It maintains the standard assumption in economics that the individual's cognitive processes are sophisticated and forward looking, but it also allows for circumstances in which affective processes can override cognitive priorities and distort the individual's effort profile. In particular, the individual's daily performance is assumed to have an affective significance depending on how it compares to a personal goal or reference level. Consistent with evidence from neuroscience, the affective system is assumed to value effort more highly when the individual has not yet achieved this more narrowly defined goal. Furthermore, the affective system is assumed to become increasingly aroused as the goal becomes more immediate, leading to the prediction of an increasing effort profile, or goal gradient, leading up to a goal.

The alternative model is able to explain important facts about effort decisions in the workplace that are difficult to explain from a purely cognitive perspective. One example is the new evidence of a goal gradient from data on the within-day effort profiles of bicycle messengers. The pattern found among messengers is inconsistent with a purely cognitive model, because a windfall gain in the morning does not affect the financial incentives to work in the afternoon (and leads to only a small change relative to the long-term income goals of the worker). On the other hand, the pattern also could indicate that the lucky morning pushes the messenger closer to a daily income goal, triggering the goal gradient and leading to more intense effort early in the afternoon. Later in the afternoon, when other messengers are still approaching their goals, the lucky messenger may have already surpassed the goal and thus works less hard. Another example is the important finding in previous studies that a worker's total daily effort is often unchanged, or even decreases, in response to a temporary increase in the wage. This contradicts a central prediction of a purely cognitive model that a worker should work harder when financial incentives are high. The alternative model can explain this perverse effect of financial incentives, however, because it allows for affective, as well as financial, valuation of effort: a higher wage allows a worker to reach a daily earnings goal more quickly and thus causes the affective valuation of effort to drop earlier in the day. If affect was a sufficiently important component of the worker's motivation to begin with, reaching the goal earlier could lead to a net drop in total daily effort.

The answer to the question of whether affect leads to better or worse decisions depends partly on the benchmark used. In our model, affect causes the worker to work too hard when a narrowly defined goal is close, and not hard enough when the goal is surpassed. In contrast, a purely cognitive perspective effort should be constant over time. For welfare calculations, our premise is that the affective system's payoff should be ignored. Affective experiences (for example, anticipated joy from completing the project) do inform the cognitive system in important ways about whether to engage in the project in the first place. However, the focus of our analysis was on how to best work on such projects, and, given this perspective, we argue that the payoff to the affective system should be ignored. We thus conclude that affect distorts decisions relative to the optimal benchmark. However, the severity of these distortions critically depends on the narrowly defined goal.

We have so far sidestepped the issue of where these goals come from. We can imagine different sources of these goals; these sources matter in judging the welfare loss due to the affective system's influence on behavior. One possibility, a straightforward extension of our model, is to integrate a conscious choice of these goals by the individual herself. One approach would be to let the cognitive system set the goal before the workday or workout starts, and the productivity of effort (which is in part randomly determined) is known. The cognitive system could then choose a goal for the affective system that will result in an effort allocation that is closest to what the cognitive system would desire in the absence of affective distortions of effort choices. It is obvious that goals which are too low or too high are not optimal, as they make the affective system complacent (that is, if the goal is surpassed without any effort) or desperate (that is, if the goal is so high such that no effort level can reach it). Such goals make the distortions in the effort profile strongest. A goal that minimizes the average distortions caused by the affective system will be optimal. Thus, we predict that when individuals choose goals for themselves, affect will do comparatively little harm. In fact, such a model also gives a rationale as to why individuals may set narrowly defined daily goals for themselves rather than broad monthly goals. If the affective system is strongly influenced by the proximity to the goal, medium-term goals (for example, monthly goals) may create larger distortions in effort than short-term daily goals.

As a second possibility, one can envision a model in which a third party sets the goal for the individual. A broad literature (Locke and Latham 1990) is consistent with the interpretation that others can also influence the affective system's target. An area in which our research could be applied fruitfully is the examination of how firms may use goal setting as an additional device to elicit effort from employees. Providing incentives (for example, pay-for-performance), is costly for the firm; hence, goal setting to elicit effort may be an attractive low-cost alternative. In this case, the firm has an incentive to set the goal such that the affective system "freaks out" maximally, providing the highest possible overall effort. However, our analysis implies that such goal setting exacerbates the negative impact of the affective system on the individual's welfare. Firms will have to at least partially compensate workers for this negative impact through a higher fixed salary, but the firm still sets more challenging goals than the individual would choose for himself. To summarize, the extent of damage done by the affective system depends on who chooses the narrowly defined goals. If the individual himself gets to choose the goal, our model predicts that the goal will be chosen to minimize damage done by the affective system. However, third parties, and specifically employers, may have incentives to use the goal strategically to their advantage, exacerbating the distortions by the affective system.

The views expressed herein solely reflect those of the authors, and not necessarily those of the Federal Reserve Bank of Boston or the Federal Reserve System.

Notes

1. This chapter was written for both a psychology and economics audience. Where it is appropriate we define terms that may be unfamiliar to researchers in either discipline. For example, we use the term *emotion* as it is used in psychology, to refer to a specific feeling state, such as anger, sadness, or joy. In all other cases we use the more general term from psychology, *affect*.
2. For example, in Camerer et al. (1997) and in other cabdriver studies it is not clear whether wage variation is exogenous to effort choices. For a discussion of this point, see Fehr and Goette (2007) and Farber (2005).

3. Intuitively, the insensitivity of λ to small z_t follows from the assumption that the individual plans over the entire time span needed to achieve Q. With this time horizon in mind, the individual uses any windfall gain in progress to reduce work effort by a small amount in every future period. Given that a lucky day leads to a change in z_t that is very small relative to Q, the resulting change in effort in any single future period will be essentially zero.

4. This final assumption corresponds to the notion of strong loss aversion (Neilson 2002) and implies a kink in $v()$ at zero. Given these assumptions, $v()$ is equivalent to the "Kahneman-Tversky" value function, proposed by Kahneman and Tversky (1979) as a description of reference-dependent evaluation of outcomes. In this sense our model is similar to Wu, Heath, and Larrick (2002), who propose a dynamic, value-function-based model of working towards a goal. An important difference is that they assume the individual is completely myopic. We assume that the affective system is myopic, but allow for forward-looking decision making on the part of the cognitive system.

5. This does not mean that the individual is "naïve" and is ignoring the impact of current effort on the decisions of future selves; the individual still has a strategic interest in encouraging future selves to adhere to current period preferences. Rather, the assumption is that the individual does not incorporate the willpower costs of future selves directly into the current period utility function, and thus would, if possible, force future selves to exert maximum willpower without regard for discomfort experienced by future selves.

6. We obtained permission to conduct the survey from the Committee for the Protection of Human Subjects at the University of California, Berkeley.

7. Fatigue spillovers could be incorporated by making the slope of the cost function for effort in period t an increasing function of effort exerted in previous periods, as we do in Goette and Huffman (2005).

8. Because our dependent variable is bounded below by zero, this necessarily implies that the variance of the error term differs between observations.

9. These findings are also broadly consistent with the predictions of the reference-dependent model of labor supply in Koszegi and Rabin (2005), which predicts that an unexpected increase in morning earnings can lead to a drop in effort in the afternoon. However, their model has only two periods, morning and afternoon, and thus cannot predict the goal gradient that we observe. This reflects the different focus of their research: they focus on modeling the role of expectations in determining the reference point rather than the role of affect as a source of motivation to work towards a reference point.

References

Benhabib, Jesand, and Alberto Bisin. 2004. "Modeling Internal Commitment Mechanisms and Self-Control: A Neuroeconomics Approach to Consumption-Saving Decisions." Mimeo. New York University.

Bernheim, B. Douglas, and Antonio Rangel. 2003. "Emotions, Cognition, and Savings: Theory and Policy." Mimeo. Stanford University.

———. 2004. "Addiction and Cue-Triggered Decision Processes." *American Economic Review* 94(5): 1558–90.

Bertrand, Marianne, Esther Duflo, and Sendhil Mullainathan. 2004. "How Much Should We Trust Differences-in-Differences Estimates?" *Quarterly Journal of Economics* 119(1): 249–75.

Camerer, Colin, Linda Babcock, George Loewenstein, and Richard Thaler. 1997. "Labor Supply of New York City Cabdrivers: One Day at a Time." *Quarterly Journal of Economics* 112(2): 407–41.

Chen, Keith M., Venkat Lakshminarayanan, and Laurie Santos. 2005. "The Evolution of Our Preferences: Evidence from Capuchin Monkey Trading Behavior." Unpublished manuscript. Yale University.

Chou, Yuan K. 2002. "Testing Alternative Models of Labor Supply: Evidence from Cab Drivers in Singapore." *The Singapore Economic Review* 47(1): 17–47.

Cohen, Jonathan D. 2005. "The Vulcanization of the Human Brain: A Neural Perspective on Interactions Between Cognition and Affect and Optimality in Decision Making." Working Paper. Department of Psychology, Princeton University.

Farber, Henry. 2005. "Is Tomorrow Another Day? The Labor Supply of New York City Cab Drivers." *Journal of Political Economy* 113: 46–82.

Fehr, Ernst, and Lorenz Goette. 2007. "Do Workers Work More When Wages Are High? Evidence from a Randomized Field Experiment." *American Economic Review*. Forthcoming.

Fudenberg, Drew, and David Levine. 2006. "A Dual Self Model of Impulse Control." *American Economic Review* 96(5): 1449–76.

Goette, Lorenz, and David Huffman. 2005. "Incentives and Within-Day Effort Profiles: Evidence from Natural Experiments with Bicycle Messengers." Unpublished manuscript. University of Zurich.

Goette, Lorenz, David Huffman, and Ernst Fehr. 2004. "Loss Aversion and Labor Supply." *Journal of the European Economic Association* 2(2–3): 216–28.

Heath, Chip, Richard Larrick, and George Wu. 1999. "Goals as Reference Points." *Cognitive Psychology* 38(1): 79–109.

Heilizer, Fred. 1977. "A Review of Theory and Research on the Assumptions of Miller's Response Competitions Model: Response Gradients." *The Journal of General Psychology* 97(1): 17–71.

Hull, Clark. 1934. "The Rats' Speed of Locomotive Gradient in the Approach of Food." *Journal of Comparative Psychology* 17: 393–422

Kahneman, Daniel, and Amos Tversky. 1979. "Prospect Theory: An Analysis of Decisions Under Risk." *Econometrica* 47(2): 263–91.

Kivetz, Ran, Oleg Urminsky, and Yuhuang Zheng. 2005. "The Goal Gradient Hypothesis Resurrected: Purchase Acceleration, Illusionary Goal Progress, and Customer Retention." *Journal of Marketing Research* 43(1): 39–58.

Koszegi, Botond, and Matthew Rabin. 2005. "A Model of Reference-Dependent Preferences." Unpublished manuscript. University of California, Berkeley.

Locke, Edwin A., and Gary P. Latham. 1990. *A Theory of Goal Setting and Task Performance*. Englewood Cliffs, N.J.: Prentice Hall.

Loewenstein, George, and Ted O'Donoghue. 2005. "Animal Spirits: Affective and Deliberative Processes in Human Behavior." Unpublished manuscript. Cornell University.

McClure, Samuel M., David Laibson, George Loewenstein, and Jonathan D. Cohen. 2004. "Separate Neural Systems Value Immediate and Delayed Monetary Rewards." *Science* 306(5695): 503–7.

Mischel, Walter, Ozlem Ayduk, and Rodolfo Mendoza-Denton. 2003. "Sustaining Delay of Gratification Over Time: A Hot-Cool Systems Perspective." In *Time and Decision: Economic and Psychological Perspectives on Intertemporal Choice,* edited by George Loewenstein, Daniel Read, and Roy F. Baumeister. New York: Russell Sage Foundation.

Mischel, Walter, Ebbe B. Ebbesen, and Antonette Zeiss. 1972. "Cognitive and Attentional Mechanisms in Delay of Gratification." *Journal of Personality and Social Psychology* 21(2): 204–18.

Mischel, Walter, Yuichi Shoda, and Monica L. Rodriguez. 1989. "Delay of Gratification in Children." *Science* 244(4907): 933–8.

Neilson, William S. 2002. "Comparative Risk Sensitivity with Reference-Dependent Preferences." *The Journal of Risk and Uncertainty* 24(2): 131–42.

Satpute, Ajay B., and Matthew D. Lieberman. 2004. "Integrating Automatic and Controlled Processes into Neurocognitive Models of Social Cognition." *Brain Research* 1079(1): 86–97.

See, Kelly E., Chip Heath, and Craig Fox. 2003. "Motivating Individual Performance with Challenging Goals: Is It Better to Stretch A Little or A Lot?" Working Paper. Fuqua School of Business.

Shidara, Munetaka, and Barry J. Richmond. 2002. "Anterior Singulate: Single Neuronal Signals Related to Degree of Reward Expectancy." *Science* 296(5573): 1709–11.

Shidara, Munetaka, Thomas G. Aigner, and Barry J. Richmond. 1998. "Neuronal Signals in the Monkey Ventral Striatum Related to Progress Through a Predictable Series of Trials." *The Journal of Neuroscience* 18(7): 2613–25.

Shiv, Baba, George Loewenstein, Antoine Bechara, Hanna Damasio, and Antonio Damasio. 2005. "Investment Behavior and the Dark Side of Affect." Mimeo. University of Iowa.

Thaler, Richard H., and Hersh M. Shefrin. 1981. "An Economic Theory of Self-Control." *Journal of Political Economy* 89(2): 392–406.

Tom, Sabrina, Craig Fox, Christopher Trepel, and Russell Poldrack. 2007. "The Neural Basis of Loss Aversion in Decision-Making Under Risk." *Science* 315(5811): 515–8.

Tversky, Amos, and Daniel Kahneman. 2000. *Choices, Values, and Frames.* Cambridge, Mass.: Cambridge University Press.

Wu, George, Chip Heath, and Richard Larrick. 2002. "A Value-Function Based Model of Goal Behavior." Unpublished manuscript. Graduate School of Business, University of Chicago.

· 13 ·

The Impact of Emotions
on Wage Setting
and Unemployment

LORENZ GOETTE AND DAVID HUFFMAN

T RADITIONALLY, models of economic decision making assume that individuals are rational and emotionless. However, the neglect of emotion in economic models explains their inability to predict important aggregate outcomes in the labor market. This is demonstrated by the example that far fewer nominal wage cuts are observed in labor markets than are predicted by traditional economic models. Firms frequently cut real wages, or purchasing power, of workers by increasing nominal wages by less than the inflation rate, but they seldom cut nominal wages. This pattern suggests that workers exhibit a special resistance to nominal wage cuts, which is hard to explain if they are purely rational.

Economists have tried to explain the infrequency of nominal wage cuts by maintaining the assumption that individuals are emotionless and relaxing the assumption that they are cognitively sophisticated. In particular, if individuals suffer from a cognitive limitation known as "money illusion," they fail to subtract the inflation rate from changes in the nominal wage and thus interpret all nominal wage increases as leading to higher purchasing power. This mistake would make workers more resistant to a nominal wage cut during a time of zero inflation than to a nominal wage increase during a time of high inflation that implies exactly the same decrease in real wages. The problem with the money illusion explanation is that it means either that individuals are unable to perform subtraction, or that they underestimate the true inflation rate. Both of these conditions appear counterfactual. People are able to perform subtraction in many domains, and there is strong evidence that, on average, individuals actually have well-calibrated inflation expectations, even during times of very low inflation (Mankiw, Reis, and Wolfers 2003).

In contrast, strong resistance to nominal wage cuts is best understood in terms of a model in which, consistent with evidence from psychology and neuroscience, salient features of a situation trigger emotional responses and sway judgment of the entire situation (Loewenstein 1996; Hsee and Rottenstreich 2004). We therefore argue that cutting the nominal wage leads to a reaction that is mainly dominated by emotions. On the other hand, we hypothesize that an increase in the nominal wage produces a more reflective evaluation, because there is no immediately salient feature: the individual needs to compare the inflation rate to the wage change before it becomes clear whether the change increases or decreases utility. Because the individual arrives at an understanding of the implications through a more reflective process, the ultimate emotional reaction is more tempered in this case.

We test the predictions of this model by asking individuals how they would react to different hypothetical wage changes in different economic environments. The subjects used in our experiment are familiar with wage offers and making these kinds of decisions. We find that cuts in nominal wages trigger strong emotional reactions above and beyond the emotional reaction caused by a real wage cut, achieved by increasing the nominal wage by less than the rate of inflation. On the other hand, varying the size of an increase in the nominal wage has no impact on emotional evaluations, holding the real wage constant. Thus, our evidence suggests that individuals are not "fooled" by nominal changes in general, as hypothesized in the money illusion explanation, but rather they have an emotional reaction to the salient qualitative aspect of the situation. The results suggest that wage rigidity can be explained by a strong emotional reaction, triggered by the salient reduction in utility that occurs only in the case of a nominal wage cut.

The existing empirical literature is consistent in this model as well. There is evidence that individuals strongly resent nominal wage cuts and retaliate against the employer if the employer cuts their wage. It is also clear that employers shy away from using nominal wage cuts; looking at the distribution of wage changes in representative data sets, we find that many workers receive wage freezes, but very few receive a cut in their nominal wage.

Taken together, this evidence strongly suggests that, in the absence of strong emotions triggered by wage cuts, wages would be lower than they are now. Thus, it is tempting to conclude that emotions make workers better off, because they protect workers from nominal wage cuts. Such a conclusion would be premature, however. If nominal wages are kept high, there are consequences for the prices that firms charge for their products. In an economic model, it is straightforward to show that the resulting price changes lead to lower employment. The evidence shows that downwardly rigid wages do indeed lead to higher unemployment, implying that the same emotions that prevent nominal wages from falling also lead, indirectly, to some other individuals losing their jobs. Thus, while it is clear that emotions play an important role in explaining stylized facts about the labor market, it is far from clear whether emotions improve outcomes in the labor market.

The Role of Emotions in Wage Setting

A basic economic framework allows us to analyze employment relationships and the ways that emotions may influence wage formation. This model of employment relationships incorporates three features. The first concerns the kinds of formal agreements that can be part of an employment contract, and the other two capture important aspects of the preferences of employees.

Contractual Incompleteness

Employment contracts are inherently incomplete. They do not specify all actions that an employee is required to take in all possible contingencies in a way that is enforceable by a third party (Milgrom and Roberts 1992). One cause of incompleteness is the cost of identifying and writing down all possible contingencies. Incompleteness can also arise even when it is clear to both the employer and employee what action is appropriate in a particular instance, but verification by an outside party is difficult or impossible. Together, these obstacles ensure that contracts are incomplete.

Contractual incompleteness confronts the employer with a motivational problem of how to motivate an employee to behave in the interests of the firm when there are limited possibilities for enforcement. Several strategies have been proposed; for example, employers could pay a wage that makes employees better off than their next best alternative, thereby creating an incentive to behave in the employer's interest in order to keep the job.[1]

Reciprocity

Paying high wages to motivate performance is particularly effective if employees have reciprocal preferences (that is, if they respond to kind actions by the employer—that is, high wages—with kind actions—that is, more effort than could be contractually enforced).

George Akerlof and Janet Yellen (1984) review the extensive literature in social psychology and incorporate key findings regarding reciprocity into a formal model of the labor market. It is notoriously difficult to verify the predictions of such a model using field data, however, as alternative explanations abound. A viable alternative is to test the behavioral predictions in laboratory experiments that mimic a labor market with incomplete contracts. In a series of experiments, Ernst Fehr and colleagues show that reciprocity can indeed have an important impact on labor market outcomes (Fehr, Kirchsteiger, and Riedl 1993; Fehr, Gaechter, and Kirchsteiger 1997; Fehr and Gaechter 2000). In these experiments, firms consistently pay wages above the market-clearing wage, and employees provide more effort than can be explained by selfish preferences alone.[2]

Reference-Dependent Evaluations

The labor-market experiments reviewed in Ernst Fehr and Simon Gaechter (2000) show that reciprocity is a potentially important behavioral force in the labor market. However, integral to the notion of fairness is a standard of comparison, or reference-point, which makes clear which types of actions are "kind" or fair.

Daniel Kahneman, Daniel Knetsch, and Richard Thaler (1986) provided some of the first field evidence on the importance of reference points in fairness judgments. For example, they show that the fairness of a wage depends on how it compares to the wage paid to the employee in the past (see results for questions 2 and 3 in their paper). They argue that transactions are coded as either gains or losses relative to the reference transaction, and evaluations are characterized by loss aversion (that is, they are characterized by a tendency for losses to be more painful than a gain of similar size is enjoyable) (Tversky and Kahneman 1991).

More recently, Eldar Shafir, Peter Diamond, and Amos Tversky (1997) show even more convincingly that the past wage is an important reference point in evaluating the current wage. Furthermore, both studies find that it is the past money wage, rather than the real wage, which appears to act as a reference point. For instance, these researchers present respondents with two scenarios: a small nominal wage cut when inflation is zero, and a small nominal wage increase when inflation is moderate. The parameters are chosen such that in both scenarios, the change in the purchasing power (that is, the nominal wage change minus inflation) is the same. They find that individuals view the nominal wage cut as unfair, but they evaluate the other scenario, which involves the same change in the real wage, much more favorably. Importantly, both studies appeal to money illusion in order to explain why nominal wage increases are coded as gains, even when they do not keep up with inflation. Economists have regarded this final argument with a fair amount of skepticism (McLaughlin 1994). The use of the nominal wage as a reference point has the strong flavor of a very basic form of irrationality and produces strong affective reactions in economists, because it implies that individuals are incapable of calculating the real wage (that is, subtracting the inflation rate from the nominal wage change). In support of this skepticism, introspection suggests that individuals are in fact able to perform additions and subtractions in many situations, and evidence from surveys shows that inflation expectations are actually quite accurate (Mankiw, Reis, and Wolfers 2003). Thus, while reference dependence clearly plays an important role in determining reciprocal responses, it is desirable to provide an alternative explanation—which does not involve an inability to perform addition or subtraction—for why nominal wage increases do not provoke strong reactions.

This issue can be looked at from the perspective of dual-process models in which decision making depends on the interaction of two systems: a reflective system, and an impulsive, or affective, system.[3] This model maintains the assumption that the individual is cognitively sophisticated (that is, the reflective system is assumed to be able to add and subtract). On the other hand, in certain circumstances the individual is assumed to experience emotions, or affect, which can override reflective decision making. In line with evidence on the nature of affective evaluation, the affective system is assumed to respond more strongly to salient features of a situation. In the case of wage changes, we hypothesize that the nominal wage change is much more salient than the inflationary environment within which the wage change occurs. Thus, the affective system responds primarily to the nominal wage change. On the other hand, we propose that the reflective system primarily cares about the final purchasing power derived from a wage change, and we assume that the reflective system is able to calculate the real wage by subtracting the inflation rate.

Since the wage cut unambiguously reduces disposable income, we also hypothesize that a nominal wage cut triggers an immediate and strong evaluation from the affective system without the need for further deliberation. When the wage change is positive, however, some reflection is required to determine whether the wage change is an improvement or not: the individual must subtract the inflation rate from the nominal change in order to determine whether the wage increase will make the individual better off or worse off than the prior year. Thus, we hypothesize that a nominal wage increase produces less of a response from the affective system and instead activates the reflective system more strongly.[4] Consistent with many examples from the literature on conflicts between affective and reflective decision making, we assume that the affective system can strongly skew the response of the reflective system when it is highly aroused.[5] On the other hand, when the affective system is not strongly aroused, behavior is assumed to correspond more closely to the goals of the reflective system. The resulting dual-process model can easily generate strong responses to a nominal wage cut. However, the same model can produce more measured responses to a nominal wage increase, in which the individual clearly behaves as if she can add and subtract.

Evidence on Emotions Triggered by Wage Cuts

Undergraduates nearing graduation at the University of Zurich were recruited to participate in a study on wage changes. Initially, subjects were asked to imagine a situation in which they had been working at a firm for about a year, during which time they had received no feedback regarding their performance. They were asked to imagine that it was now the end of the year, and that they had been called in for a meeting with their boss to discuss their salary for the next year. The subjects were then presented with a first scenario in which the boss proposed a specific wage change, and they were informed about the current inflation environment. They were asked to try their best to imagine how they would react to this wage change and to indicate how well a list of emotions provided to them characterized their reaction. They had to indicate their answers on a seven-point scale, with *one* indicating that the emotion in question did not describe their reaction at all, and *seven* indicating that it described their reaction accurately. Following this rating, they were presented with two additional scenarios. The first scenario asked them to imagine that, as in many workplaces, there were some tasks that needed to be done to ensure smooth operation of their firm, but that the person performing these tasks would go largely unrewarded for doing so. They were asked how likely they were to do these tasks following the meeting with their superior (again using a seven-point scale). They were then asked how likely it was that they would look for a new job following the meeting (on a seven-point scale). After this first scenario, subjects were posed with a second scenario in which the hypothetical wage increase was 5 percent higher, and the whole procedure was repeated.

Table 13.1   The Treatment Conditions

Wage Changes in Scenario 1

		Nominal Wage Change	
		1 Percent Cut	1 Percent Increase
Real Wage	2 percent decrease	A	B
Change	4 percent decrease	C	D

Wage Changes in Scenario 2

		Nominal Wage Change	
		4 Percent Increase	6 Percent Increase
Real Wage	3 percent increase	A'	B'
Change	1 percent increase	C'	D'

Source: Authors' calculations.

There were four different treatments in the first scenario. Table 13.1 provides an overview over the different conditions. Each subject was in either treatment A, B, C, or D. Subjects in treatment A in the first scenario were in A' in the second, and so on. Hence, all comparisons between A, B, C, and D (and their primed counterparts) measured between-subject variation. The others were identified by within-subject comparisons.[6]

Results

Figure 13.1 presents the emotional reactions to the different wage changes, plotting the mean score for each emotion. The top panel of figure 13.1 shows scores for treatments A, B, C, and D. The bottom panel shows the scores for treatments A', B', C', and D'. Comparing treatments A and B, which involved a 2 percent decrease in the real wage, to C and D, in which the real wage was cut by 4 percent, we see that a larger real wage cut leads to more anger and disappointment. However, comparing A to B, and C to D, we also see that the emotional reaction is consistently stronger in cases in which there was a nominal wage cut compared to cases where there was not, holding the change in the real wage constant. Linear regression results, presented in table 13.2, tell a similar story. The dependent variable for each regression is the corresponding emotion score. As explanatory variables, we include dummy variables for each of the possible real wage changes (from all scenarios), so that the effect of a nominal wage cut is identified by comparing A to B, and C to D. Because each subject participated in two scenarios, we adjusted the standard errors to correct for possible correlation of the error term across

Figure 13.1   Emotional Reactions to Different Wage Scenarios

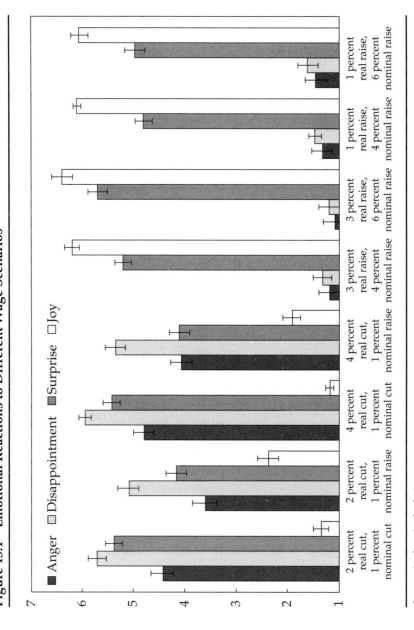

Source: Authors' calculations.

Table 13.2   Emotions Aroused by Different Scenarios of Wage Changes

Dependent Variable	Anger	Disappointment	Surprise	Joy
Nominal Wage Cut	0.7750	0.6041	1.2608	−0.8896
	(0.2126)	(0.1799)	(0.1798)	(0.1559)
2 percent Real Wage Cut	−0.4132	−0.2537	0.0094	0.3120
	(0.2118)	(0.1781)	(0.1791)	(0.1532)
1 percent Real Wage Raise	−2.6542	−3.8096	0.7685	4.1165
	(0.2003)	(0.2000)	(0.2210)	(0.1791)
3 percent Real Wage Raise	−2.9165	−4.0913	1.3393	4.3463
	(0.1867)	(0.1809)	(0.2055)	(0.1794)
Constant	4.0513	5.3538	4.1359	2.0012
	(0.1810)	(0.1633)	(0.1660)	(0.1450)
p-value that coefficient on nominal wage raise is zero in augmented regression	0.912	0.976	0.059	0.63
R-Squared	0.55	0.73	0.11	0.76
N	554	554	554	554

Source: Authors' calculations.
Note: Dependent variables are measured on a seven-point scale to indicate whether the emotion describes their reaction to the proposed scenario. One indicates the lowest level of agreement, seven indicates the highest level of agreement. Robust standard errors, adjusted for clustering on individuals.

observations for the same subject. Despite this conservative calculation of standard errors, we find a highly significant effect of a nominal wage cur: anger and disappointment are clearly higher, and joy is clearly lower when a nominal wage cut is involved, holding the real wage change constant. Interestingly, the subjects also appeared more surprised by a real wage cut if it involved a nominal wage cut. Real wage changes clearly also matter for the evaluations, and the coefficients on the corresponding dummy variables indicate that these effects are quite large. For example, going from A to A', or B to B', we find large shifts in the evaluation of the wage scenario. Interestingly, when we compare A to C, and B to D, we find impacts that are much smaller, even though they entail the same difference in the real wage change. The difference between the two comparisons is that going from A to A' is comparing a real wage loss to a real wage gain, while going from A to C is comparing a large loss to a small loss (or to a small gain in the case of comparing A' to C'). The difference in the results in these cases suggests the presence of strong loss aversion with respect to the real wage.[7]

The design of the study also allows us to examine whether there is something per se about a nominal frame that leads to a strong emotional reaction, or whether strong emotional reactions are confined to the case of nominal wage cuts. If a nominal frame affects evaluation in general, it should be true that the different nominal wage increases in the second set of scenarios lead to different emotional evaluations. However, inspection of figure 13.1 already suggests that our results are not driven by an emotional reaction to nominal wage changes in general. For example, while we find a clear effect of a nominal wage cut on the joy ratings in C relative to D, we find no effect on joy ratings when there is a difference in the size of a nominal wage increase, as shown by a comparisons of A' to B', and C' to D'. To test this more formally, we ran the same regressions as reported in table 13.2, but also included the nominal wage change as an additional explanatory variable in each of the regressions. In table 13.2, we report the p-values of these coefficients. As can be seen, there is not a single significant effect of the size of the nominal wage change at conventional significance levels, while the nominal wage cut dummies remained highly significant. Thus, difficulty with disentangling nominal from real changes does not explain our results.[8] Rather, only nominal wage cuts appear to evoke a strong emotional reaction, holding the real wage change constant.

It is also noteworthy that the effect of a nominal wage cut is quantitatively large. For example, the coefficient measuring the impact of a nominal wage cut is approximately twice as large as the coefficient measuring the impact of a change in the size of a real wage cut, from 4 percent to 2 percent.

The Consequences of Wage Cuts

Figure 13.2 displays results based on the two measures of loyalty to the employer. We find that nominal wage cuts undermine the loyalty the employee has toward the employer. Interestingly, the effect is much stronger for the tendency to look for a new job (possibly because refusing to do the unrewarded tasks also hurts fellow workers). Again, the results do not appear to be driven by confusion about nominal versus real changes in general. We report p-values in table 13.3 showing that the data do not support this hypothesis.

How do these results compare to the results of other studies? Truman Bewley (1999) conducted interviews with 288 compensation managers and personnel officers. In these free-form interviews, almost 70 percent of managers spontaneously indicated that work morale would suffer in response to a nominal wage cut, 40 percent expressed fear of higher turnover and lower productivity in this situation, and 15 percent expected even more extreme reactions such as sabotage and theft. The

Figure 13.2   Changes in Job Loyalty in Different Job Scenarios

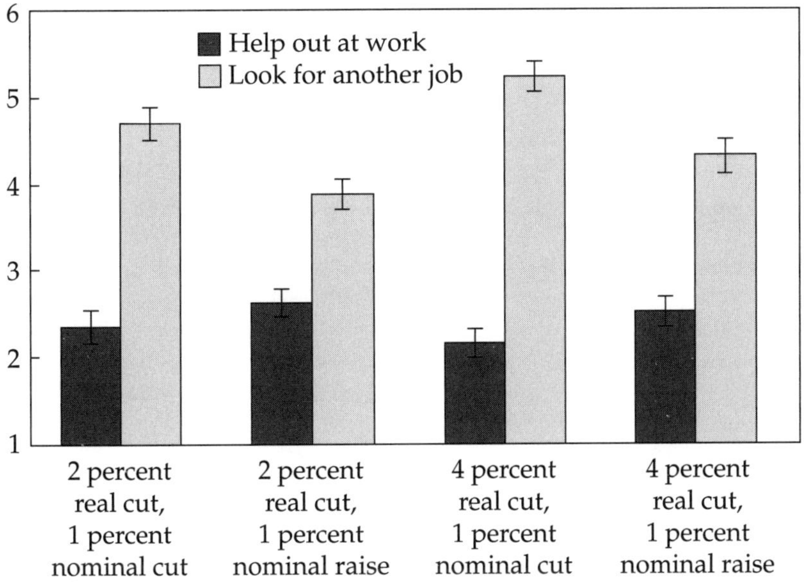

Source: Authors' calculations.

results obtained in our study are thus consistent with Truman Bewley's evidence. In a more recent study, Alexandre Mas (2005) examines the impact of final-offer arbitrations between municipalities and police officer unions on subsequent law enforcement. The results he finds are striking: in municipalities in which an arbitrator ruled against the police officers, arrest rates tend to decrease over the subsequent year.[9] Furthermore, larger "losses" relative to the level desired by the police officers lead to a larger drop in the arrest rate. On the other hand, larger "gains" do not significantly increase arrest rates. The results presented by Alexandre Mas (2005) are thus consistent with a model in which individuals care about outcomes relative to a reference outcome. While the results do not speak to the point of whether nominal wage cuts lead to lower effort of workers, they do show that outcomes below a salient reference point lead to lower effort.[10]

Overall, these results provide a strong rationale for why firms might shy away from nominal wage cuts, especially when the desired nominal wage cut is small.

Table 13.3   Loyalty Towards Employer in Different Wage Change Scenarios

Dependent Variable	Willingness to Help Out	Will Look for New Job
Nominal Wage Cut	−0.3073	0.8665
	(0.1688)	(0.1807)
2 percent Real Wage Cut	0.1525	−0.4876
	(0.1691)	(0.1807)
1 percent Real Wage Raise	2.8469	−2.4079
	(0.1702)	(0.1769)
3 percent Real Wage Raise	3.0545	−2.5477
	(0.1789)	(0.1935)
Constant	2.4987	4.3491
	(0.1467)	(0.1642)
p-value that coefficient on nominal wage raise is zero in augmented regression	0.764	0.477
R-Squared	0.57	0.51
N	554	554

Source: Authors' calculations.
Note: Dependent variables are measured on a seven-point scale to indicate whether they would engage in the behavior described in response to the proposed scenario. One indicates the lowest level of agreement, seven indicates the highest level of agreement. Robust standard errors, adjusted for clustering on individuals.

Evidence of Downward Nominal Wage Rigidity

This model predicts that nominal wage cuts occur less often than if workers were emotionless. To examine the relevance of this prediction in the field, one needs data on individual wage observations. A mass point at 0 percent wage changes, and a discontinuous drop in the density of the wage changes below zero, would be evidence of downward nominal wage rigidity (DNWR), as it might arise from behavioral forces.

One approach to testing for DNWR is thus to calculate a histogram of wage changes, and assess the extent of a spike at nominal zero and asymmetry around zero. Studies that take this approach using data on the U.S. labor market include those conducted by Kenneth McLaughlin (1994), David Card and Dean Hyslop (1996), Shulamit Kahn (1997), and David Lebow, Raven Saks, and Beth Anne Wilson (2003). The results indicate that some, but not much, nominal wage rigidity exists. Indeed, in an average year during the sample periods in these studies, about 20 percent of the workforce received nominal wage cuts, even though labor productivity rose quite rapidly and inflation was quite high.

A possible concern with these studies is that they understate the extent of DNWR. Wage data is known to contain a large amount of measurement error because individuals do not remember exactly how much they earn (Bound and Krueger 1991). Using polluted wage data can produce measurement-error artifacts that look like nominal wage cuts. Indeed, when one examines the results from studies that use data known to be free of measurement error (for example, personnel files), there are almost no wage cuts (Baker, Gibbs, and Holmstrom 1994; Wilson 1999; Fehr and Goette 2005). In most of these datasets, wage cuts are less than 1 percent of all wage change observations, while there is a massive pileup at nominal zero. Similarly, studies that ask directly about nominal wage changes (instead of panel studies that ask about wages at two points in time) find wage change distributions that look more like the evidence from personnel files. George Akerlof, William Dickens, and George Perry (1996) conducted such a survey in Washington, D.C., in 1994. They found that less than 1 percent of the sample experienced wage cuts, and those that did experience cuts had extraordinary circumstances. We find very similar results in a phone survey that we conducted in the fall of 2004 in Zurich, Switzerland (N = 240). We find that a large number of individuals have unchanged nominal wages in a given year, while only about 1 percent experienced a cut in their nominal wage.

Given that evidence from personnel files, as well as evidence from surveys asking directly about wage changes, suggests that measurement error masked a considerable amount of DNWR in previous studies, more recent studies using survey data try to correct for measurement error using more complicated statistical models. Joseph Altonji and Paul Devereux (2000) allow for measurement error in the data and find that, once one takes measurement error into account, there is a marked degree of wage rigidity, even in panel data on wages. Peter Gottschalk (2005) finds similar results using a different identification strategy for measurement error. DNWR also appears to be a very robust phenomenon and is not easily malleable in response to changes in economic conditions. For example, Ernst Fehr and Lorenz Goette (2005) examine whether, after a long period of inflation, individuals give up their resistance against wage cuts. They use data from Switzerland in the 1990s, a period marked by a significant recession but very low inflation rates. If anywhere, this is the type of environment in which one would expect to see wage cuts. However, Fehr and Goette find that after four years of virtual price stability, there are very few wage cuts (about 5 percent), while approximately 60 percent of the workers received wage freezes.

Given that many of the studies in this field differ in terms of method, the country considered, and the type of data used, it is difficult to compare results across studies. In an effort to overcome this problem, thirteen country teams have formed the International Wage Flexibility Project, and they plan to use the same type of correction for measurement error on all data sets (Dickens and Goette 2005). The first results of this project (Dickens et al. 2006) indicate that nominal wage rigidity is strong in most of the countries considered.

Thus, once one controls for measurement error, labor-force surveys led to the same finding as personnel files and direct questions about wage changes: nominal wage cuts are very rare, and even after a long period of low inflation, there is no measurable tendency for wage cuts to become more frequent. But to what extent do firms anticipate this and pay lower wages to begin with, because they know that, to some extent, any wage increase is nonreversible? As presented in detail by Michael Elsby (2005), a fall in inflation gives firms an incentive to increase the compression of wage raises (because a given wage increase is more likely to be irreversible at low inflation rates). Indeed, in British and U.S. data, Elsby (2005) finds that the distribution of wage raises is more compressed when inflation is low. However, there are two points to keep in mind with this result: First, measurement error in the data can generate a pattern that looks exactly the same as "compression," and Elsby does not correct for mea-surement error. Secondly, his results imply that compression fails to offset the impact of DNWR, even though compression is overestimated and DNWR is underestimated due to measurement error.

Implications

The evidence in this area implies that wages are higher than they would be in the absence of DNWR. It is tempting to interpret this as a positive effect of emotions on economic outcomes at the individual level: because firms anticipate retaliation in response to a nominal wage cut, workers are in a better bargaining position, and thus are to some extent shielded from wage cuts.

There is, however, a second channel through which emotions can affect labor-market outcomes. Suppose, for instance, that inflation is zero. If, as the evidence suggests, DNWR increases average wages, profit-maximizing firms will try to pass on some of the additional costs to their customers by increasing product prices. This, in turn, tends to lead to lower market demand, which may cause firms to hire fewer workers. In this way, DNWR can create higher unemployment. This prediction is quite difficult to test, however, because it requires either estimating a fully specified general equilibrium model of an economy, or it requires detailed estimates of what wages would have been in the absence of

DNWR. Akerlof, Dickens, and Perry (1996) make a first attempt at building a model along these lines and estimate their model using postwar data from the U.S. The model explains the variation in inflation and unemployment remarkably well. More strikingly, the authors then conduct an out-of-sample prediction for inflation and unemployment during the Great Depression, during which, at times, the inflation rate was negative. Given the unusual inflationary environment, this sample period provides a particularly interesting test of whether a model incorporating DNWR explains the path of macroeconomic aggregates. Their model, estimated on postwar data, predicts employment, output, and prices in the 1930s very well. These results suggest that a large part of the drop in gross domestic product (GDP) during the Great Depression must be attributed to the downward rigidity of nominal wages at that time. Fehr and Goette (2005) use their econometric model to calculate the extent to which DNWR affected wages in separate geographical labor markets and industries. They find a robust and positive correlation between unemployment and the wage sweep up in a labor market. Again, this finding suggests that DNWR reduced employment considerably during the low-inflation episode in the 1990s in Switzerland.

It should be noted that not all studies find an association between the extent of DNWR and economic outcomes. For example, David Lebow, Raven Saks, and Beth Anne Wilson (2003) find evidence at the microlevel of DNWR. Yet, they find no correlation between unemployment and DNWR as estimated in their data. Similarly, David Card and Dean Hyslop (1996) find little evidence that DNWR plays an important role in hindering labor-market adjustment: they examine whether in high-inflation years, wage changes are more responsive to unemployment than in low-inflation years, but they find little evidence to support this hypothesis.[11] One should keep in mind, however, that both studies considered a period with rapid average nominal wage growth, and hence, DNWR did not have much of an impact on average wages anyway. The country comparisons conducted by William Dickens et al. (2006) are also supportive of the view that nominal wage rigidity has an impact on the real side of the economy. They estimate models similar to those in Fehr and Goette (2005) and find that DWNR is associated with higher unemployment.

In summary, there is an often overlooked difficulty in answering the question of whether emotions lead to better or worse decisions. While emotions may benefit an individual worker, by strengthening the worker's bargaining position and discouraging firms from making wage cuts, it is far from clear that emotions benefit workers overall. Evidence indicates that DNWR can lead to higher unemployment, which does not benefit workers overall. Hence, even in cases in which emotions make individuals unambiguously better off, equilibrium effects can counteract, and perhaps fully reverse, these benefits.

The views expressed herein solely reflect those of the authors, and not necessarily those of the Federal Reserve Bank of Boston or the Federal Reserve System.

Notes

1. These mechanisms are known as efficiency wages. See George Akerlof and Janet Yellen (1986) for a survey. See also Bentley MacLeod and James Malcomson (1998) for a formal discussion of the role of bonus payments in this context.
2. See also Martin Brown, Armin Falk, and Ernst Fehr (2004), who show that labor-market outcomes can change dramatically if even a small fraction of labor-market participants have reciprocal preferences. Intuitively, this is because the presence of reciprocal types gives selfish agents an incentive to mimic reciprocal behavior; this causes them to cooperate with the employer until they switch to a strategy of defection towards the end of their employment relationship. See also Alan Krueger and Alexandre Mas (2004) for a study that uses field data. Their study shows that a firm's unkind actions can trigger strong behavioral responses. They look at data for a tire manufacturer, and document a surge in tire failures after the firm announced worse employment conditions for a part of the workforce. Given that technology and the quality of inputs appear to have remained unchanged, Krueger and Mas conclude that the tire failures were due to a retaliatory reduction in work effort.
3. This type distinction is common to many dual-process models. See, for example, Fritz Strack and Roland Deutsch (2004) and Ajay Satpute and Matthew Lieberman (2006).
4. Christopher K. Hsee and Yuval Rottenstreich (2004) provide experimental evidence that is relevant for this point: emotionally-charged priming questions (for example, questions about the emotions aroused by the word "baby") lead subjects to evaluate a subsequent economic transaction in emotional terms (that is, subjects' willingness to pay for a bundle of music CDs was relatively insensitive to the amount of CDs in the bundle). Meanwhile, a prime involving deliberative thinking (for example, simple math problems) triggered evaluation of the transaction in deliberative terms (that is, willingness to pay responded to quantity).
5. George Loewenstein (1996) discusses various examples in which affective processes come to dominate deliberative decision making as arousal of affective processes increases.
6. The most important results in this study are identified using between-subject variation. We are confident that our other findings, based on within-subject variation, would also hold up in a between-subject design as well.

7. One should keep in mind, however, that these comparisons rely on within-subject comparisons. We are confident that, qualitatively, the same results would result in a between-subject design.
8. This contrasts with the finding of Eldar Shafir, Peter Diamond, and Amos Tversky (1997) that money illusion affects judgment in general. However, the types of questions they used asked individuals what they thought *others* would do in a given scenario, not what they themselves would do. Ernst Fehr and Jean-Robert Tyran (2001) show that there is a tendency to overestimate the extent to which other individuals are prone to money illusion.
9. Alexandre Mas (2005) is careful to check whether districts in which the arbitrator ruled against the police differed from districts where the arbitrator ruled in favor of the police. He finds no difference in arrest rates and other characteristics of the police force before the arbitration is announced.
10. In the case of final-offer arbitration, there is a good reason why the current nominal wage should not be relevant. Before a wage bargain comes to the point of final-offer arbitration, the parties involved have gone through a lengthy process of unsuccessful negotiations. Thus, it is particularly likely that the cases that do reach this stage are ones in which the parties feel particularly strongly about their desired outcome.
11. Joseph Altonji and Paul Devereux (2000) examine how individual-level labor-market outcomes are correlated with whether an individual received a wage cut, wage freeze, or wage raise. They find no systematic pattern. A pattern is not to be expected, however, since the theory makes no strong predictions regarding individual-level outcomes.

References

Akerlof, George, and Janet Yellen. 1984. "The Fair Wage-Effort Hypothesis." *Quarterly Journal of Economics* 105(2): 255–83.

———. 1986. *Efficiency Wage Models of the Labor Market.* Cambridge, Mass.: Cambridge University Press.

Akerlof, George, William Dickens, and George Perry. 1996. "The Macroeconomics of Low Inflation." *Brookings Papers on Economic Activity* 1: 1–76.

Altonji, Joseph, and Paul Devereux. 2000. "The Extent and Consequences of Nominal Wage Rigidity: Evidence from Panel Data." *Research in Labor Economics* 19: 383–437.

Baker, George, Michael Gibbs, and Bengt Holmstrom. 1994. "The Wage Policy of a Firm." *Quarterly Journal of Economics* 109(4): 921–55.

Bewley, Truman. 1999. *Why Wages Don't Fall During Recessions.* Cambridge, Mass.: Cambridge University Press.

Bound, John, and Alan Krueger. 1991. "The Extent of Measurement Error in Longitudinal Earnings Data: Do Two Wrongs Make a Right?" *Journal of Labor Economics* 9(1): 1–24.

Brown, Martin, Armin Falk, and Ernst Fehr. 2004. "Relational Contracts and the Nature of Market Interactions." *Econometrica* 72(3): 747–80.

Card, David, and Dean Hyslop. 1996. "Does Inflation 'Grease the Wheels' of the Labor Market?" In *Reducing Inflation: Motivation and Strategy,* edited by Christina Romer and David Romer. Chicago, Ill.: University of Chicago Press.

Dickens, William T., and Lorenz Goette. 2005. "Estimating Wage Rigidity for the International Wage Rigidity Project." Unpublished report. Brookings Institution, Washington.

Dicken, William T., Lorenz Goette, Erica L. Groshen, Steinar Holden, Julian Messina, Mark E. Schweitzer, Jarkko Turunen, and Melanie Ward. 2006. "The Interaction of Labor Markets and Inflation: Micro Evidence from the International Wage Flexibility Project." Unpublished report. Brookings Institution, Washington.

Elsby, Michael. 2005. "Evaluating the Economic Significance of Downward Nominal Wage Rigidity." Unpublished manuscript. London School of Economics.

Fehr, Ernst, and Simon Gaechter. 2000. "Fairness and Retaliation: The Economics of Reciprocity." *Journal of Economic Perspectives* 14(3): 159–81.

Fehr, Ernst, and Lorenz Goette. 2005. "The Robustness and Real Consequences of Downward Nominal Wage Rigidity." *Journal of Monetary Economics* 52(4): 779–804.

Fehr, Ernst, and Jean-Robert Tyran. 2001. "Does Money Illusion Matter?" *American Economic Review* 91(4): 1239–62.

Fehr, Ernst, Simon Gaechter, and Georg Kirchsteiger. 1997. "Reciprocity as a Contract Enforcement Device." *Econometrica* 65(4): 833–60.

Fehr, Ernst, Georg Kirchsteiger, and Arno Riedl. 1993. "Does Fairness Prevent Market Clearing?" *Quarterly Journal of Economics* 108(2): 437–59.

Gottschalk, Peter. 2005. "Downward Nominal Wage Flexibility: Real or Measurement Error?" *Review of Economics and Statistics* 117(3): 556–68.

Hsee, Christopher K., and Yuval Rottenstreich. 2004. "Music, Pandas, and Muggers: On the Affective Psychology of Value." *Journal of Experimental Psychology* 133(1): 23–30.

Kahn, Shulamit. 1997. "Evidence of Nominal Wage Stickiness from Microdata." *American Economic Review* 87(5): 993–1008.

Kahneman, Daniel, Daniel Knetsch, and Richard Thaler. 1986. "Fairness as a Constraint on Profit-Seeking: Entitlements in the Market." *American Economic Review* 76(4): 728–41.

Krueger, Alan, and Alexandre Mas. 2004. "Strikes, Scabs, and Tire Separations: Labor Strife and the Production of Defective Bridgestone/Firestone Tires." *Journal of Political Economy* 112(2): 253–89.

Lebow, David, Raven Saks, and Beth Anne Wilson. 2003. "Downward Nominal Wage Rigidity: Evidence from the Employment Cost Index." *Berkeley Electronic Press: Advances in Macroeconomics* 3(1).

Loewenstein, George. 1996. "Out of Control: Visceral Influences on Behavior." *Organizational Behavior and Human Decision Processes* 65(3): 272–92.

MacLeod, Bentley, and James Malcomson. 1998. "Markets and Motivation." *American Economic Review* 88(3): 388–411.

Mankiw, Gregory, Ricardo Reis, and Justin Wolfers. 2003. "Disagreement About Inflation Expectations." In *NBER Macroeconomics Annual 2003,* edited by Mark Gertler and Kenneth Rogoff. Cambridge, Mass.: MIT Press.

Mas, Alexandre. 2005. "Pay, Reference Points, and Police Performance." *Quarterly Journal of Economics* 121(3): 783–821.

McLaughlin, Kenneth. 1994. "Rigid Wages?" *Journal of Monetary Economics* 34(3): 383–414.

Milgrom, Paul, and John Roberts. 1992. *Economics, Organization, and Management.* Saddle River, N.J.: Prentice Hall.

Satpute, Ajay, and Matthew Lieberman. 2006. "Integrating Automatic and Controlled Processes into Neurocognitive Models of Social Cognition." *Brain Research* 1079(1): 86–97.

Shafir, Eldar, Peter Diamond, and Amos Tversky. 1997. "Money Illusion." *Quarterly Journal of Economics* 112(2): 341–74.

Strack, Fritz, and Roland Deutsch. 2004. "Reflective and Impulsive Determinants of Social Behavior." *Personality and Social Psychology Review* 8(3): 220–47.

Tversky, Amos, and Daniel Kahneman. 1991. "Loss Aversion in Riskless Choice: A Reference-Dependent Model." *Quarterly Journal of Economics* 106(4): 1039–61.

Wilson, Beth Anne. 1999. "Wage Rigidity: A Look Inside the Firm." Federal Reserve System Discussion Paper, 1999–22, Washington.

Wilson, David, Raven Saks, and Beth Anne Wilson. 2003. "Downward Nominal Wage Rigidity: Evidence from the Employment Cost Index." *Advances in Macroeconomics* 3(1): 1–30.

· 14 ·

The Mind and the Body:
Subjective Well-Being in
an Objective World

JONATHAN LEVAV

F OLLOWING an afternoon of intense lovemaking with General
Scheisskopf's wife, Captain Yossarian, the hero of Joseph Heller's *Catch-
22*, argues with his lover about the role of God in creating life's miseries.

> Yossarian asks, " 'What in the world was running through that warped,
> evil, scatological mind of His when He robbed old people of the power to
> control their bowel movements? Why in the world did He ever create
> pain?' "
> " 'Pain?' " she retorts. " 'Pain is a warning to us of bodily dangers.' "
> Yossarian replies, " 'Oh, He was really being charitable to us when He
> gave us pain! Why couldn't He have used a doorbell instead to notify us, or
> one of his celestial choirs? Or a system of blue-and-red neon tubes right in
> the middle of each person's forehead?' "
> " 'People would certainly look silly walking around with red neon tubes
> in the middle of their foreheads,' " responds Scheisskopf's wife. (Heller
> 1955/1961, 184)

Silly or not, a neon light in lieu of feeling pain would certainly simplify
the task of those who study how painful (or pleasurable) experiences
affect human well-being. Instead, researchers must assess the impact of
these experiences on well-being by measuring a diffuse set of mental or
physical neon lights that flicker inconsistently.

Social and cognitive psychologists investigate the effect of life experiences on people's subjective, or self-reported, judgments of well-being or happiness. These judgments are assessed using surveys consisting of single- or multi-item measures that ask about satisfaction with life in general, satisfaction with certain attributes in particular, happiness, and mood (for example, the Subjective Well-Being and Life Satisfaction scale; Pavot and Diener 1993). Although some scales are used more than others, there is no standard methodology. Respondents are asked to rate their current state, evaluate the state of others, or predict their state in the future given the occurrence of a life event or change in circumstance. Sometimes ratings are assessed repeatedly at random over time (for example, the Ecological Momentary Assessment [EMA]) or at the end of the day in diary format using recollected emotions (for example, the Day Reconstruction Method [DRM]); other times, surveys are used in cross-sectional or between-subject designs. From the responses obtained, psychologists deduce conclusions about the factors, events, or circumstances that influence happiness.

Physicians ascertain well-being objectively by measuring the impact of various experiences (events or circumstances) on people's physical and mental health. Sometimes these measurements are conducted by physical examination and other times by using diagnostic survey instruments (for example, the American Psychiatric Association's *Diagnostic and Statistics Manual IV* [*DSM IV*]). Some of these instruments consist of checklists that rely on subjective reports of subjective experience (for example, sadness) or on subjective reports of objective experiences (for example, lethargy or nightmares). The composite score on the checklist indicates a diagnosis. Study designs vary depending on the availability of data. In some cases, measurements are conducted prior to and following a life event; in other studies, patients' health is assessed after an event and is compared to suitable controls.

Each of these approaches—the psychological and the medical—is an effort to reveal a consistent, detectable "signal" of well-being. Surprisingly, they often lead to opposite conclusions: while judgments of subjective well-being (SWB) show little or no correlation with objective circumstances, physicians find that life events and circumstances are highly related to objective well-being (OWB).

It is important to understand how such a contradiction might arise and what it might signify. In exploring these questions, we are motivated by the increasing interest in the field of hedonic psychology and subjective well-being as a basis for public policy (Kahneman, Diener, and Schwarz 1999). Thus, these questions raise the issue of whether it makes sense to use emotions to help not only individual decision making, but also *policy* decision making.

Well-Being: Two Views

There are critical conceptual discrepancies between the conclusions of the psychological and medical literatures about the effects of life events and circumstances on well-being. This review helps to frame the discussion on the effect of life events on people's future happiness; however, it is far from exhaustive (for comprehensive reviews, see Kahneman, Diener, and Schwarz 1999; Diener 1984; Diener et al. 1999; Strack, Argyle, and Schwarz 1991).

Subjective Well-Being

Objective Circumstances: Money Can't Buy Happiness.   Most people report that they are happy. The striking absence of correlation between increasing income and SWB over time and within nations (Easterlin 1974, 1995; Diener et al. 1999; Csikszentmihalyi 1999; Diener and Biswas-Diener 2002) as well as the fact that demographics explain little variance in SWB judgments (Diener 1984; Kahneman et al. 2004) are common themes in the SWB literature (Schwarz and Strack 1999). Even in countries characterized by abject poverty, the average of people's responses to questions such as "how satisfied are you with your life these days?" is above the midpoint of the scale (Diener and Diener 1996).[1] While some authors have presented evidence supporting a moderate correlation between SWB and income (Diener et al. 1993; Diener, Diener, and Diener 1995; Diener and Biswas-Diener 2002), these differences exist only *between* countries. Changes in wealth over time *within* countries are not associated with changes in SWB (Diener and Suh 1999). For instance, although real income doubled between 1945 and 1970, SWB in the United States remained unchanged (Diener and Oishi 2000; the same is true for Japan; Easterlin 1974). One explanation for this has been suggested by Ruut Veenhoven (1991), who reasoned that income only has an effect insofar as it enables fulfillment of basic human needs, and anything superfluous to their fulfillment does not impact judged happiness (Csikszentmihalyi 1999; Diener et al. 1993).

Other objective circumstances that laypeople would commonly associate with elevated SWB also demonstrate a surprising lack of impact on people's judgments. In a study measuring physician- and self-ratings of health and well-being using multi-item scales for happiness and life satisfaction, Morris Okun and Linda George (1984) find that physical health is unrelated to SWB. Likewise, Jason Riis et al. (2005) show that hemodialysis patients are just as happy as healthy controls. David Schkade and Daniel Kahneman (1998) report that the weather, too, has little effect on happiness. The authors compared judgments of life satisfaction and various specific life attributes elicited from students in midwestern and California universities. While the Californians were happier with their weather than the midwesterners, despite sunnier skies their reported overall life satisfaction was equal to their midwestern counterparts.

Some life events—rather than ongoing circumstances such as the weather—also seem to have an insubstantial effect on SWB over time. Daniel Gilbert et al. (1998) posit that people's affective forecasts of responses to emotional events neglect their "psychological immune system." The authors document several examples (including the dissolution of a romantic relationship, failure to achieve tenure, electoral defeat, negative personality feedback, and rejection by a prospective employer) in which people's affective forecasts overestimate the durability of the negative effect of an event on SWB. In their research, the long-term (and sometimes the not-so-long-term) impact of these events is insignificant.

Hedonic Adaptation.   The most dramatic demonstration of the seemingly minimal impact of life events on long-term well-being is Philip Brickman, Dan Coates, and Ronnie Janoff-Bulman's (1978) study of lottery winners and accident victims in Illinois. Life-satisfaction ratings of lottery winners were not significantly higher than controls. More surprisingly, accident victims (quad- and paraplegics) rated their SWB above the midpoint of the scale, suggesting that they were happy (however, they were still a bit lower than controls). This finding has been treated by researchers in the field as a quintessential example of "hedonic adaptation," or adaptation to stimuli that are hedonically relevant (Frederick and Loewenstein 1999).

Hedonic adaptation has been implicated as the primary reason that objective circumstances and life events appear to have such small effects on SWB (Frederick and Loewenstein 1999). The construct was first discussed in Philip Brickman and Donald Campbell's (1971) influential essay on the "hedonic treadmill" (which refers to the notion that people adapt to improving circumstances to the point of affective neutrality). Essentially, the treadmill hypothesis suggests that once an individual has adapted to a circumstance—even a circumstance such as paraplegia—it does not affect his or her SWB. Taken literally, however, the hedonic treadmill implies that one is never able to feel sustained pleasure. Although evidence for adaptation to circumstances and events abounds, it is not extreme enough to warrant a treadmill description (Kahneman 1999).

Various other studies have examined adaptation in a broad spectrum of domains (Frederick and Loewenstein 1999). Physical attractiveness (Diener, Wolsic, and Fujita 1995), incarceration (Flanagan 1980), solitary confinement (Suedfeld et al. 1982), and even bereavement (Wortman and Silver 1987) do not seem to affect SWB in the long term.

In conclusion, people generally seem to be able to adapt to dramatic positive and negative life events and return to their previous levels of SWB (that is, above the midpoint). There are a few notable exceptions, and there are also individual differences that determine people's ability to adapt completely to an event (Lucas et al. 2003). The exceptions include adaptation to noise (Weinstein 1982), to widowhood for some individuals (Lucas et al. 2003), and to job loss among males (Clark, Diener, and Georgellis 2001; Lucas et al. 2004).[2]

Stability in SWB: Genetics, Personality, and Set Points.   Logic suggests that adaptation alone cannot explain the resistance of SWB judgments to objective circumstances and life events. As Paul Costa and Robert McCrae (1980) comment, "If happiness were solely the outcome of processes of adaptation, we would expect that all individuals would answer that they were 'neutral' on the dimension of happiness" (677). Research on the role of genetics and personality confirms the hypothesis that SWB is biologically determined to a substantial degree, rather than the outcome of an adaptation process. The lack of correlation between OWB and SWB becomes less surprising given the abundance of findings that suggest a SWB "set point," resembling the one for body weight (Diener 2000).[3] If SWB is determined by such a set point, it is plausible that Californians and midwesterners are equally happy despite the vast differences in their weather.

The set point hypothesis is supported by the surprising strength of correlation between SWB and genetic factors. David Lykken and Auke Tellegen (1996) studied the SWB of monozygotic and dizygotic twins who were reared together and who were reared apart. Their data reveal a correlation of 0.52 between the SWB of monozygotic twin pairs reared apart, compared with a correlation of –0.02 between the SWB of dizygotic twins reared apart. This suggests a strong effect of heritability on reported SWB and leads the authors to proclaim, "We are led to conclude that individual differences in human happiness . . . are primarily a matter of chance" (189). According to this view, it is little wonder that objective circumstances do not matter to subjective well-being.

The genetic evidence is buttressed by a number of other studies that demonstrate the temporal consistency of SWB and the importance of personality moderators (Costa and McCrae 1980; Magnus et al. 1993; Diener and Larsen 1984). Temperament studies show that characteristic emotional styles emerge at an early age and may be biologically based, hinting at an inborn bias to experience pleasant and unpleasant affect (Diener and Lucas 1999).

While personality may dictate stable mean SWB over the long term, single SWB responses do vary in accordance with objective circumstances or events (Costa and McCrae 1980; Headey and Wearing 1989; Diener and Larsen 1984). Bruce Headey and Alexander Wearing's (1989) dynamic equilibrium model accounts for this apparent discrepancy by stipulating that a person has a "normal" (equilibrium level of SWB that can be predicted from personality data). When events occur, SWB deviates from equilibrium levels, but over time equilibrium is restored. The authors lend credence to this contention using data that show that life events explain variance above and beyond personality factors. Eunkook Suh, Edward Diener, and Frank Fujita's (1996) finding that only recent events matter to SWB also supports Headey and Wearing's model.

However, in rare circumstances life events can lead to a permanent shift in an individual's set point. Richard Lucas et al. (2004) use longitudinal data from a German panel which tracked, among other variables, employment history and life satisfaction. They find that, on average, previously unemployed panelists did not return to their original SWB levels even following a year or more of reemployment. The authors suggest that unemployment may be one of a few life events that lead to permanent changes in SWB set points.

Objective Well-Being

Adversity, Stress, and Pathology.   Research on the effects of life events and circumstances on SWB focuses primarily on the role and limits of adaptation. The opposite phenomenon, sensitization, is an increasingly intense response to a constant stimulus and is rarely discussed in the SWB literature (Frederick and Loewenstein 1999; for notable exceptions, see Weinstein 1982, Clark, Diener, and Georgellis 2001; Clark, Georgellis, and Sanfey 2001). This scarcity may reflect the fact that the domains where sensitization occurs in SWB judgment are, in reality, relatively few. Do life events and circumstances really have little effect on people's lives in the long term? Such a conclusion seems implausible; I argue that effects of sensitization resulting from life events and circumstances occur along a dimension that is entirely different from subjective reports: physical and mental health.

To be fair, SWB researchers are interested in which factors affect *judgments* of well-being, not some objective measure such as immune-system functioning. But if one goal of hedonic psychology is to inform policy decisions, a more comprehensive view of well-being is imperative. In this spirit, I present two robust, ubiquitous effects from the epidemiological literature that seem opposed to some of the basic conclusions from the SWB literature: the dose-response effect and the vulnerability effect.[4] As in the SWB review section, the studies presented are for illustrative purposes only; studies on dose-response and vulnerability are too numerous to cover here.

Dose-Response Effect.   The dose-response effect refers to the "increasing incidence of a disease with the increasing or decreasing exposure to [an] agent" (Armstrong, White, and Saracci 1992, 13). *Dose* refers to exposure and *response* refers to the incidence or expression of disease. Epidemiologists consider dose-response as one crucial criterion for the presence of a causal relationship between a stressor (physical or psychological) and an illness or disorder (Weiss 1981). While the conceptualization of dose may be controversial and is often dependent on the context of measurement (for example, duration versus intensity), the primacy of dose-response as an indicator of causality is considered elemental (Armstrong, White, and Saracci 1992; Lee-Feldstein 1989; Weiss 1981).

A dramatic illustration of dose-response comes from a study of Polish-born female Jewish Holocaust survivors and a matched sample that lived in prestate Israel during World War II (Fenig and Levav 1991). The authors classified the survivors according to degrees of victimization (that is, according to dose): displaced in the former Soviet Union, not in concentration camp; confined to a camp in the former Soviet Union; stayed in a ghetto; stayed in hiding; worked in forced labor; and lived in an extermination camp. Their dependent measure (that is, response) consisted of a twenty-seven-item self-reported demoralization scale, a measure of nonspecific psychological distress including self-esteem, sadness, perceived physical health, anergia, insomnia, and several other dimensions (Dohrenwend et al. 1980).[5] After controlling for socioeconomic status, the authors found a significant increase in demoralization scores corresponding to severity of victimization. Respondents living in prestate Israel showed the lowest degree of demoralization, while those who survived extermination camps scored nearly twice as high (a statistically significant difference). The remaining respondents fell between these two extremes: survivors from ghettos or hiding indicated higher demoralization than those simply displaced in the former Soviet Union.

Many authors have observed dose-response both cross-sectionally and over time (that is, within subject) in the relationship between income, socioeconomic status (SES), and other demographic variables, and risk of morbidity and mortality (Breeze et al. 2001; Brunner et al. 1999; Hemingway et al. 2000; Kohn, Dohrenwend, and Mirotznik 1998; Marmot, Shipley, and Rose 1984; Singer and Ryff 1999; Power and Matthews 1997; Weich and Lewis 1998). Others have observed that the dose-response in the SES-health relationship is actually mediated by perceived control (Bobak et al. 2000; Marmot 1999). Note that these findings largely deviate from the conclusions encountered in the SWB literature about demographic variables and happiness.

Vulnerability.   Vulnerability, which is sometimes called *stress sensitization,* refers to an individual's likelihood of initial disease onset (Dohrenwend 1998a). Sensitization is the process by which a person becomes more vulnerable due to experiencing a prior stressful life event or circumstance. An individual is considered more vulnerable or susceptible if a relatively lower dose of a stimulus (or stressor) prompts a response (Lazarus 1987). The terms *hardening, resilience,* or *inoculation* are used to denote the opposite case, when an individual's previous encounter with a stressor makes him better able to cope with a future stressor. Evidence of resilience in the epidemiologic literature is relatively rare (Rutter 1993). In general, vulnerability can be manifested in two ways: a lower threshold for response when a stressful event is encountered, given a past stressor (that is, like a statistical interaction); or a greater likelihood for disease onset relative to a control group which did not experience the stressful event (that is, like a main effect).

One of the most striking characteristics of vulnerability is its expression many years (and even decades!) after the stressful life event (Levav 1998). For instance, a study of elderly Israeli Holocaust survivors' psychological response to the Persian Gulf War found that survivors reported significantly greater feelings of danger, emotional distress, and anxiety than non-Holocaust survivor controls, even after controlling for a wide range of background variables (Solomon and Prager 1992).

Several studies have documented the effect of previous trauma on the onset of post-traumatic stress disorder (PTSD) resulting from a more recent stressor. Combat veterans who experienced child abuse, for instance, were far more likely to report combat-related PTSD than veterans who suffered little or no physical punishment during childhood (Zaidi and Foy 1994). Breslau et al. (1999) conducted a study in a large-scale community sample and found that victims of trauma (based on the *DSM IV*'s definition) were significantly more likely to experience PTSD from the more recent, "index" trauma than were control respondents who had not suffered previous trauma.

Vulnerability can also be assessed by comparing the incidence of disease in a sample of people previously affected by a stressful event or circumstance to an unaffected control group. Here, too, the manifestation of vulnerability can take place years or decades after the initial stress, as is demonstrated by evidence of elevated prevalence of PTSD in Vietnam War and World War II veterans (Dohrenwend 1998a; Goldberg et al. 1990; Keane 1998). Stanislav Kasl, Eunice Rodriguez, and Kathryn Lasch (1998) review studies suggesting that, after controlling for socioeconomic status and a number of behavioral variables, mortality risk is greater for men who were previously unemployed, even five years following continuous reemployment. Interestingly, this is the one domain in which permanently decreased levels of SWB have been found: Andrew Clark, Yannis Georgellis, and Peter Sanfey (2001) observe depressed levels of SWB among unemployed men even four years following reemployment, a phenomenon they term *scarring*. This finding is qualified by the fact that those who had been unemployed in the past do appear to adapt to future unemployment—their SWB is nearly as high as normal as when they are unemployed.

Other research has focused on the effects of stress on the onset of exclusively physical illnesses such as cancer (Fox 1995). One example is Itzhak Levav et al.'s (2000) study of cancer incidence following bereavement. The authors found an increased likelihood of certain types of cancer among Israeli parents who lost an adult son in the 1973 Yom Kippur War or in a traffic accident between 1970 and 1977. Furthermore, the demise of bereaved parents that had been diagnosed with cancer *prior* to their bereavement was faster relative to parents who had been diagnosed post-bereavement. Recall that psychologists have found that SWB is restored to normal levels some relatively short time (approximately one year) following bereavement (Wortman and Silver 1987), with the caveat that some widowers do not completely adapt even eight years after their spouse's death (Lucas et al. 2003).

Connecting Stress and Vulnerability.   The notion that immune system changes follow exposures to stress—which in turn might lead to increased vulnerability—is supported by substantial convergent evidence (Cacioppo 1998), although in some cases it is accompanied by some debate (Cohen and Rabin 1998; Faragher and Cooper 1997; McGee, Williams, and Elwood 1996). In addition to the studies reviewed above, several studies that examine the consequences of stress on the immune system on a cellular basis obtain significant effects (Benschop et al. 1998). One such example comes from a series of experiments by Janice Kiecolt-Glaser and colleagues (Kiecolt-Glaser et al. 1997; Kiecolt-Glaser et al. 1998) that document alterations in blood pressure and hormone levels among newly-weds, older couples, and professed happy couples who were participating in a thirty-minute "conflict session." Another study found that dental students required extended healing time for a biopsy wound inflicted three days prior to a major examination compared to an identical wound inflicted during the summer vacation (Marucha, Kiecolt-Glaser, and Favagehi 1998). Third, research on allostatic load indicates that cumulative wear and tear on the bodily systems charged with maintaining physiological balance in the face of stress is associated with increased morbidity[6] (McEwen and Seeman 1999; Singer and Ryff 1999). Specific chemical compounds released during allostasis have been found to mediate cellular changes, which later prompt actual diseases and disorders (McEwen and Seeman 1999).

Two Views: Synthesis and Implications

Discrepant Event "Processing" Times

The SWB literature presents a substantial body of evidence supporting the conclusion that objective circumstances do not correlate with judgments of well-being, and that people generally tend to adapt to life events and circumstances. After an initial period during which the event affects SWB judgments, happiness levels eventually return to some equilibrium level. On average, this equilibrium level is above the midpoint of the scale (that is, most people are happy) (Diener and Diener 1996). Dose-response and vulnerability lead to conclusions opposite from those offered by SWB researchers. The dose-response relationship documents a significant correlation between objective circumstances or events and measures of objective well-being (that is, health). Vulnerability entails sensitization that results from these events or circumstances, leading to diminished levels of health in the future.

If both literatures investigate people's response to similar or identical events, how is it possible that these findings coexist? An easy answer to this question is that each group of researchers is asking a different question and using different methodologies and samples. However, I argue that it is worthwhile to probe this apparent contradiction more deeply.

The juxtaposition of the two literatures and their conclusions should be of particular interest to SWB researchers because of their focus on the causes and correlates of happiness. It is indisputable that at any point in time one can be both poor and happy, as well as both rich and unhappy. SWB measures do appear to capture accurately people's present (and relatively recent) affective state (Diener 1984). Forecasts of SWB, on the other hand, are quite inaccurate (Gilbert et al. 1998; Kahneman 1994). This has prompted some SWB researchers to deduce that many of the lay beliefs about factors that govern happiness are false (Kahneman, Diener, and Schwarz 1999). The evidence for dose-response and vulnerability challenges this inference. People's affective forecasts might be faulty due to information-processing limitations (Simon 1955) or motivated reasoning (Taylor 1989), and not necessarily because a certain event does not affect their happiness. The medical literature in this area indicates that some negative and positive events have, respectively, a detrimental or salutary effect on the risk of disease onset. Illness, at one point or another, clearly negatively impacts a person's happiness; likewise, social support positively impacts happiness.[7] Thus, the medical literature suggests that events and circumstances *do* affect happiness, but they are mediated by a set of immune responses whose manifestation occurs many years later, when memory for the precipitating events or circumstances has faded.

Another way to explain my argument is that a life event (or an extended circumstance) may register multiple "memory traces." Judgments of well-being tap into people's "cognitive memory" of the event. According to this interpretation, the phenomenon that only recent events matter to SWB (Suh, Diener, and Fujita 1996) is due simply to memory decay. Any kind of delayed effect depends on the presence of an appropriate cue to retrieve a memory trace of the event from long-term memory. For instance, an accident victim who appears to have adapted to this event may relive the trauma many years later when driving by another accident scene.[8] As past events become more distant in time, their memory trace diminishes; this makes it seem as if they are no longer important to one's affective state. Such is adaptation. Evidence from the medical literature, however, suggests that a trace of the event may register in a sort of "bodily memory" in the form of vulnerability. The presence of illness associated with a previous stress (or improved health as a result of a positive event or circumstance) implies that the body has become sensitized due to the very same event to which the cognitive system seems to have adapted. Furthermore, sensitization may persist long after the event has passed (Glaser et al. 1998). Our body fails in what our mind appears to manage: forgetting.

People's failure to reflect their immune or other health-related cellular changes in judgments of SWB is actually unremarkable when considered on its own. Evidence on verbal reports of causal relationships between stimuli and particular responses indicates that people often have little ability to introspect directly on higher-order cognitive processes (Nisbett and Wilson 1977). It seems perfectly plausible that the same inability would extend to the domains of immunity and health. More direct evidence comes from a study by Baumann and Leventhal (1985), which demonstrates that people are unable to predict correctly their true blood pressure, despite their belief to the contrary. This inability to introspect—as well as the evidence from studies about sensitization—suggests a dual-level processing of events and circumstances. The conscious level is captured by SWB judgments, in which adaptation might signify that processing is complete. On the subconscious level, cellular or other unspecified changes occur. Some (and probably many) events or circumstances leave no permanent changes at the cellular level, just as they seem to leave none at the cognitive level. However in other cases, the change persists or precipitates other processes whose effects may take years to manifest. (Potential pathways are discussed by numerous authors; Friedman, Charney, and Deutch 1995; Linville 1987; Ryff and Singer 1998; Sapolsky 1999; Taylor 1989). The evidence I have reviewed in this chapter hints at a discrepancy in the "processing time" of an event at the biological level with respect to the processing time at the conscious, or cognitive judgment, level: biological processing times appear to be lengthier than cognitive processing times.

Connecting Objective and Subjective: Subconscious Mental Structures

Mental Structures and OWB.   That the processing times of the cognitive and biological systems might be discrepant does not necessarily imply that the process' "resolution" will yield discrepant outcomes. Long-term immune sensitization coupled with adaptation in judgment (that is, "divergence") is only one potential outcome. Cognitive and biological adaptation (that is, "convergence") is at least equally likely in many situations. Simply put, not every life event is life changing; not every breakup with a significant other leads to lifelong heartbreak. The context of life events is crucial to understanding their effect on SWB and health.

How do we distinguish those events whose resolution on the cognitive level differs from their resolution on the biological level? The work of Ronnie Janoff-Bulman and Irene Frieze (Janoff-Bulman 1989, 1992; Janoff-Bulman and Frieze 1983) provides an important initial clue. Along with others (Antonovsky 1979, 1987; Lazarus 1987; Lewin 1935; Parkes 1971, 1975), they have argued that people operate on the basis of important assumptions, or schemas, about the world that typically go unquestioned in the course of daily life. These schemas are the subconscious mental structures that define how incoming information is assimilated in our minds, and they represent "an internally consistent and systematic means for organizing and interpreting experiences" (Gluhoski and Wortman 1996, 417). One property of these assumptions is that they are relatively inaccessible by introspection (Parkes 1971). Another (unfortunate) property is that, while generally similar, researchers have yet to produce a single, standard set of assumptions and the scales to measure them. Antonovsky's (1987) *sense of coherence*, for instance, includes the constructs *comprehensibility, manageability,* and *meaningfulness.* The assumptive world model proposed by Janoff-Bulman (1989) incorporates schema on the benevolence of the world, the meaningfulness of the world, and the worthiness of self. Despite their differences, these researchers seem to be tapping similar underlying psychological constructs.

The dislocation engendered by some stressful life events challenges the assumptive world, and forces the individual to question its validity (Parkes 1971; Wortman and Silver 1987). According to Janoff-Bulman (1989), coping is a process characterized by an attempt to assimilate the new negative information from the life event into the old assumptions, often requiring their revision in order to create a new schema about one's world. In several studies she found that even many years following their victimization, there were persistent differences between the assumptive worlds of victims and controls. Similar results were obtained by Gluhoski and Wortman's (1996) community study on the impact of trauma on world views, including fatalism, justice, perceptions of vulnerability, and self-view. Trauma consisted of the death of a spouse, the death of a parent, the death of a child, job loss, life-threatening illness, or physical assault. The enduring change in the assumptive world indicates that life events can permanently alter more than our biology; they can also change the subconscious mental structures that serve as the lens through which we view our world.

Evidence from studies of OWB suggests a link between change in these mental structures and risk of morbidity. People with altered schemas are generally more vulnerable to mental disorders, even many years after exposure to a stressor (Horowitz 1986; Lazarus 1987, Lazarus and Delongis 1983). Patients diagnosed with PTSD or adjustment disorder, for instance, possess altered mental schematizations of the world (Horowitz 1986). These changed schemas might be viewed as signals of the sensitization that was set into motion by stressful life events or circumstances. The lasting effects of trauma on the assumptive world, and the fact that change in the assumptive world is linked to risk for morbidity, may provide a hint as to whether an event precipitated divergent processing outcomes on the cognitive and biological levels (that is, if it prompted a change in a person's schemas about the world).[9] The benefits of this schema formulation as a predictive tool for the study of well-being will be discussed in subsequent sections.

Mental Structures and SWB.   How does SWB pertain to this discussion? The duration of the process by which individuals assimilate new information into their assumptive world may explain the finding that only recent events matter to SWB (Suh, Diener, and Fujita 1996). Horowitz (1986) argues that, although the new event information is assimilated into existing mental models, it is stored in memory in a particularly active form of coding and tends to be revisited often. The effect of recent events on SWB judgments might be attributed to this assimilation process: the event is still actively *felt*. Over time, the event's meaning is incorporated into the person's schema and its codification in short-term memory decays (Horowitz 1986). Decay from active memory might be signaled by the restoration of SWB to its previous levels (that is, adaptation). However, the epidemiological evidence indicates that while SWB may recover, the body shows long-term vulnerability: years may pass until a person suffers from the medical symptoms traceable to a stressful life event or circumstance. Perhaps this explains why high SWB can coexist with low physical health (Watson and Pennebaker 1989).

Memory decay is but one explanation for the phenomenon that a changed assumptive world no longer appears to affect SWB. The nature of psychological judgment provides a complementary account. Cognitive judgments represent evaluations of change relative to a reference point, and not a representation of absolute stimulus levels (Kahneman and Tversky 1979, 1984). The reference point refers to the adaptation-level state defined by the past and present context of experience (Helson 1964; Kahneman and Tversky 1984), which is the lens through which we process stimuli. An assumptive world may be viewed as a reference point for judgments of well-being: it is a subconscious summary of our past and present. In fact, Parkes (1971) posits that schema transition is complete only when people are no longer aware of the new postulates that govern their world perceptions. Incorporated into our subconscious mental structures, past events or present circumstances exert little effect on self-reported measures of current well-being.

But past events might exert an effect on judgment via different pathways. Some people's assumptive worlds might be particularly resistant to events and circumstances, while others' might be less so. One possibility is that, once altered, certain assumptions might become more chronic than others for certain people. "Chronics" would be more affected by events that relate to the chronic assumption (but are not necessarily related to the event that precipitated the chronicity). The impact of such events on both SWB and OWB may be magnified for these types of people more so than for others. It is possible, for instance, that the unemployment experienced by Lucas et al.'s (2004) respondents precipitated the chronicity of an assumption, which might account for the lowered SWB set point even following reemployment.

Recall that one form of vulnerability stipulates a lower threshold for response to future stresses due to exposure to a prior stress. A measure of chronicity may provide a method to capture the lowered threshold because presumably a less extreme event will trigger a questioning (or requestioning) of the more chronic assumption. Researchers might then be able to classify people based on the chronicity of their assumptions. Prior "wear and tear" appears to have a cumulative effect on the body's ability to cope (McEwen and Seeman 1999; Ryff and Singer 1998); chronic assumptions might be one reflection of this process.

Finally, this discussion suggests an amendment to the meaning of reference points in SWB research. An underlying assumption in the SWB literature is that after an event affects judgment and equilibrium is restored, it is incorporated into the person's existing reference point or "endowment" (Tversky and Griffin 1991). I propose that the notion of a reference point as a summary of subconscious mental structures that are correlated with a set of objective health outcomes implies that people might sometimes actually adapt (cognitively) to a meaningfully *different* reference point. Stated differently, one could imagine a continuum of reference points. If an event precipitates change in the assumptive world, a person might shift to a qualitatively different reference point, associated with a different probability of disease than his previous one. This formulation allows for adaptation and sensitization to co-occur (the former in the subjective domain of well-being judgment and the latter in the objective domain of health). The challenge is to predict which events will not simply be incorporated into the previous reference point (that is, cognitive adaptation), but also precipitate a true reference-point shift (that is, physical sensitization). That is, when does an event-processing-time discrepancy lead to divergent processing resolution?

Schema-Change Models and Well-Being

Relying on the schema concept permits us to appeal to existing models of schema change in order to generate predictions about the effect of various events and circumstances on the assumptive world and the consequent impact on well-being. Note, however, that we need not restrict ourselves to schema-change models; any kind of category- or stereotype-change model applies. There are important implications of schema-change models to the study of well-being, and such models might indicate situations in which adaptation in judgment and sensitization in health occur concurrently.

Renee Weber and Jennifer Crocker (1983) summarize three models of stereotype or schema change: bookkeeping, conversion, and subtyping (for similar models of learning, see Rumelhart and Norman 1976). In the bookkeeping model, stereotype change occurs in an incremental process wherein each instance of disconfirming evidence elicits a minor change, and a substantial change occurs due to the accumulation of disconfirming instances. Typically this model applies to situations in which disconfirming information is dispersed in a larger pool of information (for example, encounters with African Americans in a primarily Caucasian society). In contrast, conversion is a dramatic change as a result of very salient events of relatively large magnitude (for example, riots or other major trauma). Finally, subtyping considers stereotypes as hierarchical structures that become finer and more complex with experience. Discrepant information is assimilated through the creation of subtypes of preexisting categories (for example, "Dave typically behaves well except when he is around John"). Subtyping generally occurs when there are instances of information that are inconsistent with a trend in a relatively small pool of information.

If an assumptive world functions like any other schema or category, it should change according to the schema-change models. All of the research on assumptive worlds is based on responses to very salient, traumatic events. The resulting change can be viewed through the lens of a conversion model: a major event leads to a dramatic alteration in schema. Such a change can be characterized by a divergent response along the dimensions of subjective and objective well-being. Judgments of well-being seem to respond to the event for a relatively short time, followed by a restoration of previous SWB levels. Sensitization, however, occurs along the dimension of physical and mental health, and it has long-term consequences.

In what other cases would one expect divergent patterns of SWB and OWB? While major trauma may be one instance, fortunately most of life's events are less extreme. Poverty, for example, is an adverse circumstance but not a traumatic event. Instead, it presents some relatively constant challenges and difficulties over time. The bookkeeping model seems the best-suited mechanism of schema change for such an example. The constant challenges may gradually change a person's assumptive world, or simply accumulate over time to effect a major change. Recall that psychologists find little or no correlation between objective circumstances and SWB, while epidemiologists find a clear relationship between SES and health. Furthermore, research on the allostatic load shows the cumulative effects of daily, "minor" stresses on morbidity (McEwen and Seeman 1999). It appears then that if objective circumstances are schema disconfirming over time, these schemas about the world change; however, the manifestation occurs primarily in health rather than in SWB (and only in the long term). Future research might trace the changes in assumptive worlds over time and correlate them with patterns of change in SWB and OWB in order to document divergence between the two. A longitudinal panel such as the German panel used by Lucas and colleagues (2004) could be useful for such an effort.

There are many situations, however, where events or circumstances fail to appreciably affect health in the long term, even though they might affect judgment for a short time. Final exams might depress a student's mood, but they are unlikely to have a long-term effect on either OWB or SWB. In such cases, there will not be a divergent response pattern; both SWB and OWB will rapidly return to their equilibrium state. Quite simply, most of the time people cope with whatever event life offers, positive or negative. Linville (1987) shows that people with finer multiple categories of self-aspect or greater self-complexity (e.g., wife, lawyer, tennis player, friend) cope with stress better than people with fewer categories or lower self-complexity (e.g., wife, lawyer). She finds that self-complexity moderates the incidence of stress-induced illness and depression. In related research, Hugh Morgan and Ronnie Janoff-Bulman (1994) report that subjects with higher positive self-complexity are better able to adjust to trauma than subjects with lower self-complexity. Indeed, people might develop a high degree of self-complexity by subtyping events in an effort to cope with them. Faced with some disconfirming information, a person with well-developed coping skills can treat the event as unrepresentative of life in general by subtyping it into a subcategory of an existing schema. For instance, if something uncontrollable occurs in a life that generally appears controllable, a person might qualify his assumption on controllability by thinking something like, "Generally I can control my destiny except in situations involving my mother." Linville's work indicates that such a person is less likely to become ill, which suggests that the person will not exhibit divergence between SWB and OWB.

Interestingly, most of the events that Gilbert et al. (1998) report exert little effect on actual happiness are the kinds of events that might be interpreted by people through a subtyping mechanism. Dissolution of romantic relationships, negative personality feedback, or one's favored candidate losing an election are exactly the kind of generally unrepresentative life events that most people would subtype. The authors argue that people's affective forecasts are inaccurate because they neglect their capacity to cope. One plausible hypothesis is that the "coping" that they refer to is, in fact, the ability to subtype. Although they do not mention it specifically, their description of the mechanisms that comprise people's "psychological immune system" is reminiscent of subtyping.

(More) New Avenues for Well-Being Research

Several other propositions for future research emerge from this discussion. Of pressing importance is a study that will test *a priori* which events or types of events lead to cases of divergence between SWB and OWB. The schema-shift models (or other similar category-change or learning models) merely provide an overarching structure for such a taxonomy. They suggest that events and circumstances that cause change in the assumptive world through bookkeeping and conversion will show long-term adaptation in judgment coupled with increased vulnerability to disease. In contrast, events that are subtyped into subschema will show no long-term effects on either SWB or OWB. But which events fit which model? Currently there is no systematic account of types of events and circumstances, and their effects on SWB, assumptions, and health. One motivation of this chapter is to suggest how these different domains might interact and to highlight the need to consider them concurrently rather than as separate approaches to a similar problem. Future research might simultaneously study disease onset in light of life events, altered assumptions, SWB, and immunological changes (Wortman and Silver 1987). The existence of a "mind-body problem" suggests that such research might reveal interesting links that illuminate the mental and physical pathways which affect our well-being.

A related proposition is both an avenue for future research as well as an important caveat to the arguments in this chapter. Certain events and circumstances have been defined as stressors without an elaboration on the specifics that define their context. Nonetheless, context is of paramount importance for comprehending the consequences of life events (Dohrenwend and Dohrenwend 1981; Rutter 1993; Dohrenwend 2000). Expected bereavement, for instance, is easier to overcome than sudden bereavement (Wortman and Silver 1987). Likewise, divorce from an abusive spouse is not akin to divorce due to financial strain or religious disagreement. Context is especially relevant to the present discussion because it provides an important clue as to whether or not an event's processing will yield divergent outcomes in SWB and OWB. With expected bereavement, for instance, a person may have an easier time assimilating the event to his or her assumptive world, perhaps avoiding an adverse health outcome. Bruce Dohrenwend (2000) proposes a set of life-event dimensions that contribute to the degree of an event's impact. These include valence (positive or negative), fatefulness (that is, the degree of control over an event's occurrence), predictability, magnitude, centrality to goal fulfillment, and physical impact. Future research on happiness may test the effect of these dimensions on judgments of SWB. Most SWB research to date has not classified events according to such overarching attributes. Such a typology has proven useful in psychiatric epidemiology; it might be equally illuminating in SWB research.

Note, however, that Dohrenwend's (1998b) dimensions are different than those characteristics that determine whether an event will elicit assumptive world change through bookkeeping, conversion, or subtyping. His dimensions assess the *degree* to which an event or circumstance is disconfirming of an existing assumption, and thus they assess the likelihood of its assimilation to existing schemas. The applicability of one or another schema-shift model, on the other hand, is determined by the *structure* of the information (for example, whether it is dispersed in a large or small sample, or its salience). Both degree and structure might become useful factors for characterizing events. A potential research pitfall is that these two variables may be fully confounded at times. For instance, salience is not only a matter of degree, but it is also a component of structure.

Some Caveats

A number of caveats to this discussion are in order. The first concerns my focus on negative life events and circumstances. Hedonic psychologists are oriented toward the study of pleasure and happiness, and pain and suffering only afford a share of the spotlight (Kahneman, Diener, and Schwarz 1999). My arguments should be applicable nonetheless. Pleasurable events—that is, vacations, weddings, or raises—may spur a "positive" schema change. For instance, one might think, "The world is more controllable than I thought." Perception of control in fact has been both linked to stress buffering (Taylor 1989) and offered as a possible contributor to resilience (Rutter 1993). Similarly, social supports can buffer against demoralization (Fenig and Levav 1991). Research in the growing field of positive psychology has revealed a strong association between positive emotional states and healthier cardiovascular and immune systems (Salovey et al. 2000). Nurturing can sometimes even reverse the deleterious cumulative effect of allostatic load and promote better health (Singer and Ryff 1999). A compelling example of the salutary effect of positive events is reported in a study showing that Academy Award winners outlive nonwinners by 3.9 years (Redelmeier and Singh 2001). Just as with stress, the benefits of happy events to immune functioning manifest in the long term, apparently beyond the point where hedonic adaptation takes place.

Second, the assumptive world might be just one of several factors that influence a reference-point shift. Robert Emmons (1986) reports that positive affect, negative affect, and life satisfaction are strongly associated with people's ability to strive to achieve their goals. Likewise, Dohrenwend (1998b) uses "centrality" to describe the degree of an event's threat to the fulfillment of goals considered important by an individual. Goals and world assumptions could in fact be related: an event that prevents the achievement of a goal may induce an assumption to change. This possibility underscores the need for a more precise specification of the composition of the assumptive world, as well as the need to understand mediators that determine the short- and long-term impact of a life event or circumstance.

Goals may be especially important because they function as the link between the research on responses to serious or extreme situations and daily hassles (for example, a long daily commute or airport noise).

Dohrenwend (1998b; 2000) suggests that many examples of daily stress share the centrality of stress caused by extreme situations. Even mundane circumstances such as particularly long commutes, for instance, can obstruct one's path to goal fulfillment. The highly subjective element of this path—unlike extreme situations which threaten basic human needs—makes it particularly challenging to investigate.

Third, whereas I have considered individual differences in SWB, I have omitted their role in OWB research. The heated debate on the "causation-selection issue" indicates that their importance cannot be understated (Dohrenwend et al. 1992; Dohrenwend 2000). Nonetheless, abundant evidence indicates that genetic factors alone cannot account for the etiology of many diseases (Dohrenwend 2000). Support for the importance of personality factors in disease onset therefore does not undermine the validity of the arguments on how epidemiological findings might affect SWB.

Prediction Errors and Public Policy

The notion of discrepant event processing times qualifies the sources of bias in SWB prediction into two categories: The first type of prediction error is a consequence of the inability of people to anticipate the biological changes that will affect future SWB (by way of OWB); these are instances when processing resolution results in divergent outcomes in judgment and health. Identifying such an error requires a complicated longitudinal study in which SWB assessments are followed up by a more in-depth medical examination some time following the event in question. The second type of error is a result of judgment biases, such as over- or underweighting the effect of an item in question on a criterion variable. These errors are difficult to correct, and their extent is often difficult to detect. Usually in these cases, respondents neglect their impending adaptation to the event in question and fail to realize that this process will preserve their sensitivity to stimulus differences (Frederick and Loewenstein 1999).

Sources of misprediction are particularly important when applying SWB research findings to public policy, because the assertion that a certain element does not contribute to happiness may be a result of one type of misprediction or the other. If, for instance, a policy maker has reason to believe that the misprediction is a result of the failure of SWB measures to capture biological changes, then he or she might be justified in acting paternalistically and discount the results of an SWB survey. Of course, this requires a comprehensive understanding of what types of events or circumstances are associated with which type of misprediction.

Paternalism might be defensible in cases of environmental pathogens, for example. The apparent paradox of poor health (and other objective circumstances) and high SWB has prompted SWB researchers to the counterintuitive conclusion that unhealthy people can also be happy. While the data support their assertion, and it is indeed possible that unhealthy individuals experience happy lives, the implications of their conclusions for public policy should give us pause. A policy that neglects health outcomes because they do not affect SWB in the relative long term should be rejected. From a practical standpoint, the long-term effects on OWB complicate matters; the timetables of policy makers may lead them to optimize SWB because changes in happiness are immediate, whereas changes in health often are not.

Despite its counterintuitive results, SWB research deals with a question that is intuitively important. This discussion is intended to provide a conceptual link between SWB and OWB, not to question the validity of SWB research or its usefulness for public policy. Typically the first question that physicians ask their patients is how they are doing (that is, what is their subjective well-being). However, a physician also follows this question with a comprehensive medical examination, including objective indicators such as blood pressure and heart rate. Often it is lifelong behaviors, such as diet, that influence pathology. A patient's simple answer to the question may or may not reflect this.

Accordingly, an attempt to ascertain the effect of an event or circumstance through measures of affective judgment (that is, through SWB) fails to capture sufficiently its consequences. This becomes especially important when extracting public-policy recommendations from responses to SWB questionnaires. Failure to realize the multiple effects of an event and their timing can lead to policies that are detrimental to the goal of increasing a population's well-being. Various philosophers and scientists have advocated different definitions of this goal (Ryff and Singer 1998; Ryff 1989; Diener, Sapyta, and Suh 1998); these debates are beyond the scope of this paper. Irrespective, any policy must pass Shane Frederick and George Loewenstein's (1999) commonsense test: "Assuming that future research provides a deeper understanding of hedonic adaptation, is it likely that such information would cause people to conduct their lives differently? Would they stop wearing seatbelts with the assurance that they would get used to being paralyzed?" (320). Certainly not. The commonsense test implicitly appeals to a broad perspective which takes both SWB and OWB into account. The schema formulation I have discussed suggests one approach to integrate both forms of well-being. Admittedly, this suggestion needs empirical validation in future research.

Yossarian Revisited

Perhaps Scheisskopf's wife was right. Pain—both physical and emotional—is indeed a warning of bodily dangers. A temporary change in subjective well-being in response to a stressful life event or circumstance *can* portend danger for mental and physical health in the sometimes distant future. Epidemiological findings demonstrate the link between stress and disease, and between emotional dislocation and physical suffering.

But Yossarian's protestation also rings true. Our task as researchers and the task of policy makers would indeed be simpler if people signaled pain through neon tubes lodged in the center of their foreheads. One of the limitations of a unidimensional focus—either SWB *or* OWB—is that it treats single measures as faithful proxies of Yossarian's imaginary neon lights. The co-occurrence of adaptation in judgments of SWB and sensitization of the immune system underscores the need to study human well-being as a multidimensional phenomenon. Studying well-being solely by means of judgment elicitation provides a partial (but useful) picture because many events that yield a temporary peak or valley in present-moment SWB lead to a more substantial effect in future OWB. There are, indeed, many wires leading to the light on our forehead, all of which must be considered and, together, provide a signal that is a viable measure for public policy. Future research will help untangle the paths of and connections between these different wires. It is a mystery worth unraveling.

Notes

1. SWB researchers take these data to mean that most people are happy (Diener and Diener 1996). This assertion is a bit problematic because it assumes that the SWB judgments are made on a ratio scale. The interpretation of these data should be viewed in light of this caveat.
2. Note, however, that men who have been unemployed more often in the past do seem to adapt to their current unemployment status much more than men who have not been previously unemployed (Clark, Georgellis, and Sanfey 2001).
3. A "set point" is the level of a given physical variable under normal conditions. For instance, a weight set point is the approximate weight a person tends to carry in most situations, except for extreme famine or overeating.
4. The studies presented here are for illustrative purposes only; studies on dose-response and vulnerability are too numerous to cover here.
5. Demoralization can be understood as one's mental body temperature. Elevated scores indicate that something is wrong, but their cause is uncertain (Dohrenwend, Levav, and Shrout 1986).

6. Allostasis is the "ability to adapt to change while maintaining physiological systems within normal operating ranges," and allostatic load is the "the wear and tear that results form chronic overactivity or underactivity of allostatic systems" (Singer and Ryff 1999, 97–98).

7. In support of this assertion, it is worth mentioning that Diener, Sandvik, and Pavot (1991) find that happiness is the frequency, not the intensity, of positive affect. Imagine a person who is undergoing chemotherapy; in general, he or she is more likely to indicate a greater frequency of negative affect than a similar person not in treatment. Therefore, one could say that the sick person is less happy.

    A second point worth mentioning in this context is that my argument in this section implies a rather obvious methodological criticism of some of the SWB research, which claims to show that objective circumstances do not matter to happiness. In particular, I suggest that some of the data obtained are a result of a simple selection bias. For instance, asking a bereaved parent with cancer about his life satisfaction in a survey setting—but not when he is undergoing cancer treatment or when he drives by the cemetery where his son is entombed—will grossly underestimate the frequency of his negative affect and consequently will make it seem as if he has adapted to his bereavement. Yet, according to Edward Diener, Ed Sandvik, and William Pavot's (1991) definition, the bereaved parent should be considered less happy. Note that the recently developed DRM technique overcomes some of these limitations, as participants are asked to recall their day as a series of snapshots. The EMA method is still problematic because participants can ignore the beeper's prompt to complete the mood scales. The same is true of the DRM method, except that participants are asked to complete the survey at the end of the day, when they are presumably available to do so.

8. A real-life example of such reliving comes from an interview with a friend of a victim of the Korean Airlines disaster in 1983: "Every time I get on a plane, especially on long flights over water, I return to his death, to the horror of what he must have experienced" (White 1999, 15).

9. Admittedly, this notion is a bit tautological because a divergent outcome is signaled by a schema shift, but a schema shift indicates a divergent outcome. This issue is resolved in the discussion of how the schema-shift idea can be used to make predictions.

References

Antonovsky, Aaron. 1979. *Health, Stress, and Coping*. San Francisco, Calif.: Jossey-Bass.

———. 1987. "Health Promoting Factors at Work: The Sense of Coherence." In *Psychosocial Factors at Work and Their Relation to Health*, edited by Raija Kalimo, Mostafa A. El-Batawi, and Cary L. Cooper. Geneva: World Health Organization.

Armstrong, Bruce K., Emily White, and Rodolfo Saracci. 1992. *Principles of Exposure Measurement in Epidemiology*. Oxford: Oxford University Press.

Baumann, Linda J., and Howard Leventhal. 1985. "I Can Tell When My Blood Pressure Is Up, Can't I?" *Health Psychology* 4(3): 203–18.

Benschop, Robert J., Geenen Rinie, Paul J. Mills, Bruce D. Naliboff, Janice K. Kiecolt-Glaser, Tracy B. Herbert, Gieta van der Pompe, Gregory E. Miller, Karen A. Matthews, Guido L. Godaert, Stephanie L. Gilmore, Ronald Glaser, Cobi J. Heijnen, Joel M. Dopp, Johannes W. Bijlsma, George F. Solomon, and John T. Cacioppo. 1998. "Cardiovascular and Immune Responses to Acute Psychological Stress in Young and Old Women: A Meta-Analysis." *Psychosomatic Medicine* 60(3): 290–6.

Bobak, Martin, Hynek Pikhart, Richard Rose, Clyde Hertzman, and Michael Marmot. 2000. "Socioeconomic Factors, Material Inequalities, and Perceived Control in Self-Rated Health: Cross-Sectional Data from Seven Post-Communist Countries." *Social Science and Medicine* 51(8): 1343–50.

Breeze, Elizabeth, Astrid E. Fletcher, David A. Leon, Michael G. Marmot, Robert J. Clark, and Martin J. Shipley. 2001. "Do Socioeconomic Disadvantages Persist into Old Age?: Self-Reported Morbidity in a 29-Year Follow-Up of the Whitehall Study." *American Journal of Public Health* 91(2): 277–83.

Breslau, Naomi, Howard D. Chilcoat, Ronald C. Kessler, and Glenn C. Davis. 1999. "Previous Exposure to Trauma and PTSD Effects of Subsequent Trauma: Results Form the Detroit Area Survey of Trauma." *American Journal of Psychiatry* 156(6): 902–7.

Brickman, Philip and Donald T. Campbell. 1971. "Hedonic Relativism and Planning the Good Society." In *Adaptation level theory: A Symposium,* edited by M. H. Appley. New York: Academic Press.

Brickman, Philip, Dan Coates, and Ronnie Janoff-Bulman. 1978. "Lottery Winners and Accident Victims: Is Happiness Relative?" *Journal of Personality and Social Psychology* 36(8): 917–27.

Brunner, Eric, Martin J. Shipley, David Blane, George D. Smith, and Michael G. Marmot. 1999. "When Does Cardiovascular Risk Start?: Past and Present Socioeconomic Circumstances and Risk Factors in Adulthood." *Journal of Epidemiology and Community Health* 53(12): 757–64.

Cacioppo, John T. 1998. "Somatic Responses to Psychological Stress: The Reactivity Hypothesis." In *Advances in Psychological Science, Vol. 2: Biological and Cognitive Aspects,* edited by Michel Sabourin, Fergus Craik, and Michel Robert. East Sussex, England: Psychology Press.

Clark, Andrew, Ed Diener, and Yannis Georgellis. 2001. "Lags and Leads in Life Satisfaction: A Test of the Baseline Hypothesis." Mimeo. University of Illinois.

Clark, Andrew, Yannis Georgellis, and Peter Sanfey. 2001. "Scarring: The Psychological Impact of Past Unemployment." *Economica* 68(2): 221–41.

Cohen, Sheldon, and Bruce S. Rabin. 1998. "Psychologic Stress, Immunity, and Cancer." *Journal of the National Cancer Institute* 90(1): 3–4.

Costa, Paul T., Jr., and Robert R. McCrae. 1980. "Influence of Extraversion and Neuroticism on Subjective Well-Being: Happy and Unhappy People." *Journal of Personality and Social Psychology* 38(4): 668–78.

Csikszentmihalyi, Mihaly. 1999. "If We Are So Rich, Why Aren't We Happy?" *American Psychologist* 54(10): 821–7.

Diener, Edward. 1984. "Subjective Well-Being." *Psychological Bulletin* 95(3): 542–75.

———. 2000. "Subjective Well-Being: The Science of Happiness, and a Proposal for a National Index." *American Psychologist* 55(1): 34–43.

Diener, Edward, and Robert Biswas-Diener. 2002. "Will Money Increase Subjective Well-Being?: A Literature Review and Guide to Needed Research." *Social Indicators Research* 57(2): 119–69.

Diener, Edward, and Carol Diener. 1996. "Most People are Happy." *Psychological Science* 7(3): 181–5.

Diener, Edward, and Randy J. Larsen. 1984. "Temporal Stability and Cross-Situational Consistency of Affective, Behavioral, and Cognitive Responses." *Journal of Personality and Social Psychology* 47(4): 871–83.

Diener, Edward, and Richard E. Lucas. 1999. "Personality and Subjective Well-Being." In *Well-Being: The Foundations of Hedonic Psychology,* edited by Daniel Kahneman, Ed Diener, and Norbert Schwarz. New York: Russell Sage.

Diener, Edward, and Shigehiro Oishi. 2000. "Money and Happiness: Income and Subjective Well-Being Across Nations." In *Subjective Well-Being Across Cultures,* edited by Ed Diener and Eunkook M. Suh. Cambridge, Mass.: MIT Press.

Diener, Edward, and Eunkook M. Suh. 1997. "Measuring Quality of Life: Economic, Social, and Subjective Indicators." *Social Indicators Research* 40(1–2): 189–216.

———. 1999. "National Differences in Subjective Well-Being." In *Well-being: The Foundations of Hedonic Psychology,* edited by Daniel Kahneman, Ed Diener, and Norbert Schwarz. New York: Russell Sage.

Diener, Edward, Marissa Diener, and Carol Diener. 1995. "Factors Predicting the Subjective Well-Being of Nations." *Journal of Personality and Social Psychology* 69(5): 851–64.

Diener, Edward, Ed Sandvik, and William Pavot. 1991. "Happiness Is the Frequency, Not the Intensity, of Positive Versus Negative Affect." In *Subjective Well-Being: An Interdisciplinary Perspective,* edited by Fritz Strack, Michael Argyle, and Norbert Schwarz. Oxford: Pergamon Press.

Diener, Edward, Jeffrey J. Sapyta, and Eunkook Suh. 1998. "Subjective Well-Being Is Essential to Well-Being." *Psychological Inquiry* 9(1): 33–37.

Diener, Edward, Brian Wolsic, and Frank Fujita. 1995. "Physical Attractiveness and Subjective Well-Being." *Journal of Personality and Social Psychology* 69(1): 120–9.

Diener, Edward, Ed Sandvik, Larry Seidlitz, and Marissa Diener. 1993. "The Relationship Between Income and Subjective Well-Being: Relative or Absolute?" *Social Indicators Research* 28(3): 195–223.

Diener, Edward, Eunkook M. Suh, Richard E. Lucas, and Heidi L. Smith. 1999. "Subjective Well-Being: Three Decades of Progress." *Psychological Bulletin* 125(2): 276–302.

Dohrenwend, Barbara S., and Bruce P. Dohrenwend. 1981. *Stressful Life Events and their Contexts.* New York: Prodist.

Dohrenwend, Bruce P. 1998a. "Overview of Evidence for the Importance of Adverse Environmental Conditions in Causing Psychiatric Disorders." In

Adversity, Stress and Psychopathology, edited by Bruce P. Dohrenwend. New York: Oxford University Press.

———. 1998b. "Theoretical Integration." In *Adversity, Stress and Psychopathology,* edited by Bruce P. Dohrenwend. New York: Oxford University Press.

———. 2000. "The Role of Adversity and Stress in Psychopathology: Some Evidence and its Implications for Theory and Research." *Journal of Health and Social Behavior* 41(1): 1–19.

Dohrenwend, Bruce P., Itzhak L. Levav, and Patrick E. Shrout. 1986. "Screening Scales from the Psychiatric Epidemiology Research Interview." In *Community Surveys of Psychiatric Disorders,* edited by Myrna M. Weissman, Jerome K. Myers, and Catherine E. Ross. New Brunswick, N.J.: Rutgers University Press.

Dohrenwend, Bruce P., Patrick E. Shrout, Gladys Egri, and Frederick Mendelsohn. 1980. "Nonspecific Psychological Distress and Other Dimensions of Psychopathology." *Archives of General Psychiatry* 37(November): 1229–36.

Dohrenwend, Bruce P., Itzhak L. Levav, Patrick E. Shrout, Sharon Schwartz, Guedalia Naveh, Bruce G. Link, Andrew E. Skodol, and Ann Stueve. 1992. "Socioeconomic Status and Psychiatric Disorders: The Causation-Selection Issue." *Science* 255(5047): 946–52.

Easterlin, Richard A. 1974. "Does Economic Growth Improve the Human Lot?: Some Empirical Evidence." In *Nations and Households in Economic Growth,* edited by Paul A. David and Melvin W. Reder. New York: Academic Press.

———. 1995. "Will Raising the Incomes of All Increase the Happiness of All?" *Journal of Economic Behavior and Organization* 27(1): 35–47.

Emmons, Robert A. 1986. "Personal Strivings: An Approach to Personality and Subjective Well-Being." *Journal of Personality and Social Psychology* 51(5): 1058–68.

Faragher, E. Brian, and Cary L. Cooper. 1997. "Letter to the Editor." *Psychological Medicine* 27(2): 497–8.

Fenig, Shmuel, and Itzhak L. Levav. 1991. "Demoralization and Social Supports Among Holocaust Survivors." *Journal of Nervous and Mental Disease* 179(3): 167–72.

Flanagan, Timothy J. 1980. "The Pains of Long-Term Imprisonment." *British Journal of Criminology* 20(2): 148–56.

Fox, Bernard H. 1995. "The Role of Psychological Factors in Cancer Incidence and Prognosis." *Oncology* 9(3): 245–56.

Frederick, Shane, and George F. Loewenstein. 1999. "Hedonic Adaptation." In *Well-being: The Foundations of Hedonic Psychology,* edited by Daniel Kahneman, Ed Diener, and Norbert Schwarz. New York: Russell Sage.

Friedman, Matthew J., Dennis S. Charney, and Ariel Y. Deutch, editors. 1995. *Neurobiological and Clinical Consequences of Stress.* Philadelphia, Penn.: Lippincott-Raven.

Gilbert, Daniel T., Elizabeth C. Pinel, Timothy D. Wilson, Stephen J. Blumberg, and Thalia P. Wheatley. 1998. "Immune Neglect: A Source of Durability Bias in Affective Forecasting." *Journal of Personality and Social Psychology* 75(3): 617–38.

Glaser, Ronald, Janice K. Kiecolt-Glaser, William B. Malarkey, and John F. Sheridan. 1998. "The Influence of Psychological Stress on the Immune Response to Vaccines." *Annals of the New York Academy of Sciences* 840(1): 649–55.

Gluhoski, Vicki H., and Camille B. Wortman. 1996. "The Impact of Trauma on World Views." *Journal of Social and Clinical Psychology* 15(4): 417–29.

Goldberg, Jack, William R. True, Seth A. Eisen, and William G. Henderson. 1990. "A Twin Study of the Effects of the Vietnam War on Posttraumatic Stress Disorder." *Journal of the American Medical Association* 263(9): 1227–32.

Headey, Bruce, and Alexander Wearing. 1989. "Personality, Life Events, and Subjective Well-Being: Toward a Dynamic Equilibrium Model." *Journal of Personality and Social Psychology* 57(4): 731–9.

Heller, Joseph. 1955/1961. *Catch-22.* New York: Dell.

Helson, Harry. 1964. *Adaptation-Level Theory: An Experimental and Systematic Approach to Behavior.* New York: Harper and Row.

Hemingway, Harry, Martin Shipley, Peter Macfarlane, and Michael Marmot. 2000. "Impact of Socioeconomic Status on Coronary Mortality in People with Symptoms, Electrocardiographic Abnormalities, Both or Neither: The Original Whitehall Study 25 Year Follow Up." *Journal of Epidemiology and Community Health* 54(7): 510–6.

Horowitz, Mardi J. 1986. "Stress-Response Syndromes: A Review of Posttraumatic and Adjustment Disorders." *Hospital and Community Psychiatry* 37(3): 241–9.

Janoff-Bulman, Ronnie. 1989. "Assumptive World and the Stress of Traumatic Events: Applications of the Schema Construct." *Social Cognition* 7(2): 113–36.

———. 1992. *Shattered Assumptions: Towards a New Psychology of Trauma.* New York: Free Press.

Janoff-Bulman, Ronnie, and Irene H. Frieze. 1983. "A Theoretical Perspective for Understanding Reactions to Victimization." *Journal of Social Issues.* 39(2): 1–17.

Kahneman, Daniel. 1994. "New Challenges to the Rationality Assumption." *Journal of Institutional and Theoretical Economics* 150(1): 18–36.

———. 1999. "Objective Happiness." In *Well-Being: The Foundations of Hedonic Psychology,* edited by Daniel Kahneman, Ed Diener, and Norbert Schwarz. New York: Russell Sage.

Kahneman, Daniel, and Amos Tversky. 1979. "Prospect Theory: An Analysis of Choice Under Risk." *Econometrica* 47(2): 263–91.

———. 1984. "Choices, Values, and Frames." *American Psychologist* 39(4): 341–50.

Kahneman, Daniel, Edward Diener, and Norbert Schwarz, editors. 1999. *Well-Being: The Foundations of Hedonic Psychology.* New York: Russell Sage.

Kahneman, Daniel, Alan B. Krueger, David A. Schkade, Norbert Schwarz, and Arthur A. Stone. 2004. "A Survey Method for Characterizing Daily Life Experience: The Day Reconstruction Method (DRM)." *Science* 306(5702): 1776–80.

Kasl, Stanislav V., Eunice Rodriguez, and Kathryn E. Lasch. 1998. "The Impact of Unemployment on Health and Well-Being." In *Adversity, Stress and Psychopathology,* edited by Bruce P. Dohrenwend. New York: Oxford University Press.

Keane, Terence M. 1998. "Psychological Effects of Military Combat." In *Adversity, Stress and Psychopathology,* edited by Bruce P. Dohrenwend. New York: Oxford University Press.

Kiecolt-Glaser, Janice K., Ronald Glaser, John T. Cacioppo, and William B. Malarkey. 1998. "Marital Stress: Immunologic, Neuroendocrine, and Autonomic Correlates." *Annals of the New York Academy of Sciences* 840(1): 656–63.

Kiecolt-Glaser, Janice K., Ronald Glaser, John T. Cacioppo, Robert C. MacCallum, Mary Snydersmith, Cheongtag Kim, and William B. Malarkey. 1997. "Marital Conflict in Older Adults: Endocrinological and Immunological Correlates." *Psychosomatic Medicine* 59(4): 339–49.

Kohn, Robert, Bruce P. Dohrenwend, and Jerrold Mirotznik. 1998. "Epidemiologic Findings on Selected Psychiatric Disorders in the General Population. "In *Adversity, Stress and Psychopathology,* edited by Bruce P. Dohrenwend. New York: Oxford University Press.

Lazarus, Richard S. 1987. "Individual Susceptibility and Resistance to Psychological Stress." In *Psychosocial Factors at Work and Their Relation to Health,* edited by Raija Kalimo, Mostafa A. El-Batawi, and Cary L. Cooper. Geneva: World Health Organization.

Lazarus, Richard S, and Anita DeLongis. 1983. "Psychological Stress and Coping in Aging." *American Psychologist* 38(3): 245–54.

Lee-Feldstein, Anna. 1989. "A Comparison of Several Measures of Exposure to Arsenic." *American Journal of Epidemiology* 129(1): 112–24.

Levav, Itzhak. 1998. "Individuals Under Conditions of Maximum Adversity: The Holocaust." In *Adversity, Stress and Psychopathology,* edited by Bruce P. Dohrenwend. New York: Oxford University Press.

Levav, Itzhak, Robert Kohn, Jose Iscovich, Joseph H. Abramson, Wei Yann Tsai, and Daniel Vigdorovich. 2000. "Cancer Incidence and Survival Following Bereavement." *American Journal of Public Health* 90(10): 1601–7.

Lewin, Kurt. 1935. *A Dynamic Theory of Personality.* New York: McGraw-Hill.

Linville, Patricia W. 1987. "Self-Complexity as a Cognitive Buffer Against Stress-Related Illness and Depression." *Journal of Personality and Social Psychology* 52(4): 663–76.

Lucas, Richard E., Andrew. E. Clark, Yannis Georgellis, and Ed Diener. 2003. "Reexamining Adaptation and the Set Point Model of Happiness: Reactions to Changes in Marital Status." *Journal of Personality and Social Psychology* 84(3): 527–39.

———. 2004. "Unemployment Alters the Set Point for Life Satisfaction." *Psychological Science* 15(1): 8–13.

Lykken, David, and Auke Tellegen. 1996. "Happiness is a Stochastic Phenomenon." *Psychological Science* 7(3): 186–9.

Magnus, Keith, Edward Diener, Frank Fujita, and William Pavot. 1993. "Extraversion and Neuroticism as Predictor of Objective Life Events: A Longitudinal Analysis." *Journal of Personality and Social Psychology* 65(5): 1046–53.

Marmot, Michael G. 1999. "Epidemiology of Socioeconomic Status and Health: Are Determinants Within Countries the Same as Between Countries?" *Annals of the New York Academy of Sciences* 896(1): 16–29.

Marmot, Michael G., Martin J. Shipley, and Geoffrey Rose. 1984. "Inequalities in Death: Specific Explanations of a General Pattern?" *The Lancet* 1(8384): 1003–6.

Marucha, Phillip T., Janice K. Kiecolt-Glaser, and Mehrdad Favagehi. 1998. "Mucosal Wound Healing Is Impaired by Examination Stress." *Psychosomatic Medicine* 60(3): 362–5.

McEwen, Bruce S., and Teresa Seeman. 1999. "Protective and Damaging Effects of Mediators of Stress: Elaborating and Testing the Concepts of Allostasis and Allostatic Load." *Annals of the New York Academy of Sciences* 896(1): 30–47.

McGee, Rob, Sheila Williams, and Mark Elwood. 1996. "Are Life Events Related to Breast Cancer?" *Psychological Medicine* 26(4): 441–7.

Morgan, Hugh J., and Ronnie Janoff-Bulman. 1994. "Positive Versus Negative Self-Complexity: Patterns of Adjustment Following Traumatic Versus Non-Traumatic Life Experiences." *Journal of Social and Clinical Psychology* 13(1): 63–85.

Nisbett, Richard E., and Timothy D. Wilson. 1977. "Telling More than We Can Know: Verbal Reports on Mental Processes." *Psychological Review* 84(3): 231–59.

Okun, Morris A., and Linda K. George. 1984. "Physician- and Self-Ratings of Health, Neuroticism and Subjective Well-Being Among Men and Women." *Personality and Individual Differences* 5(5): 533–9.

Parkes, C. Murray. 1971. "Psycho-social Transitions: A Field for Study." *Social Science and Medicine* 5(2): 101–15.

———. 1975. "What Becomes of Redundant World Models? A Contribution to the Study of Adaptation to Change." *British Journal of Medical Psychology* 48(2): 131–7.

Pavot, William., and Edward Diener. 1993. "Review of the Satisfaction with Life Scale." *Personality Assessment* 5: 164–72.

Power, C., and S. Matthews. (1997). "Origins of Health Inequalities in a National Population Sample." *The Lancet* 350(9091): 1584–9.

Redelmeier, Donald A., and Sheldon M. Singh. 2001. "Survival in Academy Award-Winning Actors and Actresses." *Annals of Internal Medicine* 134(10): 955–62.

Riis, Jason, George F. Loewenstein, Jonathan Baron, Christopher Jepson, Angela Fagerlin, and Peter A. Ubel. 2005. "Ignorance of Hedonic Adaptation to Hemodialysis: A Study Using Ecological Momentary Assessment." *Journal of Experimental Psychology: General* 134(1): 3–9.

Rumelhart, David E., and Donald A. Norman. 1976. "Accretion, Tuning and Restructuring: Three Modes of Learning." *Technical Report No. 63.* Center for Human Information Processing, University of California, San Diego.

Rutter, Michael. 1993. "Resilience: Some Conceptual Considerations." *Journal of Adolescent Health* 14(8): 626–31.

Ryff, Carol D. 1989. "Happiness Is Everything, Or Is It?: Explorations on the Meaning of Psychological Well-Being." *Journal of Personality and Social Psychology* 57(6): 1069–81.

Ryff, Carol D., and Burton Singer. 1998. "The Contours of Positive Human Health." *Psychological Inquiry* 9(1): 1–28.

Salovey, Peter, Alexander J. Rothman, Jerusha B. Detweiler, and Wayne T. Steward. 2000. "Emotional States and Physical Health." *American Psychologist* 55(1): 110–21.

Sapolsky, Robert M. 1999. "The Physiology and Pathophysiology of Unhappiness." In *Well-Being: The Foundations of Hedonic Psychology,* edited by Daniel Kahneman, Ed Diener, and Norbert Schwarz. New York: Russell Sage.

Schkade, David, and Daniel Kahneman. 1998. "Does Living in California Make People Happy? A Focusing Illusion in Judgments of Life Satisfaction." *Psychological Science* 9(5): 340–6.

Schwarz, Norbert, and Fritz Strack. 1999. "Reports of Subjective Well-Being: Judgmental Processes and their Methodological Implications." In *Well-Being: The Foundations of Hedonic Psychology*, edited by Daniel Kahneman, Ed Diener, and Norbert Schwarz. New York: Russell Sage.

Simon, Herbert A. 1955. "A Behavioral Model of Rational Choice." *Quarterly Journal of Economics* 69(1): 99–118.

Singer, Burton, and Carol D. Ryff. 1999. "Hierarchies of Life Histories and Associated Health Risks." *Annals of the New York Academy of Sciences* 896(1): 96–115.

Solomon, Zahava, and Edward Prager. 1992. "Elderly Israeli Holocaust Survivors During the Persian Gulf War: A Study of Psychological Distress." *American Journal of Psychiatry* 149(12): 1707–10.

Strack, Fritz, Michael Argyle, and Norbert Schwarz. 1991. *Subjective Well-Being: An Interdisciplinary Perspective.* Oxford: Pergamon Press.

Suedfeld, Peter, Carmenza Ramirez, John Deaton, and Gloria Baker-Brown. 1982. "Reactions and Attributes of Prisoners in Solitary Confinement." *Criminal Justice and Behavior* 9(3): 303–40.

Suh, Eunkook, Edward Diener, and Frank Fujita. 1996. "Events and Subjective Well-Being: Only Recent Events Matter." *Journal of Personality and Social Psychology* 70(5): 1091–1102.

Taylor, Shelley. 1989. *Positive Illusions.* New York: Basic Books.

Tversky, Amos, and Dale Griffin. 1991. "Endowment and Contrast in Judgments of Well-Being." In *Subjective Well-Being: An Interdisciplinary Perspective*, edited by Fritz Strack, Michael Argyle, and Norbert Schwarz. Oxford: Pergamon Press.

Veenhoven, Ruut. 1991. "Is Happiness Relative?" *Social Indicators Research* 24(1): 1–34.

Watson, David, and James W. Pennebaker. 1989. "Health Complaints, Stress, and Distress: Exploring the Central Role of Negative Affectivity." *Psychological Review* 96(2): 234–54.

Weber, Renee, and Jennifer Crocker. 1983. "Cognitive Processes in the Revision of Stereotypic Beliefs." *Journal of Personality and Social Psychology* 45(5): 961–77.

Weich, Scott, and Glyn Lewis. 1998. "Material Standard of Living, Social Class, and the Prevalence of the Common Mental Disorders in Great Britain." *Journal of Epidemiology and Community Health* 52(1): 8–14.

Weinstein, Neil D. 1982. "Community Noise Problems: Evidence Against Adaptation." *Journal of Environmental Psychology* 2(2): 87–97.

Weiss, Noel S. 1981. "Inferring Causal Relationships: Elaboration of the Criterion of 'Dose-Response.' " *American Journal of Epidemiology* 113(5): 487–90.

White, Daniel. 1999. "A Grief Observed." *Princeton Alumni Weekly*, December 15, 1999: 10–15.

Wortman, Camille B., and Roxane C. Silver. 1987. "Coping with Irrevocable Loss." In *Cataclysms, Crises, and Catastrophes: Psychology in Action. The Master Lectures, Vol. 6.*, edited by G. R., VandenBos and B. K. Bryant. Washington: American Psychological Association.

Zaidi, Lisa Y., and David W. Foy. 1994. "Childhood Abuse Experiences and Combat-Related PTSD." *Journal of Traumatic Stress* 7(1): 33–42.

Index

Numbers in **boldface** refer to additional figures or tables.